D0882004

THE ROUGH GUIDE TO

New York City
Restaurants

2004 EDITION

www.roughguides.com

credits

Series editor Mark Ellingham
Text editor Samantha Cook
Production Rachel Holmes
Cartography Maxine Repath
Photography Nelson Hancock

publishing information

This edition published October 2003 by
Rough Guides Ltd, 80 Strand, London WC2R 0RL.
Penguin Putnam, Inc. 375 Hudson Street, NY 10014, USA.

distributed by the Penguin Group

Penguin Books Ltd, 80 Strand, London WC2R ORL
Penguin Putnam, Inc. 375 Hudson Street, NY 10014, USA
Penguin Books Australia Ltd, 487 Maroondah Highway,
PO Box 257, Ringwood, Victoria 3134, Australia
Penguin Books Canada Ltd, 10 Alcorn Avenue,
Toronto, Ontario, Canada M4V 1E4
Penguin Books (NZ) Ltd,182–190 Wairau Road, Auckland 10, New Zealand

Typeset in Bembo and Helvetica to an original design by Henry Iles.
Printed in Spain by Graphy Cems.

A catalogue record for this book is available from the British Library.
ISBN 1-84353-098-8

THE ROUGH GUIDE TO

New York City Restaurants

2004 EDITION

by
Daniel Young

with additional contributions by
Sean Brady, Andrea Strong, Laurie Woolever

ROUGH
GUIDES

About the author

Daniel Young splits most of his time and meals between his hometown New York, where he was the restaurant critic of the *Daily News* from 1996–2000, and Paris, where he authored the *Paris Café Cookbook*. He is a member of the James Beard Restaurant Awards Committee. His most recent cookbook, *Made in Marseille*, was published in 2002 by HarperCollins. He has written extensively about food and restaurants for *Gourmet*, *Bon Appetit*, *Condé Nast Traveler*, *The New York Times*, *The Los Angeles Times*, and *The International Herald-Tribune*. As the original "Eats" columnist of the *Daily News* he reviewed New York's inexpensive restaurants from 1985–1996.

Acknowledgements

A heartfelt thanks to my colleague, mentor, and friend Arthur Schwartz for his invaluable counsel and encouragement and to Steven Biondolillo, Ray Chen, Alan Cohen, Steven Forbis, Mark Giles, Mitchell Brower, Irene Sax, and Jeff Weinstein for their insight, wit, and exceptional taste. I also wish to express my gratitude to the contributing reviewers Sean Brady, Andrea Strong, and Laurie Woolever as well as the fearless dining companions who made each restaurant visit a memorable one: Mary Barone, Diana Biederman, Nina Blaine, James Chew, Anne de Ravel, Leslie Laurence, Robert Lovenheim, JoAnn Makovitsky, Jody Melnick, Marco Moreira, Neil Manson, Anahita Mekanik, Bob Nicolaides, Olivier Wittman, Pamela Wittman, and the always lovely Vivian Constantinopoulos. In bringing this revision to fruition I am indebted to Robert Shepard for helping to advance and shape the project in so many important ways; to Jonathan Buckley for insisting upon excellence in every phase of planning and production; to my editor Samantha Cook for her tenacity and keen eye; and to Maxine Repath for her meticulous work on the maps. Finally, I profited as much as ever from the love, support, and verve of those two marvelous New Yorkers, Mimi Young and David Young.

Help us update

We've tried to ensure that this edition of the *Rough Guide to New York City Restaurants* is as up-to-date and accurate as possible. However, New York's restaurant scene is in constant flux, and standards, of course, do go up and down. If you feel there are places we've underrated or overpraised, or others we've unjustly omitted, please let us know. Comments or corrections are much appreciated, and we'll send a copy of the next edition (or any other *Rough Guide* if you prefer) for the best letters. Please address letters to Daniel Young at: Rough Guides, 345 Hudson Street, New York, NY 10014, USA; Rough Guides Ltd, 80 Strand, London WC2R ORL; or send email to: mail@ roughguides.co.uk

contents

contents

Queens 355

The Bronx 395

Staten Island 403

Index 409

introduction

The great quality, diversity and magnitude of the New York restaurant scene may go a long way towards explaining the notoriously neurotic behavior of the city's diners. Only in this worldly metropolis of 18,000 restaurants does the simple act of settling upon a place to eat provoke the despair that comes from passing up hundreds of outstanding options. This, the revised and thoroughly updated edition of **The Rough Guide to New York City Restaurants**, narrows the field to 321 enthusiastically recommended restaurants, none of which is exorbitantly priced. Each is covered in a full-page outline filled with New York attitude, candid criticisms, detailed food descriptions and commentary, specific suggestions and prices. These reviews will offer you invaluable assistance in making the best picks given your particular tastes, cravings, whereabouts and budget—whether you're looking for a paper-napkin taqueria or linen-clothed trattoria, old hamburger joint or new American bistro, homey Thai hideaway or edgy French brasserie. The guide consequently affords you that great New York luxury of being very, very choosy.

The Rough Guide to New York City Restaurants 2004 is organized by **location**. If you know where you plan on being or in which part of the city you'd like to eat, consult the chapter in question and compare the dining options in that area. Detailed neighborhood maps help you pinpoint each restaurant. If you prefer to choose by **cuisine**, check the index in the back of the guide.

Whether you have a lifetime, a week or 22 minutes to devote to dining out in **Manhattan**, **Brooklyn**, **Queens**, **the Bronx** or **Staten Island**, it will be virtually impossible to flip through the pages of this guide and wish you were somewhere else. New York is not the be-all and end-all, thank goodness. The city of immigrants depends heavily on culinary capitals and unspoiled hinterlands the world over for inspiration. Nevertheless, this guide makes a very solid case for it being the greatest dining destination on the planet.

The restaurants

The New York City's restaurant landscape is more enticing and more competitive today than ever before. Better trained, more widely traveled chefs are continually challenged and inspired by the high standards they themselves set. More ethnic cuisines are ably represented. Breads are infinitely superior. Wine lists and wine-and-food pairings are more adventurous. Service staffs are better informed. Farm-fresh, organic produce, much of it from the city's Greenmarkets, has become prevalent. Hudson Valley foie gras and Brooklyn-made chocolate rival their French counterparts. And where prices have changed a dollar or two from 2003 to 2004, they are almost as likely to have gone down as gone up.

This guide explores such **current trends** and developments as the emergence of the long disparaged Upper West Side as a serious dining neighborhood, the progression of Nuevo Latino and Asian fusion, the mainstreaming of Turkish and Korean cooking, the preparation of sushi and sashimi with a Latin or Caribbean beat, the rediscovery of open-fire cooking, and the bourgeois-bohemian colonization of Brooklyn, including the emergence of the waterfront district DUMBO (Down Under the Manhattan Bridge Overpass). The craze for fashionably contoured pizzas is reflected in the mad popularity of newcomers like Apizz, Caserta Vecchia, Celeste, Gonzo, and Otto.

You will also read here about great **New York classics** ranging from the legendary—the Grand Central Oyster Bar, Katz's Deli, Dominick's, Gage & Tollner, Nathan's Famous—to the peerless yet lesser known—Barney Greengrass, Totonno Pizzeria

introduction

Napolitano, The Pub Room at Keens Chop House—to the comparatively obscure—Gino, Prime Burger, Mei Lai Wah.

Pricing, costs, and tipping

Value was a decisive consideration in choosing which restaurants to include. Not every place that made the final cut is inexpensive. Often, a pricey meal can be more of a bargain than a cheap one. Still, although you can spend upwards of **$100** for dinner and feel like you got more than your money's worth, the guide's emphasis on value made it necessary to exclude very expensive restaurants. At every featured restaurant it is possible, if not always likely, to eat a full dinner, beverage, tax and tip included, for less than $50.

Each review features a **dollar spread** that indicates the minimum and maximum amount you are likely to spend on a meal, tax and tip included. The first figure relates to what you could get away with, perhaps by sharing an appetizer, skipping dessert, or ordering the least expensive dishes. The second figure estimates what a meal would cost without any such economizing. Diners with an insatiable thirst for cocktails, fine wines, bottled waters, and after-dinner drinks may leave the upper limit far behind. But in most instances, the cost of a meal will lie somewhere within the middle of the spread.

A **service charge**, though included in this guide's estimates, will not appear on the dinner check, except at restaurants that apply one for large groups. It is customary to tip between 15 and 20 percent of the check total, depending on how generous you are feeling and how good the service was. Many use the 8.625% **sales tax** that appears at the bottom of the check as a guide to calculate the proper tip. They double the tax to an amount totalling 17.25% of the check total and then round out that figure up or down as they feel appropriate.

No Smoking

Smoking is no longer permitted in New York City restaurants and bars. The **comprehensive smoking ban** went into effect on March 30, 2003.

Rough Guide Favorites

To guide you towards the five favorites in some essential categories, here follows some "best ofs".

Best Breakfast

Best Brunch

Best Sandwiches

introduction

Best Soups

B&H, East Village	p.28
Café Glechik, Brighton Beach, Brooklyn	p.313
Grand Central Oyster Bar, Midtown East	p.187
Second Avenue Deli, East Village	p.51
Veselka, East Village	p.56

Best Low-End Hamburger

Corner Bistro, West Village	p.152
Junior's, Downtown Brooklyn	p.294
Paul's Palace, East Village	p.48
The Prime-Burger, Midtown East	p.194
Tony's Burger, Murray Hill	p.233

Best High-End Hamburger

Balthazar, SoHo	p.124
Joe Allen, Midtown West	p.213
Pastis, West Village	p.165
Pub Room at Keens Chop House, Garment District	p.182
Union Square Café, Union Square	p.80

Best New York-Style Pizza

Arturo's, Greenwich Village	p.83
Deninos, Staten Island	p.406
Mario's, The Bronx	p.399
Nunzio's, Staten Island	p.407
Totonno Pizzeria Napolitano, Coney Island, Brooklyn	p.319

Best Roast Chicken

Five Points, NoHo	p.89
Flor de Mayo, Upper West Side	p.271

Home, West Village   p.157
Pollos a la Brasa Mario, Jackson Heights, Queens   p.391
Thomas Beisl, Fort Greene, Brooklyn   p.326

Best Steak Frites

À Table, Fort Greene, Brooklyn   p.323
Balthazar, SoHo   p.124
Diner, Williamsburg, Brooklyn   p.349
Florent, West Village   p.154
Les Halles, Lower Manhattan   p.146

Best Tuscan

Bar Pitti, Greenwich Village   p.85
Beppe, Gramercy Park   p.62
Col Legno, East Village   p.33
Pepolino, TriBeCa   p.139
Tuscany Grill, Bay Ridge, Brooklyn   p.287

Best Desserts

Babbo, Greenwich Village   p.84
City Bakery, Flatiron District   p.66
Payard Bistro & Patisserie, Upper East Side   p.257
Tavern at Gramercy Tavern, Gramercy Park   p.79
Thomas Beisl, Fort Greene, Brooklyn   p.326

Best Wine List

Cité Grill, Midtown West   p.208
Enoteca I Truli, Gramercy Park   p.72
Gramercy Tavern, Gramercy Park   p.79
Otto, Greenwich Village   p.93
Tommaso's, Bensonhurst, Brooklyn   p.286

introduction

Best Outdoor Dining

Best for Kids

Best for Groups and Parties

Best in Theater District

Best Local Haunts

Gino, Upper East Side p.252
Joe Allen, Midtown West p.213
Superfine, DUMBO p.296

Best Late Night

Cafeteria, Chelsea p.6
Florent, West Village p.154
Kansuh, Little Korea p.179
Uncle George's, Astoria, Queens p.369
Veselka, East Village p.56

Best Perennially Hip

Café Luxembourg, Upper West Side p.268
Florent, West Village p.154
Indochine, NoHo p.90
Odeon, TriBeCa p.138
El Quijote, Chelsea p.10

Best Old New York Decor

Gage & Tollner, Downtown Brooklyn p.292
Grand Central Oyster Bar, Midtown East p.187
Katz's Delicatessen, Lower East Side p.117
Locanda Vini & Olii, Clinton Hill, Brooklyn p.325
Pub Room at Keens Chop House, Garment District p.182

Most Worth the Wait

Al Di La, Park Slope, Brooklyn p.329
Celeste, Upper West Side p.269
Craft Bar, Gramercy Park p.67
Pearl Oyster Bar, West Village p.166
The Tavern at Gramercy Tavern, Gramercy Park p.79

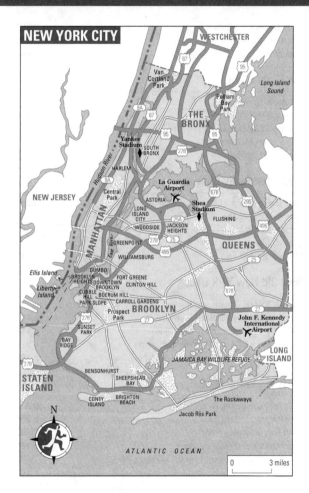

NEW YORK CITY

WESTCHESTER

Van Cortland Park

Long Island Sound

Pelham Bay Park

THE BRONX

Yankee Stadium

SOUTH BRONX

HARLEM

La Guardia Airport

Hudson River

NEW JERSEY

Central Park

ASTORIA

Shea Stadium

LONG ISLAND CITY

WOODSIDE

JACKSON HEIGHTS

FLUSHING

MANHATTAN

East River

GREENPOINT

WILLIAMSBURG

QUEENS

DUMBO

BROOKLYN HEIGHTS

DOWNTOWN BROOKLYN

FORT GREENE

CLINTON HILL

Ellis Island

Liberty Island

COBBLE HILL

BOERUM HILL

PARK SLOPE

CARROLL GARDENS

Prospect Park

BROOKLYN

John F. Kennedy International Airport

LONG ISLAND

SUNSET PARK

BAY RIDGE

JAMAICA BAY WILDLIFE REFUGE

STATEN ISLAND

BENSONHURST

SHEEPSHEAD BAY

CONEY ISLAND

BRIGHTON BEACH

The Rockaways

Jacob Riis Park

N

ATLANTIC OCEAN

0   3 miles

MANHATTAN

THE BRONX

HARLEM

Columbia University

NEW JERSEY

Cathedral of St. John the Divine

FREDERICK DOUGLASS BLVD

A.C. POWELL BLVD

LENOX AVENUE

MADISON AVENUE

PARK AVENUE

LEXINGTON AVENUE

THIRD AVENUE

SECOND AVENUE

FIRST AVENUE

W. 110TH ST.

E. 110TH ST.

W. 96TH ST.

E. 96TH ST.

BROADWAY

Hudson River

American Museum of Natural History

Central Park

UPPER EAST SIDE

E. 86TH ST.

W. 79TH ST.

Metropolitan Museum of Art

UPPER WEST SIDE

COLUMBUS AVE

E. 79TH ST.

Lincoln Center

E. 72ND ST.

MIDTOWN WEST

W. 57TH ST.

Museum of Modern Art

THEATER DISTRICT

W. 42ND ST.

Rockefeller Center

MIDTOWN EAST

E. 57TH ST.

QUEENSBORO BRIDGE

E. 50TH ST.

GARMENT DISTRICT/ LITTLE KOREA

ELEVENTH AVE

New York Public Library

Grand Central Station

Empire State Building

Chrysler Building

NINTH AVE

Penn Station

SEVENTH AVE

BROADWAY

MADISON AVENUE

PARK AVENUE

MURRAY HILL/ KIPS BAY

E. 34TH ST.

United Nations

CHELSEA

WEST 23RD ST.

FIRST AVE

FLATIRON DISTRICT/ GRAMERCY PARK/ UNION SQUARE

E. 23RD ST.

WEST VILLAGE

W. 10TH ST.

UNION SQUARE

QUEENS

East River

GREENWICH VILLAGE /NOHO

WEST 14TH ST.

E. 14TH ST.

HUDSON STREET

PRINCE ST

EAST VILLAGE

SOHO

CANAL ST.

EAST HOUSTON ST.

FRANKLIN D. ROOSEVELT DRIVE

TRIBECA

LITTLE ITALY/ NOLITA

LOWER EAST SIDE

Woolworth Building

Former Site of World Trade Center

City Hall

EAST BROADWAY

CHINA- TOWN

WILLIAMSBURG BRIDGE

WALL ST./ LOWER MANHATTAN

MANHATTAN BRIDGE

Battery Park

BROOKLYN BRIDGE

BROOKLYN

N

0   1 mile

Downtown

Chelsea

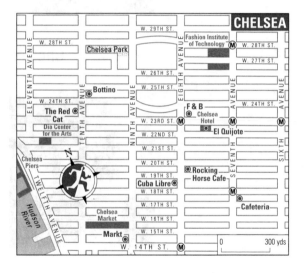

CHELSEA

W. 29TH ST.

W. 28TH ST.

Chelsea Park

Fashion Institute of Technology Ⓜ W. 28TH ST.

W. 27TH ST.

W. 26TH ST.

W. 25TH ST.

Ⓞ Bottino

W. 24TH ST.

The Red Ⓞ Cat

Dia Center for the Arts

Chelsea Piers

Chelsea Market

Markt Ⓞ

W. 23RD ST. Ⓜ

W. 22ND ST.

W. 21ST ST.

W. 20TH ST.

W. 19TH ST.

W. 18TH ST.

W. 17TH ST.

W. 16TH ST.

W. 15TH ST.

W. 14TH ST. Ⓜ

F & B Ⓜ

Ⓞ Chelsea Hotel Ⓜ Ⓜ

Ⓞ El Quijote

Ⓞ Rocking Horse Cafe Ⓞ

Cuba Libre Ⓞ

Ⓞ Cafeteria

ELEVENTH AVENUE

TENTH AVENUE

NINTH AVENUE

EIGHTH AVENUE

SEVENTH AVENUE

SIXTH AVENUE

TWELFTH AVENUE

Hudson River

N

0   300 yds

Bottino

🍴 Weighing the beautifuls (decor, garden, people) against the unremarkables (food, service, cordiality) should help determine your relationship with this glamorous trattoria. But then again you may ultimately be swayed by the X factor: Bottino's forgive-all bread pudding ($6). At any rate, Daniel Emerman and Florentine chef Alessandro Prosperi have fulfilled their ambition to do for Chelsea's gallery scene what Barocco, their other trattoria, did for

**Lunch $20–55
Dinner $35–75**

Address 246 10th Ave, between 24th & 25th Sts
☎212/206-6766
Transportation C,E to 23rd St
Open Sun & Mon 6–11.30pm, Tues–Sat noon–5.30pm & 6–11.30pm
Accepts All major credit cards
Reservations Required

TriBeCa's in the 1980s. Situated opposite Manhattan's Getty—the gas station, not the museum—this spin-off is hip, noisy, breezy, and vaguely Tuscan. There's no pretension on the forthright menu, in the simple dishes, or hanging from the white-painted brick walls.

The art of Bottino is in how architect Thomas Lesser's mid-century modern decor preserves fixtures from an old hardware store. The antiquated wood shelving, in a bar furnished with Charles Eames bentwood chairs, still stocks liquid treatments—but today it's moderately priced Pinot Grigios and Chianti Classicos rather than lacquers and paints. The sparse dining room keeps its tin ceiling and worn hardwood floors. And then there are the gardens, two outdoor spaces so enchanting they provide Bottino's most unfortunate challenge: what to do about diners who don't want to leave, and what to do about diners kept waiting for their tables.

The single candle on each garden table takes the idea of romantic lighting a bit too far. After dark, you can't see a thing. Bring along a penlight to read about such appetizers as the grilled eggplant salad with arugula, shaved Tuscan Pecorino cheese, balsamic, and excellent olive oil ($9), or the tuna tartare topped with cubed beets, arugula, and red onion ($12). Main courses are generally decent. The cooks, unlike the reservations crew, know their limits. It's impossible to fault the grilled steak ($27), with its juicy, pristine slices of New York strip, sautéed broccoli rabe, and lumpy mashed potatoes, or the spaghettini with fresh shrimp, sea scallops, and clams in a peppery tomato garlic wine sauce ($16). Besides its famed vanilla bread pudding, Bottino has a second stellar dessert in its smooth and genuine tiramisu ($6).

Chelsea

Cafeteria

🍴 Originally, the glass-paneled, garage-door facade and stark-white modernism of Cafeteria evoked a Richard Meier knockoff better suited to the West Coast than the West Side. The name itself didn't really fit, either, intimating a humble, counter-service institution rather than the LA-fashioned import of a self-consciously stylish, table-service commissary.

**Lunch $18–40
Dinner $30–65**

Address 119 7th Ave at 17th St
☎212/414-1717
Transportation 1,9 to 18th St
Open Daily 24hr
Accepts All major credit cards

But like a pair of leather pants, Cafeteria has become softer and comfier with repeated wear. The once stiff seating now has plenty of give for a fashion-aware, manifestly Chelsea mix of buff, protein-loading gym rats and their equally ravenous if less perfectly bodied neighbors. Members of the latter group should not, however, expect to join the former merely by eating as they do. A waffle with strawberry sour cream and crème brûlée-style topping of caramelized maple syrup is not, unfortunately, the fastest route to a fitter you.

Most happy habitués would agree on one thing: when our mothers stressed the importance of a *healthy* breakfast, they were referring to its size, as opposed to its nutritional facets. The dietary benefits of the summer berries or winter apples that garnish the tantalizing croissant French toast ($6.95) are an afterthought. And if an order of poached eggs with buttermilk biscuit, sausage, gravy, spinach, and gloppy Hollandaise ($7.95) just happens to cover all the major food groups, that's just a side benefit.

While everyone can agree about breakfasts, Cafeteria's conception of the term "appetizer" is a little quirky. Are you really expected to eat something *after* the lyrical macaroni and (two-) cheese ($5.95), the steamed mussels in cilantro tomato broth ($9.95), or the almost legendary Caesar salads with a one-eyed Susan (poached egg; $6.95) or grilled chicken ($10.95)? Are you really supposed to nosh something *before* the awesome hickory-smoked chicken club with tomato confit, avocado, arugula, and basil mayo on sourdough ($8.95) or triple-decker grilled tuna club with roasted tomatoes, arugula, avocado, and red onion ($13.95)? These sandwiches, which stretch from late afternoon to early morning, all come with large, crisp steak fries. And then there's that incredible banana pudding ($5.95)—a coffee mug filled with thick cream, sweet bananas, and butterfingers—to confront.

Cuba Libre

Seeking to cash in on both the Latin-fusion fad and anything with a Cuban beat, Robert Ianniello had to travel all the way from the dining room to the kitchen of his Little Italy restaurant, Umberto's Clam House, to find a suitable chef. There he gave Rene Garcia the chance to say *adiós* to the linguine with white clam sauce, move to Chelsea, and prepare foods closer in spirit, if not origin, to his native Mexico. Once Garcia was installed behind an iced bank of raw oysters in an open kitchen, a set of hanging copper pots within arm's reach, the rest was as easy as mixing a Cuba Libre (rum, Coke, lime juice, ice): mount palm branches and cigar memorabilia on the exposed brick walls, then crank up the bass on that cha-cha version of Rudolph the Red-Nosed Reindeer. In 2002 this potent cocktail was moved into dressier quarters across the avenue; arty color photographs of Cuba may have replaced the stogie placards, but, rest assured, the four-octave ululations of 1950s songstress Yma Sumac prevail.

Lunch $18–40
Dinner $30–65

Address 165 8th Ave, between 18th & 19th Sts
Ⓣ212/206-0038
Transportation A,C,E to 14th St; L to 8th Ave
Open Sun 11.30am–4pm & 5–11pm, Tues–Sat 11.30am–4pm & 5pm–midnight
Accepts All major credit cards

The great appeal of Cuba Libre remains its modest size and ambitions. There's neither the capacity to inebriate hundreds of cruising singles nor the need to make big statements about Nuevo Latino cookery. With an emphasis on seafood brought over from Umberto's, Garcia's pan-Latin ideas are fussy in the most innocent sense. When he refits fried, blue-cornmeal-coated oysters into their shells with smoky collard greens and salsa ($9.95), it's as if to show there's an experienced and creative chef in the kitchen. The same is true of the fresh lobster empanada stylishly set in mango lentil salad ($9.95).

The lightly sweet and smoky, delectably crusty, ancho-chile-rubbed slices of pork tenderloin ($17.95), served with sweet plantain mash and black bean sauce, allay all fears about Mojave-dry pork. Chicken stuffed with chorizo and garlic spinach ($16.95) is also juicy and tender. Seafood entrees tend to err on the sweet side. This tendency becomes a virtue when applied to desserts ($7) like fried plantains, tres leches cakes and domino (dark and white chocolate) cake.

Chelsea

F&B

In geographic terms, this franchise prototype is situated on the same landmark block as the Chelsea Hotel, the Clearview Chelsea Cineplex, and Manhattan's first Krispy Kreme donut shop. In emotional terms, the counter-service concept has occupied a warm spot in hungry New York hearts ever since its debut in summer 2001. The periwinkle walls and blond-wood counters on either side of this sleek and slender emporium may be seen as a fashion runway leading to several precious letters of the alphabet. While the F and the B give star billing to the frites and the beignets, the title sadly overlooks many marquee attractions. You may know and love them as HDs; others adore them as Ws, Fs, or TSs. Translation: hot dogs, wieners, frankfurters, tube steaks.

$6–25
Address 269 West 23rd St, between 7th & 8th Aves
☏ 646/486-4441
Transportation 1,9,C,E to 23rd St
Open Sun & Mon noon–10.30pm, Tues–Sat noon–11pm
Accepts All major credit cards
Reservations Not accepted

This being Chelsea, the HDs are not neglected when it comes to their wardrobe. These European-accented street foods have more designer outfits and de rigueur accessories than a Barbie doll. In all there are fifteen ensembles, ranging from the Great Dane (a supermodel-skinny Danish dog with remoulade, mustard, apple tomato ketchup, and cucumber; $3.50) to the shorter, plumper Country Dog (a chicken and apple wiener with German potato salad and sweet onion relish; $3.50). In terms of the meat itself, the firm garlic sausage is the pick of the hot dog litter. But veggie (smoked tofu) dogs do subtract 90 percent of the guilt and, assuming there are plenty of spicy toppings draped over them, no more than a quarter of the pleasure. The perfectly tanned Belgian-style frites ($2.50/$3.95) are lightly crisp and substantial; defying the laws of physics, the sweet potato fries ($2.95/$4.25) are uncommonly crisp. And the fried onion loops ($2.50) offer unbroken amusement. None of these requires the seven special dips, among them aioli, curry tomato, and blue cheese, on offer.

As for the beignets (3 for $3.50), these warm, pillow-shaped donut puffs offer truly profound gratification. They're available in cheese or apple; sadly, the plain version is no longer. Though their sugar coating alone unleashes a melt-in-your-mouth moment when sweet powder turns to liquid, a dessert dip addition—caramel, dark chocolate, berry, etc—is in this instance warmly encouraged.

Markt

🍴 The factory clock that glows in the middle of this Belgian brasserie is frozen at five to midnight. This may be viewed as a stroke, or, rather, five non-strokes of luck by assorted Cinderellas fearful of 12am curfews. But it should not be taken to mean that Markt, Flemish for "market," is a fairy-tale destination. Nor is it run with quartz precision. That said, you'll get good, decent cooking at this handsome haunt, which buzzes with more than enough possibilities for 150 diners stuck together in time. Many

Lunch $20–50
Dinner $30–75

Address 410 14th St at 9th Ave
☏212/727-3314
Transportation A,C,E to 14th St; L to 8th Ave
Open Sun 10am–11pm, Mon–Thurs 11.30am–11pm, Fri 11.30am–midnight, Sat 10am–midnight
Accepts All major credit cards
Reservations Suggested

huddle at the 70ft marble bar, enjoying Belgian brews, raw oysters, gratis fried mussels and, in their own way, each other. Others sit at the mahogany tables spread over a hardwood floor set with inlays of vintage decorative tiles.

Not surprisingly, the workhorse specialties, which serve as shared appetizers, main courses, beer accompaniments, or all three, are big pots of exceptionally meaty steamed mussels paired with good frites ($14–15). Mussels also stand in for snails in a variation of the French classic, escargots à la bourguignonne ($15). This gratin of mussels arrives at the table dripping in hot, garlicky butter sauce. Few main courses could be described as light. Among the traditional stews known as waterzooi, the "Mer du Nord" version ($22) gathers cod, shrimp, mussels, scallops, and salmon in a cream sauce touched with fish stock—as opposed to a fish stock touched with cream. Naturally, the whole ensemble is a knockout. Similarly, the sweet and fabulously juicy split grilled lobster ($29) swims with fennel and cherry tomatoes in a buttery Hoegaarden sauce. Meat options ($14–26) are pretty dependable. The huge portions simply add to the diet-busting damage. At lunch, baguette sandwiches (ham and cheese, beef tartare, shrimp salad) are just $7–8. And brunch entrees are just $7–10.

To finish, pare down the so-so selection of nine desserts ($7–9) to the warm-centered chocolate cake with pistachio ice cream and the Dame Blanche, a Flemish ice cream sundae with Belgian chocolate sauce.

SPANISH

El Quijote

(icon) While Cervantes' El Quijote is a masterpiece of satire, its namesake tribute in the landmark Chelsea Hotel is a kitsch-congested classic without a single iota of irony. And if the Spanish restaurant is more popular and magical than ever, it's precisely because in 75-plus years it never turned into a parody of its sentimental self. The blue-glass back-lit bar patronized by hundreds of artists—both professional and con—who've stayed for a spell in the Chelsea

Lunch $15–60
Dinner $25–60

Address 226 West 23rd St, between 7th & 8th Aves
(phone)212/929-1855
Transportation 1,9,C,E to 23rd St
Open Fri & Sat 11:30am–1am
Sun–Thurs 11:30am–midnight,
Accepts All major credit cards
Reservations Suggested

is marvelously intact. The partition of fluted wood and glass that separates them from the Naugahyde-bracketed diners is unblemished. The Dulcinea Room remains an ideal party space to celebrate, if nothing else, Dulcinea. And when a waiter praises the virtues of the veal extremeña ($14.95), an enormous casserole loaded with veal, green peppers, chorizo, and garlic in a sherry sauce, he means it. Anyone familiar with the mediocrity of this dish will appreciate just how much training and dedication that testimonial requires.

The tearing sound made whenever someone opens a menu is the same *shtshtsht* you hear when you pry apart the plastic pages of a photo album. In perusing the laminated listings you might conclude that all dishes distinguished as extremeña or "El Quijote" are similar, regardless of whether they contain veal, chicken, or beef. This is not actually true. There are only two constants: garlic and garlic. In any event, ordering requires of the diner exactly what the cooking lacks: finesse. You'd do well to start by sharing the extremes varidos ($15.95), a mixed appetizer of fried calamari, grilled shrimp (very salty), grilled chorizo, chicken croquettes, stuffed mushrooms, and maybe six or seven other items. Three people would have a chance of finishing a single order before taking on a paella. That is, one paella for the three of them.

El Quijote has long been a leading player within the local langosta circuit, a small group of apparently unrelated Spanish places in the vicinity of 23rd and 7th offering competing lobster deals. As of this writing, the 1lb steamed or broiled lobster was selling here for $17.95.

The Red Cat

Were its interior sided with Moroccan tiles rather than barn-red wainscoting, the large Moorish lanterns dropped from the wood-beamed ceiling would make perfect sense. But in a made-up farmhouse inn that recycles bent cutlery as coat hooks, those fixtures reflect only the logic of a vacationing Vermonter. "I don't care if they don't go with anything we have," asserts the insouciant traveler. "I like them, and I'm getting

$35–80

Address 227 10th Ave, between 23rd & 24th Sts
☎212/242-1122
Transportation C,E to 23rd St
Open Mon–Thurs 5.30–11pm, Fri &
Sat 5.30pm–midnight, Sun 5–10pm
Accepts All major credit cards
Reservations Required

them." Such wilful quirkiness amid the cutting-edge design and pretensions of the Chelsea art gallery scene suits a friendly, knowing restaurant where the chef cooks the way his guests eat: for pleasure over effect. "I don't care if the steak comes with potato chips," asserts the stubborn diner. "I like chive mashed potatoes, and I'm getting them, too."

In constructing his New American, Mediterranean-highlighted menu, founding chef/co-owner Jimmy Bradley gives every dish at least one hook. His food is catchy. Just one look reveals the fried shrimp appetizer ($12) to be a surefire hit. Four crisp, meaty, golden-brown jumbos hang on the rim of a martini glass like sun-bronzed legs surrounding a swimming pool. Other appetizers rely on supporting, often scene-stealing, ingredients for their sensuality. A pleasantly chewy risotto cake ($10) is upstaged by its lush champagne cream sauce enriched with poached oysters. Wonderfully gritty, toasted orzo benefits from mussels, roasted tomatoes, chives, and chile flakes ($9). Main courses accentuate the fondness chef de cuisine William McDaniel shares with Bradley for fresh herbs and garlic. There is so much chopped thyme on and around the garlic-sauced roast chicken ($18) you may wish to put on a green shirt before you order it. Sage and garlic are central to the outstanding sautéed calf's liver ($18), too, with smoky bacon and sweet onion confit clinging to every bite.

Pastry chef Colleen Grapes' desserts ($8) are, like The Red Cat, at once countrified and cosmopolitan. Instead of choosing between the pistacho semifreddo, the strawberry brown butter tart, and the peanut butter mousse with milk chocolate ganache and a graham cracker crust, headstrong diners may persuade their companions to order all three. "We don't care...We like them, and we're getting all of them."

Chelsea

Rocking Horse Cafe

🍴 In choosing the name, design, and philosophy of their distinctive Mexican bistro, Roe DiBona and Marvin Beck were inspired by architect Luis Barragan, the late Mexican modernist who loved horses and was partial to pure planes of sumptuous color as well as designs based on indigenous sources. With its walls of tomato red, lime green, and cafe-con-leche, and its grasp of genuine regional flavors, the Rocking Horse is a terrifically modish, if modest, expression of these principles. Its idea of interacting with its natural environment produces different results than the master's, largely due to that environment itself. It reinterprets the boisterous street life outside its red garage-door storefront within a rollicking shoebox of tequila-marinated merriment.

Lunch $18–45
Dinner $27–70

Address 182 8th Ave, between 19th & 20th Sts
☎212/463-9511
Transportation C,E to 23rd St; 1,9 to 18th St
Open Sun–Thurs 11am–11pm, Fri & Sat 11am–midnight
Accepts All major credit cards
Reservations Suggested

The vibrant cooking has survived the departure of innovative chef Sue Torres. Infrequent setbacks are probably due to the frenzied and cramped conditions in which the diligent kitchen and dining room staffs must cope. They need not worry. Once in the company of their companions, their Technicolor margaritas, and warm homemade tricolor tortilla chips (cilantro, black bean, ancho red) with rich guacamole and three warm relishes ($8.95), diners are more likely to be grateful for than upset by delays. The relaxed attitude is just one good reason for limiting a dinner order to pass-around appetizers like fried calamari citrus salad with chorizo croûtons ($8.95) and triple-decker wild mushroom quesadilla with Manchego cheese, white truffle oil, and jicama green apple slaw ($8.95). The second reason is that each of these stands well on its own—and besides, who's to say the steamed mussels in chipotle broth ($7.95) cannot be a main course?

There are some nifty entrees if you make it that far. Enchiladas filled with pulled chicken leg roasted in pomegranate juice and ancho chile ($14.95) boast an appealing, sweet tartness. Pan-seared salmon napoleon ($17.95) is adroitly layered with grilled chayote, smoked trout croquettes, and roasted tomatillo salsa. For dessert, go for the Valrhona chocolate tortilla ($5.95), a steamed, spongy, doubly dark-chocolatey, ring-shaped cake with cinnamon ice cream.

Chinatown

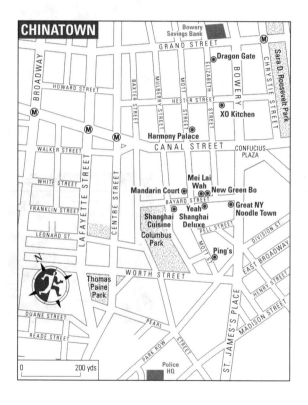

Dragon Gate

If only chef Chung Tam Keung were as demanding in his choice of venues as he is in his selection of ingredients. His prior location, May Villa, had the disadvantage of being concealed in a Chinatown shopping arcade and of replacing Phoenix Garden, a restaurant lamented for its famous salt and pepper baked shrimp. There is no history to complicate matters at Dragon Gate; only an uncertain present. Responding to an ailing economy, the owners are emphasizing $3.95–4.95 lunch specials, $3–4.75 congees, and $3.50–5.50 rice dishes over chef's specialties that are elsewhere unavailable. Some aren't even listed on the menu. The two color TVs and 3D wall posters in the blond-wooded, country-modern setup hardly lift expectations.

Lunch $7–30
Dinner $15–50

Address 92-96 Elizabeth St, between Grand & Hester Sts
☎212/274-8330
Transportation S to Grand St; 6,J,M,N,Q,R,Z to Canal St
Open Sun–Thurs 10.30am–10.30pm, Fri & Sat 10.30am–11pm
Accepts MasterCard & Visa
Reservations Not accepted

Dragon Gate serves salt and pepper shrimp ($8.95) to satisfy anyone tracing Keung's footsteps. But the real revelation is the salt and pepper "rice fish" ($7.95), so-called because the tiny, elongated fish are supposedly shaped like grains of rice (more like inch-worms if you want to be technical). The delicate, salty crunch of this delectable snack is animated, somewhat deviously, with occasional hits from razor-thin loops of sliced chiles. Another compelling dish to share as a starter, though admittedly of esoteric appeal, is the oyster pancake garnished with fresh cilantro ($8.95). With nearly as much fresh oyster as there is egg, the resulting omelette is wet, loose, and packed with oyster punch.

Feel free to dabble with such entrees as the XO-sauced chicken and beef with dried scallions, ginger, and crunchy snow peas ($8.95) or the flounder cooked two ways, fried and sautéed (market price). But be sure to get around to the crabs bundled with rice and Chinese sausage in lotus leaf and steamed ($14.95). The juices of the crab and the fatty, smoky sausage bits infiltrate the rice and give it a creamy, risotto–like consistency without sacrificing the integrity of each individual grain. And once you break into the crabs, the decor and circumstances of Chung Tam Keung's latest workplace look much improved.

Chinatown

Great NY Noodletown

It's got less ambiance than a Midwestern strip mall, with a sketchy bathroom and a silly name, but Great NY Noodletown is one heck of an after-hours Chinese restaurant, with steaming-hot grub, service that alternates between friendly and curt, and reasonable prices. At the day's intermittent rush hours, you may be asked to share a table. Have a cold Tsing Tao, or a cup of complimentary tea, and relax – the minor inconvenience is well worth it, and you may even end up bonding over the food, which will arrive when it's ready, in no particular order.

$12–35

Address 28 Bowery at Bayard St
☎212/349-0923
Transportation 6, J,M,N,Q,R,W to Canal St
Open Sun–Thurs 9am–4am, Fri & Sat 9am–5am
Accepts Cash only
Reservations For large groups

When ordering, be guided less by the name than by the window display: those hanging barbecued meats are the house specialty. Sample them all and decide for yourself which is best among crisp-skinned, tender baby pig ($6.95 with rice), sweet and succulent duck ($3.50 with rice), or roast pork loin ($4.25, with duck, inexplicably). Adventurous eaters will want to try the more exotic varieties of thick congee (rice porridge), notably the one with pork stomach ($3), which has a pleasing, fried-tofu texture and mildly liver-like taste; meatball and pork liver ($3); or frog ($6.75). Dumplings in soup are more conservative but just as pleasing; the simple shrimp variety ($3.75) is a marvel. Just about everything on the menu is enlivened with a dab of scallion, ginger, and garlic sauce, so make sure to request a bowl for the table.

Several entrees are served with flowering chives – a mature, delicious and slightly woody-stemmed version of the common herb. Sea bass with flowering chives ($9.95) is inconsistent. At best your plate comes overloaded with snowy-white pieces of gently sautéed and lightly sauced fish, but on an off night the fish chunks are overcooked and oversalted. Moist shredded roast duck with chives ($10.95) is more reliable. A variety of seafood is available baked in salt, including crispy squid ($8.95), huge scallops ($10.95), and, when they're in season (mid-spring to early summer), soft-shell crabs ($14 for two). Next door, stop by the Bubble Tea Bar, a cute cafe with a vast assortment of sweet iced drinks and fruit shakes.

Harmony Palace

Because its English name was not displayed for years, fans came to know this 500-seat dim sum palace only by its address, 98 Mott. And while its dim sum service has drawn packed houses for nearly a decade, the name Harmony Palace still means nothing to many who pine for its peerless parade of steamed, baked, fried, stuffed, wrapped, or rolled Chinese morsels. The cavernous dining room is set up as if for a banquet, with tables crowded together on the main floor and a dais for honored guests, while the gaudy decorations—glass chandeliers, gilded mythical creatures, framed displays of shark fins and Cognac bottles, illuminated photos of waterfalls—are beginning to look as worn-out as the waitresses after pushing the dim sum carts around for hours.

$10–25

Address 98 Mott St, between Canal & Hester Sts
☎212/226-6603
Transportation 6,J,M,N,Q,R,W to Canal St
Open Daily 8am–10pm
Accepts All major credit cards
Reservations Not accepted

Though dim sum service has been extended into the evening, the widest and freshest assortment is available during weekend brunch hours. You should come no later than 11am, get settled in, and, to show the staff you know what you're doing, request a pot of bo nay tea. (They serve that full-bodied black tea to Chinese and weak jasmine tea to Westerners.) Never feel pressurized into taking something you don't want or aren't sure about. You're not going to miss anything by passing on the first go-rounds. That said, rarely is the cost of experimentation—chicken feet anyone?—so little. Most items are $1.95 and nothing from the carts exceeds $3.95.

Begin with har gow, the shrimp dumplings (three to a bamboo steamer) that are elemental to dim sum. The casing here is starchy and desirably flimsy; the filling, fresh and compact. Other standards to watch for are siu mai (pork dumplings wrapped in egg noodles), pan-fried chive dumplings, steamed beef balls with watercress, and shrimp rice noodles. You could compare the last to the Buddhist roll, which is chubbier and chewier and not nearly as slippery, its lasagna-thick rice noodle enveloping a dozen chopped vegetables. Lastly, the faintly sweet house dumpling is a bulging, translucent crescent packed with peanuts, mushrooms, celery, sesame seeds, water chestnuts, and taro. They call it the Harmony Dumpling; you can call it 98 Mott.

Mandarin Court

The Chinese residents and habitués of Chinatown tend to be more loyal to chefs than restaurants. If they read in the local press that a favorite chef is moving on, they're likely to follow him. But while this game of musical woks plays out, Mandarin Court defies the rules. Its fine reputation for Hong Kong-style cuisine and, in particular, creative dim sum has outlasted the periodic turnover in kitchen personnel. As a rule, change is anathema to owner Carol

Lunch $9–30
Dinner $15–75

Address 61 Mott St, between Canal & Bayard Sts
☎212/608-3838
Transportation 6,J,M,N,Q,R,W,Z to Canal St
Open Daily 8am–11pm
Accepts All major credit cards
Reservations Not accepted

Baluyut, who has maintained the same prices for years and not fixed up the (once attractive) decor since 1988.

Such steadfastness makes a recent development all the more dramatic: an assortment of chef Po Lui's masterful dim sum is now offered *in the evening*. Although you still need to go earlier in the day for a freshly made and comprehensive selection, the dinner menu nevertheless encompasses his signature steamed scallop dumplings, steamed lotus seed buns, chicken turnovers, and bean curd rolls with oyster sauce. Prices are slightly higher at night: dumplings and rolls jump from $1.95 during breakfast and lunch to $2.95 at dinner, while the garlicky and spicy clams in black bean sauce increase from $4.95 to $5.95.

The balance of the dinner menu is supervised by chef Sam Chan, who follows his predecessors' practice of preparing Cantonese food with an occasional spicy spin. His repertoire is so comprehensive it's doubtful even Carol has sampled every dish. Diners who love moo shu, spring rolls, and other savory wraps will not want to miss the minced oysters in lettuce ($11.95)—a hash of dried oysters, vermicelli, Chinese sausage, and vegetables wrapped tableside with fresh cilantro in an iceberg leaf, and then dunked in thick hoisin sauce. Sweet and snappy sautéed prawns are set against the double crunch of mustard greens and green beans ($14.95). And Peking duck ($32) is divided into two courses. The crackling skins are first served with steamed buns and shaved scallion, while the duck meat is shredded and paired with various accompaniments. Duck dow miu, for example, gets young pea shoots.

Mei Lai Wah

(🍴) Before the 1980s Hong Kong invasion filled Chinatown with glitzy dining palaces, dim sum was largely the province of modest tea rooms and coffee houses run by immigrants from China's Taishan County. A case in point is the antediluvian Mei Lai Wah, which, with a six-stool counter on the left, tiny and tattered booths on the right, and creepy panels above, resembles a sinister Chinatown hideout in some 1960s thriller. This impression is reinforced by the prices—50¢ to $1.40—hand-printed on the wall menu. Undiscovered by downtown hipsters or slumming suburbanites, the coffee house endures as a proletarian haunt filled with Chinese working men who peruse newspapers in the morning, discuss what they've read in the evening, and sip strong coffee or tea no matter the hour.

$5–15

Address 64 Bayard St, between Mott & Elizabeth Sts
☎212/925-5435
Transportation 6,J,M,N,Q,R,W,Z to Canal St
Open Daily 7am–11.30pm
Accepts Cash only
Reservations Not accepted

As tempting as the booths are, their worn Naugahyde faded to the color of a regular coffee, the round table in the back is the best place to sit. It affords a mesmerizing view into a red-painted kitchen from another world. Giant woks and steam pots are set over old stoves fed by prehistoric gas pipes. Buns and pastries are loaded into an antiquated oven. A cook hacks up everything—whole chickens, blubbery pork skin, bamboo shoots—on a round, concave chopping block. And trays of steaming-hot dim sum keep coming. Sample the puffy, bready buns fresh from the oven or steamer and you'll never accept them again any other way. The roast pork bun (60¢) is filled with salty (saltiness at Mei Lai Wah is a given) diced pork marinated in oyster sauce. The larger "Special Big Bun" ($1.10) contains pork, chicken, sausage, egg, and mushroom. Technically, it's a meal. The oval-shaped sausage bun (60¢) is a Cantonese hot dog.

Siu mai dumplings ($1.40 for three) are so big they resemble pork meatballs. The beef rice noodles ($1.40) are overstuffed with unctuous braised meat. And the plump shrimp dumplings ($1.40), though mealy, have plenty of minced bamboo shoots. Among desserts (50¢), the custard tart is pleasantly flaky, while the apple turnover and almond cookie are, respectively, the wrong and right kind of dry.

New Green Bo

The demise in 1998 of Say Eng Look was seen as a painful irony by devotees of that venerable Chinatown institution. The last of the city's old-line Shanghai dining palaces was closing just as a new generation of more modest eateries was making Shanghai-style dumplings, cold delicacies, and red cooking the talk of Mott Street. Sadly, the now retired owner of Say Eng Look never looked back. But his wife Helen Hsu did. She helped open New Green Bo, whose utilitarian ways first came as a shock to

Lunch $10–30
Dinner $15–45

Address 66 Bayard St, between Mott & Elizabeth Sts
℡212/625-2359
Transportation 6,J,M,N,Q,R,W to Canal St
Open Daily noon–11pm
Accepts Cash only
Reservations Not accepted

old-timers familiar with its grand, flamboyant forerunner. But those Chinatown regulars who, through reverse snobbery, actually prefer the no-frills style, instantly loved the place. Ms Hsu's departure and recent renovations have not diminished New Green Bo's humble and admittedly esoteric charm.

You should order in stages so that all the food does not come at once. From the winning selection of nineteen cold appetizers you'll enjoy thinly sliced braised beef in a sweet soy ginger sauce ($4.95), vegetarian mock duck (irresistible strips of cilantro-garnished bean curd inserted with mushrooms; $4.50), and ultra-crisp shards of crispy fried eel ($6.95), which, coated in honeyed ginger and scallion sauce, become pure candy. The two varieties of Shanghai-style dumplings ought not to be taken as an either/or. Go ahead and get them both: the elongated pan-fried pork beauties ($4.25) *and* the shao lung bao ($6.25), better known among non-Chinese as "soup dumplings." Besides their crab and pork filling, the dangerously explosive shao lung bao also contain jellied meat juices that turn to hot liquid upon steaming.

Main-course standouts include seaweed-battered yellow fish fillets ($12.95); stewed pork bundled in bean curd skin ($8.95); and whole red snapper ($11.95) with the rich, sweet-and-sour brown sauce typical of Shanghai's braised—or "red-cooked"—dishes. Ready for a long-term love affair? Then introduce yourself to tong po pork ($8.55)—truly luscious barbecue-like sandwiches that you assemble yourself with hot steamed buns, baby bok choy, and sweet, wondrously fatty red-cooked pork.

Ping's

Since Chuen Hui Ping won't tell people where he's cooking at any particular time, it would be nice if the darling of the food press volunteered to wear an electronic tracking device. After leaving Triple Eight Palace, his first New York platform for contemporary Cantonese cuisine infused with Hong Kong-style theatrics and regional Chinese, Thai, and Japanese influences, in 1996, Ping pinballed between four restaurants. Even now that he's cut back his movements to two newish Ping's restaurants—one in Queens (83–02 Queens Blvd; ☎718/396-1238), the

Lunch $8–45
Dinner $20–45

Address 22 Mott St, between Mosco & Worth Sts
☎212/602-9988
Transportation 6,J,M,N,Q,R,W to Canal St
Open Mon–Fri 10am–midnight, Sat & Sun 9am–midnight
Accepts MasterCard & Visa
Reservations For large groups

other this handsome, modern, cherrywood-paneled Chinatown duplex— Ping generally avoids his kitchens during service hours, an aversion increasingly common among entrepreneurial star chefs.

With or without his hands-on participation, the food presentation alone merits a look-see. Mini-woks, mini-casseroles, and ceramic soup bowls are brought directly to the table and set atop steel stands, releasing their rigorously aromatic vapors right under your nose. Brilliantly colored and choreographed dishes are elegantly arranged on round, rectangular, triangular, or shell-shaped plates. Beyond the visuals, Ping's spicing is usually spot-on. Deceptively basic seafood dishes—snails with black bean sauce ($10.95); marvelously crunchy, juicy, salty, sautéed shell-on jumbo shrimp with black pepper sauce ($16.95)—are customized so that Ping's beloved ginger, garlic, scallion, and cilantro can take on a variety of supporting roles. Though dim-sum-style appetizers are vastly improved, many diners start with a seafood dish or Thai-styled mussels with peppers and spicy basil sauce ($12.95) to share.

In the recent past, Ping's hand was clearly missed in elaborate fusion entrees such as steamed whole chicken ingeniously inlaid with ham and mushrooms ($29.95). Now that dish must be ordered in advance. Though his lieutenants can handle Dungeness crab steamed with ginger and scallion, they don't get the variation with lemon butter broth. That's no slight. Their elusive superior is probably the only Chinese chef in New York who does.

Shanghai Cuisine

🍴 Shanghai, the "Paris of the Orient", has been portrayed as a harbor of intrigue ever since it was opened to foreign trade in 1842. Its reputation as a hotbed of shady fortunes was well established when, in the 1932 film Shanghai Express, Marlene Dietrich's prostitute remarked: "It took more than one man to change my name to Shanghai Lily." Today, however, it's the city's braised and not its brazen temptations that attract attention. And Shanghai Cuisine is an

**Lunch $10–30
Dinner $20–45**

Address 89 Bayard St at Mulberry St
☎212/732-8988
Transportation 6,J,M,N,Q,R,Z to
Canal St
Open Daily noon–10.30pm
Accepts Cash only
Reservations Not accepted

enticingly genuine platform for the city's specialty, red-cooking, whereby meats and fish are blanketed in the honeyed flavor of sweetened soy sauce. A second treat from China's Jiangsu province consists of wine-marinated meats often consumed with beer. Their sweet and sour offer a bold alternative to the spicy sameness of Szechwan and the subtlety of Canton. Appropriately, the restaurant's casual corner space stands out in the Chinatown crowd. Attractive French doors are backed by bamboo shades, while a brick wall is adorned with old posters that owner Josephine Feng picked up at a Shanghai flea market.

Slices of braised beef scented with star anise ($5.25), the Shanghai equivalent of pot roast, provide the easiest introduction to the cold appetizers. Consider also the vegetarian mock duck ($5.95), with mushrooms and bamboo shoots tucked into glistening strips of bean curd skin, and spicy cabbage in vinegar ($3.95) sharpened with mustard and fresh cilantro. The mania for shao lung bao (pork and crab "soup" buns; $5.50) overshadows the delight of another specialty, pan-fried pork dumplings ($3.75)—juicy potstickers with golden-crisp bottoms and delicate seams.

Nothing quite prepares you, however, for the salty, fatty drama of the crispy duck entree ($12.95). Of the other entrees, red-cooking sauce turns up in a variety of braised dishes: atop a whole yellow fish ($12.95), over crisp strips of fried chicken with chopped garlic, scallions, and ginger ($11.95), or around fatty pork shoulder ($11.95). But finest of all are the tender, juicy ground-pork balls ($12.95)—sometimes called "lion's head"—served in an elegant laurel of crunchy baby bok choy.

XO Kitchen

(🍴) Had a French-trained, media-savvy chef introduced XO's custardy gratin of razor clams, he would have been hailed as a genius. And had this genius served a squab as outrageously lacquered, roasted, and underpriced as XO's $7.95 rendition, he would have been reclassified just as quickly as a lunatic. Maybe there are no mad geniuses toiling towards immortality behind the XO counter. But in spinning out more than 150 of the pop-Chinese foods captivating young diners in Hong Kong, Taipei, and New York, these cooks assemble some remarkably imaginative, amusing, and cheap chow. Ordering is, however, a difficult business. Because some dishes are repeated in different menu categories, the eager servers rarely get your order exactly right. Moreover everything comes out at once.

**Lunch $8–25
Dinner $8–35**

Address 148 Hester St, between Elizabeth St & The Bowery

☎212/965-8645

Transportation 6,M,N,Q,R,W to Canal St

Open Sun–Thurs 8am–11pm, Fri & Sat 8am–11.30pm

Accepts Cash only

Reservations Not accepted

Though the repertoire is largely devoid of the fusion fiascos (French toast peanut butter sandwiches, anyone?) featured at other westernized Chinese cafes, the coupling of French-style escargot and American coleslaw ($5.95) is curious. Those bizarre baked razor clams with cheese ($4.95) are niftier. The "Appetizers" section of the menu is confusing. It covers a few entrees, including the essential salt-baked shrimp ($7.95), while excluding such starters as the seafood and ham dumplings (a clever but leaky adaptation of Shanghai soup dumplings; $4.95) and dim-sum-style steamed rice noodles ($2.50–2.75). Watch out for bones in the otherwise commendable sliced fish version.

Congees and noodle soups ($3.50–6.95) presented in small cast-iron cauldrons are the warm-up acts to the high drama of sirloin steaks ($13.95) delivered on sizzling iron platters. Tableside, the waiter douses each enormous steak with a good half-cup of black peppercorn sauce, mushroom sauce, or, best of all, chopped garlic sauce—thus splattering every unprotected garment within a 4ft radius. Don't leave before sampling the fresh papaya chunks with honeydew soup and ice cream, the warm egg custard pudding with ice cream (both $3.95), or any other dessert you may be trying for the first and possibly last time.

Yeah Shanghai Deluxe

When they opened Yeah Shanghai across the street from the very popular New Green Bo (see p.20), the owners weren't thinking they could make it on overflow business alone. They were going to offer something different. This, no doubt, partly explains the ersatz tropical garden with fountain and footbridge in the middle of an otherwise generic Chinatown eatery. But while the appeal of the plastic palms is fleeting at best, it's the figurative flowerbed the cooks carve out of fish that draws most attention. Chrysanthemum fish ($12.95), for example, consists of fried fish clusters shaped like flower heads that, with the aid of a sweet-and-sour sauce, undergo a miraculous color change from golden to reddish orange.

Lunch $7–40
Dinner $15–40

Address 65 Bayard St, between Mott & Elizabeth Sts
℗212/566-4884
Transportation 6,J,M,N,Q,R,W,Z to Canal St
Open Mon–Thurs 11am–11pm, Fri & Sat 10.30am–midnight, Sun 10.30am–10pm
Accepts Cash only
Reservations Not accepted

Why elaborate on the cold Shanghai appetizers if the mere mention of the ingredients—hairy beans, ox tongue, beef stomach—turns Westerners off? Because a combination plate of the cold starters ($13.95 for four delicacies) is Yeah Shanghai's best point of departure—far more interesting than the usual steamed buns and pan-fried dumplings. Either way, you want to get into the entrees as quickly as possible. There's lots to cover in the seafood category alone. A lovely, pale-pink mound of sautéed shrimp surrounded by a glistening green laurel of pea shoots ($12.95). Yellow fish fried two ways, seaweed battered (that's the norm) and wrapped in bean curd skin ($12.95). Sliced, sautéed, and sizzling eel draped with Shanghai brown sauce (reduced soy sauce; $19.95). Or even, for the adventurous, fleshy sea cucumber bejeweled with caviar-like shrimp eggs and the same brown sauce ($21.95).

As for the meats, few chef's specialties anywhere can beat the drama of mau tai (paper-wrapped) chicken ($17.95), a stuffed whole bird marinated for three hours, wrapped in lotus leaf, foil, and cellophane, and steamed. When a waiter cuts open the mummified bird, the perfumed vapors of ginger, mushroom, and garlic drift overhead. You could also go for the pork meatball casserole known as "lion's head" ($10.95), which carries cellophane noodles as well as the customary greens (in this case crunchy baby bok choy).

East Village

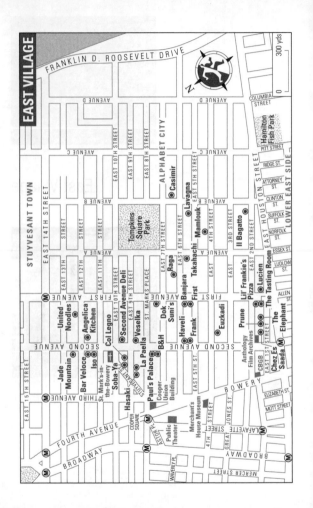

EAST VILLAGE

FRANKLIN D. ROOSEVELT DRIVE

STUYVESANT TOWN

Tompkins Square Park

ALPHABET CITY

Hamilton Fish Park

LOWER EAST SIDE

300 yds

AVENUE D
AVENUE C
AVENUE B
AVENUE A
FIRST AVENUE
SECOND AVENUE
THIRD AVENUE
FOURTH AVENUE
BROADWAY
BOWERY
LAFAYETTE STREET
EAST HOUSTON STREET

COLUMBIA STREET
PITT STREET
RIDGE ST
ATTORNEY ST.
CLINTON ST.
SUFFOLK ST.
NORFOLK ST.
ESSEX ST.
LUDLOW ST.
ALLEN ST
ELIZABETH ST.
MOTT STREET
JONES ST.
GREAT JONES STREET
MERCER STREET
WAVERLY PL.
ASTOR PL.
COOPER SQUARE
ST MARKS PLACE
STUYVESANT ST.

EAST 14TH STREET
EAST 13TH STREET
EAST 12TH STREET
EAST 11TH STREET
EAST 10TH STREET
EAST 9TH STREET
EAST 8TH STREET
EAST 7TH STREET
EAST 6TH STREET
EAST 5TH STREET
EAST 4TH STREET
EAST 3RD STREET
EAST 2ND STREET
EAST 1ST STREET
EAST 15TH STREET

Casimir
Lavagna
Mamlouk
Il Bagatto
Jade Mountain
Bar Veloce
Iso
St Mark's-in-the-Bowery
Soba-Ya
United Noodles
Angelica Kitchen
Col Legno
Second Avenue Deli
Veselka
La Paella
B&H
Dok Suni's
Raga
Banjara
Takahachi
First
Haveli
Frank
Euzkadi
Hasaki
Paul's Palace
Cooper Union Building
Merchant's House Museum
Public Theater
Prune
Lucien
Lil' Frankie's Pizza
The Tasting Room
Anthology Film Archives
CBGB
Chez Es Saada
The Elephant

Angelica Kitchen

To appreciate Angelica Kitchen you don't need to believe that eating something that once swam, flew, or roamed the earth is the moral equivalent of throwing an old lady in front of a bus. The oak, picnic-style tables of this warm, bright, organic vegetarian are perpetually packed with nose-ringed, heavily tattooed vegans, stylish, yoga-mat-carrying model-types, fresh-faced young professionals, and mature hippies. The eclectic crowd is proof that vegetarian cuisine, when prepared with wit and imagination, can appeal to a diverse and happy audience. Regulars are wont to call the hotline to hear about specials like tofu squares roasted in a thyme mustard vinaigrette with porcini and walnut sauce even on days when they have no plans to come in for dinner.

$7–35

Address 300 East 12th St, between 1st & 2nd Aves
☎212/228-2909
Transportation L to 1st Ave; 4,5,6,N,R to 14th St–Union Square
Open Daily 11.30am–10.30pm
Accepts Cash only
Reservations Not accepted

VEGETARIAN

Salads are fresh, enormous, and stunning. Even the simple house salad gets dressed up with a colorful tangle of shredded carrots, beets, daikon, red and green cabbage, and crisp pea shoots ($3.75/$5/$7.75). Soups change daily ($3.25/cup, $4/bowl) and are invariably hearty and tasty. Thankfully, the three bean chili ($7.50/$10) never comes off the menu: it's a thick stew packed with lentils, kidney and pinto beans, homemade seitan, sun-dried tomatoes, and a heavy hit of spicy chiles, all topped off with tofu sour cream. The dragon bowls ($5.95–9.95), one-pot macrobiotic meals brimming with rice, beans, tofu, and steamed vegetables, are very healthy, and alas very bland. You'll need to add lots of soy sauce.

Large sandwiches are loaded with flavor. In one favorite, thick slices of lemon-herb tofu are joined by roasted vegetables and almond parsley pesto between chunky slices of mixed grain or wheat-free sourdough spelt bread ($7.50). The warm tempeh Reuben ($7.50) is a clever twist on the classic, with cumin-marinated tempeh, sauerkraut, and tofu Russian dressing (not at all bad) assembled between slices of caraway bread with lots of oomph. Home-baked desserts vary: working your way through the apple banana crumb pie with maple tofu whip ($5) is a dream, but the plodding effort required to enjoy the wheat-free, upside-down pear ginger cake with raspberry sauce ($5) is just too much to ask.

VEGETARIAN

B&H

🍴 Today they classify the joint as "vegetarian." But the eight globe lights that hang down from the ceiling like black-stemmed lollipops illuminate a living Formica memory: the Jewish dairy restaurant. That once prevalent East Village/Lower East Side institution has been reduced to the obscenely narrow dimensions of a hallway, with room for six tables-for-two and a dozen counter stools. The action at the counter is itself a piece of Second Avenue theater played in several languages and accents. The Hispanic grillman is backstaged by Ukrainian and Polish women stirring up soups from another century, while the counter contingent is a nutritionally correct community of hip and haggard, wholesome and sickly, scholarly and street-educated. The prevailing melancholy could transform Reese Witherspoon into a sallow-skinned loner.

$5–15

Address 127 2nd Ave, between St Mark's Place & 7th St

☎212/505-8065

Transportation 6 to Astor Place; N,R to 8th St

Open Daily 6.30am–10.30pm

Accepts Cash only

Reservations Not accepted

Happily, the superlative soups restore color to all complexions: double-thick lima bean, hot rich borscht, salty split pea, and a matzoh ball variety that challenges the Second Avenue Deli's (see p.51) pricier rendition for best downtown. So good are they that regulars enter the days of the week when their favorite is featured (for curative cabbage soup, it's Mondays and Thursdays) as recurring appointments in their PDAs. You need not be a mathematician to figure out that at a $3.25 bowl of soup is a better value than a $2.95 cup. But you would need a behavioral psychologist to explain the motivation behind the small price differential. Both come with two slices of sweet, crusty, tan-colored, unbraided challah bread freshly baked in loaf pans. This foundation for the solid and unfussy French toast ($4.60) will replace any previous notions of challah you might have.

Plenty of other used-to-be standards hold up very well: perfect made-to-order blintzes ($6.50), year-round matzoh brie ($4.60), vegetarian chopped liver sandwich ($4.50). Wheatgrass juice and carrot juice are freshly squeezed antidotes for a number of ills and woes, not least of them a fear of B&H's vulnerability. One day it will close and a small New York food light—actually eight hanging food lights—will go out.

Il Bagatto

Il Bagatto's 1995 arrival in Alphabet City augured a turnaround for that then squalid, crack-ridden, last-to-be gentrified section of the East Village. It's been packed nearly every night since, first with appreciative locals and soon after with slumming uptowners pleasantly shocked to find such knowing, rustic cooking in so unlikely a location. At the time, the prevailing idea of Italian sophistication at busy pasta joints around nearby Second Avenue was adding

$22–55

Address 192 East 2nd St, between Aves A & B
☎212/228-0977
Transportation F,V to 2nd Ave
Open Tues–Thurs 6–11.45pm, Fri & Sat 6pm–12.30am, Sun 6–10.30pm
Accepts Cash only
Reservations Suggested

ITALIAN

strawberries to mixed salads. Il Bagatto limits such quirks to red Christmas lights and spooky grape vines strewn on the brick walls of its dark, noisy, cramped dining room. The downstairs bar/lounge is a merry purgatory for tolerant diners waiting on their table.

All start with a basket of lightly oiled, occasionally warm focaccia flecked with sea salt. The wondrous antipasto Il Bagatto ($8), billed as a sampler plate from an antipasti table no one has actually ever seen, can include a slice of spinach frittata, caramelized pearl onions, grilled zucchini and eggplant, a chickpea salad, and gently stewed lentils and tomatoes. It's not going to change your life, but, true to Italian style, each vegetable, free of excessive seasoning, can express its true self. Although New York's tomato season is tortuously brief, the kitchen manages to procure sweet love apples year round. Even the January tomatoes spooned atop the grilled, garlic-rubbed, must-have bruschetta ($5) have personality.

Chef-owner Beatrice Tosti's homemade pastas are demonstrably superior to versions in the same low end of town and price range. Gnocchetti verdi e blu ($11), those tiny, feathery spinach gnocchi, are inseparable from their pungent Gorgonzola sauce. Tortellini con ragu ($10.50) are smothered with the love of a toothsome veal ragu. Beyond stuffed and unstuffed pasta (even simple penne and spaghetti soar), the saltimbocca alla Romana ($14.50) is a generous veal scallop nattily cloaked in prosciutto and fried sage leaves and sided with potatoes roasted to their amber-hued peak. For dessert, go for the tartufo ($6), a cocoa-rolled ball of chocolate ice cream and lusciously eggy, frozen zabaglione.

Banjara

INDIAN

(🍴) In the New York restaurant universe, everything is relative. Had Banjara opened elsewhere with the same menu, decor, and staff, it could well be admired for its affordable menu, cozy informality, and cute, delivery-friendly reformatting of traditional Indian dishes. But because it's spread out in two adjacent storefronts at the bottom of a block packed with dirt-cheap Bangladeshi joints, Banjara is instead tolerated as the

$15–45

Address 97 1st Ave at 6th St
℡212/477-5956
Transportation 6 to Astor Place; F,V to 2nd Ave
Open Mon–Thurs 3pm–midnight, Fri–Sun noon–midnight
Accepts All major credit cards

expensive and quasi-fancy place on East Sixth, with refined service and cuisine that's too precious by half. This is only to be expected when the $17.95 that you're fairly charging for a fistful of charcoal-broiled prawns buys a complete dinner at your next-door neighbor's.

Location should not matter in a place named after a colorful gypsy tribe from Rajasthan who've roamed the 22 states of India. And it certainly becomes irrelevant once you appreciate that Tuhin Dutta is, to our knowledge, the only chef in Manhattan preparing Indian-style dumpakht. The subcontinent's counterpart to British meat pies, American pot pies, and French *en croûte*, dumpakht (the name and origin are Persian) is a centuries-old concoction. A mildly spiced stew is encased in a pastry and then baked, effectively sealing in its juices until the diner's fork breaks the lid. Banjara prepares four dumpakht varieties in a lightly salted shell that supposedly contains only water, salt, and flour: lamb ($12.95), chicken ($12.95), shrimp ($17.95), and vegetable ($11.95). Even without the benefit of a pastry, Dutta does a splendid job keeping his tandoori dishes moist. The adraki chop ($17.95) consists of ginger-spiced grilled lamb chops that exit the clay oven in superbly succulent shape. There are few better chops at this price anywhere.

The "cutesy" label does fit several of the appetizers, including the dhakshin se shuru ($6.95), a Southern Indian mixed dish of bite-sized idli (steamed rice and lentil cakes) and mini-dosa (potato-filled pancakes) that are nothing more than teasers. The condiments (mango chutney, raita, lemon pickles) and breads, however, are outstanding. When ordering a plain, garlic, or potato-stuffed nan, be sure to ask for it "dry." Otherwise it comes needlessly slathered in ghee (clarified butter).

Bar Veloce

The Italian films that play silently on the plasma TV at Bar Veloce are not meant to be a distraction. Concerned that people might clog the front of his narrow wine bar, owner Frederick Twomey wanted only to introduce some movement in the rear of a confined space. A second benefit was unforeseen: If your companion, existing or prospective, has his or her back to a screening of Fellini's *La Dolce Vita*, the English subtitles are there to be used like some cinematic Cyrano. Need an icebreaker?

$20–40

Address 175 2nd Ave, between
11th & 12th Sts
☎212/260-3200
Transportation L to 1st Ave;
4,5,6,N,Q,R,W to 14th St–Union
Square
Open Daily 5pm–3am
Accepts All major credit cards
Reservations Not accepted

ITALIAN

"It may seem strange but I know you well" flashes across the bottom of the screen. Is the conversation getting too heavy? Then repeat as follows: "If you're going to be serious I shan't listen to you." Is he or she resisting your charms? Then pass on the immortal message: "Let yourself be dominated body and soul."

Choosing just the right Italian wines, panini, and various bread-topping tidbits requires no prompting from Marcello Mastroianni. You need only consult the menu, which has a list of bruschetta (toasted bread with toppings), panini (grill-pressed sandwiches), tramezzini (small sandwiches on untoasted bread), and easy-to-share platters on one side and a list of thirty young wines, each with a modestly helpful description, on the reverse. The harmless 1999 Aglianico from Cantina del Taburno in Sicily ($7/glass) and the fruity 1998 Nebbiolo d'Alba from Luca Abrate in Piedmont ($14/glass) are among the bottles suspended behind the polyurethaned plywood bar, which displays architect Anthony Caradonna's ultra-cool blueprint.

The design of the slender sandwiches—the prosciutto di Parma panino ($8) with its melted mesh of mushrooms, truffle oil, and Fontina, for example, or the dainty, triple-decker tramezzino of black olive paste, arugula, and pristine mozzarella on white bread ($4)—also merits favorable notice. And *la dolce vita* practically oozes out of the dreamy dessert panino of Nutella and gelato ($5)—a crunchy cross between a hazelnut wafer bar and a Felliniesque ice cream sandwich.

There's another Bar Veloce at 17 Cleveland Place, Little Italy (☎212/966-7334).

Casimir

(🍴) The lazy ceiling fans and dim globe lights suggest a low-voltage locale beside a Mediterranean port. The ochre-painted walls are hung, as we imagine all authentic Parisian bistros to be, with mirrors distorted by age and rusty placards advertising brands of classic French drinks. But just as the magic of the movie *Casablanca* is a reflection of Hollywood's making, not Europe's or Morocco's, the enchantment of Casimir reflects a blend of ingenuity and budget sophistication

$30–50

Address 103–105 Ave B, between 6th & 7th Sts

☎212/358-9683

Transportation 6 to Astor Place

Open Sun–Thurs 5.30pm–midnight, Fri & Sat 5.30pm–1am

Accepts AmEx

Reservations Required

more at home on Avenue B than on the boulevard Saint-Germain. Its owners and origins, though Parisian, have found their special place, like so many emigrés before them, near the Lower East Side. The great ambition of Casimir is not only to make possible a pretty good order of steak frites for $14, but also to keep their eye on what the pricey, trendy eateries are up to uptown. Signs of trickle-down gastronomics include salads covered with Jackson Pollock-like splatters of balsamic vinegar and vertically assembled entrees poked with a mad flourish of fresh herb stems. Somewhere in the kitchen is a pent-up painter or, at the very least, a frustrated florist.

Best among the appetizer arrangements (mostly $7.50) are the toss of sautéed chicken livers, sweet balsamic, greens, and fried onions; the sliced blood sausage with sautéed apples and mashed potatoes; and the "Velodrome" salad with enough arugula, shaved parmesan, and garlic croûtons for two adults to share.

The main course menu offers lots of appealing places to go. For simplicity, take the superbly crisp-skinned duck confit ($14). For diversity, go in the direction of a bouillabaisse ($14) that freely borrows seafood—salmon, halibut, tuna, monkfish, mussels, etc—from every fish dish on the menu. For domesticity, hop on for the hamburger New Orleans ($12)—a fat, juicy, two-fisted, five-napkin job topped with bacon and grilled onions and slipped into a ciabatta roll. Desserts ($5–6) are uneven,but you could do worse than go for the molten chocolate cake, truly an abstract work of art.

Col Legno

🍴 On a block brimming with Japanese food outlets of every shape and color, Col Legno stands out for its Tuscan plainness. A single room in the requisite shade of golden sienna (can you even buy white paint in Tuscany?) has a conical wood-burning pizza oven tucked in the corner. Col Legno means "with wood" and is probably a pun referring to the pizza oven and apple-wood grill, but it can also describe the technique whereby a violinist strikes the

$25–55
Address 231 East 9th St, between 2nd & 3rd Aves
☎212/777-4650
Transportation 6 to Astor Place; N,R to 8th St
Open Tues–Sun 6–11.30pm
Accepts AmEx
Reservations Suggested

ITALIAN

strings with the wooden part of the bow. Inside the spacious, semi-open back kitchen, a rustic table (does this Italian region permit any other kind?) can be reserved for up to ten people. The resolutely unassuming restaurant attracts NYU grad students and faculty, ticketholders from the Public Theater or the more avant-garde P.S. 122, and neighborhood regulars with persistent yearnings for honest Florentine food.

Except for seasonal shifts in ingredients and upward ticks in the low-to-moderate prices, the trattoria menu has changed very little over the years. It's a welcome break from trendy eateries where everything has to be new and the recitation of specials requires a superhuman attention span. Consistency and hospitality of this high standard are plusses in themselves. Chef-owner Chris Trilivas is always on hand to ensure the integrity of his recipes, starting with soup ($5)—a brothy white bean purée with rosemary in the winter or a purée of cold tomato, red bell pepper and basil in summer—or perhaps fried baby artichokes flattened and splayed in the Roman "Jewish" style ($7.95). Country bread imported from Hoboken and several wines under $20 keep all appetizers in the very best company.

Among pastas, only the spinach lasagna doesn't inspire lasting loyalty. Try the pappardelle with rosemary-scented wild boar ragu ($13.95) or the spaghetti with mint-flavored black olive paste ($12.95) and you'll have a hard time coming back for anything else. That would be a shame, though. The wood-grilled, fennel-infused pork chops ($14.95) are dandy. And the rosemary-rubbed bistecca ($15.95) is one of the best grilled steak bargains in the city. Right up to the hazelnut gelato ($5.50), Trilivas hits all the right notes.

East Villlage

Dok Suni's

🍴 Though several chefs, restaurateurs, and journalists can claim some credit for guiding Korean food into the Manhattan mainstream, Jenny Kwak and her mother Myung Ja are indisputably the city's original pioneers of kimchee chic. Back in 1993, the idea of a hip Korean place that didn't limit itself to tabletop barbecue was outrageous, and might have stayed that way too if Kwak, then 19, wasn't so naïve. "I didn't know better," she recalls. "Just coming out of

$25–50
Address 119 1st Ave, between St Mark's Place & 7th St
☏212/477-9506
Transportation 6 to Astor Place
Open Sun & Mon 4.30–11pm, Tues–Sat 4.30pm–midnight
Accepts Cash only
Reservations Not accepted

school, I was so excited to be eating the food I loved again." A year later, the small, dark, cramped space was filling up early and staying full late with quasi-trendy clubbers, NYU students, and in-the-know audiences from the catty-cornered P.S. 122. Nowadays, Dok Suni's cachet even extends to the 'burbs. Pierced and savvy waitresses have grown accustomed to serving saketinis to Benetton-clad couples who've hooked up through Internet dating services.

The menu is country Korean mom's food with a couple of ethno twists, best exemplified by the jalapeno chicken ($12.95), battered, pan-fried chicken nuggets with jalapenos, soy sauce, and garlic sauce. It's supposed to be a main course, but it certainly doesn't have to be. You'd be wise not to choose it over two stellar appetizers, though: the fritter-like kimchee pancakes with soy and vinegar dipping sauce ($5), and the o-bok salad of green perilla leaves and barley noodles in a tangy-spicy mustard and vinegar dressing ($9). Traditional broths and stews, like the feel-good miso stew with tofu, zucchini, and mushrooms, or the vegetable dumpling soup in an egg-drop beef broth, are, at $9.95, delightfully affordable. In each there's a meal for one or an appetizer for three.

No main course can beat the tender, slow-broiled pork ribs in a spicy chile pepper and garlic sauce ($14.95). But you should still try the broiled squid with mixed veggies in a spicy red pepper sauce ($14.95), assuming you haven't already had the cornmeal fried squid starter, and bibimbop ($13.95), the catch-all rice dish tossed hot or cold with that deadly red pepper sauce. Before leaving, say "an-nyong-hi" with a shot of the sweetened cinnamon drink.

The Elephant

🍴 An anchor tenant smack in the middle of East Village's restaurant row, the mouse-sized Elephant shows no signs of slowing down despite having enjoyed several years happily spilling out onto the sidewalk. With its softly glowing zinc bar, sprays of red Christmas lights, dangling banana bunches, beaded curtains, and zebra-striped banquettes, this diminutive Thai bistro generates a seductive, psychic warmth that helps you put up with, and even enjoy, the jostled wait for a tiny table. It helps to set yourself up

$15–45

Address 58 East 1st St, between 1st & 2nd Aves
☏212/505-7739
Transportation F,V to 2nd Ave
Open Sun–Thurs noon–4pm & 5.30pm–midnight, Fri & Sat noon–4pm & 5.30pm–1am
Accepts Amex
Reservations Suggested

with a glass of sangria ($7) ladled from the bowl behind the bar and watch the loud, thirsty, and beautiful crowd shout at themselves over the bass-rumbling music.

It's prudent not to get distracted by the French-inflected options (and staff), but to order as you would at a favorite Thai takeout. Hot and sour soup with lime leaves and prawns ($6.75) and summer rolls with shrimp ($6.75) are light, well-balanced expressions of standards. The plentiful and eminently biteable grilled calamari ($7.75) is set off by a vibrant salad of spinach, frisée, mango, and a stealthy leaf or two of cilantro dressed with tamarind and lime. Moist if unremarkable chicken satay ($8.75) begets a thick, sweet peanut dip. As a main course, wildly over-priced pad Thai ($16.75) earns its place on a grownup white dinner plate. The peanuts taste freshly ground, the bean sprouts stand to attention, and the large and tender tiger shrimp abound in a piping hot jungle of spice-tinged rice noodles.

The beef in an eponymous salad ($17.75) is discernibly seared to order, and is served with a puff of steaming jasmine rice, shredded mint leaves, and harmlessly silly swirls of mango purée and spicy red pepper that one associates with mid-90s decadence and dime-store squirt bottles. Order dessert ($6.50) if you must, but prepare for a letdown after the decisive, clear flavors of your savories. The lemongrass and lime tart with passionfruit sorbet alone comes close to approximating the cool and sexy heat of earlier courses.

BASQUE

Euzkadi

Euzkadi is a political name meaning either "Basque Fatherland," or, here on East Fourth Street, "budget bistro opportunistically highlighting a hitherto overlooked regional cuisine that we the owners don't really know all that well." The design, though not patently Basque, does have the feel of a hideaway for romantic bohemians if not radical separatists. Outside, brickwork paved into the tiny sidewalk terrace is inlayed with a broken-tile mosaic spelling "Euzkadi." Inside, small wood tables, bentwood chairs, red banquettes, and stark ceiling fans are crammed into a dark, noisy, smoky room in which round-cornered, wood-framed antique mirrors are hung on the exposed-brick walls. As getting up and down from tables is a strain both on you and your neighbors, it's a good idea to visit the restroom before settling down to eat.

$28–55

Address 108 East 4th St, between 1st & 2nd Aves
☎212/982-9788
Transportation F,V to 2nd Ave
Open Sun–Thurs 5.30–11pm, Fri & Sat 5.30pm–midnight
Accepts All major credit cards
Reservations Required

Chef Serge Buzkowski isn't Basque, but he apparently owns a fine Basque cookbook or two which he's put to good use. You'll have no trouble digesting your meal, or your dinner check, and you will get a diverting, three-course immersion in the key components of Basque table: garlic, peppers, olives, shellfish, salt cod, fennel, beans, and potatoes, but, oddly, not rice (unless ordered as a side dish). Top starters include grilled octopus with a tomato, ham, and olive sauce; sautéed calamari piperade with stewed onions, peppers, and tomatoes; and, on special, perfectly grilled sardines with herb oil (all $7).

About half the entree choices are served "a la plancha," meaning they're sizzling on a cast-iron skillet. All are $14. The best (stunning pink duck breast) and worst (cooked-out skate) have recently been eliminated, leaving behind three solid options: prawns, whole fish, or pork chops. Menu changes outside this category are frequent, so be careful not to get too attached to the marvelously flaky, roasted cod encrusted in black olives ($15). Something equally good is likely to come along. Among desserts (all $6), the sensation is the fig brochette speared with rosemary. But the prune clafoutis, quince tarte tatin, and chestnut rice pudding all use their flavors well.

First

🍴 There was a time, not so long ago, when the East Village was a culinary ghetto nourished by curry-in-a-hurry, pierogi-in-a-pinch, and fettuccine-on-the-cheap. Nothing high-rent or high-minded. This did not deter Sam DeMarco, an energetic and talented chef, from attempting in 1994 a first on First with First, a self-consciously slick, steel-accented spot that soon became the after-work chefs' haunt for globally aware contemporary American cuisine. DeMarco clearly had vision. It wasn't the neighborhood that gave life to the chef

$25–75

Address 87 1st Ave, between 5th & 6th Sts

☎212/674-3823

Transportation 6 to Astor Place; N,R to 8th St

Open Mon–Thurs 6pm–2am, Fri & Sat 6pm–3am, Sun 11am–4pm & 5pm–1am

Accepts All major credit cards

Reservations Recommended

NEW AMERICAN

and his groundbreaking restaurant. It was the other way around. Consequently, he's the pioneer who deserves much of the credit—or blame—for the ensuing influx of trendy, pretentious, and pricey bistros.

It is easy to see now why First was so quickly accepted. DeMarco's creativity is playful and amusing, two attributes plainly obvious in his signature appetizers: fiery Buffalo lollipop wings with warm blue cheese fondue ($9/$14); Mexican seafood tacos packed with rock shrimp, cheese, and black beans ($11); a quartet of mini-cheeseburgers with a vat of thin, crisp, 22-carat fries ($14); fried "Asian" oysters, golden and virtually greaseless, paired with wasabe mayo ($11)—once, if you can imagine, an original idea.

If you're still hungry after those must-haves, the entrees won't let you down. Moist, buttery, sage-roasted chicken is teamed with a rustic butternut squash gratin ($19), while soy-honey marinated duck comes with a pile of fluffy kasha and a blackberry Burgundy sauce ($24). And for the ultimate in beef indulgence for two: a juicy 42oz porterhouse with steak fries ($75). Share it with someone "special" (ie, they're paying), or sneak in instead on a Sunday night for spaghetti and meatballs (not quite as large as cue balls) with garlic bread ($18). The full menu is available at the bar. It's usually three-deep with martini-swigging hipsters drawn to the infamous Tiny Tinis: a dozen creative concoctions available in three sizes—medium ($8), large ($14), and gigunda (read: pass out fast for $22). These 'tails are guaranteed to quench your thirst and make you forget your worries or your name, whichever comes first.

East Village

Frank

(🍴) The good fortunes of Frank Prisinzano and his Neapolitan-Sicilian-Pugliese-American baby have ushered in a new era for cheap, physically challenged Italian joints. Whereas its predecessors wowed the hungry masses by fitting such uptown fashions as tricolore salads, flavored pastas, and anything remotely Tuscan into a low-rent, no-frills mold, Frank's formula is based on indulging nostalgic yearnings for yummy tummy food. The flea market jumble of mix-and-match tables, baroque mirrors, sepia-toned family photos, and bric-a-brac create an irresistible setting for old-fashioned, red-sauced satisfaction.

Lunch $11–50
Dinner $18–50

Address 88 2nd Ave, between 5th & 6th Sts

☎212/420-0202

Transportation F,V to 2nd Ave; 6 to Astor Place

Open Sun–Thurs 10.30am–12.30am, Fri & Sat 10.30am–1.30am

Accepts Cash only

Reservations For large groups

Curiously, Frank's feel-good foods don't belong to any single place or era. Like the decoration, they comprise a contrived hodgepodge reflecting both the owner's Italian roots and New Yorkese ingenuity. A golden oldie like garlic bread ($3.95; $7.25 topped with Sicilian salted anchovies), for instance, looks nothing like the article of red-checkered tablecloth pasts. But its mere suggestion hits the right note and its thick layer of chopped roasted garlic suggests grandmotherly excess. Similarly, the Tuscan crostino nero ($6.95), smeared with mashed chicken livers, may be new to many of us, yet it has the qualities of something comfortingly familiar. Certainly, the menu's use of the word "gravy" for tomato ragu invites all sorts of warm associations with a happy American childhood. That gravy coats both the rigatoni al ragu ($9.95) and the polpettone ($11.95), the mammoth meatball that leads otherwise sensible people to endure long waits and cramped conditions. The main course worth knocking elbows with strangers for is fava e cicoria ($13.95), a soothing purée of fava beans with chicory and roasted vegetables. Desserts succeed mostly in bumping up the check.

With 400 Italian wines and a cellar capacity of 1560 bottles, Frank likely offers more wines per square foot than any restaurant in America, allowing you to pair a $200 Barolo with a $12 meatball.

Hasaki

Despite the huge number of sleekly designed sushi bars in NYC, nightly waits endure at the overcrowded and deceptively uninviting Hasaki. Many spend so much time huddled in the doorway and on the steps outside it that that they ought to pay rent for the space. First-timers told of Madonna sightings and celebrity regulars are baffled to behold a place so thoroughly devoid of glamor. The only features that might possibly be called decorative—at a stretch—are the empty wooden wall

$25–65

Address 210 East 9th St, between 2nd & 3rd Aves
℡212/473-3327
Transportation 6 to Astor Place; N,R to 8th St
Open Mon–Fri 5.30–11.30pm, Sat & Sun 1–4pm & 5.30–11.30pm
Accepts All major credit cards
Reservations Not accepted

JAPANESE

frames that could, after a few glasses of sake, be mistaken for surreal windows. There are just two viable reasons to be here: for exceptional sushi artistry at a moderate price or to flirt with one of the singles waiting in the vestibule.

When sitting at the bar you quickly become aware that the graceful sushi chefs are not a trio of equals. The even-tempered Kawano, stationed to your left, appears to do most of the heavy lifting. When an order comes in for a house specialty, say the naruto zukuri ($14)—sea urchin rolled in a meticulously fluted tube of squid and then thinly sliced—the assignment is his. A request for the comparatively routine, yet exquisitely perfumed, roll of ume (plum) paste and shiso leaf ($3.50), on the other hand, may go to any one of the chefs.

While the best bet is to order what you like, know that there are some winners in some unlikely places. The precise cut of the carrots in the futomaki ($6) is itself worth the price. And the yellowtail special ($6) is indeed that: an inside-out roll of lush yellowtail pieces, carrot, and scallion all coated in flying fish caviar. Individual pieces of Portuguese octopus ($2.50), Japanese red snapper ($4), and the mackerel-like shima-aji ($5) shine, as literally does anything with eel, warmed in a Bagel Best toaster oven before being draped over rice. Finally, notice the details: the impossibly fine strands of nori (purple seaweed), the faintly coarse wasabe, the lingering fragrance of the pickled ginger. With jewels as precious as these, who cares how lackluster the box they come in?

Haveli

This bold attempt to upgrade East Village Indian dining can no longer be regarded as an experiment. The frosted-glass storefront of the stylish, design-conscious Haveli is now a Second Avenue fixture, as is its host Mohammed Hazim. And once you've been exposed to the rich, complex cooking of chef Siradul Islam (who, like most of the chefs in the area's Indian restaurants, hails from Bangladesh), a

$20–55

Address 100 2nd Ave, between 5th & 6th Sts
℡212/982-0533
Transportation 6 to Astor Place; F,V to 2nd Ave
Open Daily noon–midnight
Accepts All major credit cards

return to one-note curries and generic spice blends is problematic. Indeed, the downside of your trying the $8.95 mushroom shaag will be your subsequent distaste for the mushy, $5.95 versions that used to make you happy. As it happens, the cost of being so spoiled is rarely this reasonable. Only near East Sixth could Haveli's moderate prices be described as exorbitant. Move this place uptown and it would be the pride of the neighborhood.

The pleasures may be as subtle and soothing as rasam ($3.95), a Southern Indian soup with lentils, sesame, and the gentle tang of curry leaf, or as jazzy and jaunty as do-piaz curry (lamb cooked with plenty of onions and an orchestra of spices; $9.95). The distinct, wholewheatness of the flaky paratha ($2.50) is not lost when that bread is filled with onions or potatoes. To go with it, spinach raita ($2.95) is a lovely alternative to the cucumber version. Poori bhajee ($3.50), an appetizer of fried chickpeas and fluffy poori bread, is nicely salted and almost lemony. The sautéed "Bombay" chicken livers ($3.95) are pleasantly spiced. And vegetable pakora ($3.95) are superbly fresh and far-from-greasy fritters.

Yogurt-marinated tandoori entrees—mixed grill ($15.95), murgha tikka (boneless chicken breast chunks; $11.95)—are unexpectedly succulent. But the best grilled dish must be the reshmi kabab ($15.50), a skewer of chicken chunks buzzed with ginger and garlic. Another house specialty that's practically a New York exclusive is the chicken, lamb, and vegetable balti ($14.95). A British cooking craze that originated in Northern Pakistan, balti refers to the sizzling, cast-iron bucket in which the meats, tomatoes, cilantro, and spices are cooked and served. Come dessert, homemade mango ice cream ($2.50) leaves you thinking, "Isn't mango the best fruit in the world?"

Iso

(🍴) That Iso is closed on Sundays would seem to support the maxim that you shouldn't eat seafood in a restaurant on the day when there are no fresh fish deliveries. But this never-on-Sunday rule mistakenly assumes restaurants are serving all their fish the day they get it. In fact, you would feel more secure eating sashimi on a Sunday at Iso than on other days at many other places. Iso, the older man behind the sushi bar, has proven himself to be one of Manhattan's shrewdest fish buyers. The view from the sidewalk is telling: the menu posted in the window relies heavily on specials, determined by what fresh fish Iso chooses to buy from purveyors, while the line of regulars waiting to get in assures rapid and regular turnover.

$25–60

Address 175 2nd Ave at 11th St

☎212/777-0361

Transportation 6,N,Q,R,W to 14th St-Union Square; L to 1st Ave

Open Mon–Sat 5.30pm–midnight

Accepts All major credit cards

Reservations Not accepted

The ceiling's network of black piping and spotlights may suit an off-off-Broadway theater, but their purpose in a cramped eatery is not immediately clear. The three fixtures of note are the stainless-steel sake pitchers, the logo of circling dolphins and human figures designed by the late artist and former regular Keith Haring, and Iso herself, the sweet, mop-topped hostess who answers to the same name as her husband. The amiable waiters go into performance mode when reciting such specials as marinated mackerel with garlic and marinated grated onion ($7.50); sea urchin on the half-shell ($9.50); extremely tender orange clam sashimi with a sharp ponzu sauce ($10.50); and rolled and steamed monkish liver ($9.50)—the Japanese foie gras—that manages to be both unctuous and light. The bonito sashimi appetizer ($9.50) is a pleasure.

The benefit of the stage lighting becomes clearer when the sashimi combo ($22) makes its entrance. It consists of six large, lush, and astoundingly fresh fish chosen by Mr Iso. The sushi special combo ($21) with nine pieces and a tuna roll is similarly stunning. The green tea (hot water and a tea bag) and desserts are disappointments. After consuming all this great fish, every day is wrong for apricot Grand Marnier cake ($5.75) or triple chocolate mousse cake ($6.75).

East Village

Jade Mountain

(🍽) Historically, "Chow Mein" bill-boards like the red-neon original hung here between the windows of apartments 2A and 3A were looked up to as lighthouses for the hungry and the dislocated. Nighttime navigators returning from long absences at war, at work, or at the corner saloon recognized them as the first sure sign home was near. Others saw them as beacons when home—or, more precisely, the kitchen—was the last place they wanted to be. This relic desig-nates the last of the Manhattan Chinese

$7–30

Address 197 2nd Ave, between 12th & 13th Sts

☎212/533-3770

Transportation L to 1st Ave; N,R,Q,W to 14th St–Union Square

Open Sun–Thurs 11.30am–11pm, Fri & Sat 11.30am–midnight

Accepts Cash only

Reservations Not accepted

chop suey houses as we, our grandparents, and Ralph Kramden under-stood them to be. Who made the slightest distinction between such regional cuisines as Szechwan and Hunan, Hong Kong and Shanghai, Fukien and Canton, Shantung and Taiwan at a time when all neighbor-hood Chinese restaurant menus were broken down into two regions, column A and column B?

Forlorn Jade Mountain faithfully preserves the genuine chop suey parlor experience. Its menu upholds such forgotten classics as pork chop suey ($4.50), chicken egg foo yung ($4.50), moo goo gai pan ($6.25), lobster Cantonese-style ($15.95), and nine varieties of chow mein ($4.50–7.95). These may be ordered from columns A and B in value-oriented family meals—as if the prices were not low enough.

None of this is to suggest that Jade Mountain is a very good "good restaurant." It is, however, a very good "bad restaurant." The kitchen does do "bad"—greasy, starchy, gloppy, salty, phoney, or merely bad-for-you—food extremely well. And though we may congratulate ourselves for faithfully reading the food pages and learning how to eat better, our new-found sophistication should not deny us the pleasures of an occa-sional cheap chowdown. Besides, there is culinary merit at Jade Mountain: witness the butterfly shrimp ($8.75), which predates the cur-rent fashion for bacon-wrapped seafood by decades, and the war sho op, which requires a whole duck to be fried, boiled, skinned, and boned before the meat can be ground, stuffed back into the skin, cut into cubes, sautéed, and topped with toasted almonds and brown sauce. That's a lot of labor for $7.50.

Lavagna

🍽 At first glance, Lavagna appears too perfect to be the rustic East Village *trattoria del giorno*. The exposed-brick and burgundy walls come across as overly polished, the untarnished pressed-tin ceiling gives the impression of bronze plastic, and the yellow-glass shades of the wrought-iron, 1950s-Gothic chandeliers seem to have been salvaged from a New Jersey roadhouse rather than a Tuscan osteria. Inside the kitchen, the double-stone-

$25–60

Address 545 East 5th St, between Aves A & B
☎212/979-1005
Transportation F,V to 2nd Ave
Open Sun–Thurs 6–11pm, Fri & Sat 6pm–midnight
Accepts All major credit cards
Reservations Suggested

arched, copper-encased, wood-burning oven is surely a rich kid's toy. And the knowledge that Sami Kader also owns Le Tableau, the French *bistro du jour* on the same block, fuels speculation that Lavagna is the skilled forgery of an opportunist.

Nothing is as palpably calculated as executive chef Amanda Frietag's Italian adaptations. Her cooking is way too good for what they're charging. Something suspicious is going on and we're determined to get to the bottom of it—especially if it takes dozens of visits to do so. What's this business with the soft polenta matched to a lush, sautéed sweetbread ragu with wild mushrooms and white truffle oil ($9)? That's a great main dish. And what's this fritto misto (mixed fry; $9) doing in the top appetizer position normally reserved for calamari? The freshly fried and speedily delivered tiger shrimp (so *that's* what shrimp taste like!), sea scallops, fennel, and zucchini are incredible.

Pastas too are suspiciously first-rate. The fresh pappardelle with braised, mega-shredded rabbit, thyme, and olives ($14) is phenomenal. Specials like fresh tagliatelle with shredded duck confit, chopped leeks, and cremini mushrooms ($16) display unusual delicacy for so harried a kitchen. Of the meats and fish, the grilled pork chop ($15) reveals itself to be a juicy sensation—once you can tear yourself away from the accompanying velvety chestnut flan. And wood-roasted whole red snapper ($38 for two) is solid. The flat crust of the intriguing pizzettes ($9) presaged the current craze for flat, cracker-crisp, designer pizzas. For dessert ($7), consider the superb pistachio biscotti plate served with a sweet Sicilian wine for dunking. *Then* try to figure out what is really going on with this amazing restaurant.

Lil' Frankie's Pizza

This spin-off of the madly popular Frank (see p.38) begins with the same set of sentimental, mismatched curios—dinette tables, cutlery, and dishware; old family photos; gilded mirrors—which give that Italian eatery such charm. The low prices, and the lines outside the door during peak times, are also reminiscent of its forerunner. The great departure here starts with the wood-burning brick pizza oven, supposedly built with real Neapolitan lava from

$15–45
Address 19 1st Ave, between 1st & 2nd Sts
☎212/420-4900
Transportation F,V to 2nd Ave
Open Sun–Thurs 11am–2am, Fri & Sat 11am–4am
Accepts Cash only
Reservations For large groups

Mount Vesuvius, and concludes with a lofty rear dining room that features beautiful dark-wood wine racks, a lacquered floor adorned with happy flowers, and, painted on the wall above a round communal table, a cherub-faced sun. The only thing that could make this sky-lit space feel airier would be to remove its ceiling entirely—which is hardly necessary since there is already a backyard patio for warm-weather dining.

Though the cracker-thin pizzas ($6.95–13.95) lack the pleasing chewiness and puffed rims of a classic New York pie, the 12-inch disks are nevertheless crisp and unexpectedly light, allowing you to dig more deeply into the menu. First-rate toppings range from the Napoletana, with tomatoes, garlic, oregano, capers, black olives, Sicilian salted anchovies, and—as is proper with authentic anchovy pizzas—no cheese, to the Polpettini, with tomato, mozzarella, fresh sage, and baby meatballs the size of blueberries.

The most welcome surprise is the quality of the other foods cooked in the intense heat of that brick oven. The stemless wood-roasted Portobello ($8.75), plated with sweet roasted tomato and peppery arugula, is clearly the best appetizer. Only the house-cured tuna ($7.95), served with white beans, red onions, parsley, and olive oil, comes close. The whole roasted eggplant ($4.95) is sliced open at the table and thus still steaming as you scoop out its softened, smoky pulp. Talk about a pure pleasure! And the oven-roasted chicken, with sage, capers, lemon juice, and a side of mashed potatoes ($10.95), is a joy from first bite to last. Decent tiramisu ($6.75) and panna cotta ($5.95) appear overpriced in comparison to the budget-priced pizzas and savories.

Lucien

(🍴) Lucien Bahaj has worked in the French Riviera and Manhattan, two locales where $80 can amount to pocket change. But at this magical little rendezvous of Gallic charm and New York verve, that measly amount buys a bottle of fruity red, garlicky escargots, steak frites, and warm chocolate cake. Lucien's notion of New York glamor, though admittedly more black turtleneck than blue collar, is a world apart from a manic restaurant scene fueled by helium dinner checks and status-bestowing tables. When settled down into one of the makeshift bistro's old chairs and young wines, you can even see the rationale, if not the sanity, of Bahaj's most outrageous claim: the Lower East Side is more beautiful, he says from experience, than France's Mediterranean coast. The narrow space, with ochre walls, dark wood, and somber globes emitting Left Bank melancholy, is shaped like a telephone headset. Small dining areas in the front and back are connected by the four-seat bar that faces a kitchenette.

$30–75

Address 14 1st Ave, between 1st & 2nd Sts
☏212/260-6481
Transportation F,V to 2nd Ave
Open Daily 11am–2am
Accepts All major credit cards
Reservations Suggested

FRENCH

The menu as executed by Cisse, the French-trained Senegalese chef, makes no distinction between first and second courses. You might start by sharing an order of mussels marinières ($14) with enough meaty mollusks to occupy three diners and enough buttery white wine broth to drench three sliced baguettes. Or you might assert your individuality with your very own and very garlicky Provençal fish soup ($6). Either way, be sure to pass around the grilled fresh sardines ($8) and the chunky, peppery salmon tartare ($10).

Among three steak frites variations ($20), all of them served with bronzed shoestring fries, you want the grill-striped flank steak. The squab "Christopher" ($26) is a tougher call. Considering the rough-and-ready setting, it's a rather preposterous idea. Inspired by a specialty of the acclaimed Parisian restaurant Taillevent, it uses all of Lucien's vertical space to stack tender roast squab with good-quality foie gras and sautéed Portobellos. The dessert menu lists three outstanding options: the chocolate cake, the crème brûlée, and the chunky, beautifully caramelized tarte tatin. Any one of these makes $6 go a long way.

Mamlouk

On a block of grimy, weather-beaten tenements, Mamlouk's dated distressed-wood facade is no more convincing than a pair of antiqued blue jeans from J Crew. But the seductive inducements within the dark and diminutive dining space—gracious service; pure, vibrant, flavors; and a six-course, $30 prix fixe (and choice-fixed) repast—may soon have diners pushing for a third seating to follow the regularly packed ones at 7pm and 9pm. With no menu and only the entree option (meat or fish) for expressing personal choice, Mamlouk is not for control freaks. But anyone willing to trust the owners and staff who've honed their skills at the lovely Moustache restaurants (see p.164) can relax among stacks of silk and velvet cushions and prepare to be well fed.

$37–60

Address 221 East 4th St, between Aves A & B
☎212/529-3477
Transportation F,V to 2nd Ave
Open Tues–Sun 7–11pm
Accepts All major credit cards
Reservations Suggested

Dinner typically begins with a plate of crunchy, pickled vegetables—carrots, radishes, cucumbers, sweet peppers, and so on. Next, a modest bread salad, or fatoush, is eclipsed by a mezze of babaganoush, vinegary grape leaves stuffed with rice and olives, rich, herb-inflected labnee (strained yogurt), and artichoke salad all accompanied by warm pita bread. The single, crusty falafel to follow is paired with a deep-fried filo triangle oozing feta cheese plus, for dipping, a sweet tahini dressing. At the midway point you want to sit back, sip a glass of white or red from the short list, or maybe take a mid-prandial puff on some fruit-enhanced tobacco from a hookah ($15 for the table)—although most people wait until after dining to do that.

Representative of main courses is the astounding stew of chickpeas, yogurt, garlic, nutmeg, and the most incredibly tender chicken you'll ever meet. The stew is flecked with squares of sautéed filo, whose nutty, caramelized flavor pervades every bite. There is fragrant jasmine rice alongside, as well as a tangy mixture of chickpeas, eggplant, tomato, and cilantro that cuts the richness of the stew. Course five may be lamb kebabs with an acidic tomato and parsley compote, and with it, an unremarkable okra stew that you can safely skip to make room for the finale, a sweet cheese baklava topped with chopped pistachios and drizzled with rosewater syrup.

La Paella

(🍴) Folding your legs in this tiny Spanish kitchen/tapas bar, an anomaly on a block chock-full of Japanese eateries, is as tricky as bending your fingers in the hip pocket of a pair of tight-fitting Levis. That's not to say that getting comfortable is impossible, especially with the aid of a limb-loosening sangria or sherry with a plate of ceviche ($9) and a couple of pleasing tapas ($4–12; try the potato-omelet-like tortilla española or the

$25–60
Address 214 East 9th St, between 2nd & 3rd Aves
☎212/598-4321
Transportation 6 to Astor Place; N,R to 8th St
Open Sun–Thurs 5–11pm, Fri & Sat 5pm–midnight
Accepts MasterCard & Visa

Basque cheese sampler). Soon you're about ready to declare your love for one of the paellas. But wait! Beautiful paellas should not be assessed on the basis of first impressions. Such responses are clouded by the dizzying vapors released from a steaming-hot paella as the two-handled pan of saffron-scented rice, shellfish, and sausage is delivered to an expectant table. As a consequence, judgment should be delayed until the fifteenth forkful, when the excitement and temperature are diminished, the choice seafood and meats are depleted, and the now tepid rice is at its most vulnerable. Remember, a paella is above all a rice dish. The rest is clothing, make-up, and accessories.

At their best, the short, plump grains of rice in two mildly flavored paellas—the Catalana (chorizo and chile peppers) and the Marinera (langoustines, clams, shrimp, mussels, squid)—possess a moist, almost sticky coating. In the Negro, the rice absorbs the flavor of squid and squid ink, while in the Verdura, the grains are strictly vegetarian. In the Basque, meanwhile, the rice does battle with nearly all the ingredients contained in its sibling paellas. Each one costs between $24 and $36 and is enough for two.

Desserts ($7) have never been a strong suit at La Paella, but you have to admire the management's fortitude for sticking with them since 1995 through thick (tedious chocolate mousse) and thin (flan-like crema Catalan that should be as creamy as crème brûlée). Such loyalty, so unencumbered by taste considerations, is truly rare. The cheesecake is an inoffensive lightweight.

Paul's Palace

🍴 This greasy spoon may be a hole but it sure isn't Jackson Hole, the local chain known for its soft, fatty, face-stuffing variation the crusty New York burger. The one-and-only Paul's Palace does a superior, indie version of Jackson Hole's notorious hardhat burger. The hardhats in question are stainless steel cups which are fitted over the half-pound mounds of loosely packed chopped beef as they sizzle on the griddle. This effectively steams them in their own grease. As you sink your teeth into a Paul's

$6–20

Address 131 2nd Ave, between St Mark's Place & 7th St
☎212/529-3033
Transportation 6 to Astor Place; N,R to 8th St
Open Sun–Thurs 11am–midnight, Fri & Sat 11am–1am
Accepts Cash only
Reservations Not accepted

burger, the meat crumbles and spills out from the sides of the bun. You can swallow this squashy, five-napkin job without even chewing.

There's a real Paul, who obviously woke up one day and said, "I'd like to make a great burger for my friends." The pals in question seem to be skinny rockers smoking up a storm in leather jackets and leopardskin-patterned tights, along with every off-duty cop and firefighter in lower Manhattan. The occasional drag queen, too. Most of the neon-streaked scenery is in black and white, from the checkered contact paper sloppily pasted under the counter and over the tabletops to the framed posters of movie legends. Whimsical placards herald such specialties as the "Lo Calorie Burger," so called because the cheeseburger comes with no bun. We'd hate to shake the hand of anyone who'd just handled one of those.

You can get a burger with anything you want (fried egg, chili con carne, *da woiks*). A plain burger is $3.70. A bacon cheeseburger draped with ham, mushrooms, tomatoes, and onions is $8.75; $10.60 with frozen steak fries (you don't want these, especially considering the proximity of Pomme Frites, an excellent takeout just a few doors away—it's tempting to smuggle in a bag of Pomme Frites' frites under your coat). Nothing on the menu beyond the burger and the chocolate egg cream ($1.50) should be taken seriously. The hot dog ($1.25) is sorrier than the fries. But were we to perish from unsanitary food-service choices, we'd want it to be from the garlic pickles supplied gratis in bowls passed from table to table.

Prune

Chef-owner Gabrielle Hamilton thought she could prevent Prune from becoming trendy by loading her menu with the nutritionally incorrect indulgences we might relish more often were there no judgmental friends and mirrors to stare back at us. Her strategy backfired. The fame shared by chef and bistro alike reflect an enduring rage for rustic, soulful cooking. Distressed mirrors mounted over the long wooden banquette and the zinc bar look just the part. But the absence of bread on the small, butcher-paper-covered tables seems odd. Perhaps it is Hamilton's ruse to unburden diners of that great dilemma: to butter or not to butter. Instead, she performs the business on our behalf, floating rafts of bread into a variety of dishes in many guises: buttered, deep-fried, drenched with garlicky meat drippings or, in one pajama party dessert dream, as butter-and-sugar sandwiches dunked in half-and-half.

$40–80
Address 54 East 1st St, between 1st & 2nd Aves
☎212/677-6221
Transportation F,V to 2nd Ave
Open Mon–Thurs 6–11pm, Fri 6pm–midnight, Sat 10am–3.30pm & 6pm–midnight, Sun 10am–3.30pm & 5–10pm
Accepts All major credit cards
Reservations Required

The pattern of unfettered indulgence is established with appetizers such as the sweetbreads with bacon and capers ($14), the roasted marrow bones ($13), and duck liver poached in enriched chicken stock ($14). The once mandatory fried oysters with thick homemade tartar ($9) must now be poached off the bar menu. Leading the entrees, roast suckling pig ($21) accompanied by pickled tomatoes, black-eyed peas, and aioli beats the braised short ribs piled over Yorkshire pudding for the distinction of most decadent main course. Roofing the assortment of succulent piglet meat with not one but three layers of cracking skins attests to a chef who truly loves to eat. Desserts ($6–9), though less auspicious, always display an interesting wrinkle: warm chocolate cake paired with sour cream ice cream, for example, or panna cotta spiced with cardamom.

Brunch, featuring nine different Bloody Marys ($8), is the new, very hot, hot meal at Prune. You might as well call it "brunchner": adventurous specials like a batter-fried, triple-decker Monte Cristo sandwich ($10) and a grouping of grilled lamb sausage, raw Malpeque oysters, broiled tomatoes, and grilled peasant bread ($16) can be the caloric equivalents of three-meals-in-one.

Raga

If people go gaga for Raga, it's due to their finding so inventive a bistro in a neighborhood where cheap knock-offs are the norm. Whereas new currents in music, theater, and fashion typically originate around the East Village and Lower East Side before drifting uptown, culinary tides have tended to flow in the opposite direction. Raga's Indian fusion menu, on the other hand, debuted a year before such cooking became trendy north of Fourteenth Street. Initial resistance was on economic rather than creative

$25–65

Address 433 East 6th St, between
1st Ave & Ave A
☎212/388-0957
Transportation F,V to 2nd Ave; N,R
to 8th St
Open Tues–Thurs 6–11pm, Fri &
Sat 6pm–midnight, Sun 6–10.30pm
Accepts All major credit cards
Reservations For large groups

grounds. Raga stands just east of a block packed with lovably cheap Bangladeshi joints. Locals accustomed to paying less for an Indian meal than others typically spend for checking in their coat were taken aback by Raga's comparatively high prices and high-minded food. But they soon gained a measure of tranquility from the decor. Brick and plaster walls painted paprika red are dimly lit by bare, saffron-yellow bulbs. High, straight-backed banquettes divide the snug room into cozy subsections.

The use of tropical flavors, Asian spices, and Indian curries and garnishes brings new life to the New American repertoire. Toasted cumin added to a lime dressing transforms a salad with perimeter points of garlicky and roasted portobellos ($5). Seared sea scallops benefit from a tomato and black cardamom chutney ($9). The must-have starter consists of mussels steamed in tomato broth, lemongrass, and Asian spices ($8). A terrific trio of samosas–shiitake, sundried tomato, goats cheese–comes with a traditional outfit of mint and tamarind chutneys ($6).

Certain entrees could have come out of the kitchen of a Southeast Asian restaurant, notably the salmon wrapped in banana leaf with coconut rice ($15). Other good entrees include filet mignon du jour, a beautiful hunk of meat rubbed, to take one example, with homemade garam masala and topped off with a velvety cashew paste ($22), and the pan-roasted chicken ($14) treated with yogurt, ginger, and cranberry—juicier than any Tandoori chicken in memory. The technicolor vegetable platter with basmati rice and raita ($12) is gloriously unmushy. Among desserts, basmati rice pudding with saffron and pistachios ($7) and chocolate soufflé with raspberry sauce ($7) merit your devotion.

Second Avenue Deli

Those who think the Jewish deli-catessen experience is limited to corned beef and pastrami need to refine their expectations when coming to this full-service, family-friendly deli. Smoked meat sandwiches ($9.95) are not the forte of the sole surviving kosher deli on a stretch of Second Avenue once dotted with such establishments and the Yid-dish theaters they fed off. Regrettably, skilled purveyors of kosher pastrami and corned beef have all but disappeared.

JEWISH DELI/KOSHER

Even Abe Lebewohl, the late, great, and dearly missed owner of the Second Avenue Deli, lamented the so-so quality of his pickled meats. The popularity of the pastrami here only goes to prove, paraphrasing an old Sinatra standard, "when you're not near the pastrami you love, you love the pastrami you're near."

The standard of the Jewish/Eastern European cooking, however, is unchallenged. You'd need to be invited into the home of a Jewish mother or grandmother to find a comparable matzoh ball soup ($4.75) or chopped liver appetizer ($7.95). The only viable complaint about them would ordinarily be considered a virtue: they embody compro-mise. The matzoh balls are neither floaters (light and fluffy) nor sinkers (dense and heavy) but something between the two. The chopped chicken livers are neither pasty nor chunky. No such culinary diplo-macy influences the gefilte fish (poached fish quenelles; $8.50). Their sweet freshness has no known detractors.

Forgoing an appetizer would reflect poor judgment were it not for the all-inclusive pleasures of the legendary chicken-in-the-pot ($17.95). It contains world-class chicken soup, noodles, matzoh balls, and enough chicken for dinner tonight and lunch tomorrow (chicken salad anyone?). Twosomes could also split the classic Roumanian tenderloin steak ($22.95). No other restaurant in America serves cholent ($7.95) every day. The Lebewohl family bills this slow-cooked and typically leaden Sabbath stew of fatty meats, beans, and potatoes as the Jewish cassoulet. As a side dish, outstanding fries ($4.50) possess the color of a Jerusalem sunset. For dessert, the rugelach ($3.50) and chocolate babka (more chocolate than cake; $3.95) do the trick.

East Village

Soba-Ya

(icon) This is as close to modern Tokyo as you can get in NYC for under $30 per person. Small, sleek, serene, and immaculate, the blond-wood noodle house gets a recurring ring—or at least a ring tone—of authenticity from the home-sick, cell-phone-holding Japanese students, many from nearby NYU dorms, who form the core clientele. Much to everyone's relief, Soba-Ya is a sushi-free zone. There's already too much darn sushi in this neighborhood.

$12–40

Address 229 East 9th St, between 2nd & 3rd Aves
℡212/533-6966
Transportation 6 to Astor Place; N,R to 8th St
Open Sun–Thurs noon–4pm & 5.30–10.30pm, Fri & Sat noon–4pm & 5.30–11pm
Accepts All major credit cards
Reservations Not accepted

Most begin by choosing from an adventurous assortment of elegant small-plate "delicacies" to go with a beer or a fine sake, among them daily items like homemade shrimp shumai (dumplings; $6.50), squid stuffed with sticky rice ($5.50), boiled spinach ($4.50), assorted seaweed salad ($6), Japanese mountain yam ($4), sliced duck breast ($7.50), and chilled sesame tofu ($4.50). Regulars know to keep an eye out for such specials as sesame-flavored (or sometimes chile-detonated) tuna tartare with quail egg and scallion ($6), grilled sea and bay scallops with miso sauce ($6.50), and warm herring with seasoned rice ($3.50). And every table seems to get at least one order of edamame (green soybeans; $3). Next up, the glorious homemade soba (brownish buckwheat noodles) are served in bowls of chilled or hot broth. Among the eight cold soba selections, you'd do best to go for either the salted salmon roe option ($12.50) or the alternative with whipped yam, an enduring fascination that could easily be mistaken for egg drop soup ($11.50). It's also avail-able in a hot version. From the nine hot sobas choose the variety with gently battered tempura shrimp (not at all greasy; $13.50) or another topped with a high pile of shredded herbs and vegetables ($10).

Udon—the thick, white, chewy, spaghetti-like Japanese wheat noodle—may be substituted for the soba in all its hot and cold varieties. Good tempura, seasoned rice bowls, adorable bento-styled lunch boxes, and the best wasabe honey ice cream in the area round out the list. All told, you'll get a near flawless meal and, considering what other Japanese noodle houses of this caliber charge, a phenomenal bargain.

Takahachi

Anytime the words "sushi" and "cheap" appear in the same sentence, as they do throughout the East Village, it's a risky proposition—though that doesn't dissuade fearless young sashimi fans from packing themselves in at even the most dubiously dingy joints. Takahachi's decor is hardly high-style Japanese and not likely to inspire confidence straight off. But look closer and you'll find that the terribly crammed quarters are adorned with some nice wall hangings, light-wood fixtures, and horizontal lines—the most noticeable of which leads out the door and vestibule. As for the sushi—it won't win any design awards, but it is simple, fresh, bountiful, and absurdly cheap. And it's a friendly place, the affable hosts and overworked servers eager to establish good relations with their repeat customers. As if superbly inexpensive sushi were not enough of an enticement, free goodies are occasionally handed out (a nibble of this, a bottle of that) to loyal habitués.

£12–40
Address 85 Ave A, between 5th & 6th Sts
☎212/505-6524
Transportation F,V to 2nd Ave; 6 to Astor Place
Open Sun–Thurs 5.30pm–midnight, Fri & Sat 5.30pm–12.30am
Accepts All major credit cards
Reservations Not accepted

A deluxe sushi for two, including an extra hand roll of choice, is just $28. And the two maki trios are winners: "Avenue A" ($11) features tekka (raw tuna), California, and yellowtail rolls; rolls in the superior "Avenue B" ($12) hold eel, buttery yellowtail, and nicely broiled salmon skin. Not bad as far as pre-selected sushi combos go. From the a la carte menu, nasu hasami (a sandwich of eggplant tempura stuffed with whitefish; $4.50) and kinuta maki (cucumber-wrapped eel, avocado, and seaweed; $6.50) are chopstick-stopping sensations.

Cooked food selections are pretty good too. The shumai (crab potstickers; $5) are infinitely more delicate than anyone has a right to expect. And the sake aspara make ($5), consisting of five fried asparagus rolls wrapped in salmon and seaweed, makes a terrific appetizer. The blackened tuna ($7.50), however, is one of only a few bad ideas listed on this menu. Noodle soups, broiled fish platters, and tempura all offer good value, while kushiyaki (Japanese barbecue) make for great beer snacks: grilled skewers of marinated squid, shrimp, shiitake, and bacon-okra varieties are just $2 apiece; the bean curd and asparagus, $1.50.

The Tasting Room

Even in the East Village, an area saturated with cute eateries, there's something instantly appealing about this closet-sized, exposed-brick room enticingly framed by its large picture window. Peering in, you'll spy about a dozen tables, each about an inch apart, crowded with open bottles of wine and small square plates filled with the inspired, market-driven creations of chef Colin Alevras. At the door you'll find Colin's wife Renée, who invariably greets you with a grin. And if you are lucky enough to score a table at their restaurant, you'll be reminded that an exceptional dinner comes from a combination of many things—food, wine, space, service, and, perhaps most of all, the people that make you feel at home.

$35–75

Address 72 East 1st St, between 1st & 2nd Aves
℡212/358-7831
Transportation F,V to 2nd Ave
Open Tues–Sat 5.30–11pm
Accepts MasterCard, Visa
Reservations Required

The menu lists about a dozen seasonal, Greenmarket-inspired dishes, each in two sizes—"Tastes" ($6–15, the size of a large appetizer) or "Shares" ($12–30, similar to a large entree). The best way to go, given the lure of Alevras' creative cuisine, is to order many tastes. Warm roasted baby eggplant sprinkled with fresh feta is a delight—the slightly salty cheese a clever foil for sweet chunks of rosemary-scented eggplant ($6/$11). Luscious scallops the size of giant marshmallows are marinated in soy sauce tinged with chiles, mint, and lime ($13/$25). Use the soft ciabatta bread on the table to mop up every last drop. Sheep's milk cheese, cured olives, and caramelized wild onions mingle in a tangle of fresh homemade fettuccine soaked in a meaty lamb jus ($13/$25), while braised and roasted duck leg ($11/$21) rests on a bed of hominy along with collard greens. The gumbo sauce gives it a sneaky kick.

The cheese plate, like the extraordinary, 300-bottle wine list, is all-American, and you should leave room to indulge ($15/$29). Desserts rotate, but if Renée's grandmother's cheesecake ($6) is on, order the whole thing and see if you can sweet-talk Renée into giving you the recipe. Truth be told, it just won't taste as good. Home is nice, sure, but it's not The Tasting Room.

United Noodles

🍴 The compact vehicle for Thai chef
Paul Chantharavirooj's general
assembly of world noodles is a modular,
space-age dining car colored white, off-
white, and off-off white. Designer Kit
Thahong uses Eames chairs, Saarinen-
like tables, and Panton-inspired curves to
create a mid-century-modern idea of a
21st-century people-mover. Were it in fact
designed fifty years ago, United Noodles

$28–50
Address 349 East 12th St, between 1st & 2nd Aves
☏212/614-0155
Transportation L to 1st Ave
Open Daily 5–11pm
Accepts AmEx

might have been predicting an era when shipping East Villagers to Italy,
China, and other noodle production superpowers would become more
efficient than importing their fettuccine and wontons back home. With
eye-level mirrors over sleek banquettes and silver bulbs reflecting softly
upward into round ceiling hollows, this would be a neat attraction even if it
never left East 12th. That, in any event, is an outcome to wish for.

Chantharavirooj cooked at top kitchens on both American coasts,
Patina in LA and Union Pacific in New York, before developing his own
fusion menu composed of imaginative with-noodle dishes. His UN is
no mere noodle shop. Its sophisticated identity was established within a
month of its 2002 opening by two appetizers: the tower of wontons
($6), a narrow napoleon of diced apple, pineapple, and orange layered
with shrimp and crunchy wonton skins; and the peanut-sauced forest
mushroom rolls ($7), which, with their slanted tops, together resemble a
miniaturized cathedral constructed of rice paper. A third starter destined
for distinction is the mixed sashimi plate ($8) paired with persimmon
purée or, more recently, a mango purée. You might order and polish off
all three and then ask for the check.

That isn't to suggest entrees like the braised short ribs with cherry
tomatoes, Chinese watercress, and monstrously large ribbons of pappardelle ($15) or the cider-glazed cod with sweet potato purée and
spinach ($15) are not commendable. It's only that Chantharavirooj's
intricate inventions and subdued flavors work better in smaller doses.
The mushroom-stuffed chicken linguine and garlic pepper sauce ($13),
for example, should probably be shared. As for a warm chocolate cake
with poached pear and apple cinnamon espresso caramel ($7), better that
you claim sole ownership, and share only your sweet recollections of it.

East Village

Veselka

(🍴) Many New Yorkers are convinced that Veselka's alternately irritable, inattentive, and sloppy service was a much better fit before the recent makeover. The negligence suited a place as worn, constricted, and difficult to discard as an old pair of jeans. Now that the Ukrainian coffee shop has transformed itself into a bright, airy, unsoiled, and—whisper it—attractive place to eat, the Eastern bloc hardships lost much of their

$9–30
Address 144 2nd Ave at 9th St
☎212/228-9682
Transportation 6 to Astor Place; N,R to 8th St
Open Daily 24hr
Accepts All major credit cards
Reservations Not accepted

old country color. Veselka nevertheless endures, like a cup of strong java or a bowl of hearty soup, to stimulate or soothe a disparate crowd of East Villagers. Its frank informality still attracts that extraordinary mix of characters—artists, students, middle-income bohemians, elder Eastern Europeans—that gives the neighborhood its abundant creative energy. Sometimes it seems as though every customer should either be writing a screenplay or having one written about them.

A homemade soup ($2.95/$3.90)—cabbage, vegetable, mushroom barley, split pea, lentil—is compulsory, as are pierogi (Polish dumplings; $6.75) filled with potato, cheese, mushroom, sauerkraut, ground meat, spinach, or even sweet potato. Those pockets of goodness may be ordered boiled or, defying good judgment, fried. Both soup and pierogi accompany four combination dinner plates. The vegetarian deluxe plate ($9.95) assembles a salad, a meatless stuffed cabbage, and mushroom-sauced kasha to go with a pierogi trio. The deluxe meat combo ($10.25) includes a pork- and beef-stubbed cabbage, a grilled kielbasa, and a beet salad. Though the American standards—burgers, sandwiches, specials of the day—are generally less satisfying, you can't complain about the stalwart BLT ($6.25) or the milk shakes ($3.95) and ice cream sodas ($3.75) made with Ben & Jerry's.

The no. 4 breakfast special ($7.75), served until noon on weekdays and 4pm on weekends, includes an order of fluffy banana buckwheat pancakes, eggs, juice, and coffee, plus a choice of bacon, ham, kielbasa, sausage, or corned beef hash. Or you could take another kind of late breakfast, just as satisfying in its way: a simple chunk of coffee cake (or a slice of homemade poppyseed bread) with a cup of high-octane black java.

Flatiron District, Gramercy Park & Union Square

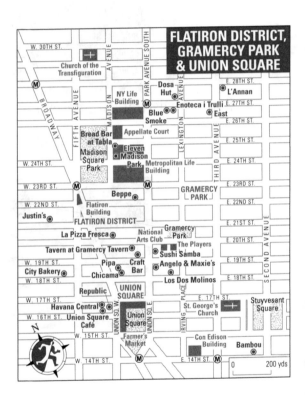

FLATIRON DISTRICT, GRAMERCY PARK & UNION SQUARE

W. 30TH ST.

W. 28TH ST.

Church of the
Transfiguration

E. 28TH ST.

L'Annan

NY Life
Building

Dosa
Hut

E. 27TH ST.

Enoteca i Trulli
East

Blue
Smoke

E. 26TH ST.

PARK AVENUE SOUTH

PARK AVENUE

MADISON AVENUE

FIFTH AVENUE

BROADWAY

LEXINGTON AVENUE

THIRD AVENUE

SECOND AVENUE

Appellate Court

E. 25TH ST.

Bread Bar
at Tabla

Madison
Square
Park

Eleven
Madison
Park

W. 24TH ST.

E. 24TH ST.

Metropolitan Life
Building

W. 23RD ST.

E. 23RD ST.

Beppe

GRAMERCY
PARK

W. 22ND ST.

E. 22ND ST.

Flatiron
Building

Justin's

FLATIRON DISTRICT

E. 21ST ST.

La Pizza Fresca

National
Arts Club

Gramercy
Park

E. 20TH ST.

Tavern at Gramercy Tavern

The Players

W. 19TH ST.

Pipa

Craft
Bar

Sushi Samba

E. 19TH ST.

City Bakery

Chicama

Angelo & Maxie's

W. 18TH ST.

Los Dos Molinos

E. 18TH ST.

Republic

W. 17TH ST.

UNION
SQUARE

E. 17TH ST.

Havana Central

St. George's
Church

Stuyvesant
Square

W. 16TH ST.

Union Square
Café

Union
Square

UNION SQ W

UNION SQ E

IRVING PLACE

W. 15TH ST.

Farmer's
Market

W. 14TH ST.

Con Edison
Building

Bambou

E. 14TH ST.

0   200 yds

Angelo & Maxie's

This steakhouse/cigar bar takes its name from the song "Lullaby of Broadway," in which lyricist Al Dubin identified Angelo's and Maxie's as the hot spots where daffodils entertain. Given a choice between seeing smug carnivores chomping fat stogies, or watching daffodils sing and dance, we'd take the daffodils. Still, the place does showcase a few very good, very large steaks at affordable prices. The theme park-like entrance opens into a cigar store and a long bar mobbed with carousing hunks and slender cuts who create their own kind of meat market. Behind it, a clubby dining room with semicircular Hollywood booths, rich-wooded walls, and tall round pillars is encased in fluted, tobacco-colored mahogany.

STEAKHOUSE

Lunch $25–70
Dinner $35–85

Address 233 Park Ave South at 19th St

☎212/220-9200

Transportation 6 to 23rd St

Open Mon–Thurs 11.30am–3pm & 5–11pm, Fri 11.30am–3pm & 5pm–midnight, Sat 5pm–midnight, Sun 4–10pm

Accepts All major credit cards

Reservations Suggested

Appetizers, salads, and sides are big enough for family-style sharing. Two favorites: chopped shrimp salad in a subtle mustard vinaigrette ($13.95) and angel-hair onion rings ($6.95/$9.95, like all side dishes). Bluepoint oysters ($9), hash browns, and creamed spinach are satisfactory, but the shrimp in the Busby Berkeley-style shrimp cocktail ($11.75) too often possesses zero flavor. From the raw bar, a two-person sampler ($28) will keep a couple busy and happy for thirty minutes.

The kitchen merits most kudos for turning out distinctly flavored, precision-cooked steaks. The 26oz on-the-bone rib-eye ($25.95) protrudes from both ends of a plate as wide as Park Avenue. For value, it's challenged only by the firm, velvety, grilled filet mignon ($24.75) and the tender, 16oz charbroiled sirloin ($23.95). The porterhouse for two ($48.50), with T-bone and filet mignon portions, requires its own zip code; at the other end of the scale, the 10oz burger on a husky onion bun ($12.50) slashes your bill but not your enjoyment. A good alternative to beef: whole roasted chicken ($18.50) with an intense garlic-lemon-pepper crust. Desserts designed for couples—chocolate bread pudding ($8), deep-dish apple pie ($8)—can feed foursomes.

There's another Angelo & Maxie's at 1285 6th Ave, Midtown West (☎212/459-1222).

L'Annan

The true test of an ethnic restaurant's neighborhood status is the junk quotient: are there enough quick, affordable, caloric impulse foods to ease the pain of bad video rentals, surprise visits from the in-laws, or Knicks' fourth-quarter collapses? A cheery spin-off of a nearby Chinese noodle shop, L'Annan certainly comes up with the goods, without sacrificing the lighter, healthier side of Vietnamese cooking. The waitstaff and owners are Chinese, and the rushed service is familiar from local Chinese stand-bys. But this corner spot is distinguished by dark wood tables, Hollywood booths and a striking aluminum lighting fixture suspended over the bar.

> **Lunch $7–25**
> **Dinner $15–40**
>
> Address 393 3rd Ave at 28th St
> ☎212/686-5168
> Transportation 6 to 28th St
> Open Sun–Thurs
> 11.30am–11.30pm, Fri & Sat
> 11.30am–12.30am
> Accepts All major credit cards
> Reservations Accepted

Routine appetizers—spring roll ($4.50), summer roll ($4.95)—are humdrum. But the delicately encased shrimp sui mai (pot-shaped dumplings; $4.50) and the steamed slippery rice crêpes banh cuon ($5.25) are splendid. Goi ga ($5.50), a refreshing salad of shredded baby greens and big loops of tender calamari, is enormously refreshing. And canh chua ($2.50–5.95), a mildly hot and sour soup with pineapple chunks, straw mushrooms, and bean sprouts is practically curative.

Heading the long entree list is curry tom ($12.35), a mild red curry with prawns, green beans, okra, eggplant, bell peppers, onions, and bamboo shoots. You can't order better than fresh whole fish ($13.95) in an oniony lemongrass sauce. And then there are the junk dishes: no. 39 ($9.50), a Vietnamese take on the Chinese takeout addiction, General Tsao's chicken, consists of fried chunks of chicken in a cloying honey soy sauce. Number 49 ($9.95) contains unnaturally tender chunks of beef in a thick, chunky peanut sauce. As unimpressed as you may initially be with either, you will not be able to stop eating them. For dessert, red bean and green tea ice creams ($2.70) cleanse the palate—especially useful for anyone who has ordered nos. 39 or 49.

There's another L'Annan at 121 University Place, Greenwich Village (☎212/420-1179).

Bambou

Bambou is a dreamscape that extends Manhattan's longest crosstown street even further, taking you to a guesthouse on a Caribbean plantation. Its sensuously lit bar/lounge decked out with tropical plants, flowers, and fruits is separated from an intimate dining room by French windows and ivory drapes. The green-and-white color scheme looks very Ralph Lauren, at least until you notice the big picture of Bob Marley smoking something other than a cigar. The beautiful people huddled at candlelit tables also appear to be perma-

$35–80

Address 243 East 14th St, between 2nd & 3rd Aves

☎212/358-0012

Transportation L to 3rd Ave; 4,5,6,N,Q,R,W to 14th St-Union Square

Open Sun 11am–3pm, Tues–Sat 6–11pm

Accepts All major credit cards

Reservations Suggested

nent fixtures. But they are here on their own volition to experience Bambou's upscale, nouvelle, West Indian-fusion cooking.

Looking forward to the *soupe du jour* can be agony when the odds of it actually being the scintillating eggplant soup with a chorus of sweet, spicy, and smoky notes ($9) are pretty long. Lucky thing there are the steamed mussels ($11) and their piquant, coconut-enhanced broth—great for sourdough sopping—to fall back on. Demonstrating coconut's versatility, the broth has none of the sweetness of "A Shrimp Called Bambou" ($9)—crunchy, coconut-battered shrimp certain to invite poaching from fellow diners. You could also go for the crisp crabcake ($13), which has avocado butter, chive oil, and balsamic molasses syrup to counteract its fiery kick.

Despite their upscale aspirations, main courses rarely stray too far from their roots. Rather than mess too much with familiar dishes like grilled jerk chicken with avocado and rice-and-peas ($20) or braised oxtail with lima beans ($20), Bambou gives its Caribbean menu a French accent—or vice versa—by introducing dishes like a two-alarm bouillabaisse Caraïbe ($26) and a succulent shell steak ($25) marinated with an Arawak spice mix made mostly of Caribbean peppers. The grilled vegetable roti ($18) is assembled as a napoleon. The fine dessert assortment (all around $8–13) features an elegant, sorbet-topped fruit cocktail, a nice rum sponge cake and the requisite warm chocolate soufflé cake.

ITALIAN

Beppe

Italian trade groups, travel editors, and foodies vying to promote some undiscovered region or other as "The Next Tuscany" share a common obstacle: if their wholehearted response to Beppe is any indication, New York Italophiles are perfectly content with the original one. Chef-owner Cesare Casella's mid-block farmhouse is a fabulous fiction of oak-planked antique flooring, dark-wooded ceiling beams, and walls brushed in ochre and burnt sienna. The rustic dining room is warmed by a stone fireplace.

$40–85

Address 45 East 22nd St, between
Broadway & Park Ave South
☏212/982-8422
Transportation 6,N,R to 23rd St
Open Mon–Sat noon–2.30pm &
5.30–10.30pm
Accepts All major credit cards
Reservations Suggested

The Lucca-born chef, previously of Il Cantinori, Coco Pazzo, and Il Toscanaccio, here expands a notion of Tuscan cooking that he himself helped shape. His cuisine is simple, robust and earthy. But from countrified roots stems a menu of means: Casella has the resources to explore, procure, and thoroughly amuse; his clientele, the wherewithal to finance pastas priced in the high-teens and secondi pushing $30.

The infamous Antibaci ("no kissing"), a $10 garlic and onion tasting, has been retired (no longer must you cross the street when you run into a Beppe diner), but not, fortunately, the grilled handmade sausage ($10) spiced with a secret renaissance blend (cinnamon, nutmeg, cardamom—you figure out the rest) from an old apothecary in Lucca. Among recommended pastas, "butcher's spaghetti" ($17) combines crumbled pork sausage and the Lucca blend with a New World influence, tomato. Potato gnocchi hold up beautifully to the weight of a wild boar ragu enriched with red wine and powdered bitter chocolate ($18). There are more fabulous flavors endowing the spicy, Scotch-soaked shrimp sweetened with chestnut honey ($29). Beppe's fried chicken ($26) owes much of its critical acclaim to the surprise of finding it and three other specialties of the American south—collard greens, black-eyed peas, fried green tomatoes—on a Tuscan plate. Pastry chef Vera Tong's extreme chocolate tasting—chocolate panna cotta, chocolate semifreddo, and a tiramisu layered with chocolate sponge cake ($11)—is unmistakably pro-*baci*.

Blue Smoke

BARBECUE

Ever walk into a restaurant and know that you won't want to leave? It's a rarity to be expected every time you step into this down-home barbecue joint from Danny Meyer and partners—the same team that brought us Union Square Cafe (see p.80) and Gramercy Tavern (p.79). Here's why: the messy, sticky, spicy, juicy grub is just plain fun. At the long steel bar, smiling crowds stand three-deep, frosty, perspiring mugs of handcrafted Blue Smoke Ale in hand. And in the lively, rustic dining room, tables are packed with after-work suits, yuppie families, sexy waifs and the men who chase them (newsflash: waifs eat ribs) all wiping sticky barbecue sauce from their cheeks with one hand while reaching for more 'cue with the other.

Lunch $16–55
Dinner $25–70

Address 116 East 27th St, between Park & Lexington Aves
☎212/447-7733
Transportation 6,N,R to 28th St
Open Mon & Tues 11.30am–11pm, Wed–Sat 11.30am–1am, Sun 5–11pm
Accepts All major credit cards
Reservations Suggested

Executive chef/pit master Kenny Callaghan spent eight years at Union Square Cafe before moving over to man Blue Smoke's custom-made, applewood-filled smoke pits, each one the size of a VW van. Texas-style smoked beef brisket ($15.50) and pulled pork ($14.50) are tender and intensely flavored, but the real showstoppers are the fall-off-the-bone ribs. Choose from Memphis baby back ($14.25/$21.95), St Louis spare ribs ($13.95/ $19.95), or Texas salt and pepper beef ($14.50/$22.50), all dry-rubbed with a secret spice mix before getting thrown in the pit where they melt in their own fat, rotating for twelve to sixteen hours on the rotisserie. Glazed in a molasses, brown sugar, cayenne, and tomato sauce, these racks demand lots of finger licking.

To pair up with your rack-o-ribs, don't miss the three-sausage sampler with pickled onions and okra ($9.50) and a pint of microbrew to put out the fire. Other stars include hush puppies with jalapeno marmalade ($3.50) and collard greens braised to spinach tenderness in bacon fat ($4.95). Pit beans ($3.95) are ingenious. Callaghan lets them roll around on the rotisserie just to ensure they have enough fat and flavor. Pastry chef Jennifer Giblin's best work is the sort of banana cream pie ($5.95) you could actually imagine enjoying being thrown in your face.

Bread Bar at Tabla

(⚐) Sure, Bread Bar is positioned beneath Tabla, the new-American, Indian-spiced, too-expensive-for-this-guide standout, in terms of prestige, splendor, and location. But once you're seated in a round-backed chair and sipping a Tablatini (Absolut citron, pineapple juice, lemongrass) you won't be able to regard Bread Bar as a cut below anything. For one thing, the terrazzo-floored

$10–50

Address 11 Madison Ave at 25th St
☎212/889-0667
Transportation 6,N,R to 23rd St
Open Mon–Fri noon–10.30pm, Sat & Sun 5.30–11pm
Accepts All major credit cards

room is beautiful. The suspended ceiling floating over the perimeter oval tables doubles as the floor for the Tabla dining room upstairs. It encircles a mosaic-rimmed oculus that throws open the entire duplex. Furthermore, the multiple-choice menu fashioned for Bread Bar by chef Floyd Cardoz is more representative of Goa, his ancestral region, and better suited to grazing, sharing, and snacking than the prix-fixe ones he creates for Tabla.

This being a Danny Meyer production (see Blue Smoke, p.63, Tavern at Gramercy Tavern, p.79. and Union Square Cafe, p80), the tunic-clad servers are absurdly well trained. Say the word "vegetarian" and they'll instinctively prod you towards the savoy cabbage masala with mustard seeds, curry leaves, and coconut ($8) or braised cauliflower with tomato, ginger, and cumin.

Matching tandoori breads ($4–8) to custom chutneys and raitas ($3–4) is a question of personal taste. The crunch of the tiny chickpea dumplings implanted in the bhoondi raita, made with organic yogurt, goes particularly well with the give of the lightly puffed sourdough naan. You'll want to split (with yourself if you're dining alone) a corn-roti pizza ($13) topped with creamed spinach and goat cheese; the heat here is pointed but not painful. Three sandwiches could easily have diners creeping downstairs from Tabla: pulled lamb and mashed potatoes on naan; hanger steak with horseradish raita on naan; and braised oxtail in a wrap. For pastry chef Susan David's desserts ($6–8) there's no need to sneak down *or* up. They're the same here as at Tabla. Order the conical vanilla kulfi (Indian ice cream), the pumpkin crème brûlée, or the chocolate-covered almond kulfi pop and you'll feel certain you selected the best one.

Chicama

First, ABC Carpet & Home reconstructed an old Brazilian farmhouse inside its Broadway store as the setting for an authentic Tuscan trattoria. When that didn't work, they changed the drapes, brought in chef Douglas Rodriguez, New York's founding godfather of contemporary, Pan-Latin-American cooking, and—voilà—rechristened the restaurant Chicama. Rodriguez and some of his staff were lured away from the seminal Nuevo Latino restaurant Patria by the promise of a larger space, a front section built entirely around a ceviche bar, and a kitchen equipped with a eucalyptus-burning rotisserie. More than anything, the change of venue afforded first Rodriguez and his successor, Alex Rodriguez (no relation), the freedom and luxury to exercise greater control. Though Alex is still tempted to make a sensation with every dish and thus prone to excesses, he now succumbs less than before.

Lunch $35–75
Dinner $40–85

Address 35 East 18th St, between Broadway & Park Ave South
☎212/505-2233
Transportation 6,L,N,Q,R,W to 14th St-Union Square
Open Mon–Thurs noon–3pm & 6–11pm, Fri noon–3pm & 5.30pm–midnight, Sat 5.30pm–midnight, Sun 5.30–10pm
Accepts All major credit cards
Reservations Suggested

NUEVO LATINO

Combination ceviches ($13–16) adorably served over ice in little glass fish bowls teach you to appreciate these piquant assortments of citrus-marinated raw fish as bracing cold soups. The hot chills of the Thai ceviche, with squid and tuna, are sent up and down your spine by the pungency of the lemongrass, ginger, lime, basil, and fish paste juices. In addition, all parties should pass around at least one order of the mixed and multicolored (parsley green, squid-ink black) empanadas ($11–14). You will also want one anticucho (Peruvian barbecue; $14) platter featuring spicy shrimp, chimichurri-bedecked chorizo, and tender little chunks of beef tenderloin in place of the more traditional beef hearts.

Frequent menu changes make it difficult to single out entrees. Still, it's worth mentioning the succulent, Peruvian-Chinese "chifa" rotisserie duck marinated in soy sauce, ginger, and chiles ($25). The mariscada Caribbean ($26), with its rich assortment of mussels, clams, octopus, and grilled langoustines over coconut rice, is another winner ($29). Desserts ($9) are not remotely skippable. There's warm churros with dulce de leche sauce and hot chocolate for double dunking, and a memorable coconut tapioca pudding.

City Bakery

Before there was a City Bakery, the great tart universe was split into two factions: those who preferred a triangular wedge cut from a large round pie and those who favored a crustier, individually sized tartlet. Around the Flatiron District and Union Square there is no longer this divisive dessert debate. The community has rallied around the tartlet format, its greatest New York champion, baker Maury Rubin, and the café/bakery that, appropriate to is name, is deemed an essential municipal utility.

$6–25

Address 3 West 18th St, between 5th & 6th Aves
☎212/366-1414
Transportation F,V to 14th St; L,N,Q,R,W to 14th St-Union Square; 1,9 to 18th St
Open Mon–Sat 7.30am–7pm, Sun 9am–5pm
Accepts All major credit cards
Reservations Not accepted

The sleek, industrial design for this lofty space, with narrow lanes to the left and right of the elongated, U-shaped counter, obliges you to maneuver dangerously close to the tantalizing displays of Rubin's signature baked goods. Besides the illustrious tartlets (all $4.50), among them tapioca cherry, cranberry carrot, crème brûlée, and Milky Way, you'll find some of the best croissants, chocolate chip cookies, homemade marshmallows, lemonades, and hot chocolates ($3–3.50) in town. Seating is at high-backed banquettes against both walls and on the cozy mezzanine where many creative professionals essentially keep office hours.

To the rear, a hot-foods station features a soup bar (tomato-vegetable, $4.50/$5.50/$6.50, is the house specialty), mamaligah (Jewish grits), and burnt-edged macaroni-and-cheese ($8.50/lb) all prepared by chef Ilene Rosen. Everything at the premium salad bar is $12/lb—not at all bad for the likes of Rosen's poached salmon with wasabe dressing. Side-course options have included roasted green beans with fennel seed and sweet potatoes with grilled pineapple and cilantro. Pressed sandwiches are prepared and served from behind a rounded, seven-stool counter. True, the option with melted halloumi (a salty Cypriot cheese), grilled radicchio, and three-alarm harissa on wholewheat baguette ($5) is a pungent little marvel. But it's the grilled chocolate sandwich ($4) you want to know about: two paper-thin slices of white toast with French dark chocolate that, caving into the heat and the pressure, dissolves into the realm of dream.

Craft Bar

(icon) Craft Bar does for the wine bar menu what Craft the highbrow restaurant does for contemporary American cuisine: pares it down to the bare and beautiful essentials. Executive chef-owner Tom Colicchio's first-come, first-served spin-off trims its daily entree selection to one fish, one meat, and one pasta. It's possible the limited choice will deter some from returning, but that may just be wishful thinking. During prime-

$25–60

Address 43 East 19th St, between Broadway & Park Ave South
☎212/780-0880
Transportation 6,N,R to 23rd St
Open Daily noon–midnight
Accepts All major credit cards
Reservations Not accepted

time hours there is not only a wait for a table. There's also a wait for the wait, meaning a place to sit or stand at the bar opposite its 500-capacity grid of chain-netted bottle hammocks. Although the high design is typical of the area's trendy gathering spots, the sound-absorbing ceiling and well-informed, solicitous service scale down the usual noise and non-sense.

A gleaming stainless-steel kitchen stretches across the rear of the dining area, making it absolutely clear who the stars of this show are. Anyone distracted by the kitchen view is not necessarily bored by their dinner date. They could well be trying to figure out how to prepare the fried stuffed sage leaves ($6)—five golden mini-logs tightly packed with ground sausage. Other bar snacks that do double duty as appetizers include salumi (Italian cured meats; $9 each, $16 for an assortment) and a dreamy bruschetta topped with tomato and poached egg ($7).

Main courses are programmed by chef de cuisine Marco Canora in the manner of a cable network that airs the same shows throughout the day but only on that day. Lasagna ($15) is on Sundays, braised pork belly ($17) on Tuesdays, and never the twain shall meet. Thursdays have folks shouting T.G.I.T., thanks to the roasted (and grill-marked) sardines with grapefruit and fennel ($16) and the creamy risotto with shrimp, saffron, olive oil, and great individual grain integrity ($15). Pastry chef Karen De Masco's dark gingerbread with quince butter ($8) and apple fritters with caramel ice cream ($8) run continuously, like the bulletins on CNN—and in this instance the news is all good.

Flatiron, Gramercy Park & Union Square

Los Dos Molinos

Were you cruising Route 66 on a Nabokovian quest for seedy motels, kitschy tourist traps, and elusive truths, Los Dos Molinos could very well be your Shangri-la. The brick walls, dimly lit as if for illicit encounters, are covered with holsters, sombreros, kachina dolls, synthetic chile peppers, and Mexican folk art. The snag is that this is not even the southwest side of Manhattan, much less the country, and even the cranked-up country-western tunes and the prodigious 3oz of tequila in a frozen margarita goblet ($10) can't make big city folk buy into the fiction. Only with the arrival of the two salsa pots—tangy green and smoky, throat-stinging red—do things begin to heat up.

$14–50

Address 119 East 18th St, between Park Ave South & Irving Place
Ⓣ212/505 1574
Transportation 4,5,6,N,L,Q,R, W to 14th St–Union Square
Open Tues–Thurs 11am–3pm & 5–9.30pm, Fri 11am–3pm & 5–11pm, Sat 3–11pm
Accepts MasterCard, Visa
Reservations For large groups

Los Dos Molinos—"the two (chile) grinders"—is an outpost of the well-liked New Mexican-style cantinas of the same name in Arizona. As a warning to East Coast gringos, the menu carries a disclaimer about the liberal use of hot chiles. As it turns out, the sauces are no more unbearable that any Lexington Avenue vindaloo. Still, the biting, paste-like chile sauces, the homemade tortillas, and the oval dinner plates that extend from here to next Thursday represent a welcome north-of-the-border break from "real" Mexican. You're no more likely to complain about the cheerfully inauthentic Mexican pizza ($11) than the absurdity of listing this giant thing as an appetizer. Likewise, you'll be too busy sinking your chips into the pleasurably goopy guacamole ($5.50) to worry much that the genuine stuff is supposed to be chunky.

Everything is made to order, from the tostada covered with beans and succulent shredded beef ($6.25) to the cheese-stuffed, batter-fried chile relleno platter ($14.25). Shrimp Veracruz comes as six snappy shrimp alongside fiery red rice, chile beans, and a blistered, nan-like tortilla ($19.95). The best entree by a mile, however, is the Adovada ribs ($18.95): fatty, tender, just-this-side-of-mushy, off-the-bone pork ribs marinated in that red chile stuff. The thought of a dessert may not come easily, but the sopapillas ($5.75), fried pillows of dough drizzled with honey, are not to be missed.

Dosa Hut

Expectant Dosa Hut devotees struggle to control their emotions as they take their places in this modest, pink-walled eatery. Just as the last minutes of a long journey can seem to drag on for hours, the whole business of menus, ordering, and waiting is grueling for the disciples of Veerappan Gownder. Having followed that dosa-master from Pongal, another Southern Indian vegetarian place in Manhattan's Little India, to here, they're all too familiar with the thrill when one of his enormous, paper-thin cones made from a fermented rice-and-lentil batter is set before them.

$10–30

Address 102 Lexington Ave, between 27th & 28th Sts
212/725-7466
Transportation 6 to 28th St
Open Tues–Fri noon–3pm & 5–10pm, Sat & Sun noon–10pm
Accepts All major credit cards
Reservations Not accepted

A select minority exhibit sufficient patience to share appetizers. Such fresh, cleanly fried fritters as onion pakoda, spinach bhajjia and chickpea-coated eggplant bhajjia (all $3.95), served with two chutneys—sweet date and lethally hot, small-podded hari mirch (green chile)—may be ordered in a mixed $6.95 platter that also includes a fried minced-vegetable cutlet. The wholewheat breads, both poori puffed to a full sphere ($3.95 plain, $5.95 with mashed potatoes) and thin, flaky paratha ($3.95 stuffed with peas, potatoes, radishes, or fenugreek leaves), are outstanding.

The spectacular, golden-brown, paper sada masala ($6.95)—one of 16 dosas—are marked with the signature swirls made when Gownder slowly pours the batter onto the griddle. Too delicate and unwieldy to be easily attacked with a knife and fork, the dosas are best dealt with by breaking off a piece, topping it with some of the accompanying spicy mashed potatoes, adding a drizzle of tamarind-sweetened sambar (lentil sauce) and/or a hit of coconut chutney, rolling it all up, and popping it in the mouth. It is crisp and yielding, tart and sweet, fiery and earthy. Dosas also come in the form of folded, wheat-rice flour pancakes, as in the onion rava ($8.50) filled with chopped onions and fresh cilantro. With the ends of the half-moon dosa hanging out on both sides of the plate, this too seems impossible to manage. It comes as some relief that payasam ($2.95), a sweet pudding of coconut milk and mung bean, is easily consumed with only a spoon and enthusiasm.

JAPANESE

East

🍴 Kaiten—"revolving"—sushi is a craze in Tokyo that, for some reason, has never truly taken off in New York. Individual servings of sushi, along with Japanese appetizers, desserts, and various tidbits are covered with clear plastic hoods and placed on a conveyer belt that rotates past diners who can then pick what they like. Prices are calculated according to the color or pattern on each plate. At cheery, modish East, the floodlit sushi bar is shaped like an elongated tuning fork with seating around the outside and, between the prongs, an assembly station where sushi chefs do their wrapping, rolling, and pressing. Once they've transferred each preparation to the appropriate plate, quick as a flash they load it onto the conveyer belt that choo-choos clockwise.

> **$16–55**
>
> Address 366 3rd Ave, between 26th & 27th Sts
> ☎212/889-2326
> Transportation 6 to 28th St
> Open Mon–Fri noon–10.30pm, Sat & Sun 1–10.30pm
> Accepts All major credit cards
> Reservations Not accepted

In truth, the fresh sushi at East is distinguished by neither size nor artistry. But the prices are reasonable and the whole kaiten thing is fun. It's like the supermarket-style perfume shops that let you try everything. You may well regret the loss of personal service, but you can't resist the temptation. East regulars take pride in stacking up their finished plates into multicolored towers eight, twelve, or even fifteen layers high, while sneering at neighbors whose stack climbs no higher than four or five stories. Plate prices are as follows: $1 for white (California roll, salmon skin); $1.50 for pink (striped bass, spicy tuna roll); $2 for green (sardine, scallop-eel-cucumber), $2.50 for red (orange clam, tuna), $3 for blue (spicy yellowtail, toro-scallion roll); $4 for checker (sea urchin, dragon roll); $5 for gold (jumbo clam, toro).

Fishy, esoteric selections like scallop and herring roe tend to be best. Elaborate concoctions like the green Green River, an inside-out roll of eel, cucumber, and avocado speckled with nori, go too heavy on the rice. Standard pieces—salmon, yellowtail, mackerel—are fine. The pink, green, and white little balls that revolve past you a hundred times are fortunately not priced as a sum of their colors. These sweet, yummy, red-bean-filled rice cakes are a red-plated dessert.

Eleven Madison Park

(🍴) The planter boxes behind Eleven Madison's tufted, black-leather banquettes must be bugged. How else to explain the fact the servers know exactly what diners want before they have a chance to ask? Such responsiveness, whether achieved through eavesdropping or something as prosaic as professionalism, is the hallmark of restaurateur Danny Meyer. His informal, unpretentious idea of multi-starred sophistication pervades this soaring rhapsody to Manhattan's Gilded Age. Through the vaulted entrance that corners a bulky Art Deco skyscraper, a towering ground-level space has been updated, like chef Kerry Heffernan's classically inspired cuisine, with sensitivity and good taste. Though rings of halogen lights hang down from period ceiling lamps, it's the terrazzo floors, Deco detailing in marble, wood and bronze, and giant arched windows that dazzle most.

Lunch $30–65
Lunch $40–100

Address 11 Madison Ave at 24th St
☎212/889-0905
Transportation 6,N,R to 23rd St
Open Mon–Thurs 11.30am–2pm &
5.30–10.30pm, Fri 11.30am–11pm,
Sat noon–2pm & 5.30–11pm, Sun
11.30am–2pm & 5.30–10pm
Accepts All major credit cards
Reservations Required

NEW AMERICAN

That is until you experience the telepathic service, exquisite food, and expertly chosen wines. The drama of Heffernan's elegant dishes is experienced through incidental dashes of secondary flavors, not through radical combinations that steal attention from the star ingredients. A raw tuna appetizer ($13) has many things going on around it: caperberries, croûtons, marinated cucumbers, outstanding Provençal olive oil. Still, the six narrow bars of pristine tuna are front and center. Tarte flambée ($12) lets smoked bacon, sautéed onions, and fromage blanc find their place, while blue hubbard squash flan with Brussels sprouts, black trumpet mushrooms, and marjoram butter ($11) is just one of the chef's many flan-tasies.

Main courses show off premium ingredients cooked to near perfection: a roasted loin and crisp braised shoulder of lamb is joined by orzo risotto and goat cheese ($29). Succulent roast chicken, its crackling, St Tropez-tanned skin up, rests in porcini broth ($25). The smoked bacon in roasted Maine lobster ($31) and Portuguese sausage in a monkfish fricassée ($25) both understand their supporting roles. At lunch, the $25 prix fixe New York market menu always features two of pastry chef Nicole Kaplan's fanciful desserts. Sadly, you only get to choose one.

Enoteca i Trulli

"There are 53 Barolos alone!" gushed the young man from Atlanta, scribbling notes into a spiral pad. "And all of them ready to drink!" Anyone as passionate about wines as this grande amatore will adore the wine bar that shares a wall, wine director, owner, Apulian ancestry, and pasta-making-mamma with the Southern Italian restaurant I Trulli. And even those unmoved by the list of some 400 bottles (how many can you drink in one sitting anyway?) will still find reasons to slot Enoteca into their

Lunch $20–60
Dinner $32–80

Address 122 East 27th St, between Park and Lexington Aves
☏212/481-7372
Transportation 6,N,R to 28th St
Open Mon–Thurs noon–10.30pm, Fri noon–11pm, Sat 5–11pm
Accepts All major credit cards
Reservations Not accepted

dining itineraries. The shapely chairs of plywood and tubular steel, the twelve-seat, white-marble bar, and the large, gold-leaf-framed mirror add up to a cozy setting for sampling Italian wines, cheeses, and cured meats. And the three-course prix fixe ($20 at lunch, $25 at dinner) is a steal.

Fourteen wine-sampling "flights" ($8.25–24.25), grouped by region, each consist of three wines poured into tasting glasses up to their 2oz lines. These let you assess the nuances of wines with comparable origins, varietals, and blends. You can then buy the one you like best, should you so desire, at Vino, the across-the-street shop co-owned by proprietor Nicola Marzovilla and wine director Charles Scicolone. On quantity alone, whole bottles like the exceptional-value 2000 Leverano Rosse from Conti Zecca in Puglia ($19 here, $12 in the shop) offer better value than the flights. Cheeses, cured meats, and olives may also be ordered as three-way samplers ($10, $10, and $4). With the puffy, tomato-and-mozzarella-filled panzerotti (baked half-moon pastries; $12), one will do.

The prix fixe might start with lightly golden panelle (fried chickpea cakes) filled with goat cheese or a chunky caponata (a Sicilian relish of eggplant, tomato, olives, red peppers, and pine nuts). Next up, home-made pastas prepared by Dora Marzovilla, the owner's mother, are usually outstanding (chewy cavatelli with chopped broccoli rabe) and only occasionally disappointing (orecchiette with an overly sweet veal ragu). To close, the gelati are superior to the cookie plate.

Havana Central

(🍴) Put the Cuban coffee shop genre into the hands of an adroit New York capitalist like Jeremy Merrin and you get a colorful restaurant/bar/sandwich counter that pleases and, to a lesser extent, disappoints in unexpected ways. Larry Bogdanow, the designer of the Union Square Cafe (see p.80) and City Hall (see p.135), has installed small booths and seating sectionals to cut the narrow confines into cozy subdivisions. Exposed brick, cement, and Edison

$10–50

Address 22 East 17th St, between Union Square West & 6th Ave
℡212/414-4999
Transportation 4,5,6,L,N,R,Q,W to 14th St-Union Square
Open Mon–Sat 11am–11pm, Sun noon–10pm
Accepts All major credit cards

bulbs hung from horizontal wood beams shape his appealing, rustic-industrial riff on a pre- or post-Castro Cuba. If you order well, maybe starting with a classic mojita ($8) or a fruity one ($9) coordinated to the tropical wall colors, and manage to overlook the sketchy service, Havana Central can be a great spot to kill the biggest of appetites with the smallest of bundles.

The Cuban sandwich ($7.95) presses mustard, pickle, Swiss cheese, and unblemished, thick slices of roast pork and smoked ham between perfect bread. Diagonally halved and sided with sweet potato fries crisper than you have a right to expect, this Cubano very nearly supersedes any desire for a half rack of those smoky, fruity, tangy, spicy BBQ ribs ($12.50 with rice and beans). The mango habanero sauce (you might want some more on the side) clings to the moist, chewy meat to provide a lusciously sloppy rib experience. Sides like mango pineapple cole slaw with raisins and fried yucca bites are good enough to be ordered as appetizers. And the house ropa vieja ($12.50), the Cuban classic of shredded stewed beef, is an arresting tangle of juicy, spicy meat.

The whole concept of the paella bar, where you start with preseasoned, precooked rice ($6) as a base and then choose veggies, meat, and seafood extras ($1–2) as you would at a salad bar, is boneheaded. With little opportunity for those additions to flavor the rice, it defies the purpose of paella. The other disaster is the virtually unchewable Cuban steak sandwich with grilled onions ($11). Happily, indulgent desserts ($4–6)—tres leches cake, fried-plantain (rather than banana) split, chocolate-dipped churros—rub sweet cream into those sore spots.

Justin's

Velvet ropes and dumbbell-shaped door handles frame the red-carpeted entrance. Just inside, great-lookers with striking duds tracing the curves of their spectacular bodies huddle five-deep at the curvilinear bar. At the reception desk, it's difficult to tell if the usual refrain, "Can't seat you 'til your entire party has arrived," is passing through the lips of the diva hostess or coming from the sound system of the superstar record producer whose house

$35–70

Address 31 West 21st St, between 5th & 6th Aves
☎212/352-0599
Transportation N,R,F,V to 23rd St
Open Sun–Thurs 5pm–midnight, Fri & Sat 5pm–2am
Accepts All major credit cards
Reservations Suggested

this is. Sounds intimidating? You would be amazed how threatening Justin's is not. By snubbing neither fan nor foodie, the swank restaurant P. Diddy named after his son raises the bar or, more literally, the dining platform, for stylish, upscale, celebrity-owned eateries. Mere nobodies led up to the candlelit tables or the all-embracing corduroy booths are treated as privileged guests. And no one here is trying to modernize or glamorize Southern and Caribbean cuisine. Rather, the creative flourishes applied to familiar dishes seem inspired only by a desire to make things better.

Up first: chicken wings in a sweet and sticky barbecue glaze ($7) are enticingly presented in a tiny, cast-iron skillet with blue-cheese dip. Great idea, nice execution. Spicy catfish fingers ($8) are so wonderfully delicate you wonder they don't fall apart when lifted out of the deep fryer. Louisiana seafood gumbo ($7) boasts an outstanding assortment of shellfish. Among entrees there's plenty to choose from and plenty to eat. Nothing tops the barbecued salmon ($22), which has just enough of that sweet glaze that embellishes the chicken, while braised short ribs ($21) benefit from their heavy sweet-and-sour sauce. Only the smothered pork chops are heavy-handed, and eminently skippable.

To close, you're unlikely to find a better sweet potato pie ($6). There are two other desserts, though, that may intrigue you: the ethereal peach cobbler pastry, and the red-velvet pound cake with cream cheese frosting—fabulous, providing you don't try to figure out what makes it so virulent a red.

Pipa

(🍴) The deliberately frayed and purposefully eccentric elegance of the in-store restaurant Pipa could well be defined as "Miss Havisham chic." Others may view its concoction of Venetian glass chandeliers, threadbare brocade, and decayed keepsakes as the result of a clever pruning of its inventory by home furnishings store ABC Carpet. Regardless, this estimation of what a Victorian attic might look like if submerged in the ocean for a century has certainly caught on with the young and restless. So few diners are over thirty years old that you might even assume there is someone at the door checking IDs.

**Lunch $15–50
Dinner $30–65**

Address 38 East 19th St, between Broadway & Park Ave South
☏212/677-2233
Transportation 6,N,R to 23rd St
Open Mon–Thurs noon–3pm & 6–11pm, Fri noon–3pm & 5.30pm–midnight, Sat 11.30am–3.30pm & 5.30pm–midnight, Sun 11.30am–3.30pm & 5.30–10pm
Accepts All major credit cards
Reservations Suggested

SPANISH

If any chef could upstage this elaborate staging it was the Nuevo Latino star Douglas Rodriguez, who devised this thrilling concept of nuevos tapas untroubled by notions of authenticity. This, like the departure of Rodriguez, goes unnoticed by the revelers who crowd the noisy dining room, communal table, and bar. Despite the impressive list of Spanish wines and sherries, most tables opt instead for a pitcher of superb sangria ($29). Moreover, no one sharing one of the enticing "cocas" much cares if the makeup of these flatbreads has come entirely from the chef's imagination. The Moroccan lamb flatbread combo ($15) consists of ground lamb *and* rosemary-seared lamb tenderloin, with raisins, pine nuts, and goat cheese. The mushroom alternative ($16) carries a herb-seasoned mushroom purée and is topped with Manchego cheese, truffle oil, and grilled Portobellos.

Two of the better tapas are the trio of fried oysters ($12)—refitted into their shells with banana lentil salad, horseradish aioli, and slab bacon—and the almond-stuffed, bacon-wrapped dates ($8), poised at the tip of endive leaves. The lamb meatballs ($9) need an accompaniment to soak up their rich salsa. Although the small plates seem best suited to Rodriguez' big excesses, his "new paella" ($24) possesses an awesome array of shellfish. It takes a good fifteen minutes to get down to the rice. Among desserts ($8), the three-chocolate terrine is a pretty confection.

La Pizza Fresca

When you fold a slice cut from a great New York pizza, its oozy overlay of molten mozzarella streams down a puddle of piping-hot tomato sauce towards the tip of the triangle. The expectation of that sensual first bite makes it difficult for natives to appreciate pies of another origin and style, including those from Naples, the birthplace of pizza Margherita. That's why chauvinistic locals may at first be cool to the authentic, soft, and dainty Neapolitan pies baked in a wood-fired brick "igloo" at La Pizza Fresca. But those who stop comparing and start relishing soon learn to cherish the city's only pizzeria to be awarded the "Attesta" certificate of authenticity by the Associazione Vera Pizza Napoletana in Naples. Though the decor merits no such accolades, wall murals do add whimsy and warmth to a narrow dining room imparted, like the pizza crusts, with the smoky aroma of the wood-fired oven.

**Lunch $20–40
Dinner $25–60**

Address 31 East 20th St, between Broadway & Park Ave South
☎212/598-0141
Transportation N,R,6 to 23rd St
Open Mon–Fri noon–3.30pm & 5.30–11pm, Sat 5.45–11pm, Sun 5–10.30pm
Accepts All major credit cards
Reservations For large groups

The exacting standards of the Associazione require the use of fresh mozzarella di bufala (Buffalo), San Marzano tomatoes, Italian olive oil, a special flour, and a wood-burning oven. The upshot is a thin, lightly charred, appealingly bubbly crust that provides gentle resistance and compression. Small individual pizzas ($9–17) come in fifteen varieties. The house pie adds the drama of explosive cherry tomatoes and black olives to the pure Margherita (tomato, mozzarella, basil). The Quattro Stagioni, with prosciutto, mushrooms, and artichokes, is also recommended.

Pizza Fresca also serves up some pretty good starters. Best of the lot is the teepee of grilled zucchini, eggplant, carrot, and peppers drizzled with balsamic, propped over salad greens, and served, as all appetizers are, with wonderfully thin, focaccia-style bread baked in the brick oven ($7.95). The cleanly fried squid ($10) and sautéed spinach ($8) are decent alternatives. Though pastas are in general no better than anything offered at other nearby Italian restaurants, the simplicity of the rigatoni alla Siciliana (sautéed eggplant woven with mozzarella, basil, and marinara; $14) does complement the elemental pizza approach.

Republic

The Asian noodle shop conforms to a new order at this soaring, whimsically designed, and frighteningly efficient Republic. Communal seating on blond-wood benches provides monastic austerity without zen-like quietude. And if the thunderous clamor and lightning-fast service still fall short of giving you the jitters, the ludicrously arty, black-and-white blowups of women with noodles wrapped around their bare bodies can always be counted on to irritate more females than they do titillate males. Be that as it may, Republic is a winner. The eating is good, the people-watching (and that includes the black-clad servers) is even better, and the cost of doing both is extremely low for so enduringly stylish a concept eatery.

$15–40

Address 37 Union Square West, between 16th & 17th Sts
☎212/627-7168
Transportation 4,5,6,L,N,Q, R,W to 14th St-Union Square
Open Sun–Wed 11.30am–10.30pm, Thurs–Sat 11.30am–11.30pm
Accepts All major credit cards
Reservations Not accepted

After ordering at most restaurants, there's usually time to wash your hands, tell a knock-knock joke or, at the very least, lay an unfolded napkin over your lap before the appetizers arrive. At Republic you must be ready to eat seconds after your server punches in your request on a hand-held keypad and instantaneously transmits it to the behind-the-counter kitchen. Luckily, dishes don't suffer from the advance prepping. The vaguely Thai, Vietnamese, and/or Japanese food is fresh, flavorsome, and never oversalted. And the occasional citrussy excesses do perk up the salads and broths. Top picks among the so-called "small dishes" include an acutely spicy cold seafood salad with shrimp, calamari, teeny bay scallops, crunchy jicama, and Thai basil ($5), grilled calamari in a scrumptious but not cloying soy glaze ($5), and a seaweed salad with cucumber, mint, ginger, and a tofu-sesame vinaigrette ($4).

The best of the noodle soup entrees is the steamed salmon with vermicelli and bean sprouts in a coconut broth ($8), but for the tastiest options you should head for the soup-less noodle section. Here you'll find galangal-marinated, lettuce-wrapped grilled beef slices paired with angel-hair rice noodles ($9) and flat, leathery strips of BBQ garlic pork with bean sprouts, mint, and scallions propped over cold vermicelli ($8). Coconut sorbet ($3) is worth staying for, if you're not in too much of a hurry to get your sore butt off the hard bench.

Sushi Samba

Due to Japanese immigration to Brazil, sushi and samba have long shared the same turf and surf. But at Sushi Samba the Brazil/Japan pairing isn't quite on the mark. Eiji Takase ("Taka"), the mastermind behind this creative restaurant, was actually inspired by the food of Peru, not Brazil. It was Lima he visited to learn about ceviche and devise a fusion cuisine, not Rio. That said, the Brazilian gimmick does work beautifully. With bossa nova pouring from its speakers, and cachaca, the Brazilian liquor, poured into its cocktails, this smash success now has a second locale in the West Village (87 7th Ave South; ☎212/691-7885) and a third in South Miami Beach.

$30–60

Address 245 Park Ave South, between 19th & 20th Sts
☎212/475-9377
Transportation 6 to 23rd St
Open Mon–Wed noon–1am, Thurs–Sat noon– 2am, Sun 1pm–midnight
Accepts All major credit cards
Reservations Required

The stunning, glass-paneled storefront of the original resembles a Mondrian pieced together with a tropical palette. The interior is wrapped in mango-orange walls and guava-red banquettes, all dotted with a touch of 1960s futurism. Overhead, a galaxy of Plexiglass domes illuminates the central sushi bar. Servers are rightly programmed to ensure that no diner overlooks the sashimi-like ceviches, best sampled in tasting platters of four ($27). To accompany the ceviche the sushi chefs play with an assortment of Japanese garnishes, setting them off with Peruvian chiles. From the apple, soy sauce, and sake dressing to the shaved coconut, coconut milk, and mango paste that anoints the sea urchin, each seems to pack more refreshing thrills than the next.

Elsewhere on the menu, chile peppers take over, sometimes to detrimental effect. Korean chile paste overwhelms a sensational yellowtail tartare ($12.50), a mistake repeated by firing the yellowtail sushi roll with minced jalapenos ($7). Nevertheless, you do learn to love the lingering buzz of hot pepper. The sweet standout among sushi is the Rainbow Dragon ($13), a beautifully crafted roll of eel, daikon sprouts, and red and yellow pepper meticulously wrapped in thin, smooth slices of mango and avocado. The same artistry inspires the el tapo ($12.50), a spicy salmon roll with a thick spread of marshmallow-like mozzarella, a pile of fried onions, and a few squiggles of mayo.

Tavern at Gramercy Tavern

Many of New York's best-value bistros profit from trickle-down gastronomics. They adapt, simplify, and slash the price of food fashions introduced by star chefs like Tom Colicchio at elite, trend-setting restaurants like Danny Meyer's Gramercy Tavern. Colicchio might have a slightly less flattering characterization of these imitations, some of them produced by ex-employees. Fortunately for him and us, the Tavern's fifty-seat tavern gives Colicchio the

$25–65
Address 42 East 20th St, between Broadway & Park Ave South
☎212/477-0777
Transportation 6,N,R to 23rd St
Open Sun–Thurs noon–11pm, Fri & Sat noon–midnight
Accepts All major credit cards
Reservations Not accepted

chance to design his own knock-offs (he does the same for Craft, his second restaurant, at Craft Bar; see p.67). You get access to the true flavors, easy elegance, and outstanding wines-by-the-glass and cheeseboard selections of a great New York restaurant without having to make reservations or loan applications.

Sure, the Tavern's tavern requires sacrifice. You'll wait for one of the smallish, cafe-style tables and you won't be seeing any foie gras after you get there. But appetizers like grilled quail with polenta, pearl onion, raisins, and pine nuts ($12) and grilled baby octopus with shaved fennel, lemon confit, and sweet pepper caponata ($12) suggest zero compromise. Colicchio's inventive associations of Greenmarket-driven, razor-sharp flavors are as salient here as they are in the dining room. The kitchen isn't cutting back. It is devising simpler dishes better suited to the comparatively compressed and informal circumstances.

If there's envy in the air, it could just as easily be felt for as by diners restricted to the Tavern menu. The marinated vegetable and buttery Taleggio cheese sandwich on ciabatta ($14) is an unfettered, hands-on delight that wouldn't fly in the dining room. Who in so formal a setting would dare lick the caper aioli that's prone to leak from that sandwich? In addition, no part of the filet mignon with mashed potatoes and balsamic-onion relish ($19.50) can be improved upon. Not even by Colicchio himself. The only complaint with desserts ($8) like the poppyseed parfait and the oatmeal stout gingerbread is that pastry chef Michelle Antonishek tires of (and consequently replaces) them much sooner than her fans do.

Union Square Cafe

As new and original as it was for its time, the beloved Union Square Cafe was already a classic on the day it opened in October 1985. It's hard for anyone to recall this block without the distinctive USC awning and, seen through the picture windows, the colorful modern art hung on its dining room walls. Someday this address will bear a plaque marking the site where restaurateur Danny Meyer pioneered and perfected the Meyer Touch, a service style that was at once friendly, casual, and omnipresent. The ensuing acclaim, first local and then national, was unprecedented for so informal a restaurant and distinguishes Meyer's achievement as a patently American success story. Given its lofty reputation, some first-timers are shocked and, in an odd way, dismayed to discover the famous Union Square Cafe to be so devoid of opulence and stiffness. Their disappointment rarely lasts through dinner, as the four-week wait for its 125 seats will attest.

Lunch $25–65
Dinner $45–90

Address 21 West 16th St, between Union Square West & 5th Ave
℡212/243-4020
Transportation 4,5,6,L,N,Q,R,W to 14th St-Union Square
Open Mon–Thurs noon–5pm & 6–10.30pm, Fri & Sat noon–5pm & 6–11.30pm, Sun 5.30–10pm
Accepts All major credit cards
Reservations Required

Chef Michael Romano's eclectic but accessible cuisine was always a great match for the service and every bit as influential. Signature dishes that were innovative then are now commonplace at contemporary American and Italian-nuanced restaurants around the country: most of the 1001 lobster (or seafood) shepherd's pies, mascarpone-creamed polentas, rare tuna steaks, and caramelized banana tarts of our dining lives can all be traced back to Sixteenth Street.

The noteworthy pricing policy is reflected in the $12.50 tag on the USC hamburger. Sure, that seems a little high for a burger. But once you get your hands on that marvel, its juices sealed in a carefully packed patty with no cracks or crevices, the lunch-only sensation is instantly appreciated as an unparalleled bargain on a poppyseed bun. Likewise, the dinner entrees, though up in the twenties ($27 for seared salmon, $26 for lemon-pepper duck, $28.50 for grilled smoked shell steak), constitute a price leap down from other elite New York restaurants.

Greenwich Village & NoHo

GREENWICH
VILLAGE & NOHO

W. 14TH ST.
W. 13TH ST.
W. 12TH ST.
New School
W. 11TH ST.
First
Presbyterian
Church
W. 10TH ST.
Village
W. 9TH ST.
GREENWICH
VILLAGE
W. 8TH ST.
Otto
WAVERLEY PL.
WASHINGTON SQ. N.
Blue Hill
Babbo
WASHINGTON PL.
Washington
Square Park
WASHINGTON SQ. S.
SIXTH AVENUE
New York
University
MACDOUGAL ST.
Bar Pitti
BLEECKER ST.
SULLIVAN ST.
Tomoe Sushi
THOMPSON ST.
Lupa
Arturo's
HOUSTON STREET
LAGUARDIA
PLACE
WOOSTER ST.
SOHO

FIFTH AVENUE
BROADWAY
FOURTH AVENUE
E. 12TH ST.
THIRD AVENUE
E. 11TH ST.
Grace
Church
E. 10TH ST.
Knickerbocker
Bar & Grill
E. 9TH ST.
ST. MARKS PL.
Cooper Union
ASTOR PL.
E. 7TH ST.
SECOND AVENUE
UNIVERSITY PL.
WAVERLEY PL.
Indochine
LAFAYETTE ST.
E. 6TH ST.
WASHINGTON
PLACE
Public
Theater
E. 5TH ST.
BROADWAY
MERCER ST.
Time Cafe
GT. JONES ST.
BOWERY
E. 4TH ST.
E. 3RD ST.
Five Points
BondSt
BOND ST.
Il Buco
Angelika
Film Theater
GT. JONES ST.
NOHO

0   200 yds

Arturo's

NYU students, Greenwich Village musicians, Italian expats, movie buffs from the nearby Film Forum and Angelica Film Center, and pizza lovers everywhere should raise a glass of inexpensive red to local kid Arturo Giunta and the friendly haunt he opened in 1957. Romantic attachments to this dowdy looking cheap-date favorite are unrelated to the presence of a bathtub in the restroom. They've more to do with the cool breeze of live jazz that blows the steam off sizzling, coal-oven-baked pizzas esteemed for their crisp and resilient crusts, pristine mozzarella, zesty (to the point of fruity) tomato sauce, and matchmaking attributes. Suitors who discard crust ends like fish bones may be hopelessly neurotic, but they do get along quite well with the shameless scavengers who scoop them up.

$15–55

Address 106 West Houston St at Thompson St

℡212/677-3820

Transportation A,C,E,F,V to West 4th St; 1,9 to Houston St; 6 to Bleecker St

Open Mon–Thurs 4pm–1am, Fri & Sat 4pm–2am, Sun 3pm–midnight

Accepts All major credit cards

Reservations Weekdays only

ITALIAN/PIZZA

A large pie, which could be shared by four people, costs between $14 and $19, depending on your choice of extra toppings: anchovies, bacon, eggplant, meatballs, mushrooms, pepperoni, peppers, onions, sausage. The Arturo's Fiesta is a tempting and fortunately not top-heavy compilation of sausage, mushrooms, peppers, and onions. A little fresh chopped garlic doesn't hurt either. A full menu of Italian food is also available and, were you to judge from the eating habits of the people who ostensibly know best, worth investigating. Just before dinnertime, the kitchen and service staffs can be seen gleefully gorging on various unidentifiable pasta concoctions. Oddly, however, while you'll never see them eating pizza, you yourself will regret any foray beyond the pizza list. The best advice is to stray no further than the inoffensive cold antipasto ($4.75) or the stuffed artichoke ($7).

Choice front-room booths near the bar and the music prove to be worth a short wait, while the sidewalk tables are ideal for moonlit summer evenings. Two rear rooms double as galleries. The paintings, though signed by an artist who, like Leonardo and Michelangelo, is widely recognized by his first name, are unremarkable. Pizza is Arturo's medium, and all should uncork a bottle of Tuscan red, preferably Santa Cristina ($22), in praise of his art.

Greenwich Villlage & NoHo

Babbo

No road atlas will help you pinpoint the origins of Mario Batali's cooking. But understanding the appeal of Batalian cuisine, with its Italian regional influences and New World inventions, is simple: its founding father crowds his plates with crisp flavors and properly cooked, piping hot food. Babbo, which is Italian for daddy, is the two-papa partnership of restaurateur Joe Bastianich (Esca, see p.210) and Batali, who's garnered national celebrity through his Television Food Network cooking show, Molto

$45–95

Address 110 Waverly Place, between 6th Ave & MacDougal St
℡212/777-0303
Transportation A,C,E,F,V to West 4th St
Open Mon–Sat 5.30–11.30pm, Sun 5–11pm
Accepts All major credit cards
Reservations Required

Mario. Babbo is quartered on two floors of a one-time coach house off Washington Square. On the lower level, beyond the oak bar, is a softly lit room that, like the menu, splits the difference between dressy and casual, upscale and rustic. From leather banquettes, couples sitting side-by-side face out towards a beautiful round service table displaying fruit, cheeses, wines, olive oils, wines, and a floral arrangement.

Appetizers establish Batali as the daddy of 100 vinaigrettes. He accents that mother sauce with spicy quince for grilled octopus ($14), or with thyme for thinly sliced testa (headcheese) coated with a mustard-seed crunch ($10). These notes never drown—or drown out—a dish. It's the tricolored beets and not the rhubarb dressing you notice most on the soppressata starter ($13).

It's fine to order a pasta in lieu of a main course, but never the reverse. Star turns include the long-running mint love letters ($18), elongated parcels of mint purée accompanied by a spicy lamb sausage ragu, and the momentous chopped beef cheek ravioli ($19) with a squab liver purée and sliced truffles. The seven-course, pasta-heavy tasting menu offers great value at $59. If you're not choosing pasta, you'll enjoy the excess of the grilled lamb chops Scottadita, a teepee of meat with Jerusalem artichokes, shiitakes, and cumin yogurt ($29), or the elegance of whole grilled branzino fish ($29) with lemon oregano jam. For dessert, pastry chef Gina De Palma wows with chocolate-sauced pistachio semifreddo ($9), orange-sauced chocolate hazelnut cake ($9), and an enchanting sorbetti-gelati tasting presented in six mini-glasses ($8).

Bar Pitti

(🍴) No one can leave Bar Pitti without a strong opinion about Giovanni Tognozzi, its bald-headed host/co-owner, and his service brigade. To cope with the nightly overflow at this bargain Florentine annex to trendy Da Silvano, tables both inside and on a hip terrace prized for its people-watching are hastily filled and hurriedly emptied in an arbitrary manner. Detractors maintain they've been seated behind others who've arrived after them and then felt bullied to eat fast and get out. Devotees insist the seating policy is

$20–55

Address 268 6th Ave, between Bleecker & Houston Sts

☏212/982-3300

Transportation 1,9 to Houston St; A,C,E,F,V to West 4th St

Open Daily noon–midnight

Accepts Cash only

Reservations For groups of four or more

fair and regard the service as prompt and professional with a flavorsome give-and-take between knowing server and diner. Though many subscribe to the second position, it may be because they're simply desperate to stay in Giovanni's good graces. The best advice is either to take pleasure in this blend of Italian brio, gusto, and impertinenza, to reserve as a party of four or more, or to come off-hours.

When, sooner or later, you do sit down, a laminated menu is immediately tossed your way while the specials blackboard is leaned against the nearest wall, empty chair, or diner's shoulder. It's the oft-running specials that interest most, with such appetizers as the heartiest of ribollitas (Florentine vegetable and bread soup; $5.50), insalata pitti (peppery arugula topped with sautéed artichokes and sheets of Parmesan; $8), grilled cuttlefish salad ($10.50), and a herb-perfumed melanzane alla parmigiana (thinly sliced eggplant casserole; $8.50) that two could easily share—as an entree!

The most requested pasta is pappardelle alla fiesolana ($10.50), its ribbons sensuously entwined with smoked bacon in a creamy tomato sauce with Parmesan. It and the similarly sauced rigatoni Pitti (with turkey sausage and peas; $10.50) can only lead to a re-evaluation of all self-imposed bans on cream sauces. Oven-roasted whole fish (market price $15–17) is dependably fresh. Ask which desserts are homemade—the waiters like this question—and you get a choice between chocolate mousse, tiramisu, and panna cotta. The tiramisu ($5.50) isn't bad, but the dark chocolate-sauced panna cotta ($6) is brilliant.

Blue Hill

Located in a townhouse just south of Washington Square, Blue Hill does cutting-edge, market-driven (as in the Union Square Greenmarket, not Nasdaq) contemporary American cuisine with bistro-styled informality. What it does not do, however, is offer bistro-styled pricing. Cheap it is not. Tremendous value and a wonderful dining experience it is. Indirect lighting hidden beneath both the high-backed banquettes and the low ceiling's recessed perforations gives a welcome impresssion of space in this confined room. This artful enhancement of volume reflects the cooking approach of co-owner Dan Barber, who, with kitchen partner Michael Anthony, brings intensity, texture, but not heaviness to his contemporary, seasonal cooking. Few chefs can do more things in more ways to a sauce, a purée, a broth, or a foamy emulsion than Dan and Michael.

$45–75

Address 75 Washington Place, between MacDougal St & 6th Ave

☎212/539-1776

Transportation A,C,E,F,V to West 4th St

Open Mon–Sat 5.30–11pm, Sun 5.30–10pm

Accepts All major credit cards

Reservations Required

A crabmeat lasagna appetizer ($14), assembled between two thin homemade pasta sheets, benefits from both the amplification of grain mustard and the intensity of spinach purée. Gently steamed foie gras ($14) is served with red wine to absorb the broth left from its garbure (Southwest French stew) of summer vegetables. Every evening, a different ceviche ($10) is featured under the "simply raw" heading: sea bass with pomegranate vinaigrette, perhaps. Rotated seasonal main courses might include poached cod with a delectable starchy vichyssoise broth ($22) and, if you're very lucky, the exceptional hanger steak ($25) with crusty, caramelized chunks of deep-pink meat joined by pancetta-laced potatoes and an astonishing loose spinach purée that's practically an ink. The poached duck ($25) is a revelation. Rounds of tender breast meat as perfectly pink as prime rib contrast with the crispness of the confit.

Be warned: since the menu changes regularly, some great relationships between dish and diner can be painfully brief. Happily, the outrageously fine chocolate brioche pudding ($10) is available every night of the year. A very good argument can be made for skipping dessert elsewhere and stopping at the bar here for an order.

BondSt

BondSt's instant allure was no shocker. Its owners had already licked the trick of flicking a switch and having hordes of beautiful people turn up before the lights go on. That the quartet behind the eternally hip Indochine (see p.930) was able to repeat its gravity-defying feat is nonetheless remarkable. Since opening in 1998, the Japanese triplex refuses to come down from its fashionable high. Inside a bleached brownstone and directly above a dark and sexy cocktail lounge/sushi bar is a deafening dining room whose stark modernity is softened by elegant lighting and gossamer fabrics. Diners may lean their backs against curvilinear booths or throw pillows, both of which are preferable to the cramped seating in the brighter, more stylized rear sushi room.

$40–80

Address 6 Bond St, between
Broadway & Lafayette St
℗212/777-2500
Transportation 6 to Bleecker St
Open Mon–Sat 6-11.30pm, Sun
6–10.30pm
Accepts All major credit cards
Reservations Required

The appeal of Hiroshi Nakahara's sushi is less about fish quality than presentation. His adorable hini zuchi, with mini-pieces of tuna, yellowtail, clam, shrimp, fluke, egg, and salmon, delights his customers *and* his bosses. The former get novel, bite-size pieces; the latter, an $18 charge for half the usual quantity of fish. The hot eel dice ($10) is beautiful propped atop an inside-out avocado roll. Arugula crispy potato roll ($6), with the crunch of finely julienned potato sticks, is a revelation.

If BondSt aspires to be the Nobu of NoHo, it helps to have one of that acclaimed restaurant's former chefs at the helm. Two of Linda Rodriguez's soups, both made with a base of dashi (seaweed and dried bonita broth), proffer Zen-like goodness: truffle and mushroom ($8), and spicy, cirtrussy crab ($8). Other good starters: sliced duck breast in a rich, fruity glaze ($12); fried monkfish in a crystalline spicy and sour salsa ($12); juicy, grilled blue water shrimp with a purée of Japanese eggplant ($14). Entrees best for sharing include broiled, miso-marinated Chilean sea bass ($25); dry-aged New York strip steak ($25); and succulent rack of lamb in an Asian pear sauce ($25). Despite the leanness of the servers and the regulars, the chocolate fondue ($16 for two) is not a gravity-defying dessert. It descends directly to the hips. The fruit alternatives ($10) are nicer anyhow.

Greenwich Villlage & NoHo

Il Buco

You might initially be drawn into Il Buco, nestled among the galleries and shops at the east end of cobbled Bond Street, out of curiosity (how much is that creepy marionette in the window?), but it's the sophisticated wine selection, effortlessly artful food, and informed, gracious service that will keep you in your big wooden chair until the last drop of Barolo is gone. Il Buco, heaped with gorgeous antiques and discreetly oozing Italian charm, succeeds in convincing you that this space has always been a warm, fire-lit Tuscan farmhouse. Co-owner Alberto Avalle hails

$20–80

Address 47 Bond St, between Bowery & Lafayette St
℡212/533-1932
Transportation F,V to Broadway-Lafayette; 6 to Bleecker St
Open Mon 6pm–midnight, Tues & Wed noon–4.30pm & 6pm–midnight, Thurs–Sat noon–4.30pm & 6pm–1am, Sun 5pm–midnight
Accepts AmEx
Reservations Suggested

from Umbria and is passionate about the exquisite olive oils from that region. A novel way to launch your meal is with a tasting of oils ($6–8 with a basket of bread for dipping), whose qualities are explained, upon request, by sommelier Roberto Paris.

Starter ingredients are wholly governed by the seasons. In autumn and winter, you'll be wooed by radishes cooked in bagna cauda ($8), a heady bath of anchovies, garlic, and a featured Umbrian oil. Spring temptations encompass a salad of fava beans and Pecorino cheese ($10), or pan-seared Portuguese sardines draped over homemade focaccia ($10)—rich, fresh fish split and seared. Thinly sliced cooked beets stand in for pasta year round in a goat-cheese-filled "ravioli"($10).

There is risotto ($18–21) on the menu every night. During strawberry season (and a few weeks past), the chef prepares an odd-sounding but exquisite version with Parmigiano-Reggiano and the red fruits that makes a great case for sweet-savory taste combinations. On other nights, octopus and mussels, their flavors highlighted with a dash of saffron, hide among the creamy kernels of Arborio rice. Other choices may include calf's liver with mashed potatoes and seasonal greens ($27)—fresh, tender, precisely cooked—while the roasted baby chicken with baby carrots and smashed fingerling potatoes ($27) reinforces the sense that you're just a few steps away from the garden, the barn, and the hills of Italy.

Five Points

(🍴) To break bread here on Great Jones Street is to emulate Al Capone, Lucky Luciano, and other members of the notorious Five Points Gang. But this place is not a re-creation of their headquarters, the New Brighton Dance Hall, nor does it have any link to the Five Points featured in Martin Scorsese's Gangs of New York. It is instead a woodsy, clamorous, New-Age-styled showcase for the Mediterranean-accented, pleasure-principled cooking of co-owner Marc Meyer, a disciple of star chef Larry Forgione.

$30–75

Address 31 Great Jones St, between Bowery & Lafayette St

℗212/253-5700

Transportation 6 to Bleecker St; F,V to Broadway-Lafayette

Open Mon–Sat 5pm–midnight, Sun 11.30am–3pm & 6–10pm

Accepts All major credit cards

Reservations Suggested

Considering the value and consistency at Five Points, the day has come when Larry might want to put Marc's name on his resumé. Meyer's bistro resembles a dining car in both shape and, with its faux train windows, appearance. Under the vaulted ceiling, a hallowed, 25-foot oak log runs the length of the room, carrying a southward flow of water.

Opening acts from the rotated menu could be the star attractions in a lesser venue. Tough deal for any entree to follow the fritto misto ($8.50), a dizzyingly delicious "mixed fry" of golden artichokes, fennel, and lemon. The oft-running brandade ($9), a garlicky purée of potato and salt cod bronzed like hash browns and inventively presented in a square iron skillet with crusty sourdough country bread, is a star turn. Alternatively, there are a couple of good seafood salads: one with lobster, asparagus, pea shoots, and fava beans ($11), and a larger dish with rare tuna, romaine lettuce, white runner beans, onions, and celery ($10). The wood-burning oven imparts character to such entrees as the baked lamb casserole ($21) and the buttermilk baked chicken ($18) with the crunch but not the guilt of fried. Try also the house-cured, double-cut pork chop ($21) and the chargrilled bacon cheeseburger ($13.50).

The smart wine list features fruity reds and whites from France's Loire Valley as well as Alsatian whites ideally suited to the fresh, aggressively flavored cooking. If there are two of you, try this dessert deal: one take the chocolate brioche pudding ($7), one take the rustic apple tart ($7), and then go halvesies.

Greenwich Villlage & NoHo

Indochine

It was a little past eight on a Thursday evening and only three tables were occupied. Could it be that Indochine, the perennially trendy haunt with higher interest rates than a loan shark, had finally hit rock bottom? Not so fast. One hour later, the French colonial bistro, with its palm-leaf wallpaper and seductive lighting, was filling up. By 9.30pm it was obvious that the only feature about the place that had dropped to new lows were the waistbands. Bare belly buttons and the flat-tummied gazelles attached to them were everywhere. The green banquettes were mostly obscured by the black garb of shoulder-to-shoulder diners. And the heady glamor throughout made every other place in town seem as, well, hopelessly unhip as, well, Indochine at 8pm.

$35–70

Address 430 Lafayette St, between 4th St & Astor Place

☎212/505-5111

Transportation 6 to Astor Place; N,R to 8th St

Open Sun–Thurs 5.30–11.30pm, Fri & Sat 5.30pm–midnight

Accepts All major credit cards

Reservations Suggested

So how's the Frenchified Vietnamese food? Certainly no worse and probably better than ever. Huy Chi Le, the Saigon native who started here in 1984 as an off-the-boat bus boy, is now the executive chef and co-owner. (He and partners Michael Callahan and Jean-Marc Houmard also own BondSt and Republic; see p.87 and p.77.) His remarkable rise might suggest that this was just the man to finally bring the entrees up to the level of the appetizers. But no. Loading up on starters and going light on—or ignoring altogether—the mains is still the best approach.

Crunchy spring rolls plucked from the hot oil come with two fillings: seafood ($8.50) or chicken ($8), with vegetables and vermicelli. Get them both. Pristine slices of deep-pink beef make up a good two thirds of the spicy beef salad ($11.50), and crisp breaded shrimp stuffed with artichoke and shiitakes ($9.50) are fitted so that their tails protrude like handles—ideal for dipping into the pimento-plum sauce. Don't miss the outstanding spare ribs ($8.50), which are marinated and grilled yet neither glazed nor sauced. The notes of lemongrass and anise turn "chewy" and "dry" into positives. If you must have an entree, try fat-rimmed roast duck with ginger sauce ($18.50); steamed sea bass fillet with fresh ginger, scallions, and asparagus ($20); or roasted five-spice Cornish hen ($18.75).

Knickerbocker Bar & Grill

Just as the waitress served the young couple crispy duck breast with duck confit, a fig-and-caramelized onion tart, and balsamic vinaigrette ($18.50), her colleague brought to the next table a T-bone steak-for-three ($84) large enough to stagger a hockey team. The guys taking on the beef checked out the young lovers' order and theirs. Then they each turned back to their companions and sneered: "Do you believe those guys, ordering something like *that* at a place like *this*!" Such encounters are commonplace at a neighborhood mainstay equally comfortable with po' boys and porcini flan, conversational lunches and live-jazz suppers, $25 Montepulciano and $350 Bordeaux, discreet celebrities and flashy nobodies, undergraduate cliques and solitary seniors. There's something undeniably reassuring about this place, with its dark-wood fixtures and comfy crescent-shaped booths, Abe Hirshfeld prints and old New York posters on the burgundy walls.

Lunch $20–55
Dinner $35–75

Address 33 University Place at 9th St
☎212/228-8490
Transportation N,R to 8th St
Open Sun & Mon 11.45am–midnight, Tues–Thurs 11.45am–1am, Fri & Sat 11.45am–2am
Accepts All major credit cards
Reservations Suggested

AMERICAN

The Knickerbocker is a deceptively nostalgic showcase for contemporary cooking. The kitchen embraces innovation as well as it preserves tradition. Perhaps too well. While such appetizers as yellowfin tuna sashimi ($9.75) or crisp flatbread with grilled lamb, sausage, goat cheese, and watercress ($10.75) are generally good, it's archaic specialties like the eccentric caviar pie ($8.75)—a cake-like wedge of egg salad, sour cream, and cream cheese "iced" with black caviar and toast points—that you won't get anywhere else. And who could resist late-night (after 10pm) snacks like the Cuban sandwich ($13.75) made with roast suckling pig, fresh turkey, and mango mustard?

Among pastas, the fettuccine with short ribs Bolognese ($15.75) skirts the divide between timeless and timely satisfactions. The famous T-bone endures ($29.50) as the house favorite, but the grilled filet mignon ($25.50) is also a power hitter. You'll go back in a flash for the seared salmon ($17.95) or, from the lunch and late-night menus, the solid Knickerbocker bacon cheeseburger ($11). For dessert, choose between the chocolate bread pudding ($6.75) and one of three banana splits ($7.50).

Lupa

(🍴) Alas the world is not perfect. Yes, at Lupa there exist adorable bowls of superlatively simple pasta for as little as $9. True, entrees on the cutting edge of hearty Roman chic do max out at $15. Sure, some dozen Italian wines are poured by the carafina, perfect for sip-sampling the moonlit Manhattan night away. Yet this 70-seat paradiso shatters its utopian scenario with one omission. A choice table has not been kept open at all times in anticipation of the possibility of your coming in. Named after the she-wolf of Roman mythology and inspired by Rome's neighborhood trattorias, Lupa is the second of four smash-hits from co-owners Mario Batali and Joe Bastianich (Babbo, Esca and Otto are the others; see p.84, p.210, and p.93). Managing partner Jason Denton ('ino; see p.158) unsnarls traffic jams in the countrified space and assists an informed service staff. Executive chef Mark Landner plays with the Italian regional influences and New World constructions that together define Mario's "Batalian" cooking.

Lunch $25–50
Dinner $35–65

Address 170 Thompson St, between Houston & Bleecker Sts
☎212/982-5089
Transportation A,C,E,F,V to West 4th St; 6 to Bleecker St
Open Daily noon–2.30pm & 5–11.30pm
Accepts All major credit cards
Reservations Restricted

Antipasti are stripped down to the basics. Citrus-curing blunts the fishiness but not the character of iridescent sardines dangling over a pilaf-like pillow of cracked wheat ($10). But go easy on the cured meats. At $10 apiece, they bloat the bill in a hurry. Forgoing pasta? At $9–14, you shouldn't. At lunch, bucatini, the thick-gauge spaghetti unrivaled for slurping but disastrous for dating, is prepared *alla gricia* with pancetta and grated pecorino romano cheese. At dinner, rigatoni gets tossed with a broccoli rabe pesto and ricotta salata cheese.

Talking main courses, braised oxtail stew ($14), unapologetically rich from first forkful to last, is no longer Lupa's undisputed king of fat-enriched excess. It is challenged by the crisp, fried pork shin with glazed rose petals ($15). For closers, the provocative wild fennel pollen panna cotta ($7) lures few away from the tartufo ($8), an ice cream treat from Rome served here with a halzelnut-chocolate sauce. When in Lupa you do as the Romans do.

Otto

🍴 Never mind that pizza ranks fifth among Otto the pizzeria's attractions. New York is infatuated with the newest collaboration of superstar chef Mario Batali and Italian vino vindicator Joe Bastianich, the co-proprietors of Babbo, Esca, and Lupa (see p.84, p.92 & p.92). Partnered with Jason Denton and Mark Landner, respectively the co-owner and chef at Lupa, they've created a hotspot where you can spend twice as

$25–65

Address 1 5th Ave at 8th St
☎212/959-9559
Transportation N,R,W to 8th St;
A,C,E,F,V to West 4th St
Open Tues–Sun 9am–11.30pm
Accepts All major credit cards
Reservations Not accepted

much time—and money—waiting for your table as you do sitting at it. The method to this madness is in the bar area: Carrara-topped mahogany counters let standees sample wines, antipasti, and each other's company until their name is called. An in-house salumeria is equipped with hand-cranked meat slicers gleaming as red as they did when they left the Berkel factory in the 1920s. The newness of Otto's vintage fixtures sets it apart from old-style trattorias and bistros whose fiction requires that 1920s fixtures look old and worn.

The mahogany and Naples-red dining areas are handsome enough but, given the dimensions of Batali's ebullience and Bastianich's wine list, oddly devoid of personality. The menu's centerfold lists 350-plus Italian wines, some poured by the quartino (a quarter-liter carafe). The pairing of wines and antipasti—vegetables ($4), meats ($8), fish ($8), salads ($8)—constitutes Otto's unmitigated temptation. Batali plays pinball with your palate, lighting up your taste buds with the pointed flavors of peppery headcheese, poached swordfish, pickled mushrooms, pristine salami, and so on. The bruschetta del giorno ($6) and fritto (fritter or fried thing) del giorno ($8) earn high-impact bonus points. The Tuesday fritto, Arancine, is a gooey, cheesy, and altogether thrilling saffron risotto rice ball filled with chicken livers.

The pizzas ($9–13), cooked in a griddle and divided into classic and house varieties, are another story. These pies fall flat. There's no chew to them. The clam pie requires your picking clam shells off the topping, and isn't worth the nuisance. The Margherita is merely respectable. To close on a high note, the gelati ($7 for two flavors) are remarkably smooth, rich, and intense.

Time Cafe

Since storming the scene in 1990, Time Cafe has joined the ranks of faded beauties whose white-hot phase has come and gone. Nowadays it's a relaxed fallback for impromptu meals, casual first dates and friendly gatherings. The high ceilings, quiet trance music, and desert photo-mural all contribute to a happily hangin'-n-drinkin'-in-LA kind of feel—even as the number 6 train rattles underneath the bleached-wood chair you'll recognize as a grownup cousin of the one you suffered in grade school.

$15–40

Address 380 Lafayette St, between Great Jones & East 4th Sts
℡212/533-7000
Transportation 6 to Bleecker St; F, V to Broadway-Lafayette
Open Sun 10am–midnight, Mon & Tues 8am–10pm, Wed–Fri 8am–10pm, Sat 10am–10pm
Accepts All major credit cards
Reservations Suggested

While too eclectic to be categorized as comfort food, the extensive menu of salads, pastas, pizzas, sandwiches, and entrees holds minimum shock value and maximum name-recognition. The homemade hummus ($7), served with a basket of warm pita bread, is light and perfectly smooth, with the barest bite of garlic. Crispy calamari ($7) is just that, served with a tangy, moderately spicy tomato sauce. Cobb salad ($14), heaving with chunks of well-seasoned grilled chicken, crumbled bacon, quartered hard-boiled egg, avocado wedges, romaine and iceberg lettuces, and a bland mustard-based vinaigrette, is an homage to the legendary Brown Derby, the Hollywood restaurant where the salad was invented. Black-sesame-crusted salmon ($17) is served smartly and simply with a pungent wasabe vinaigrette and sautéed spinach.

Most pizzas ($12) are joyously overloaded, with chicken, black beans, Jack cheese, grilled apples, and all manner of kooky ingredients sure to infuriate purists. They feel like something fabulously forgettable you'd eat while watching a game or B-movie on TV. The Time Burger ($10 plus $1 for cheese, bacon, or avocado) gets you a hefty 10oz of beef on a Parker House roll, cooked as requested, and accompanied by perfectly good fries. Among the homemade desserts, the best is the spiced apple crisp ($6.50), although there's too much of the firm, buttery crumb topping and fresh, juicy apple chunks for the relatively skimpy scoop of vanilla-bean-flecked ice cream.

There's another Time Cafe at 2330 Broadway, Upper West Side (℡212/579-5100).

Tomoe Sushi

"Nobody goes there anymore," Yogi Berra once remarked about a particular restaurant. "It's too crowded." His skewed logic could just as well be applied to this, Manhattan's most wildly popular, thoroughly uncelebrated sushi place. The skinny-downtown-intellectual-arty-NYU types who wait in line for the chance to knock elbows at drab tables in a nondescript environment do so for one reason only: oversize sushi at low-to-moderate prices. Other words that come to mind when sampling the fresh raw fish

$20–55

Address 172 Thompson St, between Bleecker & Houston Sts

☎212/777-9346

Transportation A,C,E,F,V to West 4th St

Open Mon & Wed–Sat 1–3pm & 5–11pm

Accepts AmEx

Reservations Not accepted

are "silky," "velvety," "buttery," and just plain "big." Although sushi is ordinarily measured in terms of artistry and not dimension, there is decadent pleasure to be had when taking on a nigiri with long, Rubenesque pieces of glistening tuna and salmon sensually draped over cushions of rice or, within rolls, buttery chunks of tuna that dissolve in the mouth. Besides, you get a little bit of artistry, too—Tomoe's trio of sushi chefs are skilled craftsmen.

The sushi deluxe ($25) features tuna, salmon, fluke, Spanish mackerel, orange clam, shrimp, salmon roe, flying fish roe, egg, a tuna roll, and a yellowtail scallion roll. It's serious business and clearly the exception to the rule about not ordering sushi deluxes. If there are two of you, the best strategy might be to share that platter and then do a round—or two, or three—of a la carte selections, being careful not to overlook the inside-out salmon skin roll ($5) and the piece of indomitable sea urchin ($5) that presents the ultimate challenge to chopstick dexterity. Then again, you cannot do much better than the straight sashimi deluxe ($28.50) or, for lighter appetites, the "battera" quartet—nuggets of Osaka-style pressed rice with eel, shrimp, mackerel, and salmon ($12.50).

If you're not going for sushi, at least three appetizers merit attention: the ethereal shumai (crab dumplings; $5), a deep bowl of marinated squid in spicy chile sauce ($6.75), and the yellowtail in a teriyaki-like marinade ($6). And as for the either/or of miso soup and salad with your deluxe ($2.50 a la carte)—there's no competition. While the soup is delicate and lovely, the salad is, frankly, pathetic.

FRENCH/AMERICAN

Village

(🍴) You could have walked in a second after Village's 2000 opening and asked yourself: why didn't I know about this place before? The clandestine grandeur suggests a well-used, well-loved restaurant. Relaxed first-time diners effortlessly adopt the comportment of longstanding regulars. Whether bistro or brasserie, retro or contemporary, American or French, Village has something New Yorkers know how to use. Past the crush of cosmopolitans—liquid and human—in the bar/cafe is an oval-domed, curved-glass skylight rising some 30ft over the handsome, balconied,

$25–70

Address 62 West 9th St, between 5th & 6th Aves

℡212/505-3355

Transportation A,C,E,F,V to West 4th St

Open Mon–Thurs 6pm–midnight, Fri noon–3pm & 6pm–midnight, Sat & Sun 11.30am–3pm & 5pm–midnight

Accepts All major credit cards

Reservations Suggested

Depression-era dining hall. Down below, slim bodies tightly folded into the red-and-black banquettes along the wainscoted perimeter lean close to hear each other speak. Chef-owner Stephen Lyle is quietly making noise with the beautiful-people-and-homely-food formula he mastered at Odeon (see p.138) and Independent.

Lyle's dishes are devoid of frou-frou. Though he has replaced some of the more rustic fare—pork cheeks, smoked calf's tongue, herring—with appetizers—mussels, smoked sausage—more in line mainstream American tastes, good food on a plate is still what matters. As before, no starter can match the pan-roasted oysters in a chipotle-heated crème fraîche bisque ($11) for pure excitement, through the grilled leeks with prosciutto and truffled pecorino ($8.50) come close.

Entrees revel in the rich and the unctuous. Homemade folds of ravioli, their veal stuffing braised to the brink of collapse, waft in rosemary cream and enriched veal stock ($18.50). Crushed pepper melts into the fatty juices of a New York strip steak au poivre ($24.50). Even roast salmon ($18.50) feels meaty in the company of a white bean purée. With dessert, Lyle again proves he knows what we want. No amount of praise for the doubly tangy lemon tartlet ($7.50) and the ultra-rich tapioca pudding ($7.50) is likely to talk you out of the ice cream sundae with chewy, pistachio-nutted brownie cubes ($8). And good news: the warm apple tart is back!

Little Italy & Nolita

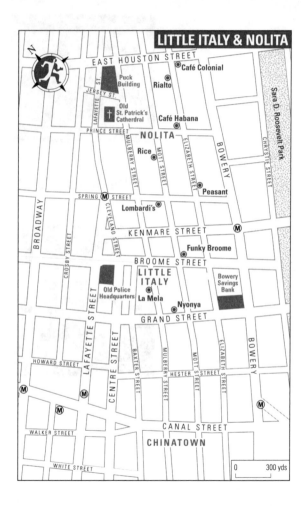

LITTLE ITALY & NOLITA

EAST HOUSTON STREET

Café Colonial

Puck Building

Rialto

JERSEY ST

LAFAYETTE ST

Old St. Patrick's Cathedral

Café Habana

PRINCE STREET

NOLITA

Rice

MULBERRY STREET

MOTT STREET

ELIZABETH STREET

BOWERY

CHRYSTIE STREET

Sara D. Roosevelt Park

Peasant

SPRING M STREET

CLEVELAND STREET

Lombardi's

BROADWAY

KENMARE STREET

M

CROSBY STREET

Funky Broome

BROOME STREET

LITTLE ITALY

Old Police Headquarters

LAFAYETTE STREET

CENTRE STREET

BAXTER STREET

MULBERRY STREET

La Mela

Nyonya

GRAND STREET

Bowery Savings Bank

BOWERY

ELIZABETH STREET

MOTT STREET

HOWARD STREET

HESTER STREET

M

M

M

M

WALKER STREET

CANAL STREET

CHINATOWN

WHITE STREET

0   300 yds

Café Colonial

(YI) The late-afternoon sun angles through the storefront picture windows on the northern fringe of Nolita. A politely worded sign offers the gentlest reminder to turn off all cell phones and beepers. Young, über-fashion plates sip cappuccinos and wait their turn to recount their day's shopping conquests. A few hours later, the recorded ballads of a soft-voiced Brazilian crooner serenade the couples compelled to sit close at small, candlelit tables. These are the easygoing, unhurried Latin rhythms that

Lunch $6–9
Dinner $9–16

Address 276 Elizabeth St at Houston St
☎212/274-0044
Transportation F,V to Broadway-Lafayette; 6 to Bleecker St
Open Sun–Thurs 8am–11pm, Fri & Sat 8am–midnight
Accepts All major credit cards

BRAZILIAN/AMERICAN

differentiate Café Colonial from any other formulaic bistro with a tile floor, marble-topped bar, and requisitely mismatched antiques. Nothing is as over these days as coordinated fashion, be it in threads, furniture, or food.

The menu is every bit as relaxed. Steamed mussels with spicy tomato sauce ($8.50 for a large bowl, $6 half order) is as far as you can get from exotic in a neighborhood that is still, after all, part of Little Italy, but it's a great starter. The spinach salad with moist slices of grilled chicken breast and velvety avocado dressing ($8.50) and the weighty hamburger Americano ($7.50) served with regulation-sized fries are the sort of post-adolescent fixations you expect from an off-campus coffeehouse.

As for entrees, the grilled organic chicken breast ($13.25) served with mashed sweet potatoes and daily vegetables could only possibly displease diners with cilantro issues. In truth, if you don't like cilantro you'll need to order very carefully here. The camarao a bahaiana ($12.95) is another cilantro-fest: shrimp cooked in coconut sauce dotted with green peppers, tomatoes, and, naturally, lots and lots of that zingy herb. Carnivores will flip for the flavorful seared and sliced sirloin ($16.75) pushed against arugula and cherry tomatoes, dressed with a rich balsamic vinaigrette and then topped with crispy, salty (what more could you want?) shoe-string fries. When it's time for dessert, skip the pedestrian Brazilian flan (what makes it Brazilian is anyone's guess; $6), and order instead the exceptional chocolate croissant bread pudding ($6).

MEXICAN/LATIN AMERICAN

Café Habana

Despite its name, its Cuban sandwich, and its roast pork, Café
Habana is not Cuban. Inspired by a legendary Mexico City luncheonette of the
same name, it dishes up inexpensive,
mostly Mexican grub from co-owner
Richard Ampudia's hometown. In moving
into a corner formerly occupied by
Bella's, itself a beloved luncheonette,
Ampudia desired only a likeable and
unpretentious place that wouldn't anger
locals sorry to see him move in. His
noble plan backfired when Nolita's shop-

Lunch $12–40
Dinner $20–45

Address 17 Prince St at Elizabeth St
☎212/625-2001
Transportation 6 to Spring St; F,V
to Broadway-Lafayette; J,M to
Bowery
Open Daily 9am–midnight
Accepts All major credit cards
Reservations Not accepted

ping scene exploded in the late 1990s. Fashionistas who were dropping
$300 on high-heeled mules at nearby Sigerson Morrison were also
flooding into this adorable dive for $7.75 chicken quesadillas slathered
with smoked Cheddar. Soon it was a challenge just to fit in, either
because the 35 seats were full or simply because you didn't have the
right haircut.

That isn't to suggest you'll get attitude from the young servers, most of
them chatty imports from the Lower East Side and Williamsburg who, if
they have any restaurant experience, do a great job of hiding it. They are,
however, friendly and do overcome madhouse conditions to deliver the
spicy slop while it's steaming hot. Tlacoyo tres marlas ($8.95), a popular
street food in Mexico City rarely seen in the US, is presented here as a
blue cornmeal cake stuffed with sundried tomatoes and goat cheese. The
chilaquiles ($7.25), a soufflé-like casserole of corn tortillas, shredded
chicken, and tomatilla salsa, is somewhat more familiar, as are the wonderfully sloppy huevos rancheros ($5.75), but the grilled chicken and
corn salad ($7.95) is a Café Habana invention. Here they take the cafe's
best single item—Mexican-style grilled corn with chile powder, Cotija
cheese, and lime ($3.50)—and expand it into a lunch plate.

At dinner, the chicken enchiladas ($10.95) have a marvellously rich,
chocolate-free mole poblano. For dessert, the flan with ricotta and cream
cheese ($3.75) is something you can get nowhere else but in the kitchen
of Ampudia's mother, a native New Yorker, who concocted it in Mexico
City while pining for her beloved cheesecake.

Funky Broome

(🍴) Nearly every Manhattan neighborhood has at least one whimsically named and fancifully designed corner spot like Funky Broome. Gray walls and lightboxes highlighted in lollipop pink, lime, and fuchsia. Elliptical indirect lighting from a pink ceiling fixture shining over glossy tabletops. Synthetic lilies and white roses glistening with imitation dew drops. The only difference is that those

$8–50
Address 176 Mott St at Broome St
☎212/941-8628
Transportation 6 to Spring St; J,M to Bowery
Open Sun–Thurs 11.30am–11pm, Fri & Sat 11am–midnight
Accepts All major credit cards

other neon-lit, storefront businesses are nail salons, while Funky Broome is a Chinese restaurant, and a serious one at that. Don't be fooled by the address that, three blocks north of Canal Street, is in the heart of Little Italy. Funky Broome's all-encompassing selection of 278 Chinese dishes is of the quality, breadth, and value you'd expect from neighboring Chinatown.

The appetizers you find all over town—pan-fried pork dumplings ($4.95), BBQ spare ribs ($5.95), cold sesame noodles ($4.50)—are generally superior at Funky Broome. But you'd do better to take advantage of such specialties as lemongrass chicken wings ($5.95), crispy beef strips ($5.95), and the wondrous, crisp, deep-fried, pinky-sized, asparagus tip bacon rolls ($6.95 for six). The same intricacy is found in fabulous entree no. 61 (it's easiest to order by number)—shrimp-stuffed tofu with baby eggplant, bell peppers, and black bean sauce on a sizzling platter ($11.95). Among other hot numbers are the 75 (stir-fried sliced fish with minced pork; $13.95) and the 47 (a mini-wok of pork-stuffed lotus roots; $10.95). Even the simplest veg dishes are delightful—for sautéed pea shoots with garlic ($11.95) or crunchy water spinach cooked in chicken broth with a little sugar and garlic ($9.95) ask for numbers 170 and 171.

A meal without rice or noodles is unthinkable. The rice dishes under the heading "Rice in Bamboo" (nos. 189–197) are cooked and served in six-inch lidded bamboo logs (essentially casseroles). They contain rice and various stewed meats, vegetables, seafood, or poultry. Top combinations (all $6.50) include pork, duck liver, and ginger; and duck, peas, and preserved veggies. Among great noodle options, the no. 208 consists of knotted vermicelli with shredded beef and black pepper ($6.95).

Little Italy & Nolita

Lombardi's

(🍴) Opened in 1994, the third incarna-
tion of America's oldest pizzeria is
a virtuoso tribute to the Neapolitan immigrant Gennaro Lombardi's milestone
achievement. Composed of two adjacent
shops down the block from the long-
closed, circa-1905, Little Italy original, the
third-generation Lombardi's is outfitted
with old photos, brick walls, a pressed-
tin ceiling, a vintage beehive-patterned
mosaic, and, more importantly, a coal-
fired brick oven. And although that old
oven was salvaged from a bakery and
not a pizzeria, it is of the type undoubt-

$8–35

Address 32 Spring St, between
Mott & Mulberry Sts
☏212/941-7994
Transportation 6 to Spring St; N,R
to Prince St
Open Mon–Thurs 11am–11pm, Fri
& Sat 11am–midnight, Sun
11am–10pm
Accepts Cash only
Reservations Not accepted

edly used by Gennaro to turn out crisp, bubbling, coal-charred
masterpizzas. During your first of hopefully several visits, be sure to get a
peek at it.

The first pies baked under the restored name and brickwork were
promising, but their charred crusts sacrificed the flour-dusted surface of
a New York classic in favor of an olive-oil sheen. Fortunately, more
recent renditions baked by Ricardo and Victor Minthali have offered
that almost powdery surface as a desirably dry counterpart to the combined ooziness of melted cheese and tomato. Now the only warranted
crust criticism is that its firmness doesn't quite support the copious toppings. There is never a need to order extra sliced mozzarella, tomato
sauce, or grated Pecorino Romano atop a six-slice small pie ($11.50 and
up) or eight-slice large pie ($13.50 and up). Additional toppings, like the
San Marzano tomatoes used for the sauce, are top quality: ricotta impas-
tata, sausage from Esposito's, Citterio pancetta, Hormel Rosa Grande
pepperoni.

The white clam pizza ($17/$21), a variety more commonly associated
with New Haven than New York, is distinguished by the density of fresh
clams atop a pie also dressed with chopped garlic, oregano, grated
Romano, and olive oil. Perhaps it might benefit from slightly fewer
clams and, in their place, the flavor and color of chopped parsley. At any
rate, the diminishing pleasure of a clam pizza as it cools and dries rein-
forces the ideal strategy for a Lombardi's outing. To assure you're always
eating something hot, go with a group and take on one pie at a time.

La Mela

The stereotype of the Little Italy Italian restaurant as a sappy, tacky, tourist trap may be unfair to Mulberry Street's prouder dining establishments. But if that description does not quite fit La Mela, it's only because it understates its trashy excesses. For anyone thinking about coming here specifically for the cooking there's just one word: fuhgeddaboudit! But groups intent on a rowdy, singing, wisecracking, chugalugging pig-out will discover these three adjacent storefronts and courtyard garden to be a blast. Fittingly, the setting, with its plastic-covered tables and fluorescent-lit walls papered with low-resolution blowups of diners caught in Polaroid moments, is not appealing in even the homey, humble, straw-Chianti-bottle sense. It's the apple of no one's eye. And the young barker who sings out "La Mela, La Mela" to restaurant-trolling passersby in his best Neapolitan inflection is not even remotely convincing. He freely admits to being Dominican, his idea being, like La Mela's, to let everyone in on the joke.

Lunch $20–40
Dinner $30–60

Address 167–171 Mulberry St, between Broome & Grand Sts
℡212/431-9493
Transportation 6,J,M,N,Q,R,W to Canal St
Open Daily 11am–midnight
Accepts All major credit cards
Reservations For large groups

ITALIAN

There is a thing called a menu here, with real food and prices ($8–12 for pastas; $12–15 for chicken, veal and seafood entrees). But this illustrated document has little to do with how things work. Basically, they keep bringing the food and you do your darnedest to put it away. Dinner starts with a hot antipasto that might contain decent stuffed mushrooms and roasted peppers and pretty good baked asparagus with Parmesan as well as a cold salad of tofu-textured mozzarella, tomato, and basil. Next up is linguine, gnocchi, and tricolored tortellini served together on a single platter, their sauces running together into a creamy, ricotta-tomato mess.

The waiter may at this moment give diners a chance to call it quits. Most move courageously on to the satisfying "meat" course of chicken scarpariello (fried, on-the-bone chunks with lemon-wine sauce), shrimp marinara, and tender veal scaloppine al limone. Dessert is a gratifying if unsightly muddle of tartufo, cannoli, cheesecake, and fruit. The check total depends mostly on how much wine you drink and the mood of the waiter.

Nyonya

Nyonya novices seem preoccupied by a mysterious specialty commonly referred to as "that." Those who don't know what "that" is simply point to some dish before asking, "What is that?" Others make a similar gesture while asserting, "I want that." Since the menu offers inadequate translations of its 144 selections, "that" is what many rely on to experience this scintillating place in Little Italy's Chinatown suburb. Targeted towards Chinese, Malaysians, and Nyonya (half-Chinese, half-Malay), the

Lunch $10–25
Dinner $15–45
Address 194 Grand St, between Mott & Mulberry Sts
☎212/334-3669
Transportation 6,J,M,N,Q,R,W to Canal St
Open Daily 11am–midnight
Accepts Cash only
Reservations Not accepted

experience is fast and frantic. Diners are not so much served as they are bombarded by dazzling flavors—chile, cilantro, peanut, ginger, garlic, coconut, lemongrass, dried shrimp.

In an open kitchen, a cook flattens rice-flour dough into paper-thin sheets for roti canal—an Indian-style crêpe served with a spicy curry dip. Everyone orders it as an hors d'oeuvre ($2.50). In a second kitchen, a team of cooks furiously fry, steam, braise, and sauté as diners surrounded by blond wood and bamboo ogle each other's orders. Eager waitresses race between kitchens and tables to reduce the interminable seconds that separate diners from their appetizers: Nyonya lobak ($6.95), say, a mixed fry of shrimp pancakes, tofu cubes, and bean curd skin dumplings; or white turnip rolls ($6.95), logs of diced white turnip, scallion, dried shrimp, and mushroom in a peanut-thickened seafood chile sauce.

One favorite "that" is steamed sea bass Teow Chow-style (seasonal price about $15–20) served in a bubbling broth over an aluminum pan heated by two oil burners. When first tasted, it seems like the salty broth has robbed the fish of flavor. Minutes later, with much of the liquid evaporated, the flavor returns to the fish. What a transformation! Entrees to order by name: sweet-and-tangy braised duck ($13.95); house special jumbo prawns ($20.95) in a spicy sauce redolent of cilantro; fried whole red snapper "Thailand style" (seasonal price $15–20) in a sweet, red sauce spiced with chile, lemongrass, and tamarind. These spicy extremes may be extinguished by various sweet iced drinks or chendor ($2.50), a refreshing dessert of shaved ice, red beans, chendor (green pea flour), and coconut.

Peasant

🍴 The best Italian restaurant in Little Italy is not what anyone would consider to be a Little Italy Italian restaurant. Peasant belongs to the neighborhood's hip enclave of Nolita, and could thus disappoint sightseers drawn to the area for more of a touristy, frolicsome dining experience (see La Mela, p.103). Even so, don't be fooled by such style signatures as the iron-and-glass storefront lounge, the sleek concrete bar, and, behind it, the capellini-thin barmaid in a tagliatelle-strapped tank top. Frank

$35–75

Address 194 Elizabeth St, between Spring & Prince Sts

☏212/965-9511

Transportation 6 to Spring St; J,M to Bowery

Open Tues–Sat 6–11.30pm, Sun 6–10pm

Accepts All major credit cards

Reservations Required

DeCarlo's region-roaming Italian cuisine constitutes a dramatic throwback to rustic simplicity. When it comes to the food, it's peasant chic that makes Peasant chic.

The smoky aroma and fiery glow emanating from open fires in the open kitchen warm the hard surfaces of the deafening dining room. The only fixture that absorbs sound is the polenta. You have to applaud the brevity of the menu, with its superb thin-crusted pizzas (go for the Margherita; $10) and wood-roasted sardines ($10), while questioning its reliance on Italian terms. Translation requests abound: "What is acciuga?" "What is fico?" "What is razza?" (Answers: anchovy, fig, skate.) This might prove tiresome were the waitresses not so well informed and the extensive list of good-value Italian wines not so easy to swallow.

You need not utter a word, Italian or English, to get crusty Sullivan Bakery bread served with ricotta cheese and olive oil. From there it is a painless transition to the hot appetizer of choice: a mini-casserole of seppiolini (cuttlefish), white wine broth, and sweet cherry tomatoes ($11). Pastas depend on their sauces. Lobster bucatini ($24) is rich in crawfish flavor, while a lush stock suffuses each grain of rice in the sweetbread risotto ($22). Meats are cooked under intense heat with great precision, from the tender rotisserie lamb ($20) to the wood-grilled T-bone ($24) topped with parsley butter. There is one classic to please Little Italy old-timers: zuppa di pesce ($24). Its lightly peppery tomato broth accommodates razor clams, baby octopus, mussels, skate, orata, langoustines, and seppiolini. The rough-hewn ricotta cheesecake proves similarly reassuring ($8).

Rialto

Chef-proprietor Sam Martinez feared the meltdown that afflicts eateries that get too hot too fast. While up-and-coming arbiters of downtown taste first called Rialto "the baby Balthazar," after the madly chic brasserie on Spring Street (see p.80), he preferred to think of it instead as "USC Jr"—in deference not to the University of Southern California but to the Union Square Cafe (see p.80). He even enlisted a USC alum to help execute a menu of reasonably priced American bistro standards interpreted with a Greenmarket shopper's vocabulary and the prerequisite Mediterranean, Tuscan, and Asian accents. Tin walls and semicircular booths in red Naugahyde give the dim, candlelit bistro a relaxed, retro flair, while beyond the smoking lounge a magical courtyard garden features a flowerbed set into its brick walls.

**Lunch $15–35
Dinner $25–65**

Address 265 Elizabeth St, between Houston & Prince Sts

☏212/334-7900

Transportation F,V to Broadway-Lafayette; N,R to Prince St; 6 to Spring St

Open Daily 11am–1am

Accepts All major credit cards

Reservations Suggested

The appetizer roster features several hot picks that could easily stand in for entrees: grilled homemade wild mushroom sausage with roasted shallot vinaigrette ($6.95); penne with asparagus, goat cheese cream sauce, and slow-roasted plum tomatoes ($12.95); crisp fried calamari with chipotle remoulade ($8.95), and Maryland crabcakes set against crunchy celery-root slaw. Main courses are a tad less reliable. Granted, the succulent roast chicken with sautéed spinach and rosemary roasted potatoes ($15.95) would be difficult to improve upon; the same goes for the Portobello napoleon layered with grilled asparagus and roasted tomatoes on a bed of white beans, brown rice, and shaved Parmesan ($14.95). But the marinated seared yellowfin tuna needs to be rescued by the wasabe mashed potatoes ($18.95).

The free range strip steak with fries ($19.95) recalls solid, pre-radicchio food, while grilled salmon ($16.95) satisfies the post-Portobello generation in various seasonal guises—recently piled over leek mashed potatoes with wholegrain mustard sauce. The banana cake ($6.50) and hot fudge sundae ($5.95) highlight a winning dessert card.

Rice

This Nolita hotspot is an Atkins dieter's worst nightmare. Every single dish involves rice in some fashion or another. As you approach, you'll spot a tribe of tragically hip neighborhood folk nibbling on rice-centric concoctions hidden in brown paper bags and using toss-away chopsticks provided at Rice's takeout. Inside, you'll find all those from the same crowd who've decided to splurge, spend the extra fifty cents, and eat at a table. The decor is sparse;

$5.50–13

Address 227 Mott St, between Prince & Spring Sts

℡212/226-5775

Transportation 6 to Spring St; J,M to Bowery

Open Daily noon–midnight

Accepts Cash only

Reservations Not accepted

seductively dark, even on the sunniest afternoon. Black, slate-like tables sit close in a narrow space. Don't be fooled by the chopsticks trapped in the brown paper napkin—the menu at Rice, though centered in Southeast Asia, features dishes cooked all over the world, including Jamaica, Mexico, India, and the United States.

Once you're seated, an overworked but capable waitress will make you feel at ease. As an appetizer, the Thai shrimp rice balls ($4.50) are an excellent choice. You'll wonder what holds these unusual alternatives to meatballs together. Spritz the half-dozen balls with the provided lime wedge for an even more intense flavor. You'll also do well with the tamales ($3). Peeling back the cornhusk of the chicken and mole tamale reveals a scrumptiously moist layer of sticky rice. Digging further (with the provided fork) reveals a mixture of plump, flavorful chicken, corn, and a superbly complex mole.

For a main course try the Thai beef salad ($5.50/$9.50). Thinly sliced beef, marinated in mint and vinegar, is grilled and placed atop shredded iceberg lettuce, carrots, and celery. Oddly, it's served with your choice of rice. Another excellent choice is the Thai chicken coconut curry ($5.50/$9.50). A creamy spicy-sweet curry of chicken, broccoli, and sweet red peppers, this dish screams for a rice accompaniment, unlike the beef salad, and, bizarrely, doesn't come with one. Even the desserts, such as the delicious Thai banana-leaf wrap ($2/$3), feature rice. This unique dessert, a sweet plantain wrapped in sweet sticky rice dotted with red beans, is completely encased in a large tropical leaf.

There's another Rice at 81 Washington St, Dumbo, Brooklyn (℡718/222-9880).

Lower East Side

LOWER EAST SIDE

EAST 2ND STREET

EAST 1ST STREET

EAST HOUSTON STREET

Hamilton Fish Park

Bereket

Katz's Delicatessen

Oliva

Grilled Cheese NYC

Paladar

STANTON STREET

aKa Café

Apizz

71 Clinton Fresh Food

RIVINGTON STREET

DELANCEY STREET

WILLIAMSBURG BRIDGE

DELANCEY STREET

DELANCEY STREET

Congee Village

Tenement Museum

BROOME STREET

GRAND STREET

Bowery Savings Bank

GRAND ST

N

Overseas Asian

W.H. Seward Park

EAST BROADWAY

HENRY STREET

CANAL STREET

STRAUS SQUARE

MADISON STREET

DIVISION STREET

0   200 yds

CHRYSTIE STREET

FORSYTH STREET

BOWERY

NORFOLK STREET

SUFFOLK STREET

ATTORNEY ST

RIDGE STREET

PITT STREET

CLINTON STREET

ELDRIDGE STREET

ALLEN STREET

ORCHARD STREET

DOW STREET

ESSEX STREET

EAST BROADWAY

MONTGOMERY STREET

ELIZABETH STREET

71 Clinton Fresh Food

$35–80

Address 71 Clinton St, near
Rivington St
☏212/614-6960
Transportation F,J,M,Z to
Delancey-Essex Sts
Open Sun–Thurs 6–10.30pm, Fri &
Sat 6–11.30pm
Accepts All major credit cards
Reservations Required

NEW AMERICAN

When this 30-seater opened behind a garage-door grid of metal and glass in 1999, the waft of greatness drew social climbers down from the high grounds of Manhattan to the then dark depths of the now trendy Lower East Side. Chef Wylie Dufresne's first dinners were attended with the excitement of Bob Dylan's early sets at the fabled Folklore Center or Eddie Murphy's stand-up acts at the Comic Strip. The cramped confines closed the distance between the open-windowed kitchen and open-minded diner, while ensuring a waiter as slender and agile as Gumby was never more than a few feet away. After four years, Dufresne left to open his own place on the opposite side of Clinton Street.

Though early habitués can be forgiven for already thinking of 71 Clinton in wistful tones, there is no justification for any sort of downgrade. Like Dufresne, chef Matt Reguin maneuvers New American cuisine in ingenious ways, ensuring that you experience the interplay of flavors and textures in the correct sequence: the bitter tickle of parsley root before the sweet kick of faintly peppery crab in a velvety soup ($10); green apples and cider-cooked lentils bringing tartness before and after a lush foie gras terrine; pickled radish, chives, Tabasco, and horseradish throughout the avocado-encased chopped Scottish salmon ($11). While menu specifics change with the seasons, the precise cooking and controlled spicing are constants.

The gritty mix of soybeans and rye breadcrumbs that tops but does not encrust the black sea bass ($24) lets diners transfer the crunchy garnish to the accompanying chive mashed potatoes. Droplets of red chorizo oil and green basil oil run into each other, but not, until you desire it, the beautifully seared sea scallops and gooey risotto cake they encircle ($25). A puddle of thick sauce under lusciously sweet, beer-braised short ribs somehow does not spill over to the chewy hanger steak that is the plate's co-star ($24). The desserts and wine selection are a letdown, if only by comparison.

Lower East Side

aKa Café

Baby bistros spawned by multi-starred chefs are no longer a novelty. What culinary luminary hasn't launched a *prêt-à-porter* alternative? Nevertheless, aKa Café embodies a novel concept in restaurant reproduction: a casual, cramped, and cheap spin-off of something already casual, cramped, and, if not cheap, moderately priced. It is found down the block from its acclaimed parent, 71 Clinton (see p.111), in a former clothing store that, according to the cursive etched on the vintage terrazzo, was called Kupersmith's. Peculiar fashions are still displayed in the shop windows, only now the models can move their lips,

Lunch $10–25
Dinner $20–45

Address 49 Clinton St, between Rivington & Stanton Sts
☏212/979-6096
Transportation F,J,M,Z to Delancey-Essex Sts
Open Mon–Fri noon–4.30pm & 6pm–midnight, Sat 6pm–midnight, Sun 11am–4pm
Accepts All major credit cards
Reservations Suggested

if not their limbs. The undersized tables barely accommodate twos and fours. Forcing threes and fives to share them is an egregious act of discrimination against odd-numbered groups. White sangria (with vodka-macerated fruit!) and fresh pear martinis only help so much.

Chef Scott Ehrlich cooks with the passion of a freshly liberated student, applying a global reach to close-to-home hankerings. One of the $8 pressed sandwiches, a gushy "slider" of chopped hanger steak, is assembled with a Gus' pickle and a Kossar's bialy (for the uninitiated, a flat round roll sprinkled with chopped onion). And while those classic accoutrements salute the Lower East Side's Jewish origins, the egg-washed empanada filled with roast turkey, smoked paprika, and Parmesan tomato marmalade ($8) honors the neighborhood's Latino and increasingly bobo (bourgeois bohemian) present. The Smithfield ham, Swiss, and pickled-pepper panini ($8)—a glorified Cubano with Reuben leanings—perhaps encapsulates this multiculturalism best of all.

If you prefer something more filling, a couple of soups ($7) and entrées ($13) allow for a conventionally configured meal. Choose the silky squash soup with popcorn crumbs over the thinner oyster soup. Among rotated entrees, barbecued trout and grilled sausage are smoky fill-ups. Braised pork practically dissolves into its celery-root purée. You'll melt, too, for the chocolate empanada with vanilla ice cream ($6) and the near-liquid dolce de leche pudding ($6).

Apizz

Sure, Apizz—a Neapolitan corruption of pizza—is pronounced ah-BEETZ. All the same, it would be more useful to refer to the annex of chef/co-owner Frank DeCarlo's Peasant (see p.105) as ah-PEECE, as in a piece of this and a piece of that. With round-cornered pizza rectangles and terracotta casseroles crowding its small tables, this friendly spinoff is so conducive to sharing you almost want to slap the stubborn

$25–65

Address 217 Eldridge St, between Stanton & Rivington Sts
℡212/253-9199
Transportation F,V to 2nd Ave
Open Mon–Sat 5–11pm
Accepts Cash only
Reservations Required

soloists who insist on ordering their own dishes. Apizz is less than five blocks from Peasant, as well as the trendy parts of Nolita and the Lower East Side, but this dreary street is hardly a haven for hipsters. Its windowless facade, foreboding even for a motorcycle shed, camouflages a cool, cozy, noisy brickhouse canteen composed of cement, brushed concrete, a wood-beamed ceiling and displays of fresh garlic and canned tomatoes.

Sullivan Bakery bread served with ricotta for spreading and chunky tomato sauce for spooning or dunking has you eating something akin to pizza before you've even ordered. The secret about Apizz is that you can order the $9 salad with bresaola, arugula, roasted peppers, and shaved Parmesan, demand bread refills, and make a thoroughly satisfying meal of it. But DeCarlo must know there's no resisting such appetizers as the mussels with white wine and tiny tomatoes that explode like cherry bombs ($11) or the lightly dusted calamari oreganata with their breading spilling into the garlicky, lemony, parsley-laden broth. The cooking juices extracted under the intense heat of the wood-flaming brick-oven, coupled with the bread deliveries, turn dinner into a sopfest.

The pizza boards, ranging from the $10 Margherita to the $12 Salsiccia (Italian sausage), are basic and fine, though perhaps a tad too cheesy and pale. Share one and then get on with the sopping. Delectable juices swim on the bottom of clay cooking vessels containing roasted whole fish ($24), baked eggplant rollatini ($17), and lush lasagna bound by a wild boar ragu ($19). Only with the buttery cinnamon apple crumb thing does the wood-fired liquefying get excessive.

Bereket

Where there is art in transition there is gyro on the cutting edge. The scope of the gyro, or kebab, extends from Paris' Latin Quarter through Amsterdam's Jordaan to New York's Greenwich Village. The oft-feared and sometimes legitimately scary mystery meat has journeyed from the great cultural centers of the Middle East, Greece, and Turkey to inspire and feed shoestring travelers, famished students, and starving artists. A window rotisserie spinning with a large mass of dripping lamb meat is a symbol of creative-creature comfort—cheap eats for the nonconformist. And at garish, friendly, 24/7 joints like this Turkish kebab house, it is no less than a fluorescent-lit beacon for late-night revelers with pre-, post-, or between-club attacks of the munchies.

$4–20

Address 187 Houston St at Orchard St

☎212/475-7700

Transportation F,V to 2nd Ave

Open Daily 24hr

Accepts Cash only

Reservations Not accepted

That Bereket, positioned on the bohemian frontier between the East Village and the Lower East Side, also draws couples, families, and working men from Turkey and other areas of the Middle East and Southeast Europe tells you there is more to this fast-food place than wee-hours chowdowns. Moreover, the superior quality of the prepared salads and appetizers demonstrates this is no ordinary kebab house. The doner kebab, as Turkish gyro is known, is clearly the big draw and the big feed. Never have you seen so much thinly sliced meat (supposedly lamb *and* beef) packed into a single pita pocket with yogurt sauce, lettuce, and tomato (a sandwich is $5). Still, the tasty shards of doner are not crisp-edged and they're no more succulent than the chicken kebab or baby lamb kebab (also $5 in a pita). Could the meat be too lean?

Nobody could dispute the appeal and freshness of the cold vegetarian dishes, which are served in sandwiches ($3), platters ($4–5), or large combination plates ($8). These last are composed of four items: perhaps crunchy white bean salad with red onion, parsley, and bell pepper; fried eggplant with stewed tomatoes; marinated leeks; and turmeric-tinted kisir (bulgur wheat) with pepper and parsley. To close there is decent baklava ($2.50), which, unlike the custardy, cinnamon-dusted rice pudding ($2.50), generally requires some chewing.

Congee Village

The very existence of Congee Village is enough to make you kiss the sidewalk and thank providence you're in New York. Only here, within earshot of police sirens closing in on the Williamsburg Bridge, could you find a tropical oasis and rice shop showcasing 29 varieties of the Chinese breakfast porridge, congee. With commendable optimism, they've placed a few faux tree stumps outside to serve as stools and tables. They're the seating option of choice for those who want to keep an eye on their parked cars. Most people, however, prefer the artificial vegetation inside the amusing, jungle-themed dining areas.

Lunch $6–25
Dinner $10–35

Address 100 Allen St at Delancey St
☎212/941-1818
Transportation F,J,M,Z to
Delancey-Essex Sts
Open Daily 10.30am–midnight
Accepts All major credit cards
Reservations Not accepted

No one skips the congee ($2.50–7.75), of course, enclosed in a bamboo casserole brimming with enough bubbling, silky rice porridge to fill five tiny soup bowls. The rising steam carries the scent of scallions and the promise of inner peace. Though shellfish varieties (fresh scallops, shrimp, squid) are generally best, the pristine chicken-abalone combo is a nice alternative. Each may be consumed with a long cruller-like pastry for dunking. But the fried bun, which comes with a sweet, condensed-milk dip, makes a better treat.

Despite the namesake specialty, the real treasure here is rice in cylindrical bamboo pots. These exotic cooking vessels are laid horizontally on serving plates. Flip open the hinged lid, scoop out some rice, and close the lid again. The rice then stays hot, absorbing the flavor of its garnishes. For bold, smoky flavor, the top bamboo pots hold rice baked either with Chinese sausage or with salty, fatty preserved duck (both $6.25). For a cleaner, less nutty taste, the mixed seafood ($6.25) buzzes with ginger and scallion. Only the Chinese mushroom and bony frog coupling ($7.75) is a letdown. Other house specialties reflect the spicier ways of modern Cantonese cooking. Sautéed crab ($9.95) carries a hot, peppery kick, while succulent chicken ($8.95) and tender sautéed short rib ($8.95) maintain a silent sizzle of dazzling flavor long after the hissing has subsided. The reddish sprocket wheels that the Chinese kids at the next table are invariably digging into are crunchy slices of lotus root in a gently bitter fermented red bean sauce ($5.50).

Lower East Side

Grilled Cheese NYC

Blink and you'd miss this petite twelve-seater, which is making quite a name for itself as the place to come for the ultimate comfort food—a perfect grilled cheese sandwich. The heady aroma of Swiss cheese wafts onto happening Ludlow Street, while inside feels less like a restaurant than the store-front apartment of someone who'd like nothing better than to make sandwiches for friends. Patrons armed with plastic cutlery casually sit at small cafe tables,

$3.50–7

Address 168 Ludlow St, between Houston & Stanton Sts
☎212/982-6600
Transportation F,V to 2nd Ave
Open Mon–Sat 10.30am–midnight, Sun 10.30am–7pm
Accepts Cash only
Reservations Not accepted

bobbing their heads in time to ambient background music as if honoring their half of the mantra that hangs from joints ceiling : "We Grill, You Chill." They stay relaxed right up until the moment that a paper or plastic plate carrying one of the cheesy concoctions is plonked down under their noses. Then they attack and devour, pausing only for the occasional breath between mouthfuls.

Some order a "I ❤ NY" cup of tomato soup ($2) to keep them distracted during the interminable three-minute wait for their sandwiches. The mild, definitely not canned soup is enlivened with fresh cilantro. Another pleasant diversion is the side salad ($2)—a not-so-small plate of spinach, tomato, onion, carrot, sprouts, roasted red pepper, cucumbers, and kalamata olives with a tangy, slightly emulsified balsamic vinaigrette.

Sandwiches ($5–7) can be custom-made from a list of three breads, ten vegetable toppings, five cheeses and five extras. Still, mortals dizzied by the smell of melting cheeses lack the concentration to make a series of such difficult choices. They opt instead for combos such as the Hamlet, a gooey mélange of Swiss, Cheddar, Black Forest ham, onion, and tomato, or the Grilled Motsy—as in "motsyrella"—with sun-dried tomato, arugula, and basil. Home-brewed cold beverages (all $2) include lime lemonade and peppermint ice tea. In the end, the only complaint is that Grilled Cheese NYC doesn't make it the way mom did—with yellow-orange American cheese singles on buttery white bread. But after a bite of any of these sandwiches, you'll realize that even moms make mistakes.

Katz's Delicatessen

Regulars of this landmark Lower East Side deli know you get a nicer pastrami sandwich (plus a sample taste!) by ordering it from—and slipping a buck or two to—a counterman than you would if you ordered it from a waiter at the tables along the wall. The tipping tradition is as essential to Katz's as the old terrazzo floor, the chestnut-colored wood paneling, the stainless-steel water fountain, and the hanging salamis. Another time-honored custom is the archaic system of distributing tickets to customers as they enter and having the servers mark off prices on them as items are ordered. Those who misplace their tickets may be required to pay the maximum amount or, heaven forbid, clean the premises.

$5–25

Address 205 East Houston St at Ludlow St
☎212/254-2246
Transportation F,V to 2nd Ave
Open Sun–Tues 8am–10pm, Wed & Thurs 8am–11pm, Fri & Sat 8am–3am
Accepts Cash only
Reservations Not accepted

The utter superiority of the pastrami sandwich ($10.50), assembled with hand-carved, black-edged, gloriously deep-pink meat freshly plucked from the steamer, is a comparatively recent development; Katz's pastrami did not supplant Carnegie Deli's (see p.204) as New York's best until the early to mid-1990s. Tender, peppery meat glistening with fatty moisture melts into the mouth. No crumbs or shreds on a sandwich, as is often the case at the Carnegie; just full slices. Don't order the pastrami lean. If you want lean, have turkey. Know too that Katz's corned beef ($10.50) tends to be a tad chewy and dry and is not up to the standards of the pastrami and the mostly remarkable brisket sandwich ($10.50). When consumed within 90 seconds of its removal from the steambath, the brisket is moist, buttery, and untainted by toughness. The frozen steak fries ($3.10) are nothing to get excited about, though they're admittedly good for what they are. They're said to be the highest grade of frozen steak fries on the market (some distinction!) and a number of people love them.

Two budget items merit consideration. The knoblewurst sandwich ($8.05) gets a decent crunch from the crisp skins of its thinly sliced, garlicky, knockwurst-like meat. And the plump, naturally encased frankfurter—just $2.50—is among the last of the great New York tube steaks.

Oliva

$30–65

Madrileno restorer-turned-restaurateur Eduardo Fontan and Belgian actor Steve Benisty have reproduced the noise level of Pamplona's Fiesta de Saint Fermín as thoroughly as Hemingway captured its furor. The vaulted concrete ceiling installed by the co-aficionados can make the voices of 40 people sound like 400. The noise, however, is just about the only good reason not to go. Though too contemporary-American to feel authentic, Oliva is an adorably cool, cozy,

Address 161 East Houston St at Allen St

☎212/228-4143

Transportation F,V to 2nd Ave

Open Sun–Thurs 5.30pm–midnight, Fri & Sat 5.30pm–1am

Accepts AmEx

Reservations Required

colorful, and affordable expression of Basque flavor. Even diners not jovial by nature become that way after a single superbly mixed mojito—the sweet minty rum drink that was another Hemingway passion, from another land and another book.

The menu was put together by former chef and ongoing kitchen contributor Joe Elorriaga, who is Basque by descent and cooking experience, American by nationality, and New Yorker by sensibility. Standards like gambas a la plancha ($12), here an appetizer of garlicky, juicy, fabulously snappy prawns blast-sautéed on a hot griddle, are good. Bacalao rellenos—roasted red peppers stuffed with a creamy salt-cod purée—is a nice rendition of a Spanish classic ($9). The recurring components of Basque cooking—tomatoes, sweet peppers, garlic—return as the foundation for clams piperrada, a rousing terracotta casserole of clams, fava beans, white beans, and chorizo ($8). Sensational cornmeal-crusted fried calamari ($8) need only the garlic mayo for embellishment.

Main courses, served on a variety of geometrically shaped plates, are somewhat less conventional and often less reliable than the starters. But roast monkfish ($16) is a rousing fiesta dish, taking on cepe mushrooms, fava beans, dried tomatoes, Yukon Gold potatoes, and Spanish olives to best advantage. And tender filet mignon au poivre ($21), sauced with a reduction of Spanish brandy (sitting in for red wine) and sided with great paprika fries, is painless enough. And the decent desserts ($5–6) offer a little something extra: mint color and flavor for the poached pear, walnut cream for the apple tart, black cherries for vanilla flan.

Overseas Asian

(🍴) When Peggy Yau opened Overseas Asian in fall 2002, it was easy to identify which diners were veterans of Ipoh Garden, her pioneering Malaysian place of the early 1990s. They were the ones staring in wonder at the undersized chandelier hanging down from the pressed-tin ceiling panel as if it was a priceless artifact from the Kings Palace. Recalling a beloved if somewhat scary dive in a then gloomy area of the Lower

$20–40

Address 49 Canal St, between Orchard & Ludlow Sts
☎212/925-3233
Transportation F to East Broadway
Open Daily 7am–11.30pm
Accepts All major credit cards
Reservations For large groups

East Side, they had difficulty connecting it to this clean, serviceable newcomer. Out of desperation, they ordered old standbys and hoped for what they didn't expect to get—the best.

Early signs were encouraging. A soothing house soup, a potluck broth containing chicken, beef, lotus root, and, in the Ipoh Garden manner, various bones of unclear origins, was folllowed by a stellar rendition of the essential Malaysian appetizer, roti canai ($1.95). Here the pancake was cut into triangles as flaky as croissants, while the chicken potato curry balanced its coconut sweetness with a late, peppery kick. Pol piah ($4.50), a steamed spring roll drizzled with hoisin sauce and red chile pepper, was meticulously assembled with an impossibly fine julienne of cucumber, chicken, beef, mushrooms, bean sprouts and maybe six other ingredients. And pieces of tender-enough squid sautéed with Chinese watercress and topped with chopped peanuts ($7.95) bore a precise, jagged cut.

Chef Lek brought a definitive end to the nostalgists' anxieties with his Monk's Head ($9.95). Filled with chicken, shrimp, baby corn, snow peas, black mushrooms, cashews, and fresh cilantro, this golden crown of fried taro surpassed even the most glorified memories of Ipoh's version. The same artistry was displayed by another classic main course, golden dragon chicken ($9.95), a clever amalgam of ground chicken and minced shrimp deep-fried to a crackling crispness. Fried whole tilapia (market price around $15) is served sizzling over an oval hot plate. Only the duck steamed with Chinese herbs ($8.95) is a comedown, mostly because the curative herbs—astragulus, codonopsis, lycium—are not served with the duck. Even so, Peggy Yau's triumphant return has been the very best medicine.

Lower East Side

Paladar

To dress properly for the backyard of Paladar you need to wear one cotton T-shirt and three pairs of woollen socks. While hot air from the heating elements swirls around the ersatz palms that act as the tent's support columns and then shoots up your back, a frigid breeze creeps under the picket fence and stings your toes and ankles. These fevers and chills certainly suit a hip, pan-Latin playground that runs very hot and cold: spicy cooking improvisations which

$20–55
Address 161 Ludlow St, between Houston & Stanton Sts
☎212/473-3535
Transportation F,V to 2nd Ave
Open Sun–Wed 5–11.30pm, Thurs–Sat 5pm–2am
Accepts Cash only
Reservations For large groups

borrow freely from Mexico, the Caribbean, and South America are intermittently extinguished by refreshing, lime-infused cocktails—mojito, pisco sour, caipirinha—and bottled beers from the same sources. Enjoyment depends only on your ability to regulate these spine-tingling temperature controls.

The menu was composed by hotshot heartthrob Aaron Sanchez, whole Latin knowhow is both inherited (his Mexican mom is *the* Zarela; see p.196) and learned (as well as Cuban at Isla, see p.160, he's cooked Nuevo Latino at Patria and Gulf coast fusion at L-Ray). For Paladar he's assembled a roster of appetizers so good you may want to construct your entire meal around them. Twin baked empanadas are stuffed with chicken picadillo (chopped) and set to advantage against a smoky potato salsa ($5.95). Chorizo and potato bring a robust satisfaction to the quesadilla with a thick roasted-tomato sauce and chipotle salsa ($6.95). And the mango and aji chile dip that accompanies lightly coated fried calamari ($6.95) is splendid.

There's little harm in main courses that top out at laughably low $14.95, even if they do lack some of the panache displayed by the starters. Braised short ribs with Mexican pozole and ancho chile broth ($14.95) disintegrate into a muddled stew. Pan-roasted fish gets lost within the coconut rice and orange chile vinaigrette ($14.95). But the hanger steak ($13.95) rubbed with a rather mild adobo (Mexican chile marinade) is one succulent slab of beef. Less ambitious items like the Cubano sandwich ($9.50) proffer greater rewards.

SoHo

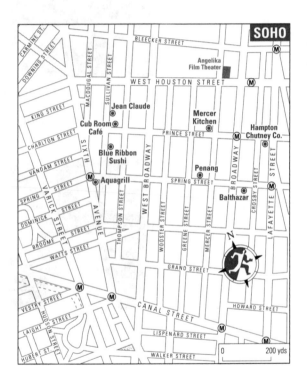

Aquagrill

Observing the bodies folded over thinly padded benches with only velvet throw pillows to cushion their backs, you are reminded that Manhattan invites two distinctly different dining postures: liquid and solid. Liquid people easily assume the shape of any container. Solids never really get comfy in loosey-goosey settings and sittings. Aquagrill, like a white-wine glass, best suits "liquids" with a nose for fish. By fitting clever seafood, able service, and a judicious wine list into a snug corner of

Lunch $25–70
Dinner $30–85

Address 210 Spring St at 6th Ave
☎212/274-0505
Transportation C,E to Spring St
Open Sun, Tues, Wed & Thurs
noon–4pm & 6–10.45pm, Fri & Sat
noon–4pm & 6–11.45pm
Accepts All major credit cards
Reservations Suggested

SoHo, chef Jeremy Marshall and his wife/sommelier Jennifer provide a low-key alternative to expense-account fish houses and oyster bars.

Great chefs tend to tire of their specialties much more quickly than their customers do, and thus update their menus prematurely. Happily, Marshall has kept on many of the hit dishes that first made a splash here in 1996. Choosing an appetizer is now, as then, a can't-miss conundrum between the pepper-crusted tuna carpaccio with avocado, lemon, and roasted Bermuda onions ($9.25); the elemental Manhattan clam chowder ($6.75); the Billi Bi mussel soup ($6.75); the roasted Dungeness crabcake Napoleon with cantilevered potato chips ($12); and the Maine lobster tossed with grapefruit, avocado, and ruby grapefruit in a champagne vinaigrette ($18.50 with enough lobster to merit the price).

The signature main course, felafel-crusted salmon over hummus with cucumbers, tomatoes, and lemon cilantro vinaigrette ($20), is intact and as enthralling as ever. Elsewhere, the changes are minor. The seared diver sea scallops ($24) now take on Peekytoe crabmeat risotto rather than crabmeat polenta—hardly a cause for protest. And the revised set-up for the roasted Florida grouper ($24) consists of baby Brusselsprouts, bacon, and caramelized pears in a butternut squash sauce. Desserts ($8.50) like the roasted caramelized grapefruit with grapefruit sorbet, the warm apple tart with cinnamon ice cream, and the chocolate-crusted deep dish walnut pie with chocolate ganache topping and vanilla ice cream confirm Marshall's mastery of casual chic.

SoHo

Balthazar

🍽 Now several trendy-restaurant life spans removed from its 1997 debut, Keith McNally's Balthazar still incites more bubbly pleasure among its 160 diners than a caseload of balthazars—giant champagne bottles sixteen times the standard volume. Re-creating the relentless élan of the great Parisian brasseries of the 1920s, arched aged windows soar over red banquettes strategically positioned on an old mosaic floor to maximize sight lines. Exquisite woodwork rambles through the vestibule, around the windows, up the pillars, and

| Lunch $22–65 |
| Dinner $30–80 |

Address 80 Spring St at Crosby St
ⓉＴ212/965-1414
Transportation 6 to Spring St; N,R
to Prince St
Open Mon–Thurs 7.30am–1am, Fri
7.30am–2.30am, Sat 8am–2am,
Sun 8am–midnight
Accepts All major credit cards
Reservations Required

under the 27ft bars. Spectacular cold seafood platters like "Le Grand", a multi-tiered, $58 extravaganza of oysters, scallops, crab, periwinkles, mussels, and gigantic shrimp, affirm the utter impossibility of not having a great time.

Co-chefs Lee Hanson and Riad Nasr excel at such French brasserie favorites as escargot with garlic butter sauce ($12.50), very good bistro steaks ($23 with awesome frites), and, as the Sunday plat du jour, rich, rustic cassoulet ($23). The serious hamburger ($11.25 lunch/$12.75 dinner) is an American imposition that's impossible to ignore. But perhaps wanting to impress *tout* SoHo, presentation is often too SoHo. Plates tend to emphasize cute over hearty. Even triumphant appetizers like the goat cheese and caramelized onion tart ($9) and the Balthazar salad ($11) of asparagus, haricots verts, fennel, ricotta salata, and truffle vinaigrette seem precious. And seafood entrees like crisp-skinned grilled brook trout ($19.50) and roasted bacon-wrapped monkfish ($22) are a tad demure.

Breads from the adjoining bakery—peasant rye, country sourdough, country baguette, white boule—provide the pleasure of crusty resistance followed by agreeably chewy surrender. The dessert approach follows the same lines as the savory one: they're either true classics—profiteroles ($7.50)—or stylized departures—banana tarte tatin with banana zabaglione ($7). Fruit tartlets and clafoutis ($8) are sweet exclamation points to a heady experience.

Blue Ribbon Sushi

The facade of Blue Ribbon Sushi is mysteriously unmarked. Were it not for the hand-lettered sign asking patrons not to sit on the steps of the adjacent building while they wait, you might completely miss this slim, handsomely low-lit place altogether. And once you find it, there's a process to gain access: give the harried-yet-congenial host your cell phone number, take a ticket, and prepare to wait for up to ninety minutes for a call-back. (There's a small lounge with wooden benches for those without cell phones.)

$30–70

Address 119 Sullivan St, between Prince & Spring Sts
℡212/343-0404
Transportation C,E to Spring St
Open Daily noon–2am
Accepts All major credit cards
Reservations Not accepted

When the call comes and you've been seated, either at a narrow wooden table or one of eight spots at the dramatically lit sushi bar, you'll be handed a piping hot towel and a menu. Those who forgo the menu in favor of omakase (chef's choice; $75 for two) may be disappointed, as the selections include surprisingly conservative, Americanized rolls and sashimi. More adventurous diners will prefer specials like ankimo ($9.50), a smooth, sweet monkfish liver pâté, served cold with a mild paste of chile radish and a light, soy-based vinaigrette, and chutoro tataki ($15.50), a watermelon-pink lump of bluefin belly tartare, topped with a raw quail egg and meant to be mixed with the super-fine shreds of spring onion and dash of sesame oil that accompany it. The appetizers from the daily menu also hold appeal, especially the various sunomono dishes ($7.25–16.50) in which oysters, clams, octopus, and jellyfish come bathed in a smooth, piquant vinegar bath.

Daily sushi and sashimi selections are divided by ocean, "Pacific" and "Atlantic," except for a short list of prime meats crafted sushi-style, including stunningly fresh, obscenely flavorsome gyu, or filet mignon with garlic sauce ($8.75). Blue Ribbon's maki (from $4 for California roll to $16.75 for lobster and black caviar roll) are uniformly excellent. While dessert at first seems absurdly beside the point, the green tea crème brûlée ($7.50) can be just the sweet, creamy, crackly thing to send you happily out the anonymous front door.

There's a second Blue Ribbon Sushi at 278 Fifth Ave, Park Slope, Brooklyn (℡718/840-0408).

Cub Room Café

(🍴) In the 1960s many people were guided by the maxim, "you are what you eat." In the 2000s, that's progressed to "you are what, where, and when you eat." And so, if your anything-but-average Joe SoHo does eat a 4.30pm order of fish and chips at an informal, kid-friendly, continuous-service eatery like the Cub Room Café, he doesn't dare tell anyone. This modest companion cafe to the more stylish Cub Room is an ideal spot for dine-down Fridays, ad-lib lunches, and other

Lunch $10–30
Dinner $25–40

Address 183 Prince St, near Sullivan St
☎212/777-0030
Transportation C,E to Spring St
Open Mon–Fri noon–10pm, Sat & Sun 11am–10pm
Accepts All major credit cards
Reservations Not accepted

impromptu escapes from the restaurant rat race. It's a countrified space, with a French-windowed storefront, wainscoted banquettes, and parquet tables set with paper napkins. The menu is a comforting blend of traditional and contemporary American cooking, the difference between which Arthur Schwartz, the host of radio show Food Talk, explained thus: in "traditional," the meat, fish, or chicken are served to the side of the mashed potatoes; in "contemporary" they're stacked over them. Cub Room Café showcases its incredibly rich mashed Yukon Golds both ways.

Copious starters include the Tuscan pizza with three cheeses and caramelized onions ($9), or the Cub cobb salad with chopped greens, spinach, chicken, bacon, egg, avocado, and blue cheese ($11). Outstanding fried calamari ($7) benefit from a chunky, peppery marinara dip and slices of garlic-Parmesan toast.

Certain entrees are simplified versions of dishes chef/owner Henry Meer prepares at City Hall (see p.135): witness the cherrywood-smoked rib-eye steak ($18). Yet as terrific as that steak is, it's difficult to make a case for it with when there's a thoroughly convincing steak frites (grilled hanger with hand-cut fries), grilled Atlantic salmon, and golden, brick-pressed roast chicken featured on the $20 three-course prix fixe. Weekend brunch features decent brioche French toast ($8.75) and a crisp potato latke with bacon and eggs ($10). Desserts ($4–5) are unchanged throughout the day: check out the nutty warm nectarine raspberry crisp and the arborio rice pudding.

Hampton Chutney Co.

Gary and Isabel MacGurn met at an ashram in Bombay, where they immersed themselves in yoga and meditation. While clearing their minds of the material world, they did their seva—selfless service—in the ashram's kitchen, where they learned a thing or two about Southern Indian cooking. Back home, partnered with chef Patty Gentry, the MacGurns have brought their know-how to less spiritual surroundings beside the chichi retailers in SoHo (South of

$9–25

Address 68 Prince St, between Crosby & Lafayette Sts

☎212/226-9996

Transportation N,R to Prince St; 6 to Spring St

Open Daily 11am–8pm

Accepts All major credit cards

Reservations Not accepted

Houston Street). On-site seating at this Indian-themed take on a wrap joint is limited to a dozen or so counter stools and a pair of high-top tables. Soft, melodic chants fill the air, and snapshots of the ashram's teachers adorn the walls. Grab a stool in front of the open kitchen, and you may even discover your own personal nirvana.

All thirteen options come in two formats made with a slightly sour fermented rice and lentil batter: dosa (a sheer, crisp, lacy crêpe filled like a fat burrito), or uttapa (pancake-style). Both are big enough to share with a friend, but you won't want to. Don't forget to choose your chutney (tomato, cilantro, mango, pumpkin, or peanut). You get one free per order, but the extra 50¢ you pay for a second will be two of the best quarters you ever spend in NYC.

Despite the veracity of the dosa batter, most fillings are no more Indian than the solid, hearty, breakfast variety ($7.95), overflowing with fluffy scrambled eggs, spinach, roasted tomatoes, and Jack cheese. Likewise, the uttapa topped with smoked turkey, Jack cheese, and balsamic roasted onions ($9.95) is the cultural equivalent of barbecue chicken pizza. Bogus, but delicious. Just add ripe avocado for an extra buck and the transformation is complete. There are several vegetarian options, including a substantial dosa filled with grilled Portobellos, roasted butternut squash, arugula, and Jack cheese ($9.45). The masala dosa ($6.95), stuffed with the traditional garam masala-spiced potato and onion filling, is one of the few choices at Hampton Chutney Co. which, though made in SoHo, could have come straight off the streets of SoIn.

FRENCH

Jean Claude

Resembling for all the world a workaday Paris bistro with a few Mediterranean accents, Jean Claude is a diminutive restaurant with an inviting red-painted exterior that can be difficult to see, crowded as the sidewalk is outside. Though reservations are accepted, you may still have to cool your heels on this civilized block of Sullivan Street or, if you're that type, stare in at the lucky diners already seated at one of the

$28–55

Address 137 Sullivan St, between Houston & Prince Sts
ⓉⒼ212/475-9232
Transportation C,E to Spring St
Open Sun–Thurs 6–11pm, Fri & Sat 6–11.30pm
Accepts Cash only

twelve tables and hope they get your "hurry up" vibe. But they probably won't, not while enjoying the warm, yellow-toned dining room, simple, elegant bistro fare and efficient service whose occasional lapses into bitchiness only add to the authenticity. The much copied formula was pioneered here by onetime waiter and now budget-bistro godfather Jean-Claude Iacovelli, who is also behind Impala Café in Greenwich Village.

Come early (6–7.30pm) on Monday through Thursday nights and you're rewarded with a remarkably reasonable $19 prix fixe menu. Whether you choose from this or a la carte, bear in mind that the daily soups tend to be a bit slapdash. A better option is the shrimp ravioli ($7.50), surprisingly light, full of ocean-fresh shrimp, and bathed in a buttery tomato sauce. The quail appetizer ($7), roasted medium-rare so that it's still pink and juicy, is served with warm, sweet glazed pear slices and a bright salad of shaved fennel and frisée. A modest medallion of New York State foie gras ($9) has its smooth and mild flavor set off nicely by a Sauternes reduction.

When it comes to entrees, the kitchen has a way with fish, including a fine sautéed skate wing whose briny caper garnish is countered by a meaty roasted Portobello cap ($14). Equally good, if short on sex appeal, is seared Atlantic salmon accompanied by a tender wedge of roasted fennel, delicate sweet peas, and crisp, earthy carrots ($15). Superbly roasted Cornish hen, smartly paired with an al dente, herb-flecked risotto and super-garlicky sautéed spinach ($14) is fine, but the pork loin with paprika sauce ($15) can be a little dry. Desserts, either crème brûlée ($6) or tiramisu, are true to form.

Mercer Kitchen

(icon) You enter superstar chef Jean-Georges Vongerichten's SoHo digs in the Mercer Hotel as you would a glam nightclub, descending a glass-walled stairway to a dark-wooded cellar partitioned like a Japanese bento box. Three long communal tables extending from the open kitchen to the salad assembly line blur the distinction between front and back of house. Candlelit tables surrounded by distressed-brick walls afford a measure of seclusion and—now that the notoriously chilly service has warmed some—romantic charm. The cuisine is

Lunch $35–75
Dinner $40–90

Address 99 Prince St at Mercer St
☎212/966-5454
Transportation N,R to Prince St
Open Mon–Sat 7–11am,
noon–2.45pm & 6pm–midnight,
Sun 7–11am, noon–2.45pm &
6–10.30pm
Accepts All major credit cards
Reservations Required

self-defined as "Provençal," a description both limiting and, considering the sun-starved premises and black-on-black fashions, somehow preposterous. The hotspot is too worldly, too unconventional, and too full of full-of-themselves New Yorkers to be positioned north of 14th Street, much less in the South of France.

   Crystal-clear flavors mark a number of appetizers: the elemental ensemble of fresh figs, prosciutto, aged balsamic, and rosemary pizza bread ($11); the salad of baby fennel, Parmesan, carpaccio-thin mushrooms, arugula, and lemon dressing ($10); the sliced and reconstructed tomato fitted with fresh basil ($11). Toppings on superbly thin, almost weightless pizzas range from artichokes, prosciutto, and Taleggio cheese ($12) to the raw tuna, shiso leaf, and wasabi ricotta pie ($17) named after Barry Wine, who introduced the concept at the defunct Quilted Giraffe.

   To derive maximum pleasure from an entree you need to adore all its components. There is no ignoring the yogurt-dill garnish and olive-vanilla-cumin sauce adorning the rotisserie chicken ($19). Perfectly grilled dorade (sea bream; $25) asks you to delight in the drama of fennel, shiitakes, and cherry tomatoes. Other joys are effortless, such as the dripping braised short ribs with sliced steak ($26) and, from the pastry oven, a wood-grilled bruschetta of buttered toast topped with peaches and plums ($7). And there's rarely any resistance to the molten chocolate cake with vanilla ice cream ($9). For the best value, go for the $25 prix fixe lunch.

SoHo

Penang

(🍴) With log-pitched huts, exposed ventilation ducts, and a tropical waterfall, Penang gives an industrial SoHo spin to the Paradise Island restaurant tradition. Among the best dining values in SoHo, it's a great, albeit small, place to introduce yourself to scintillating Malaysian cooking. And though you may be kept waiting at the sheet-metal bar for your table, the service, once you're seated, is friendly, patient, and well orchestrated, with shared appetizers arriving one at a time.

**Lunch $10–65
Dinner $22–65**

Address 109 Spring St, between
Greene & Mercer Sts; plus other
locations
☎212/274-8883
Transportation N,R to Prince St; 6
to Spring St
Open Mon–Thurs 11.30am–
midnight, Fri & Sat 11.30am–1am,
Sun noon–11pm
Accepts All major credit cards
Reservations Suggested

Servers rightly insist you begin by sharing roti canai ($4.25), a thin, neither-crisp-nor-soft, Indian-style crêpe served with a neither-thick-nor-thin curry dip containing potato and chicken, and penang lobak ($6.50), a mixed fry of tofu, pork roll, and shrimp pancake with hoisin plum and chile dipping sauces. Penang clay pot noodles and Penang chow kueh teow noodles (both $9.95) are the antithesis of one-taste wonders. The former packs five different star ingredients in its vegetable-laden broth: home-cut noodles, scallops, shrimp, squid, and an eggy gravy. The latter boasts seven co-stars: flat rice noodles, shrimp, squid, eggs, chives, bean sprouts, and a black soy chile sauce.

The pièce de résistance when it comes to ensemble dishes is sarang burang (known also as "monk's head;" $14.95), a cashew-sprinkled coronet of fried taro filled with baby corn, carrots, black mushrooms, baby mushrooms, shrimp, squid, and scallops. Other royal dishes are beef rendang (slow-cooked, almost shredded beef with a paste of ground onions, lemongrass, and chile in a thick coconut curry sauce; $12.95); kari ayam (chicken and potatoes in a red coconut curry; $11.95); and any one of three whole fish options (all $19.95): steamed striped bass with tamarind sauce, deep-fried red snapper with a spicy-pungent-fruit orange sauce, or grilled striped bass wrapped in banana leaf. The shaved ice desserts, like chendol ($5.50), with green pea flour noodles, coconut milk, and red beans, are for the adventurous only; there is no fitter finale than the warm peanut pancake a la mode ($7.50).

TriBeCa

Bubby's Pie Co

Though accepted from the outset as a wholesome, honest, unaffected neighborhood cafe and bakery, Bubby has something of a con going with its name. It was intended to suggest the Yiddish word for grandma. And you could well believe it was a genuine bubby who baked the old-world-hominess into the fruit pies, notably the mile-high apple and the sour cherry (both $5.95 for a generous wedge). But in truth, the co-founder (now sole proprietor) was no bubeleh, but a young guy named Ron Crismon. And the kitchen has never been headed by a woman old enough to have kids with kids.

Lunch $8–25
Dinner $20–60

Address 120 Hudson St at North Moore St

☎ 212/219-0666

Transportation 1,9 to Franklin St

Open Mon–Fri 8am–11pm, Sat 9am–4pm & 6pm–midnight, Sun 9am–4pm & 6–10pm

Accepts All major credit cards

AMERICAN

Still, you could say the place has grown into its name. Many of the single downtowners who first came in 1990 today push strollers through the front door of an eatery cherished for its picture windows, child-friendly outlook, and small-town vibe. Movie stars like Julia Roberts, Ed Burns, and Spike Lee slip in quietly from time to time for the same reason anyone else does: compelling breakfasts, brunches, and lunches. Sit down and a freshly baked, scone-like biscuit materializes on your distressed-wood table. As if by magic, the strawberry jam is already coating the end of your knife. Soon you are surrounded by fluffy sourdough pancakes ($8.95 weekdays, $9.95 weekends), ham and spinach-fluffed "green" eggs ($13.95), and peasant bread French toast ($8.95/$9.95), with barely a spare inch for grilled ham as thick as a steak and well-done, terrifically oniony home fries. As for lunch, the twin pulled pork sandwiches ($11.95) introduce a new emphasis on barbecue with their faintly spicy tang.

At night the side room, with its dim light, copper-topped bar, and floral wallpaper, is cozy and romantic. Crismon has abandoned his signature rosemary roast chicken in favor of a barbecued bird ($13.95) while also pushing meaty, tender-and-tart BBQ ribs ($13.95). And if entrees are sometimes delivered before appetizers are cleared, it's for the best possible reason: starters like homemade potato chips swimming in melted blue cheese and equally messy corn nachos with the works (both $8.95) are unending. You will, however, experience no difficulty getting to the bottom of the chocolate peanut butter pie ($5.95).

FRENCH

Capsouto Frères

Welcome to the wonder of Washington and Watts Streets. Since 1980, the three Capsouto frères— Jacques, Sammy, and Albert—have occupied the ground floor of a gloriously eccentric TriBeCa landmark. Built in 1892, the Fleming Smith warehouse stands near the Hudson waterfront as a golden marvel of fanciful Flemish brickwork, gables, and arched windows. Inside, the bricks and tall windows enclose a spacious loft distinguished by the pine ceiling beams that lie 14ft overhead. Romantic and unpretentious, the bistro is just as suited to young hopefuls

**Lunch $16–55
Dinner $25–65**

Address 451 Washington St at
Watts St
℡212/966-4900
Transportation 1,9 to Canal St
Open Mon 6–11pm, Tues–Thurs
noon–3.30pm & 6–11pm, Fri & Sat
noon–3.30pm & 6pm–midnight,
Sun noon–3.30pm & 6–11pm
Accepts All major credit cards
Reservations Suggested

on first dates as to old-timers celebrating silver-wedding anniversaries.

The classic French kitchen is neither oblivious to, nor preoccupied with, modern food fashions, which, like skirt lengths, constitute fads and revivals more often than they do outright inventions. The consommé of desirably chewy duck and cepe ravioli ($7.50) will satisfy any fashion-conscious diner, while those who favor a more traditional plate can contend with the blasts of garlic and nose-burning grainy mustard in the Lyonnaise pairing of sausage and warm potatoes ($6.50). And diners of all persuasions would adore the potato-chip-tiered lobster napoleon ($10).

Main courses are solid and substantial and rarely any more than that. The arugula, wild rice, and sweet raspberry butter crowding a plate of grilled quail ($17.50) could not be less photogenic, but offers plenty of good nibbling and shoveling. Likewise, the sautéed sweetbreads with wild mushrooms and baby vegetables in an unrepentantly rich brown butter sauce ($19) will never make it to a glossy magazine spread, however tasty they are. The pot au feu of vegetables in a truffled broth ($16) is a noble gesture toward caloric correctness. Forget calories when it comes to dessert, and take note: no one can truly be happy with the hazelnut crème brûlée or warm tarte tatin—though these are perfectly okay—when everyone around them is dipping into the hot recesses of chocolate, raspberry, hazelnut, or lemon soufflés (each $6.50).

City Hall

Times have never been tougher for the bratty tycoons of Wall Street and Foley Square. No to interoffice flirting. No to topless live theater. No to red meat, raw oysters, buttered anything, morning martinis, afternoon caffeine, and seven-figure bonuses. City Hall, however, indulges a generation that will no longer be denied. With a Delmonico steak gracing its menu and back-lit vintage photographs of old downtown markets lining its handsome dining room, this restaurant conjures up the chophouses, oyster bars, and cafeterias of Tammany Hall days. Yet since the city's dining

**Lunch $20–40
Dinner $40–85**

Address 131 Duane St, between Church St & West Broadway
☎212/227-7777
Transportation 1,2,9,A,C,E to Chambers St; N,R to City Hall
Open Mon–Thurs noon–2.30pm & 4–10pm, Fri noon–2.30pm & 4–11pm, Sat 5.30–11pm
Accepts All major credit cards
Reservations Suggested

scene is much better now than at any time in its history, the nostalgic appeal is ultimately not for the old foods. It's for the old rules. Arched windows, cast-iron Corinthian columns, travertine marble floors, courtly circular booths, colossal steaks, and tiered shellfish extravaganzas recall a more permissive age when fatty meat and fat politicians could be had for the money and in plain view.

City Hall has no remedies for a sluggish economy or a bear market, but it does administer temporary relief from an assortment of ailments in its bowl of chicken soup with matzoh dumplings ($8). Among appetizers, the half-salmon/half-tuna tartare ($12) and lightly fried oysters ($9.50) are exactly what you want them to be. The signature main course is the Delmonico ($28.50)—a thin, 16oz slab of charbroiled ribeye with a layer of melted Maytag blue cheese. A tuna steak encrusted with tri-colored peppercorns ($24) works beautifully, as do the sensational, goose-fat-fried hash browns (like all side dishes, $6 extra) and the split chicken ($21) cooked with rosemary and shallots in an infrared broiler to crackling perfection.

Desserts (mostly $8) may at first seem fussy. But if you're compensating for years of denial, the warm chocolate hazelnut soufflé with caramel ice cream and warm chocolate might be just the thing. Likewise, the brioche apple pudding and the cheesecake.

TriBeCa

The Harrison

When looking back at the ill-fated date and location they chose for their downtown follow-up to the well-liked Red Cat (see p.11) executive chef Jimmy Bradley and partner Danny Abrams can only shake their heads and ask themselves, "what if?" Harrison opened one month after—and nine blocks north of—the World Trade Center attacks. It's probably safe to bet that under less trying circumstances, the ensuing reservations backlog of two to three weeks might have stretched closer to two to three months. The success of The Harrison confirms Bradley's mastery of the up-to-date, feel-good food that Manhattan feels like eating. And the white-washed barnwood, antique leather banquettes, oiled walnut, and French doors give his new digs the ambiance of a TriBeCa clubhouse—just the ticket for nightly and noisy get-togethers.

$40–80

Address 355 Greenwich St at Harrison St
℡212/274-9310
Transportation 1,9 to Franklin St
Open Mon–Thurs 5.30–11pm, Fri & Sat 5.30–11.30pm, Sun 5–10pm
Accepts All major credit cards
Reservations Required

The menu, as supervised by Joey Campanaro, applies Mediterranean highlights to contemporary American comforts. (Maybe it's better to instead specify "New York" comforts, as it's uncertain that the rest of the nation is as enamored of veal cheeks and sweetbreads as New Yorkers are.) Braised veal cheeks make an early entrance in an appetizer of ricotta cavatelli (the cheese is added to the dough) dressed with oven-dried tomatoes, escarole, and Pecorino Romano ($10). Recently some lighter salads—toasted sunflower salad with beets and Parmesan ($8); endive and pear salad with candied walnuts and Maytag blue cheese ($9)—have been added to run alongside the trusty fried clams with lemon cilantro aioli ($10).

Among entrees, the spice-rubbed grilled pork chop with German potato salad and fennel slaw ($21), and the 14oz shell steak ($29) are heavy-hitters. The pan-crisped skate ($18) and signature pan-crisped chicken ($19) are heftier than you expect. (Pan-crisped is a euphemism for pan-fried.) To close, the ricotta panna cotta ($7), beignets with chilled coffee mousse and warm chocolate sauce ($8), and the warm apple crêpe with cinnamon beignets ($8) tack on a good three days to the table backlog.

Nam

In a high-windowed, ground-floor loft on Reade Street, Nam hits on a balanced mix of style, sophistication, warmth, and informality. Evocative family photos silk-screened onto the sides of hatbox-shaped lampshades illuminate the carved-wood walls with wistful memories of Saigon and Hanoi, while the chartreuse opalescence that back-lights both the dark-wooded bar and the wall display of bamboo branches casts a glowing promise of nocturnal pleasures. The fantasy is brought to life by the elemental Vietnamese cooking of co-chefs Tien Phan, Hoang Do, and Quy Tran. The lucidity of familiar flavors is so great as to make them seem mysterious and complex.

$25–65

Address 110 Reade St, between West Broadway & Church St
☎212/267-1777
Transportation 1,2,3,9,A,C,E to Chambers St
Open Mon–Thurs noon–2.30pm & 5.30–10.30pm, Fri noon–2.30pm & 5.30–11.30pm, Sat 5.30–11.30pm, Sun 5.30–10.30pm
Accepts All major credit cards
Reservations Suggested

VIETNAMESE

The irresistible bo bia ($5)—soft, rice-paper rolls of jicama, shrimp, and sausage with a chile bean dip—are a compulsory starting point. But the banh cuon—loose and slippery ravioli filled with chopped shiitakes and topped with fried shallots, basil, cilantro, bean sprouts, and lime vinaigrette ($5)—are also non-negotiable. The chao tom lets you wrap rice paper, vermicelli, crushed peanuts, lettuce, cilantro, and mint around a sugar-cane-speared brochette of ground, pressed shrimp ($8). And the goi muc—a vertical grilled calamari salad ($7)—is a thing of rare beauty.

The wonder of main courses is the way in which you can isolate and appreciate each ingredient. The drama supplied by the tomato, soft tofu, and crisp strands of ginger to steamed sea bass with noodles, shiitakes, ginger, and scallions ($18–20) is entirely unexpected. In mi xao, the stir-fried egg noodles, shrimp, chicken, pork, carrots, and peanuts ($10) are all distinct. Bun cha ($10) poses grilled chunks of desirably chewy, succulent, sweet-and-spicy barbecued pork alongside a nest of rice vermicelli and roasted peanut. The one criticism of entrees is that they rely too often on the same chile lime sauce. Lime makes a final appearance as a marinade for the mango chunks accompanying the ginger flan (a bit high at $8). Like the banana bread topped with flakes of toasted coconut ($7), it applies a stylish, tropical spin on an everyday dessert.

Odeon

🍽 The arduous burden of staying fashionable, of anticipating trends and eluding obsolescence, of securing the right tables in the right places at the right times, is lifted for an hour or two of giddy, conversational pleasure at the former site of the Tower Cafeteria. In Left Bank Paris, the Odeon is a theater and a Metro station. In Manhattan, it's a brasserie and a guarantee to feel with-it, relevant, and relieved to be nowhere else. Co-founded in 1980 by Brian McNally, Keith McNally (Balthazar, Pastis; p.124 and p.165), and Lynn Wagenknecht (Cafe

Lunch $22–60
Dinner $30–80

Address 145 West Broadway at Thomas St
☎212/233-0507
Transportation 1,2,3,A,C,E to Chambers St
Open Mon–Fri 11.45am–2am, Sat & Sun 11am–2am
Accepts All major credit cards
Reservations Suggested

Luxembourg; p.268), Odeon set the template for the retro bistro craze, not only with its 1930s look (salvaged terrazzo floor, hanging globe lights, wood-paneling, chrome details), but also in its newly minted brand of downtown cool that was practiced to look unpracticed.

The food has proved crucial to Odeon's staying power. As far as anyone knows—and hopes—there's no fashionable Odeon cookbook on the horizon. It's the absence of flashes in the pan that's so enduring; there's nothing to tire of. As on a cafeteria line, the aim is to crowd likeable food on a plate and let the diner figure out how to manage it. Disorderly salads have typically been the most challenging in this regard, especially the very satisfying frisée with crumbled Roquefort, bacon lardons, and Dijon vinaigrette ($10.50). With decent fried calamari ($9.50) or shrimp cocktail ($11) you have a better shot at keeping contents confined to plate and fork.

No matter who's manning the kitchen, steak frites (among which the superb, $13 steakburger must be included) continue to be the best choices, either as a splurge (the grilled sirloin; $26, $27.50 au poivre) or on the relative cheap (a fully functional grilled hanger with a wild mushroom garnish; $17.50). Tuna too is a great bet, either as a grilled steak ($23) or seared and then slid into a sandwich with arugula and wasabe mayo ($15.50). The roast chicken ($17.50) never disappoints. Of the desserts, look no further than the chocolate pudding ($7).

Pepolino

Stepping upstairs and then inside Pepolino is a heady experience. One moment you're inhaling the fumes from the Holland Tunnel approach; the next, you're breathing the air of a folksy Florentine trattoria. Sooner than you and yours have had time to figure out who's sitting where at the little butcher-block table, someone arrives with crusty Sullivan Bakery bread accompanied by a garlicky tomato flan, a savory custard that you spread like jam. Life at Pepolino just gets better and better.

Lunch $19–30
Dinner $25–70

Address 281 West Broadway, between Canal & Lispenard Sts
☎212/966-9983
Transportation A,C,E to Canal St
Open Mon–Fri noon–3pm & 5.30–11pm, Sat & Sun noon–midnight
Accepts AmEx
Reservations Suggested

Co-owner and pastry chef Enzo Pezone must count on one loaf of bread per diner. The next house specialty to arrive is the terrine di cozze con burro e prezzemole ($9), a ramekin of shelled mussels in a pool of melted butter, garlic, and parsley that requires several slices of toast for sopping. And then there's the Tuscan bread soup ribollita ($8). Made with cannellini beans, cabbage, thyme, and sage, this thicker-than-thick version has no visible liquid. You could feasibly drop this soup, but you couldn't really spill it. The spinach ricotta soufflé ($11) and the polenta mousse with wild mushroom and white truffle oil ($12) also reflect the rustic, herb-packed style of chef Patrizio Siddu's cooking.

Pasta is not a strong point, excepting the malfatti (spinach-ricotta dumplings) in a butter sage sauce ($11 lunch, $14 dinner) and the daily homemade lasagna ($13/$16). Among evening entrees, the chicken ($18.50) is a joy. Succulent and tender pieces of boneless breast are assembled with roasted pears, melted Pecorino cheese, and a rich wine sauce to create a melt-in-your-mouth sensation. Similarly, roast leg of lamb with artichokes ($22) is a revelation. The deboned and rolled lamb is superbly tender, if occasionally a tad dry. From the sea there is the spicy fish stew cacciucco alla Livornese ($25). And how nice of Enzo to go to the trouble of preparing such wonderful desserts (all $7) as bittersweet flourless chocolate cake, ricotta cheesecake, and panna cotta. These give the illusion of choice when in truth here is none—quite simply, bypassing the chocolate flan with caramel sauce is nothing short of a crime.

TriBeCa

Le Zinc

To truly enjoy Le Zinc, it is almost better not to know that chef David Waltuck and wife Karen are behind it. Twice the Waltucks have broken new ground for fine downtown dining, first when they opened the exacting French/New American restaurant Chanterelle in SoHo 1981, and later when they moved it to TriBeCa in 1989. Le Zinc, on the other hand, despite a few outstanding dishes, is merely a good neighborhood place. With a zinc-plate bar, Thonet bentwood chairs, and unframed art posters plastered on the

**Lunch $16–50
Dinner $25–70**

Address 139 Duane St, between
West Broadway & Church St
☎212/513-0001
Transportation 1,2,3,9A,C E to
Chambers St
Open Sun–Thurs 8am–1am, Fri &
Sat 8am–2am
Accepts All major credit cards
Reservations For large groups

high walls, the 95-seat dining room suits a high-rent district that still sees itself as arty and nonconformist. The menu seeks a comparable balance between creativity and comfort, listing Asian fusion snacks alongside bistro fare and hearty Old World selections.

If you ended up with cute Asian appetizers like the chicken satay with spicy peanut sauce ($7.50) and pulled pork in moo shu wrappers ($8.50) you wouldn't run away. But with better versions of similar things elsewhere you wouldn't make a special trip, either. The cornmeal-coated duck wings ($8.50), however, are a revelation. Chewing the fried, confit-like duck meat off the bone is the closest thing you'll ever experience to a duck spare rib. The curried onion fritters ($6) are milder than you expect, but still very good. Aunt Fanny's chopped chicken liver ($5.50) is dry.

The onion roll used for an otherwise solid bacon cheeseburger ($12.50 with first-rate fries) is detrimentally large. Objections to the grilled pork chop ($20) have nothing to do with the juicy meat and everything to do with the black pepper inexplicably dominating the apple-smoked bacon sauce. Better to keep that pepper to the grilled shell steak au poivre ($21). The roast chicken ($18.50), with fresh thyme under its crisp skin, in its sauce, and throughout the sensational stuffing made with cubes of sourdough bread and Parker House rolls, exudes true greatness. When it comes to desserts ($6–7.50), disparities are just as marked. On a night when the ice cream in profiteroles was crystalized, the top-notch pecan pie was successfully ridding the classic of its cloying gooiness.

Wall Street & Lower Manhattan

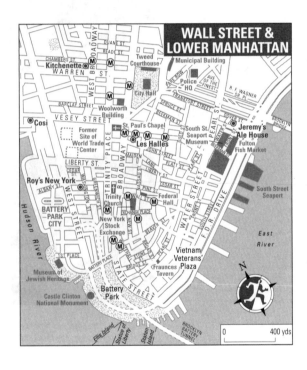

WALL STREET & LOWER MANHATTAN

Kitchenette

DUANE ST.

READE ST.

CHAMBERS ST.

WARREN ST.

Tweed Courthouse

Municipal Building

BARCLAY STREET

Police HQ

AVE. OF THE FINEST

R. F. WAGNER SR. PL.

City Hall

Woolworth Building

FRANKFORT STREET

SPRUCE ST.

BEEKMAN ST.

VESEY STREET

Cosi

St. Paul's Chapel

Les Halles

South St. Seaport Museum

FULTON ST.

Jeremy's Ale House

Fulton Fish Market

BROOKLYN BRIDGE

DOVER ST.

PEARL ST.

WATER STREET

Former Site of World Trade Center

MAIDEN

LIBERTY ST.

PLATT ST.

JOHN STREET

CEDAR ST.

LANE

LIBERTY ST.

CEDAR ST.

Roy's New York

ALBANY ST.

Trinity Church

New York Stock Exchange

PINE ST.

Federal Hall

BROADWAY

NASSAU ST.

WILLIAM ST.

EXCHANGE PLACE

BEAVER

WATER STREET

FRONT STREET

SOUTH STREET

South Street Seaport

East River

F.D.R. DRIVE

BATTERY PARK CITY

WEST STREET

GREENWICH ST.

WASHINGTON ST.

TRINITY PLACE

BRIDGE ST.

STONE

PEARL

Vietnam Veterans' Plaza

1ST PLACE

BATTERY PLACE

STATE STREET

Fraunces Tavern

Museum of Jewish Heritage

Battery Park

Castle Clinton National Monument

Hudson River

Ellis Island

Statue of Liberty

Staten Island

BROOKLYN BATTERY TUNNEL

N

0   400 yds

Cosi

Soon there may well be too many Cosis. But for the moment, the proliferation of this Paris import continues to brighten the shadowed canyons of Manhattan's sometimes dreary lunchscape. And this location, in the dining atrium of the refurbished World Financial Center, is a vital resource in a neighborhood on the mend. All sandwiches are made with the bread that makes Cosi better than "cosi cosi"—Italian for "not so bad." The delectably chewy and crusty flatbreads are baked on the premises in an iron-clad brick drum that fronts these

$7–30

Address 3 World Financial Center (200 Vesey St); plus other locations
☎212/571-2001
Transportation R to Cortland St; E to World Trade Center; 1,2,3,9,A,C to Chambers St
Open Mon–Thurs 7am–9pm, Fri 7am–8pm, Sat 8am–5pm
Accepts Cash only
Reservations Not accepted

AMERICAN

stylish eat-in/takeout/delivery cafes. Directly in front of that oven, a baker usually sets out a bowl of warm bread scraps—gratis nibbles to occupy those waiting patiently on the sandwich assembly line. Presumably the sneaky folks who grab a few scraps, suddenly discover they are no longer hungry, and then walk out are not among those concerned about Cosi's aggressive expansion.

The worry resulting from Cosi's growth, and its merger with the Zando coffee bar chain, is that the freshness of the bread and quality of the sandwich fillings will suffer. When you order a sandwich containing tomatoes, you're already likely to get slices cut from an insipid winter tomato, even in July. Fortunately, many other ingredients are decent and some are really quite good, notably grilled eggplant, roasted red peppers, and caramelized onions. You can ask for all three in the same sandwich or order instead a pre-selected combo. Best bets are the no.22 (tandoori chicken, roasted red peppers, and vinaigrette; $6.95), the no.38 (roasted turkey, Swiss, and honey mustard; $6.95), and the no.53 (ham, grilled eggplant, roasted red pepper, romaine, and Dijon mustard; $6.45).

The idea of baking bagels with the Cosi bread dough and oven was an inspired one. But the square-shaped "squagels" (95¢) are too bready and lack the hard lid produced from boiling. The sorry name (the precaution of trademarking it was probably unnecessary) doesn't help matters. Those who can think of squagels as breakfast rolls rather than bagels will appreciate the granular crust of the cinnamon raisin (good toasted), Parmesan, and Asiago cheese varieties.

DOWNTOWN

SEAFOOD

Jeremy's Ale House

Jeremy Holin anticipated the 1980s boom and 1990s bust set off by the marketplace-styled redevelopment of South Street Seaport when he pitched his deep-fryers and beer taps in a vacant space beside the Brooklyn Bridge in 1981. Whereas the developers sanitized the historic waterfront area, leasing space to franchise or touristy restaurants of little lasting interest to discerning locals, Jeremy's crude, raucous seafood tavern captured some of the grit and stench of the old harbor. Moreover, that colorful essence is likely to survive

$6–25

Address 254 Front St, between Dover St & Peck Slip
☎212/964-3537
Transportation 4,5,6 to Brooklyn Bridge-City Hall; 2,3,J,M,Z to Fulton St; A,C,E to Broadway-Nassau
Open Mon–Sat 8am–midnight, Sun 8am–2pm
Accepts Cash only
Reservations Not accepted

the pending move of the neighboring Fulton Fish Market from here to the Bronx. In truth, Jeremy's never depended upon the trade from the city's main wholesale fish market. The hundreds of customers' neckties and brassieres hanging from the garagehouse's high rafters are evidence of that, as longshoremen generally do not wear either to work. Those garments were presumably left behind by workers from another lower Manhattan market. After the close of trading on Thursdays and Fridays, the place is packed with Wall Street carousers.

At other times, the principal attractions are fish and beer, both of them cheap, fresh (the catch is brought in daily except weekends), and sold from the bar. For fried-to-order seafood there are few better batters—or deals—in town than those to be found in Jeremy's platters ($5.95–7.95 including coleslaw and passable fries). Best are the calamari, accompanied by a spicy tomato sauce, and the clams, which can be dipped into tartar sauce or cocktail sauce but, like the calamari, require only a squeeze of lemon. The smallish shrimp don't have all that much flavor. As a lower-fat alternative, grilled calamari ($6.95) are sensationally tender.

Some two dozen drafts, including such rotated notables as Pilsner Urquell, Bass Ale, Pete's Wicked Ale, Harp's Lager, Double Diamond Original Burton Ale, and Saranac Black Forest Lager, are poured by the clear-plastic pint ($2.75–4.50) or the Styrofoam, 32oz "bucket" ($4–6.75). Disciplined lunchers sworn to a one-beer limit are generally partial to the larger option.

Kitchenette

Lower Manhattan is not entirely consumed with the business of either making money or, as is frequently the case, losing it. For those who'd rather be tending a garden than a portfolio or sifting flour instead of paperwork, cozy, quirky Kitchenette, with its distressed-wood furnishings, flea market relics, and homespun pantry, is a breath of fresh air. The 9-to-5ers or, very often, 8-to-8ers are joined at communal, enamel-topped tables by moms (and nannies) and their charges drawn from their TriBeCa apart-

Lunch $9–20
Dinner $12–30

Address 80 West Broadway at Warren St
℡212/267-6740
Transportation 1,2,3,9,A,C,E to Chambers St
Open Mon–Fri 7.30am–10pm, Sat & Sun 9am–10pm
Accepts All major credit cards

AMERICAN

ments by Kitchenette's inviting pastry case, sweet (albeit scattered) service, and vaguely Southern fare. Or maybe it's just the peanut-butter-cream-filled chocolate cupcakes.

The cafe's logo cleverly incorporates a pan of eggs, sunny side up, into the letter "K"; take the not-so-subliminal suggestion and indulge in any of the hearty egg-centric breakfast or brunch options available until 4pm. Roast eggplant omelet ($8.50) includes spinach and sun-dried tomatoes and is served with so-so breakfast potatoes and buttery biscuits. Ordering the Lumberjack ($10), with two eggs, bacon, and two fluffy, mixed-berry pancakes, allows you to straddle the line between an egg selection and Kitchenette's other specialty: carbo-loaded breakfast breads and sweets.

If you're counting on a healthy lunch or dinner, go for the Middle Eastern salad with hummus, tzatziki, couscous, and grilled chicken ($9), but there's no guarantee you won't feel jealous of the guy with the $13.95 plate of buttermilk-battered, honey-fried chicken with a side of macaroni and cheese. Similar sources of envy include the tuna melt with tomato and cheddar ($7.75 lunch, $10.50 dinner) or the BLT on challah ($7.25/$10). All sandwiches are served with garlic- and pepper-dusted hand-cut fries ($2.75). As for the crusty-rimmed muffins and other goodies in that pastry case, there isn't a clinker in the bunch. The choice changes daily, but always includes gooey, cream-filled cupcakes ($3) and rich, tangy sour cream coffee cake ($3.25).

There's another Kitchenette at 1272 Amsterdam Ave, Upper West Side (℡212/531-7600).

DOWNTOWN

FRENCH

Les Halles

🍴 In a business district where an average lunch "hour" lasts 22 minutes and the after-work dinner trade is negligible, there is purportedly no place for a stylish French brasserie like Les Halles. But try telling that to the overjoyed bankers, French expats, and tourists sidling up to its ornate mahogany bar or settling into its comfy, high-backed leather banquettes. A smartly restored tavern that feels more pre-crash (1929) New York than Belle Époque Paris, Les

$25–70

Address 15 John St, between Broadway & Nassau Sts
☎212/285 8585
Transportation A,C to Broadway-Nassau; J,M,Z,2,3,4,5 to Fulton St
Open Daily noon–midnight
Accepts All major credit cards
Reservations Suggested

Halles is the Lower Manhattan offshoot of the popular bistro/butcher shop of the same name (411 Park Ave South, Gramercy Park; ☎212/679-4111) and is the second culinary home of chef Anthony Bourdain, author of restaurant tell-all Kitchen Confidential. Autograph seekers are, however, a more frequent presence than the globetrotting Bourdain.

This Les Halles has no butcher counter, but it does share with its sibling a flair for cooking with French cuts of beef, sausages, and meat fats. A little of each probably fortifies the French onion soup ($7.50) crusted with a thick layer of salty Gruyère. Bacon lardon enriches both the tartiflette ($9), a bubbling gratin of Reblochon cheese and tender fingerling potatoes, and the fine frisée salad. Nine varieties of moules frites ($9/$14.50) are each nobly presented in beautiful, copper-bottomed casseroles. Standouts include marinières (white wine, shallots, and garlic), billi-bi (saffron, cream, and vermouth) and portugues (garlic, cilantro, white wine, spicy chorizo, and tomato). The crisp, golden, salty, Les Halles frites are legendary.

Potato lovers will also like the duck parmentier ($14.50), with its strips of rich duck confit, although this duck shepherd's pie may arrive with a tepid center. Steak frites is cooked with precision—you wouldn't expect otherwise—either as a plate ($14.50) or on a crusty "French dip" baguette sandwich ($12.50) where the steak replaces the usual roast beef. Both are served with a red wine-and-shallot sauce for dipping. Decadent choucroute garnie ($16.50) assembles smoked pork loin, white veal sausage, smoked pork breast, boiled potatoes, and sauerkraut all slow-cooked in white wine. For dessert, tarte tatin ($6) is a good, basic expression of the classic.

Roy's New York

The type of restaurant tip that puzzles the most goes something like this: "I'm not a big fan of sardines, but the sardines at so and so's are outstanding." If a person doesn't much care for a certain food, wouldn't his or her fondness for a particular rendition suggest its essential character had been lost? Members of the "I'm-not-a-big-fan" club will worship this handsome crowd-pleaser for camouflaging its star ingredients in the most original ways. Roy is Roy Yamaguchi, the pioneer first of Euro-Asian cooking in LA and then of Hawaiian regional cuisine at the first Roy's in Honolulu. The fifteenth Roy's, tucked into the Marriott that was barely spared the attacks of 9/11, has toned down some of the Polynesian excesses of yore.

Lunch $25–75
Dinner $35–75

Address 130 Washington St at Albany St
☎212/266-6262
Transportation A,C,J,M,Z,2,3,4,5 to Fulton St-Broadway Nassau; 6 to Cortland St
Open Mon–Fri 6.30–10am, 11.30am–2pm & 5.30–10pm, Sat 7.30am–1pm & 5.30–10pm, Sun 7.30am–1pm
Accepts All major credit cards

Personable service and daily specials help dodge the franchise fakeness that hounds similarly conceived spin-offs. The view from the curved food bar that faces the open kitchen is one of excitement, spontaneity, and hyperactive sauce cooks who float juicy crabcakes ($12) in a pool of spicy sesame butter sauce. The crabcakes also take a ride on a dim-sum-styled canoe-for-two ($26) with salty potstickers, Szechwan-spiced baby back ribs, shrimp sticks, and chicken satay.

Fish entrees ($22–25), no matter their treatments (porcini dust, lemon-grass crust) and accessories (Thai curry red wine sauce, lobster basil truffle sauce), are flawlessly cooked. When the sauce really works—as with the wasabe ginger butter sauce, which counterbalances the delicacy of the ground macadamia nuts encrusting the shutome (Hawaiian swordfish)—the results are exceptional. Meats and birds, though less dependable in preparation, are unapologetically indulgent—garlic honey mustard short ribs ($23), say, braised to a mush. Desserts ($7–9) are just fine. Sure, the mascarpone cannoli could use more crunch. But the awesome hot chocolate soufflé is the volcano that Roy's sometimes tries too hard to be.

West Village

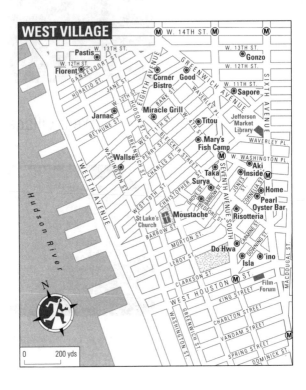

WEST VILLAGE

W. 14TH ST.

W. 13TH ST.
Gonzo

W. 12TH ST.

Pastis
W. 13TH ST.
W. 12TH ST.
Florent
GANSEVOORT ST.
HORATIO ST.
JANE ST.
BANK ST.
Corner Bistro
Good
GREENWICH AVENUE
WAVERLEY PL.
W. 11TH ST.
Sapore
SIXTH AVENUE

Jarnac
BETHUNE ST.
W. 12TH ST.
EIGHTH AVENUE
Miracle Grill
Titou
Jefferson Market Library
WAVERLEY PL.

HUDSON STREET
GREENWICH STREET
PERRY ST.
CHARLES STREET
BLEECKER STREET
Mary's Fish Camp
W. WASHINGTON PL.
Aki
Inside

Wallsé
WASHINGTON ST.
W. 10TH ST.
CHRISTOPHER ST.
GROVE ST.
Taka
Surya
SEVENTH AVENUE SOUTH
JONES ST.
CORNELIA ST.
Home
Pearl Oyster Bar

TWELFTH AVENUE

Hudson River

WEST STREET
BEDFORD ST.
St Luke's Church
Moustache
BARROW ST.
MORTON ST.
CARMINE ST.
Risotteria
DOWNING ST.
MACDOUGAL ST.

LEROY ST.
Do Hwa
Isla
'ino

CLARKSON ST.
WEST HOUSTON ST.
Film Forum

N
KING STREET
GREENWICH STREET
WASHINGTON STREET
CHARLTON STREET

VANDAM STREET

0   200 yds
SPRING STREET

DOMINICK ST.

Aki on West 4th

Turns out not everything in Manhattan is about location, location, and location. Though wedged into a narrow, brick-walled triangle on a stretch of West Village real estate relegated to merchants of sunglasses, sex toys, tattoos, electronics, flashy duds, and crummy eats, Aki nevertheless has a regular stream of diners—up to a dozen at tables and six at the fibreglass-topped sushi bar—happy to violate the cardinal rule to never set foot in a restaurant on

$20–75

Address 181 West 4th St at Jones St

℡212/989-5440

Transportation 1,9 to Christopher St; A,C,E,F,V to West 4th St

Open Sun, Tues, Wed & Thurs 6–11pm, Fri & Sat 6pm–midnight

Accepts All major credit cards

this block. Inside, every detail appears to have been achieved with great economy and creativity. Inside, photos of the specials, cut by hand from color snapshots, are displayed in peacock-shaped postcard holders. The semi-opaque, white-curtain that separates chef-owner "Siggy" Nakanishi and his sushi-rolling sidekick from the service kitchen is a silky backdrop for understated excellence.

Siggy was once private chef to the Japanese ambassador to the West Indies and the influences of that experience are everywhere. Jamaican jerk chicken comes either neatly rolled with shrimp paste and veggies alongside mango teriyaki and banana tempura ($7), or packed into a tobiko-specked sushi roll with hearts of palm, mayo, and a smoky, peppery, wasabi buzz ($8). Uni coco ($9), that cool, multicolored cocktail of sea urchin, scallop, creamy coconut, green caviar, and a fermented, plum-based ponzu sauce, is a thrill-a-second treat.

Other small plates to consider are the wondrous eel napoleon of mashed eel and pumpkin alternately layered between potato chips and fried dumpling skins ($7), and the seafood-filled yam croquette in a shiitake and inoko broth ($10). Sushi highlights include the banana boat roll with fried banana and spicy tuna ($8) and a fried oyster, avocado, and vegetable roll that starts crunchy and ends creamy. The Aki ($5) with green tea syrup and passion fruit sauce isn't merely an outstanding dessert. Its snapshot demonstrates wonderfully the brilliance of Fujicolor. Ordering by impulse, a la carte, is a liberty most Aki regulars exercise. Still, the chef practically beams when you order a tasting dinner ($35–55), which features an amuse bouche, two to four appetizers, a sushi entree, and dessert.

Corner Bistro

(YI) In the annals of preposterously named eateries, this ranks somewhere between the Jackson Diner, which is an Indian restaurant, and Seppi's, a French place. There's no problem with the appellation "Corner" for a dark old pub bounded by the picturesque intersection of two quiet streets. But "Bistro" is an odd thing to name a drinking establishment that serves only burgers, mild chili con carne, a chicken breast sandwich, a BLT, and fries. If its kitchen were a telephone booth, there wouldn't be room for long-distance calls. Ultimately, this is a classic West Village saloon. College students instinctively recognize the mahogany bar, stamped-tin ceiling, and frosty mugs of beer—both those etched in the stained-glass cabinet doors and the drinkable ones filled with Budweiser, Samuel Adams, and McSorley's—as a perfect literary backdrop for all those great American paragraphs yet to be written.

$8–20

Address 331 West 4th St at Jane St
☎212/242-9502
Transportation 1,2,3,9,A,C,E to
14th St; L to 8th Ave
Open Daily 11.30am–3.30am
Accepts Cash only
Reservations Not accepted

The pleasures of a Corner Bistro burger ($4.50) cultivate an awareness of what's very right and, by comparison, what's very wrong in the New York hamburger universe. When you bite into this chubby archetype, dressed with tomato, lettuce, raw onion, and pickle on a lightly toasted sesame seed bun, the tasty pink juice squirts out of several gaps in the leaky patty and, under the best of circumstances, forms a puddle on the bottom of the small paper plate. Were it not for that plate's fluted rim, Corner Bistro would have a serious spillage situation unknown to pretenders who make their so-called steakburgers with tightly pressed ground sirloin or some other prime, lean meat. Great, juicy burgers start with fatty, loosely packed meat. And a knowing grill man never presses out their juices with a spatula as they cook. The slender fries ($2), though good enough for frozen, are not in the same echelon.

The cozy back room is an ideal spot to nurture your burger education in small study groups. The tiny tables in the dimly lit, brick-walled space could even be called romantic. Couples have been known to declare their love for one another (a good burger will do that to you) by scratching each other's names in the wooden banquettes.

Do Hwa

You can tell how mainstream Korean food has become by how little handholding is offered at Do Hwa. This house policy of nonintervention portends all that is very good and most of what isn't about this stylish spin-off of the East Village's wondrous Dok Suni's (see p.34). The traditional cooking speaks for itself, eloquently. But the servers' indifference can make you feel rushed, abandoned or, worse, unloved.

$25–65

Address 55 Carmine St, between Bedford St & 7th Ave South
℡212/414-1224
Transportation A,C,E,F,V to West 4th St; 1,9 to Houston St
Open Sun & Mon 5–11pm, Fri & Sat 5pm–midnight
Accepts All major credit cards
Reservations Suggested

KOREAN

Named after a flower, to suggest blossoming, Do Hwa—pronounced "DOE-ha"—extends the mother-and-daughter collaboration of Myung Ja and Jenny Kwak that works so well at Dok Suni's. The home cooking is mom's; the downtown vibe is Jenny's. Architect Hassan Abouseda's dark, spare, and casual design relies on dramatic lighting, irregular geometry, and hard surfaces to create a New Age abstraction with a Korean imprint. It has just the right mix of comfort and mystery.

The menu is somewhat more adventurous than Dok Suni's. Four $23–25 per-person tasting dinners (one of them vegetarian) let groups of four sample a wide variety of the best dishes. Financially and artistically, this is the way to go. Mandu, those fabulous crescent dumplings, come boiled or deep-fried. It's easier to appreciate the meat and kimchee (spicy, pungent, fermented vegetable) fillings when they're stuffed beneath the cleaner, softer, boiled casing. And boiling sets the dumplings apart from the golden pancakes often appearing alongside them. Three barbecue dishes—kalbi (short rib), bulgogi (rib-eye), and deji bulgogi (thinly sliced pork)—feature luscious, ultra-tender meats, marinated in sesame oil, soy sauce, garlic, sugar, and kiwi juice. The meat may be plucked off the grill or wrapped in a lettuce leaf with various accessories and kimchee. The shellfish grill platter, with squid, sea scallops, lobster tail, and surprisingly tasty shrimp, is likewise superb. And the kimchee bokum bop, a stir-fry of kimchee, beef, and rice, quickly becomes an obsession. Unexceptional desserts range from a vaguely sweet chocolate cake ($8) to gingerbread with pumpkin ice cream ($8).

Florent

The view outside has changed drastically since Florent Morellet's arrival in 1985. Once the lone beacon for night owls on a desolate, difficult-to-find block in the Meatpacking District, this one-of-a-kind French diner is now surrounded by hip restaurants, bars, and boutiques. These days it's yellow taxis and stretch limos rather than transvestite hookers who troll the cobblestone streets for pick-ups. Some of the nocturnal pedestrians headed to Florent now approach with the aloof gait of reverse snobs who want nothing to do with the Johnny-come-latelies. But Florent the community leader and Florent the community eatery only get cooler with age. Cool as in hip. Cool as in tolerating anything but intolerance.

Lunch $18–50
Dinner $22–65

Address 69 Gansevoort St, between Greenwich & Washington Sts
☎212/989-5779
Transportation 1,2,3,9,A,C,E to 14th St; L to 8th Ave
Open Mon–Thurs 9am–5am, Fri–Sun 24hr
Accepts Cash only
Reservations Suggested

When it comes to selecting what to eat, usually the choices are pretty clear: thin, golden, French pancakes in the after sunrise ($6.95). Nice basic salads ($4.50–9.95), English muffin burgers with great fries ($6.95–9.75), and grilled eggplant baguette sandwiches ($7.50) during the midday. And in the evening, what else but steak frites ($14.50–17.50). But matters get more complicated during the wee small hours. The diners who are just beginning the day might not want to eat—and, hopefully will not want to drink—like the majority of people who are reaching the end of theirs. And of those who are looking for a pre-crash breakfast, there's not necessarily going to be any consensus about particular cravings.

Luckily there is a selection of stellar dishes on a decent and diverse bistro menu unconstrained by such notions as "brunch" and "supper." The moules frites ($12.50) are outstanding. And though it's hard to let go of the classic marinières version, the newfangled specials—sake, ginger, and black bean; spicy tomato and fennel—are often delightful. The rib-eye steak ($17.50), skirt steak ($14.50), and boudin noir (blood sausage) with apples and onions ($14.95) are dependable. How could they not be with those frites by their side? The creamy mashed potatoes ($4.50) are a worthy side for any dish. And several desserts—rice pudding, crème caramel, country apple tart—hit any spot you care to mention.

Gonzo

Gonzo would not be so noisy if diners stopped complaining about, well, the noise, and the sympathetic service staff stopped explaining what's been done about it. It might also be quieter if everyone used their hands, rather than knives and forks, to break into chef/co-owner Vincent Scotto's amoeba-shaped grilled pizzas. The tapestries now hung like faux window shades at least give the impression of absorbing sound, as does the very fat body of the chef por-

$25–65

Address 140 West 13th St,
between 6th & 7th Aves
℡212/645-4606
Transportation 1,2,3,9 to 14th St
Open Tues–Fri 5.30pm–1am, Sat
11.30am–1pm, Sun 11.30am–11pm
Accepts All major credit cards
Reservations Suggested

ITALIAN/PIZZA

trayed in a comical canvas by Velasco. (Scotto, who was presumably smaller when that painting was signed, could not have been its model). If you want to know what the racket is all about—and the smart money says you should—then try dropping by this townhouse on the early side, when the front bar area is still sober and the dining hall reverberating under a high, coffered ceiling is calm enough to use a cell phone (but, please, don't).

Scotto learned pizza grilling at the restaurant that pioneered the method, Al Forno in Providence, Rhode Island. He brought it to Manhattan, first at Fresco by Scotto in midtown, then at Scopa in Gramercy Park, and now, dropping prices and formality, at Gonzo. Dinner can be loosely structured around pizzas ($13–15), cicchetti (small plates; $4–7), appetizers ($8–12), pastas ($13–15), and meat and fish entrees (mostly $14–17 excluding sides). The pizza crusts, coated with olive oil and striped on the gas-heated grill, are commendably crisp, light, and not so brittle as to collapse under piles of toppings: arugula and prosciutto in one combo, Portobello and mashed potato in another, runny tomatoes and creamy splotches of mozzarella crowning a dandy Margherita.

The cicchetti to try are the chicken liver crostini blessed with thin, crisp toasts, the white beans with scant cured tuna, and the marinated sardines. For substance, bypass the pastas and consider instead fennel-crusted pork tenderloin or buttery roasted brick chicken with lemon and sage. Desserts (about $6)—chocolate hazelnut semifreddo sundae, pecan praline ice cream sandwich—are the kind you might ordinarily shout about. But, please, don't.

Good

🍽 This restaurant started as Campo, a Pan-American country kitchen bridging the cultural divide between north- and south-of-the-border cooking through its apparent affection for both. Unfortunately for chef/owner Steven Picker, his would-be diners didn't know what to make of the place. Plum-tired of explaining what Campo meant, Picker removed the farm tools from the brushed blue walls, repainted the place neutral beige, reversed the menu's mix from 60/40 Latin to 80/20 American, and—how's this for playing it safe?—changed the name to Good. "That," says Picker, "everyone understands." (If only it were true…) The doubly popular result is "New American" in its inventiveness, yet uncharacteristically down-to-earth for that classification. Another wonderful anomaly is Picker's affinity for brunch, the meal most of his peers loath.

Lunch $20–45
Dinner $25–65

Address 89 Greenwich Ave, between Bank & West 12th Sts
☎212/691-8080
Transportation 1,2,3,9 to 14th St
Open Mon 6–11pm, Tues–Thurs 11am–3pm & 6–11pm, Fri 11am–3pm & 6–11.30pm, Sat 11am–4pm & 6–11.30pm, Sun 10am–4pm & 6–10pm
Accepts All major credit cards
Reservations Suggested

Even dinner appetizers possess a brunch-like breadth. The raft of grilled sourdough topped with broccoli rabe, garlic-marinated chickpeas, and fresh ricotta ($8) is too elaborate to be called a bruschetta. The plate of tender grilled calamari ($9) assembled with chile mint vinaigrette and the fruit salad (mango, melon, watercress) is essentially two starters in one. Fried chicken tenders coated in crunchy peanut crumbs are supplemented by a toss of frisée and roasted corn vinaigrette ($8).

The moderately spicy baked green chile macaroni and cheese draped with melted mozzarella, Parmesan, and peppered Jack cheese and lightly dusted with tortilla crumbs and grated Parmesan ($15) is a must, even if you have to borrow from your next day's calorie rations. You'll enjoy too, but not without guilt, the juicy burger with slab Indiana bacon ($11) and the molasses-glazed tuna with a trio of carrot scallion griddlecakes drizzled with still more molasses, their sweetness barely cut by acidic balsamic vinegar and collard greens ($18). The dessert that Picker never let out of his sight—and neither should you—is a holdover from Campo: warm orange donuts with Mexican hot chocolate for dunking ($7).

Home

AMERICAN

It's one thing to name your restaurant Home, as David Page and Barbara Shinn did in the spring of 1993, and quite another to have your diners calling it home, as many grateful New Yorkers have been doing ever since. By decorating their unlikely venue for American comfort food with bead-board wainscoting, assorted antique wall sconces, quaint old photos, and a distressed, pine-planked floor, Page and Shinn turned a cold-water flat into something suggesting the Victorian interior of a New England walk-in closet. The full extent of their success is perhaps illustrated by recurring requests for the precise paint colors used for the walls, molded rails, wood banquettes, and tin ceiling. (Warning: their creamy colors of preference, Benjamin Moore Nos. 380 and 382, get their chartreuse cast from the yellowish lighting as opposed to any dye in the paint.) Home is, apparently, exactly what they want their own house to resemble and be.

Lunch $18–45
Dinner $28–55

Address 20 Cornelia St, between West 4th & Bleecker Sts
℡212/243-9579
Transportation A,C,E,F,V to West 4th St; 1,9 to Christopher St
Open Mon–Fri 9am–4pm & 5–11pm, Sat 10.30am–4.30pm & 5.30–11pm, Sun 10.30am–4.30pm & 5.30–10pm
Accepts All major credit cards
Reservations Suggested

You might expect Home cooking to be real home cooking. But the delicious irony is that most of us would only think of eating cornmeal-crusted oysters with roasted red pepper tartar sauce and a fennel, green apple, and red onion slaw ($10) or blue cheese, cream cheese, and butter-milk fondue with caramelized shallots and rosemary toasts for dunking ($8) in a restaurant. In this restaurant.

Most of us can only dream of a childhood that featured a succulent pork rib chop spiced with cumin, coriander, and mustard and sided with mashed butternut squash and parsley salad ($17). The juicy roast chicken with braised greens, awesome onion rings, and Home-made ketchup ($17) is an exclusive. And who among us grew up with lemony tangerine sauce to spoon over grilled whole brook trout ($17)? Only the down-to-earth desserts ($6)—dark chocolate pudding, toasted pound cake, chocolate pecan pie—finally convince you that Page and Shinn's approach to American cooking is truly homespun as opposed to Home spin.

'ino

🍽 If 'ino didn't have its picture-window view of a quaint West Village street, it would still be one of the nicest restaurants in the area. If it were forced to discontinue its long list of Italian wines, diners would simply redirect their attentions to the origins, producers, and vintages of the sodas: limonata (lemon) and aranciata (orange). If this intriguing wine bar were not also an adorable, inexpensive, snug, neighborly cafe fit for morning crosswords, afternoon day-dreaming, evening romance, and

$12–40

Address 21 Bedford St, between Downing St & 6th Ave
☎212/989-5769
Transportation 1,9 to Houston St; A,C,E,F,V to West 4th St
Open Mon–Fri 9am–2am, Sat & Sun 11am–2am
Accepts Cash only
Reservations Not accepted

midnight debates following a late screening at the nearby Film Forum, you could dream up still more excuses to claim the first open table. But change by a hair the thickness of the soppressata slices in the salami, Fontina cheese, and arugula panini and we're out of here!

Some New Yorkers bring back Tower of Pisa refrigerator magnets from their travels in Italy. Lupa (see p.92) co-owners Jason and Jennifer Denton returned with an inspiration: to open a wine bar serving the Italian bruschetta and panini they couldn't stop eating during their trip. You'll soon know how they felt. At $2 apiece, 'ino's bruschetta offer zero incentive for restraint. It's simpler to order them all than confront the dilemma between, say, the braised fennel with tapenade or the roasted vegetables and goat cheese. The $8 panini are fundamentally pressed sandwiches, yet from this modest frame come forth the great riches of Italian salumeria and formaggiaio. Honoring the latter is a scrumptious, three-formaggio grilled cheese drizzled with white truffle oil. Cured meats appear one-to-a-sandwich, as in the classic prosciutto, mozzarella, and tomato.

Breakfast at 'ino revolves around an eggy treat Americans know by a variety of names (knothole eggs, toads in the hole, eggs on a raft, and so on). Here the egg-in-the-hole is blanketed with melted, truffle-oiled Fontina and takes the name that strong men mumble in their dreams: truffled egg toast. For dessert, you could somehow survive without the Nutella panini ($5). But forgo the bruschetta topped with mascarpone and berries ($5)? Impossible.

Inside

It's tempting to explain away chef Anne Rosenzweig's West Village retreat as an economy blend of her two prior East Side restaurants, the Lobster Club and Arcadia. But its dash of comfort from the former and drizzle of inventiveness from the latter notwithstanding, Inside is too quirky to be summed up in a soundbite. Likewise, the narrow room, with African masks and photos of trees hung on the white walls, and ceiling fans suspended from the bleached-tin ceiling, is impossible to peg. The only certainty is

$30–60

Address 9 Jones St, between West 4th & Bleecker Sts
☎212/229-9999
Transportation 1,9 to Christopher St; A,C,E,F,V to West 4th St
Open Mon–Sat 6–11pm, Sun 11.30am–3pm & 5–9pm
Accepts All major credit cards
Reservations Suggested

the appeal of this smart-casual place to the over-30 and under-20 crowd—referring first to the diners' ages and then to their dollar budget for entrees. The value is astonishing.

The tight menu is a moving target of transient dishes that don't necessarily belong together. You can't even be sure who's supervising the kitchen at any given moment. Charleen Badman, formerly sous-chef at the Lobster Club, is officially the chef. But Rosenzweig's fingerprints are all over the tongs and saucepan handles. There are some welcome constants, however: the insider's favorite appetizer, the delicately crisp salt-and-pepper shrimp ($9), once a temporary visitor, now has the status of permanent resident. You are also likely to stumble upon the he-man salad, a rugged toss of bacon, blue cheese, and romaine ($8).

Understated main courses are about showing off flavors and not technique. The short ribs with fried horseradish ($18) suggest a flanken (the Eastern-European Jewish boiled beef dish) with Mediterranean leanings (tomato and green olives). In a similar vein, braised lamb stew acquires Israeli couscous, cinnamon, and garlic ($18). But the slow-cooking similitude is broken by the sautéed sea bass with shiitakes ($18), which is prepared in a flash but presented without it. The garlic fries must sit in at table whether or not they fit with your entree. Finally, if you do stop in for dinner, please insist that the banana split with peanut brittle and malted milk ice cream ($6) and the visiting gingerbread-crumb-topped fruit clafoutis ($6) be issued green cards.

West Village

Isla

🍴 The azure tiles, white-leather banquettes, potted palms, and bluish
opal tabletops transport diners either to a
poolside cabana in 1950s Havana or to
an airport lounge on a Miami-to-Rio lay-
over. Either way, Isla is some groovy
place. If the playful curves of the plastic-
mesh deck chairs and suspended orange
globe lights don't get to you, the
"cocteleria"—a selection of nine exotic
cocktails—most certainly will. And as for
the amazing creations introduced by

> ### $40–80
>
> **Address** 39 Downing St, between
> Bedford & Varick Sts
> ☏212/352-2822
> **Transportation** 1,9 to Houston St
> **Open** Mon–Wed 6–10pm, Thurs
> 6–11pm, Fri & Sat 6pm–midnight
> **Accepts** All major credit cards
> **Reservations** Suggested

pastry chef Tricia Williams—these will have you considering the uncertain
merits of a nice weight-loss program: the DOD, or dessert-only diet. The
best way to order might be to go heavy on the ends (appetizers,
ceviches, desserts) and light on the in-betweens (entrees, side courses).
Better still, come in between 6 and 8pm, when the specialty cocktails are
just $6 and bar-sized plates are no higher than $13.

Dishes, like body movements, are calibrated to Isla's compressed confines. While most of the appetizers are cleverly put together, portions can
be skimpy and, in the case of cornmeal smoked chicken and chorizo
croquetas ($9), uncharacteristically bland. New chef Christian Interlandi
has added some zing to the steamed mussels ($8). But the starter to
behold is still "La Isla" ($32), a two-person rotated assortment of lime-
marinated seafood ceviches each served on a long Lucite tray in glass
cups over ice. The presentation is spectacular and a couple of the featured ceviches (scallops in coconut milk; pristine tuna sashimi with
accents of ginger, chile, and soy) truly terrific.

Despite caveats, when main courses like roasted chicken with a gar-
banzo bean purée ($18) or filet mignon with a Cabernet-red currant
reduction and onion bread pudding ($21) are on the mark, they're truly
superb. But if cooking does get sloppy then you're ready to re-examine
the DOD. First course: an intensely rich cafe-con-leche flan remarkably
true to its flavor ($8). Second course: a fudgy, high-octane dark choco-
late cake served with guava sauce and thick vanilla cream ($7). Dessert:
the Isla parfait ($12 for two), a chocolate, coffee, and dolce de leche ice
cream sundae.

Jarnac

The distance between the far west of Manhattan and the far west of central France is greatly reduced by this tranquil and informally romantic bistro. Jarnac probably has less affinity with the hip Meatpacking District to its immediate north than with its namesake city in the Cognac-producing region of Poitou-Charentes some 3500 miles away. The engaging owner Tony Powe grew up in late French President François Mitterand's birthplace and brings to his restaurant a small-town sensibility and an easy rapport between staff and customer. This intimacy might take some time to get used to—perhaps as long as five minutes. It's atypical even for a quiet corner of West Village, whose charms are seen and felt through white-paned country windows.

$37–80

Address 328 West 12th St at Greenwich St

☎212/924-3413

Transportation 1,2,3,9,A,C,E to 14th St

Open Tues–Thurs 6–10pm, Fri & Sat 6–11pm, Sun 6–9.30pm

Accepts All major credit cards

Reservations Suggested

The monthly changing tastes of chef Maryann Terillo run more towards Southwest France and the Mediterranean than France's mid-Atlantic coast. The sophistication of her winter menus is bold. Multiple layers of flavor are applied to hearty plates, and understatement is limited to the appetizers. Even there, the restraint is restrained. Grilled scallops are teamed with a rice beans and arugula ($10.75). The butteriness of crisp-edged, sautéed sweetbreads is cut with lemon and spicy greens ($10). Black truffle garlic flan ($9.50)—wow!—seductively combines two of the headiest, most forceful flavors in the smoothest and gentlest of packages.

Of the entrees, the bubbling, garlicky casserole of cassoulet ($22) could nourish a bear on the eve of hibernation. It's crammed with great northern white beans and tomatoes fat-fed with the drippings of pork, duck confit, and sausage. The bone-in veal breast braised in pear cider ($19.75) promises to be lighter, until you contend with the roasted butternut squash and chestnuts. The fish entrees also endure substantial embellishment, be it Puy lentils and garlic sauce for oven-roasted cod ($23) or braised wild mushrooms and leeks for porcini-crusted Chilean sea bass ($25). For desserts, veer away from the chocolate and towards the fruit—warm apple crisp with crème anglaise or high-impact blueberry tart (both $8.25).

Mary's Fish Camp

For diners, splitting a bowl of ultra-creamy, bacon-laced New England clam chowder is a difficult but do-able proposition. But for Mary Redding and Rebecca Charles, co-founders of the cherished Pearl Oyster Bar (see p.166), it was an agonizing consequence of their decision to go their separate ways. In their settlement, Charles was allowed to keep Pearl. But Redding neither signed a non-compete clause nor handed over full menu custody. She instead created a snug eatery with picture windows, pressed-tin ceiling, silvery blue walls, tin-plated counter, and comparable versions of the same signature dishes less than six blocks away. Though egos may have been damaged in the process, neither party is hurting for business. Both play nightly to overflowing crowds.

> **Lunch $22–60**
> **Dinner $35–75**
>
> Address 64 Charles St at West 4th St
> ☏646/486-2185
> Transportation 1,9 to Christopher St
> Open Mon–Sat noon–3pm &
> 6–11pm
> Accepts All major credit cards
> Reservations Not accepted

When first laying eyes on Mary's Fish Camp, the perspective of past Pearl patrons is distorted. To them, the cramped, eight-table space looks roomy in comparison to the one-table Pearl. Conversely, the expanded menu seems shorter than ever. Their eyes invariably focus in on the lobster roll ($18), the life-enhancing sandwich of sweet, faintly peppery, mayonnaise-saturated lobster chunks spilling out of a toasted hot dog bun and sided with a stack of rusty-golden matchstick fries. Most adults have sufficient willpower to start first with an appetizer, maybe plump Canadian steamers ($10), fried oysters and clams with scallions and cilantro ($9), salt-crusted shrimp ($10), or the fascinating lobster knuckles ($9). Why fascinating? Whereas seafood restaurants of yore featured lobster tail because it was the least difficult, least messy part to eat, these sweet-meated claw joints are just the opposite. Forget a bib. What you need are rubber gloves and goggles.

The dinner menu lists a number of fine dishes, including grilled whole fish ($24). Still, that's a lot to spend at so casual an eatery. That's one rationale, anyway, for returning to the lobster roll or, during lunch, the fried clam roll ($12). Although the blueberry almond tart and hard-lidded, soft-centered brownie are homey delights, you may well never see beyond the monster ice cream sundae (all $6).

Miracle Grill

Thumbnail reviews often praise the original Miracle Grill (112 1st Ave, East Village, ☎212/254-2353) as the restaurant that launched TV Food Network host Bobby Flay to stardom. Others leave it on their now faded short lists of best cheap eats. Founder Lynn Loflin would rather be disassociated from her first chef and first—albeit more slowly ascending—prices. But her West Village outpost still strives to offer good food and value, even if it is no longer the miracle bargain it once was. Its two dining rooms are sparsely decorated with sandy, stucco-like walls, with lamps that emit a romantic glow all but neutralized by the bar's deafening din. To avoid the noise, come for weekend brunch. It's a good one, with fine blue-corn pancakes and all sorts of eggy things with Southwestern home fries.

Lunch $18–40
Dinner $25–65

Address 415 Bleecker St, between Bank & West 11th Sts
☎212/924-1900
Transportation 1,9 to Christopher St
Open Mon–Thurs 5.30–11.30pm, Fri 5.30pm–midnight, Sat 11am–3.30pm & 5.30pm–midnight, Sun 11am– 3.30pm & 5.30–11pm
Accepts All major credit cards
Reservations For large groups

Dinners involve lots of edible and likeable (as opposed to architectural and esoteric) food crowded on a plate, with blurred distinctions between first and second courses. At Miracle you simply can't tell the appetizers from the mains without a menu. There's no white space on the special appetizer plate of ancho-chile-seared rare tuna piled over mixed greens, red bliss potatoes, olives, and green beans ($8.95). The top starter, however, consists of soft tacos folded over hot serpents of corn-crusted catfish, sesame slaw garnish, and a cool, spicy ribbon of smoked jalapeno mayo ($10.95).

Entrees are imaginative without getting silly. Even the grilled pork chop with an orange-ancho chile sauce and sweet potato gratin ($16.95) leaves you dazzled yet not dazed. BBQ salmon, in a molasses and ancho-chile glaze ($18.95), should delight anyone intrigued by the idea, and grilled New York strip steak charred in chipotle butter ($19.95) is a terrific take on steak au poivre. Desserts ($5–6) score high on effort, low on result: ancho-chile powder is baked into a flourless chocolate cake to no real effect. The deep-fried Mexican pastry bunuelos are plunged into rather than topped or sided by ice cream.

West Village

Moustache

A mere dozen or so copper-topped tables fit into this cozy West Village hideaway. Two rugs on the walls provide a colorful backdrop for bright-faced diners and vibrant tabouleh. And the Tintin poster in the restroom never fails to amuse. All the same, your moustache-high regard for this place probably won't jump to your arched eyebrows until you start thinking of it as something more than a Middle Eastern pizzeria baking

$10–30

Address 90 Bedford St, between Grove & Barrow Sts
☎212/229-2220
Transportation 1,9 to Christopher St
Open Daily noon–midnight
Accepts Cash only
Reservations Not accepted

"pizzas." So-called, of course, because the thin-crusted, individually sized pies are made with rolled-out pita dough.

That's not to say you should overlook those pitzas ($6–10) or their fresh, Italian-style and Middle Eastern toppings. Quite the contrary. The spicy, garlicky chicken pitza is an explosive combo flavored with red pepper, scallions, parsley, and olive oil, while the traditional lahambajin puts forward a tight coalition of lamb, onions, tomatoes, parsley, and dry spices. And vegetarians will adore the green pitza ($9.50), a habit-forming trio of leeks, scallions, and herbs that makes a great appetizer. That said, you really should acquaint yourself with the outstanding Middle Eastern vegetable salads and spreads, namely babaganoush and hummus (both $4), each drizzled with a puddle of olive oil and served beside pita freshly baked in the pizza oven. The pita is so good, so fluffy—so different—that some first-timers don't even recognize it for what it is.

It's the pita which sets apart the sandwiches. The substantial merguez sandwich ($7.50) contains a thick, spicy, ground lamb sausage (instead of the typically long and skinny affair) along with onion, ripe tomato, and superbly silky tahini sauce. The slices of lamb that stuff a meaty sandwich ($7.50) are a big improvement upon the souvlaki-style chunks that typically turn kebabs into tough-going affairs. And the falafel balls ($5.50), cleanly fried to a golden-brown crisp, are rarely dry. You can get them served as a platter for a couple of dollars more. Finally, if your check does not include a $3.50 charge for the saffron rice pudding, someone has made a big mistake.

There's another Moustache at 265 East 10th St, East Village (☎212/228-2022).

Pastis

(🍴) The exhilaration of the retro haunts opened by Keith McNally —Odeon (see p.138), Cafe Luxembourg (p.268), Balthazar (p.124) and more— is equal parts illusion and reality. The access to 1920s Paris is make-believe; the connection to late twentieth-century New York glamor, wondrously genuine. In 1999, the mix of period furniture and somewhat younger celebrities instantly established Pastis as yet another hopelessly hip epicenter of munching and mingling, this time with a difference. Though McNally's foray into the fashionable Meatpacking district has inherited the fabulous breads

Lunch $20–65
Dinner $25–75

Address 9 Little West 12th St at 9th Ave
☎ 212/929-4844
Transportation A,C,E to 14th St; L to 8th Ave
Open Sun–Thurs 9am–2am, Fri & Sat 9am–2.30am
Accepts All major credit cards
Reservations Required

FRENCH

and diligent co-chefs, Riad Nasr and Lee Hanson, from Balthazar, the unfussy French cooking gives it more of a bistro soul. Pastis takes its name from the anise-flavored aperitif of Marseille. Bottles of the Ricard brand line the illuminated backbar as well as walls of the kitchen entranceway. A custom-made "zinc" bar curls into the middle of the 70-seat front barroom over a starburst mosaic floor and under a tin ceiling. Up to 100 diners are crowded into the rear space's perimeter of banquettes or around a long communal table that turns strangers into either warmhearted friends or sharp-elbowed enemies.

The kitchen turns out a host of serviceable appetizers: deeply flavored French onion soup ($8), puffy pissaladière (the Niçoise pizzette) topped with caramelized onions, black olives, and anchovies ($9) and a wonderful, terrine-like chicken and duck liver mousse ($8) to spread over both toasted slices and plain hunks of the Balthazar bread.

Among entrees, meaty skate well matched to its traditional accompaniment of capers and black butter sauce ($16) is a satisfying cholesterol chartbuster. But generally it's best not to dig too deeply into the menu and instead narrow the choice between the reliable steak frites ($22) and the always extraordinary burger ($11), both blessed with gorgeous fries, or a solid sandwich like the glazed pork and lentils ($18) or what amounts to a salade Niçoise on a baguette. Desserts ($7) are unexceptional, with chocolate mousse and crêpes Suzette beating the others hands down.

Pearl Oyster Bar

(🍴) With just eleven seats at the marble counter, eight stools against the wall, and room at a single table by the front window for up to seven Lara Flynn Boyles, this New England-style oyster bar is woefully undersized. Protracted waits for those 26 choice chairs could have you thinking that chef-owner Rebecca Charles might want to sell them as co-ops or, at the very least, time shares. But she won't even commit them to reservations. As a result, folks must endure long waits for precisely the kind of impulse seafoods—

$25–65

Address 18 Cornelia St, between West 4th & Bleecker Sts
☏212/691-8211
Transportation A,C,E,F,V to West 4th St; 1,9 to Christopher St
Open Mon–Fri noon–2.30pm & 6–11pm, Sat 6–11pm
Accepts MasterCard & Visa
Reservations Not accepted

oysters on the half-shell, salt-crusted shrimp, lobster rolls—that demand instant gratification. The alternatives are to come in for lunch, for an early dinner (about 6.15pm), for a late supper (about 10.30pm) or to wait until Pearl's expansion into the adjacent storefront has been completed.

Opened in 1997, Pearl grew out of Charles' childhood memories of summers on the Maine coast, her reverence for San Francisco's Swan Oyster Depot, and apparently also her fondness for grayish metallic colors. Everything, from the ceiling and antique oil lamps, to the pepper mill and champagne bottle wrappers—and, of course, the fish skins—bears a silvery tone. These contrast with the meals and their golden beginnings (fried oysters, jumbo lump crabcakes), middles (seared scallops, crisp matchstick fries, buttered and toasted hot-dog buns top-loaded with lobster salad), and finales (blueberry crumble, butterscotch praline parfait).

The mayo-creamed, faintly lemony, overstuffed lobster roll ($17) is an essential NYC experience. For many, not ordering it is simply not possible. The gentlest departure might be the fried oyster roll ($15), a recurring special. The sensation of those big, crunchy oysters meshing with the oozy tartar sauce is spellbinding. The advantage of the outstanding Caesar salad ($6) and New England clam chowder with smoked bacon ($5.50) is that these appetizers don't preclude your having a lobster roll afterward. But opting for grilled whole sea bass ($25) or pan-roasted cod ($17) requires, and ultimately rewards, self-sacrifice. No one is suggesting, however, that you forgo the Callebaut chocolate mousse ($5).

Risotteria

It's not surprising that New York has an eatery devoted to the preparation of risotto. The wonder is that it took well over 350 years for it to arrive. As it happens, New Yorkers might still be living in the purgatory of a risotteria-less metropolis had Joseph Pace not signed a lease for a compact corner of Bleecker and Morton. The narrow confines ruled out the idea of specializing in anything as long as fettuccine or bucatini. Even penne was out of the question. This cute

$13–45

Address 270 Bleecker St at Morton St

☎212/924-6664

Transportation 1,9 to Christopher St; A,C,E,F,V to West 4th St

Open Daily noon–11pm

Accepts All major credit cards

Reservations Not accepted

ITALIAN

space was meant for cooking rice, preferably short grain, so that sufficient room remains for the tapered kitchen, a single row of tables, and the long counter between them. A full half of the limited seating is a long cushioned sill against the picture windows. The lack of back support isn't all bad. It speeds up table turnover.

There are 45 risottos on offer, divided by rice type: Vialone Nano is shorter and thicker than Arborio and holds twice its weight in liquid. Pace recommends it for seafood and vegetables. Carnaroli, the caviar of rice, is the highest grade of superfino (short, plump, and stubby grain) and yields an ultra-creamy risotto. It's paired here with meats and hearty flavors, with a particularly successful merger of roasted pork shoulder with roasted garlic. Baldo is a versatile, quick-cooking variety of superfino presented with vegetables and cheeses. The fabulous porcini, truffle oil, and sweetcorn risotto ($10.50) brandishes the creamy consistency the Italians call all'onda, or "with waves," yet each individual Baldo grain retains its chewiness. A great Vialone Nano pick blends zucchini, oven-dried tomato, parsley, and melted Fontina ($9.50). (The intense oven-dried tomato is reason enough to order any variety.)

Terrific salads grouped by greens—romaine, arugula, spinach, mixed baby lettuce—borrow judiciously from the risotto pantry. Again, the oven-roasted tomato is particularly good, perhaps combined with arugula, shaved Parmesan, and lemon vinaigrette ($5.25 for an ample small; $11.50 for a large). Tiramisu, the lone dessert, is dandy. Still, Mr Pace should realize that New Yorkers are tired of living in a city without Carnaroli rice pudding.

Sapore

(🍴) The man who does the food buying at Sapore has a difficult job. He needs to keep an eye on the Weather Channel. If the forecast is for a clear and mild evening, he must plan on the sidewalk cafe staying open and thus buy sufficient provisions for 32 people. But if an unexpected shower rains down on dinner, the total number of diners may be as much as halved and several pounds of perishables could go to waste. More troubling still, the rainout would require that diners be conveyed to one of the tiny green tables inside the restaurant without the benefit of being able to remove the plate-glass window. Finding room for ballet dancers and jockeys poses little challenge. But fitting in anyone over 110lb without injury to fibula or furniture requires the skill of a wispy whizz in space management.

Lunch $8–20
Dinner $18–45

Address 55 Greenwich Ave at Perry St

☏212/229-0551

Transportation 1,2,3,9 to 14th St

Open Daily noon–11pm

Accepts Cash only

Reservations Not accepted

You put up with the cramped quarters either because you want to eat well and cheaply or because you desire to take a relationship to a new level. Salads contain nice assortments of fresh ingredients and are large enough to share. The tre colore adds grilled sesame chicken breast and a honey vinaigrette to the defining assortment of arugula, radicchio, and endive ($6.95). The insalata di tonno ($6.95) has lots of everything: tuna, black olives, onions, cukes, endive, even extra virgin oil. Fried calamari ($6.95) is extremely fresh—you actually taste the squid—and profitably entangled with fried zucchini. Grilled Portobellos with sautéed spinach ($7.95) are first-rate.

With pasta it's best to stick to spaghetti and keep it simple. Spaghetti al pomodoro (with tomato and basil; $4.95) and spaghetti aglio olio e peperoncino (garlic, olive oil, and hot pepper; $4.95) are far better options than anything more complicated. The same principle extends beyond pasta. The potato-wrapped veal ($11.95) is an absurdity. But the grilled chicken breast ($7.95) is basic and fulfilling. The veal scaloppine ($11.95), pounded to be extra thin, may prove to be the perfect dish for anyone who desires to get in and out of Sapore with ease. The alternative is to dine across the street at Sapore Due, which is large enough to accept credit cards, serve drinks, and admit large people.

Surya

🍽 When this mod Indian bistro first opened in 1998, its Ultrasuede banquettes flanked a battlefield where the menu's destiny was being passionately fought: Anand and Pandian, the Tamil-speaking sauciers, were refusing to talk to Jamaican chef Denzil Richards for his having the audacity to purée their rustic masala sauce. That clash illustrated both Surya's formidable challenge and its greatest strength: to provide genuine, not-strictly-vegetarian South Indian cooking with contemporary flair. And although the absurdly tall, thin, and stunning people who first packed the narrow room mostly vanished soon after the successful ceasefire, the food, furniture, and the cinnamon-dusted Tajmapolitan (Absolut, Chambord, lime juice, cranberry) have remained intact. The orange walls and lime-green pillows reflect the mid-century-modern fashion that extends to the lovely garden furnished with shapely designer stacking chairs by Arne Jacobsen.

**Lunch $15–35
Dinner $25–60**

Address 302 Bleecker St, between Grove St & 7th Ave South
☎212/807-7770
Transportation 1,2 to Christopher St
Open Mon–Thurs noon–3pm & 5.30–11pm, Fri noon–3pm & 5.30pm–midnight, Sat noon–3.30pm & 5.30pm–midnight, Sun noon–3.30pm & 5.30–11pm
Accepts All major credit cards
Reservations Suggested

The logical starter is the vegetable pakora ($5). Served with red chutney and coconut dips, these mildly spicy fritters are made with coarsely ground lentil flour for an appealingly crisp and gritty exterior. They may be paired with fried kaikari rolls ($5) consisting of turmeric- and cumin-seasoned potatoes wrapped in wonton skins. The most style-conscious appetizer consists of two firm, sautéed, sweet-and-spicy jumbo shrimp stacked at the center of a large plate carrying tamarind sauce, a decorative drizzle of curry oil, and a red pepper-and-dill garnish ($9). The vegetable korma ($12), a trail mix of lentil sprouts, black channa (dried chickpeas), onions, and cilantro, is more filling.

The star main courses are prepared with a Chittenad-style masala that graces grouper ($16), salmon ($15), haddock ($16) and rack of lamb ($26) with its rich texture and a choice mix of animated flavors, among them cinnamon, chile, curry leaf, onion, tomato, and coconut milk. Desserts ($4–6) are perfect for post-dental-surgery dining. Everything is a pudding.

Taka

Mitch, June, Reed, and David, though no doubt proud to be among the Taka regulars honored with personalized ceramic teacups, can't be too thrilled to also see their first names in this context. They would prefer you didn't learn of this sushi spot and thus compete with them for its 32 prized seats. For years they've counted on passers-by to be dissuaded by the modest room crammed with blond bentwood chairs and unsightly green tables, some of which are chipped. Moreover, additional discouragement is provided by several unremarkable cooked dishes and specials, including bacon-wrapped oysters and Japanese-style egg rolls. But finding fault with the preparation and presentation of sushi takes levels of fabrication and imagination that are beyond anybody's capabilities—and especially those of the knowing folks waiting in line nearly every night.

$25–45

Address 61 Grove St, between
Bleecker St & 7th Ave South
☎212/242-3699
Transportation 1,9 to Christopher St
Open Tues–Sun 5–11pm
Accepts All major credit cards
Reservations Suggested

"Taka" is Takaka Yoneyama, the serene sushi chef and accomplished sculptress in the white hat. It's a treat to watch her carve carrots and cucumbers or simply spread a dab of wasabi with her index finger across the length of a sushi roll. Even her plastic takeout containers have a personal style. Hers is not precise, symmetrical sushi in which man imitates machine. A methodical worker, she pauses only to choose the right serving vessel. Beautiful ceramic plates and accessories in a variety of glazes and free-form shapes are all hand-crafted and signed by Taka. Particularly lovely are the long slabs that curve up at one end like snowboards.

Rolls of raw fish, in turn, are inspired by the land. The "Mt. Rocky Roll" ($12) is an inside-out mountain peak of spicy tuna, yellowtail, cucumber, and avocado with flying-fish caviar, sesame seeds, and toasted seaweed flakes clinging to its surface. Another offering, the "Volcano" ($11), an improvised tuna roll, is garnished with salmon roe and gold leaf. It contains both chopped and whole tuna, creating an echo of textures. The first melts in your mouth instantly; the second, after a few chews. Alternatively, you would do well to leave the choosing to Taka, requesting either a sushi deluxe ($21) or sashimi deluxe ($25).

Titou

The familiarity of Titou—all warm woods, worn furniture, and Serge Gainsbourg and Edith Piaf CD—makes you realize how naturally New Yorkers have taken to the bistro format. No fanfare. No attitude. Just an attractive local hangout that lures you in off West Fourth Street like the slightly mischievous older cousin who liked to sneak you a paper cup of red wine and tell you stories about the Résistance back when you were a teenager (never mind that you both grew up in New Jersey).

$25–55

Address 259 West 4th St, between Charles & Perry Sts

☎212/691-9359

Transportation 1,9 to Christopher St

Open Tues–Fri 5.30–11pm, Sat 10.30am–3pm & 5.30–11pm, Sun 10.30am–3.30pm & 5–10pm

Accepts All major credit cards

Reservations Suggested

Chef John Light isn't inventing the wheel with his on-the-money bistro fare. Start off with a Roquefort, pear, and walnut tart ($7.95) whose base of puff pastry has a nice balance of butter and crunch. The Roquefort, rich and piquant, oozes. The fruit is fresh and firm. Alternatively, the torte with fennel, eggplant, zucchini, tomato, roasted red pepper, tapenade, and parsley coulis ($7.95) envelops a Mediterranean vegetarian tasting plate in a pastry, while the tuna tartare ($8.25) is enhanced by a sesame orange confit dressing. An appetizer of thinly sliced smoked trout ($8.25) is divinely paired with a silky horseradish crème fraîche. And a number of salads hit their marks, notably the salade Basquaise ($7.95), whose sweet roasted red pepper strips and silky Bayonne ham barely need the balsamic vinaigrette.

Steak frites ($17.95), a NYC French bistro litmus test, is usually right on the money, although those who like their meat rare are advised to say so at least twice during the height of dinner service. The crispy, salty fries are even better dunked in the meat's herbed Bordelaise sauce. Other fine choices include the juicy, well-seasoned, and nicely browned roast chicken with a truffle-oiled potato purée ($13.95) and a thick pork chop with a sweet and tart apple compote and mashed potatoes heaving with roasted garlic cloves ($13.95). Desserts are of the standard chocolate mousse and crème brûlée variety (both $6.50), each now more commonplace to West Villagers than their American counterparts, chocolate pudding and vanilla custard.

West Village

Wallsé

(🍴) This bistro's arrival in summer 2000 heralded not so much the rise of a trend as the end of a fizzle. The expected boom in new Austrian cuisine following the success of David Bouley's Danube had proven to be just another Y2K no-show until a disciple of that superstar chef conceived this more moderately priced alternative. Kurt Gutenbrunner was born in Wallsee, a village along the Danube, and cooked

$40–80

Address 344 West 11th St at Washington St
☎212/352-2300
Transportation 1,9 to Christopher St
Open Mon–Sat 6–11pm
Accepts All major credit cards
Reservations Suggested

nouvelle cuisine in Vienna and haute cuisine in Munich before relocating to New York. He worked at Bouley, Bouley Bakery, and, in a conceptual role, Danube before his talents caught the eye of another employer: himself. At Wallsé (pronounced "vall-see"), Gutenbrunner's approach differs from that of his ex-boss. He did not, for instance, put his surname in the restaurant's title. Probably a shrewd decision. Furthermore, the decor is as spare as Danube's is lush. Set over dark-wooded floors against white-painted brick walls, the Thonet bentwood chairs furnish merely an elegant hint of classic Art Nouveau styling.

The minimalism suits the chef's modern, Franco-Americanized take on Austro-Hungarian cooking. By preparing his dishes with great care and restraint, he effectively challenges the widespread image of this cuisine being all about leaden soups, stews, and cream sauces. Seasonal appetizers are downright dainty, even when they don't sound it. Case in point, the nearly weightless herb spätzle with sautéed rabbit ($12). Chilled tomato, pepper, and crawfish soup is a lasting thrill ($9), while wild cherries bestow just the right balance of sour and sweet upon sautéed foie gras ($15).

The uncharacteristic lightness extends to such entrees as the pristinely golden wiener schnitzel ($24); the goulash with tender but not mushy veal chunks ($24), and the tafelspitz (boiled beef) matched to a fabulous apple-horseradish condiment ($26). The roastbraten ($28), however, is no lightweight: fried onions top the gorgeously grilled hunk of sirloin (not roast beef). And roast chicken ($22) is saucy and succulent. For dessert, the nifty, three-disk mixed berry strudel ($8), stacked like a New Age napoleon, is obviously not your grandmother's strudel, while the sabayon-capped ice coffee is a real Viennese indulgence.

Midtown

Garment District & Little Korea

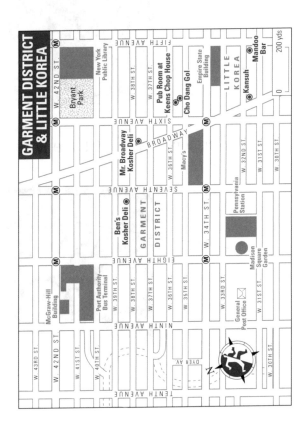

GARMENT DISTRICT & LITTLE KOREA

W 43RD ST
W 42ND ST
W 41ST ST
W 40TH ST

TENTH AVENUE

NINTH AVENUE

McGraw-Hill Building

Port Authority Bus Terminal

W 39TH ST
W 38TH ST
W 37TH ST
W 36TH ST
W 35TH ST

EIGHTH AVENUE

W 33RD ST
W 31ST ST

General Post Office

DYER AV

W 30TH ST

Madison Square Garden

Pennsylvania Station

W 34TH ST

SEVENTH AVENUE

GARMENT DISTRICT

Ben's Kosher Deli

W 32ND ST
W 31ST ST
W 30TH ST

BROADWAY

W 36TH ST

Macy's

SIXTH AVENUE

Mr. Broadway Kosher Deli

New York Public Library

Bryant Park

W 42ND ST

W 38TH ST
W 37TH ST

FIFTH AVENUE

Pub Room at Keens Chop House

Cho Dang Gol

Empire State Building

LITTLE KOREA

Kansuh

Mandoo Bar

0   200 yds

Ben's Kosher Deli

(🍴) The jazzy, Art Deco-styled, 250-seat Ben's was conceived in 1997 to be the Radio City Music Hall of Garment District delis. A gorgeous terrazzo floor leading to the counter, bar, and sprawling dining room bears a violin, a pickle, a coffee cup, and an uncorked bottle all rendered in sweeping curves. Three unfunny deli jokes are hand-stencilled in gold bands along the handsomely wooded walls. Owner Ronnie Dragoon, who also runs one Ben's in Bayside and seven on Long Island, has the know-how needed to serve 500 kosher (but not glatt) lunches in two hours on a typical workday. That's no small accomplishment. But, sadly, he lacks either the expertise, resources, or will to make a truly great deli sandwich. His restaurant is best for midday hot meals—portions are enormous—or, given that Madison Square Garden is just five blocks away, pre-game eats.

$10–50

Address 209 East 38th St, between 7th & 8th Aves
☏212/398-2367
Transportation 1,2,3,7,9,N,Q,R,W to 42nd St-Times Square
Open Daily 11am–9pm
Accepts All major credit cards
Reservations For large groups

JEWISH DELI/KOSHER

Ben's does pickle its own corned beef, piling enough slices of fat-glistening meat on rye to justify its $8.25 price. But rather than cure its own pastrami (also $8.25), Dragoon uses the low-impact product made by Hebrew National, which, despite its pink color, sufficient fat, and good mouth feel, lacks the smoky, peppery kick that's the whole point of pastrami. It's preferable, however, to the thick-sliced, rubbery brisket of beef ($8.25) that not even a quart of gravy and a 20lb mallet could save. The golden, crinkle-cut fries are excellent ($2.95). And the platter of "specials" ($10.95), oversized franks split butterfly-style for even grilling, makes an elegant presentation.

When it comes to Jewish/Eastern European standards and dinner entrees, Ben's is careful about not taking sides. The only passion is for consistency. Nicely textured matzoh balls ($3.75 with chicken soup) strike the perfect balance between "sinkers" (heavy and compact) and "floaters" (light and fluffy). Good roast chicken ($12.95) and chicken in the pot ($14.95) are mildly seasoned. Pâté-like chopped chicken livers ($6.95 for an appetizer portion) are neither light nor heavy on the onions. Only the extra-crisp potato latkes ($2.50 apiece) and the sweet coleslaw have a bias. For dessert, the rugelach (cheese cookie crescents; $11.95/lb) rule!

KOREAN

Cho Dang Gol

🍴 When coaxing a companion into joining you for dinner at Cho Dang Gol, you might want to exclude from your pitch the terms "tofu" and "bean curd" and their associations with veggie burgers and simulated dairy products. Better you pique his or her curiosity by whispering the simple question: "Do you do doo boo?" Doo boo, for the uninitiated, is the Korean term for those healthy unmentionables. And the homemade doo boo, as it is prepared and understood

$9–45

Address 55 West 35th St, between 5th & 6th Aves
☎212/695-8222
Transportation B,D,F,Q,N,R,V,W to 34th St
Open Daily 10.30am–10.30pm
Accepts All major credit cards
Reservations Not accepted

here, is not a stand-in for something else but rather a star ingredient to be appreciated for its softness and lightness and its unique ability to absorb whatever flavors it comes into contact with.

Just get your friend in through the door and let Cho Dang Gol do the rest. The dining room is a serene blend of country classic and city modern, with vertical cherrywood beams rising from the concrete floor and an abstract forest of trees outlined on the cement walls. Servers are gracious and, though their English is limited, generally ask the right questions. They rightly warn first-time non-Koreans that appetizers are too large to order as a first course, unless you're sharing. Besides, the gratis little dishes called panchan—sesame-sauced spinach, egg cakes, assorted kimchee, crunchy miniature fish (think 1:200 scale anchovies) with soy beans—do the appetite-stimulating trick. You nevertheless want to share one of the 12-inch pancakes (pa-jun), which neutralize any lingering illusions about sanctimonious eating with the pure joy of good grease. The boo-choo-pa-jun ($12) is particularly nice: a soft, golden cake striped with glistening green leeks.

The doo boo take the form of triangular, weightless wedges of goodness in such dishes as the mo-doo-boo-oh-jing-uh bok-um (best to ask for no. 4 from the pan-fried specialties list), a sizzling iron casserole of squid, mushrooms, scallions, and noodles ($15.95). The doo boo is cut into cubes for daen-jang-ji-gae (no. 4 in the main-course column), an earthenware crock holding green chiles, scallion, potato, ground beef, and a scintillating broth. All spooned over rice, the doo boo carries the flavors—and the day!

Kansuh

The no-wool, no-cotton dress code that normally applies to down-and-dirty Korean BBQ joints does not apply to Kansuh. Those who do not tuck their hair under a rubber bathing cap will not require a triple-rinse shampoo before returning to work. That's because the peppery, garlicky, charcoal-burning smoke and grease that typically permeates such places—stinking up the clothes and hair of hapless diners—doesn't occur at this comfortable,

Lunch $10–60
Dinner $22–60

Address 1250 Broadway at 32nd St
☎212/564-6845
Transportation B,D,F,N,Q,R,V,W to 34th St
Open Daily 24hr
Accepts All major credit cards
Reservations Not accepted

friendly, and versatile restaurant. So effective are the ventilation hoods over each second-floor, grill-embedded table that you could easily assume the barbecue is not actually available at the time of your arrival. But because Kansuh closes only for credible bomb threats, such an hour does not exist.

Lacking the trappings and gimmicks of touristy, novelty Korean barbecue, Kansuh is the restaurant you go back to for barbecue *after* you've begun to explore the other riches of Korean cuisine. The BBQ service begins without fanfare: an invariably kind waitress delivers a pedestrian assortment of panchan—the complimentary little plates of mung bean sprouts, scallions, Daikin radishes, and kimchee (pungent, spicy, fermented cabbage and turnips)—that precludes the need for appetizers. Then the guy with the cinder box delivers hot charcoals, loading them on either side of the grill. The waitress returns with the barbecue fixings—lettuce leaves, raw garlic cloves, sliced chile pepper, soy sauce, the hot fermented chile paste gochu jang, and, of course, the items to be grilled. The two standards are exceptionally tender bulkoki (rib-eye; $18.95) and succulent kalbi (boneless short ribs; $18.95), both marinated in soy sauce, sugar, and sesame oil. Adventurous second-timers may wish to try instead the pork, the ox-tongue, the shrimp, or, best of all, the squid in a spicy marinade (all $18.95). Once cooked, grilled items are wrapped with their accessories in a lettuce leaf, picked up with hands, dipped in soy sauce, and gobbled.

Besides BBQ, the menu lists an array of Korean specialties and sushi. You might forgo BBQ altogether and drop by for a stone-pot bop (rice casserole) or a noodle dish, both available as $6.95 lunch specials.

Mandoo Bar

True, man cannot live on mandoo alone. But near the southwest corner of 32nd and Fifth, it's worth considering. This is no place for the recovering between-meals munchaholic to be meandering. For in the storefront of Mandoo Bar is a surefire come-on: a butcher's block atop which two cooks roll, shape, stuff, and seal several varieties of mandoo — Korean dumplings — and load them row-by-row into shallow, three-sided blond-wood trays. The

$8–25

Address 2 West 32nd St, between
5th & 6th Aves
☎212/279-3075
Transportation B,D,F,N,Q,R,V,W to
34th St
Open Daily 11.30am–11pm
Accepts All major credit cards
Reservations Not accepted

window must surely be cleaned three times a day just to wipe off the noseprints left by transfixed passers-by. Once prepared, the mandoo are cooked to order in a medium-sized kettle for boiling or a wok-like casserole for pan-frying.

If the window display is meant to draw you in, the Buddhist austerity inside seems intended to hurry you out. The thin seat cushions do little to pad the backless wood benches. Only devoted monks, master yogi, and circus performers manage to stay longer than thirty minutes without fidgeting like a nine-year-old in a dentist's chair. The sleek design is, however, kind of nifty, with illuminated wall recesses and such wall messages as "Why bother?" and "Divorce Leaves a Permanent Void" to ponder.

The difference between appetizers and mains is basically six dumplings and a couple of dollars. It makes virtually no sense to order an appetizer, as you're paying more for each mandoo. Better you share entrees according to the size and appetite of your group. Each order is served with a pair of pickled radishes for picking and soy sauce, white vinegar, and Vietnamese red chile sauce for dipping. The most stunning of the mandoo varieties is the vegetable mool (10 pieces $6.99). The green casing of these boiled vegetable dumplings appears so delicate and wilted that the mandoo at first resemble a stuffed green cabbage leaf. The steamed kimchee mandoo (10 pieces $7.99), filled with tofu, pork, veggies, and kimchee, make a spicier alternative. The pan-fried goon mandoo ($6.99), packed with interwoven pork and vegetables, is crisp but not greasy. Rice and homemade noodle dishes ($7.99–10.99) are little more than menu fillers, and you'll be offered no desserts.

Mr. Broadway Kosher Deli

$8–45

Address 1372 Broadway at 38th St
☎212/921-2152
Transportation 1,2,3,7,9,N,Q,R,W
to 42nd St-Times Square
Open Sun–Thurs 9am–9pm, Fri
9am–3pm
Accepts All major credit cards
Reservations Not accepted

Mr. Broadway looks like an old-fashioned New York kosher deli with all the classic trappings. The meat counter stands opposite the cash register that guards the storefront's typically narrow entrance. Wade through the crowd of takeout customers calling orders to the countermen, and the room widens to a large dining room fitted with utilitarian chairs and Formica tabletops protected by paper placemats. Many of the customers are men wearing skullcaps and designer clothes. But it is not only the Garment District's kosher/fashion crowd filling up every lunchtime seat. Mr. Broadway may smell like an old-fashioned deli, the spice of pastrami and the vapors of the excellent matzoh ball soup ($3.75) in the air, but it has something for everyone. Tucked behind the cashier is a sushi bar. The menu has a list of Chinese and Israeli/Middle Eastern dishes.

Indeed, the last thing you want to eat here is the pastrami and corned beef. Nowadays, the main meat attraction is shawarma ($7.50 as a sandwich stuffed in pita or a crusty baguette; $11.75 as a platter with two sides). The rotating cone of ground and seasoned turkey and lamb cooks on a vertical spit by the front door, literally and symbolically upstaging the hot dog grill. True, the well-spiced, kosher hot dogs ($2.50) come in natural casings with real snap, a rarity these days. But the shawarma, sliced with a flourish, is an absolute show-stopper, succulent and savory. Order it and you get your choice from a small salad bar of Middle Eastern pickles and vegetables. Also from the Israeli/Middle Eastern section of the menu—of special note to vegetarians—is an excellent plate of mezze with a stack of hot pita ($7.75): earthy hummus, garlicky babaganoush, smooth tahini, and fiery red Turkish salad.

The chicken schnitzel ($14.75)—breaded and fried cutlets—are perfect; they go particularly well with very good Eastern European side dishes like onion-laden kasha varnishkas ($3.75), properly stodgy stuffed derma ($3.75), or one of the best potato knishes ($2.50) in the city. The Chinese kitchen turns out a credible General Tsao's Chicken ($14.95), too!

Pub Room at Keens Chop House

Legendary actress Lillie Langtry broke the gender barrier at Keens, the historic (1885) chop house best known for its handsome, oak-walled private banquet rooms and the 64,000 Church Warden pipes that adorn their ceilings. A fair number of those pipes are attached to the first-floor Pub Room, the sole consideration both of this review and of hungry, thirsty, weary, informed souls headed to or from Madison Square Garden, Macy's, and the Empire State Building. This gorgeous room of dark-stained mahogany and pine, with its masculine, polished-brown banquettes, bench-like tables, geometric-tiled floor, and vintage photos of sports figures, also has the classic style of an old New York men's club. But as an affordable and practical alternative to the $35 steaks and mutton chops served upstairs during lunch and dinner hours, the Pub Room offers great sandwiches and pub food throughout the day.

$18–45

Address 72 West 36th St, between 5th & 6th Aves
☎212/947-3636
Transportation B,D,F,N,Q,R,W to 34th St
Open Mon–Fri 11.45am–10.30pm
Accepts All major credit cards
Reservations Not accepted

It is difficult to walk on 36th from Sixth to Fifth Avenues without at least popping in for crisp ringlets of floured dusted fried calamari ($8.50) scattered with tiny halos of scallion and served with two dips: cold tomato and extra-garlicky aioli. The Caesar salad with large, salted anchovies ($7.50) also merits a detour. And once inside, a rationale can always be found for having the remarkably juicy, moderately sized steak-burger with equally good fries ($12). The steak sandwich ($18.50 with fries) is also a marvel. The grilled beef, served on a toasted and crusty baguette brushed with meat juice, is tender enough to cut into with your teeth but not too soft as to become mushy. There is only one way to spread the accompanying horseradish cream sauce over the steak sandwich, and that's quickly. The good BBQ lamb sandwich ($10.50), with thinly sliced, sauce-drenched meat posed over focaccia with red onion, is not in the same league.

Dessert desires gravitate towards two ice cream treats, the hot fudge sundae ($7) or the coffee cantata (coffee ice cream with raspberry syrup; $7.50). Should you opt instead for a classic like the warm, deep-dish, crumb-topped apple pandowdy ($7), you still get a scoop of first-rate vanilla.

Midtown East

MIDTOWN EAST

Brasserie

Anyone who remembers the Brasserie as the place they ate French toast at 4am beware: the institution long famous for 24/7 service now goes to bed at 1am (earlier on Sunday). Likewise, though it may now offer sushi, the celebrated birthplace of rotisserie baseball no longer serves rotisserie chicken. But if there's no stepping back in time at the remade Brasserie, its invitation to step down ultimately rejuvenates more effectively than a year of Botox. You escape the foyer through an open hatch and then a long, glass stairway that cuts through the center of the spacecraft stationed below. The descent beneath cascading panels of Swiss pearwood constitutes one of Manhattan's most glamorous restaurant entrances.

$30–75

Address 100 East 53rd St, between Lexington & Park Aves

☎212/751-4840

Transportation E,V to Lexington Ave; 6 to 51st St

Open Mon–Fri 7–10am & 11.30am–1am, Sat 11am–3.30pm & 5.30pm–1am, Sun 11am–3.30pm & 5.30–11pm

Accepts All major credit cards

Reservations Required

FRENCH

Designers Ricardo Scofidio and Elizabeth Diller have emphasized amusement over ostentation, creating a carefree counterpart to the Seagram Building's other restaurant-in-residence, the almighty Four Seasons. Glancing left, six booths are divided by avocado-green backs that slant from seat to ceiling. At right, gel-cushioned barstools shaped like tractor seats face a line of color monitors displaying video snapshots of patrons entering the restaurant. A frosted glass backbar appears to freeze its horizontally held bottles in time. In the expanse between, open-back Saarinen chairs hug the hips of diners in soft white vinyl.

The brasserie-style French cooking is, by comparison, a low-tech and timidly spiced collection of mostly classic dishes. Start with the escargot garlic puffs ($11) or the French onion soup ($9), then get serious about the standout cold lobster salad with a cabbage-and-frisée chiffonade, a wasabe-detonated ginger mayo, delectably crisp sesame chips, and plenty of meaty lobster at its fresh and firm best ($26). The pot au feu assembled with deliciously tender boiled short ribs and the standard accessory kit ($24) is great on the merits, great on the execution, and the bacon cheeseburger ($16), a perfectly pink chopped steak topped with oven-dried tomato and caramelized onion, is one of the best on the planet. It's a swell lead-in to the warm chocolate beignets or the cookie bowl.

Comfort Diner

You could hardly call Ira Freehof a fashion victim. The diner historian opened this affectionate tribute to the American institution years after the 1980s retro diner craze had swept in and out of town. As a result, the Comfort Diner's terrazzo tabletops, streamlined stainless-steel details, red tail lights, and kitschy 1950s wall sconces appear dated—just not in the way they were intended. Nevertheless, it's always nice to come across a restaurateur motivated by love rather than opportunism. Indeed, the challenge for Freehof is in assembling and maintaining a staff able to put his child-like enthusiasms (Mom's Meatloaf "On Her Best Day", the "Imagination Burger") into practice. And though the Comfort Diner is fun, consistency and versatility—hallmarks of a New York diner—are wanting.

$10–35

Address 214 East 45th St, between 2nd & 3rd Aves
☎212/867-4555
Transportation 4,5,6,7,S to 42 St-Grand Central
Open Mon–Fri 7.30am–11pm, Sat & Sun 9am–11pm
Accepts All major credit cards
Reservations Not accepted

What's never lacking is quantity. Even Jim Carrey would have difficulty fitting the above-par sandwich standards—BLT ($6.95), grilled chicken club ($8.50), tuna melt over a toasted English muffin ($7.95)—in his mouth. "Large plates" are way over the top. "Thanksgiving Every Day" ($12) is a self-defeating concept, reminding us why we only eat that way once a year. The plate stacks piles of roast turkey breast over stuffing and somehow fits a heap of excellent mashed potatoes, cranberry sauce, and fresh vegetables on the same plate. And there is no letting up with desserts: the fabulous house take on s'mores ($4.95), melted marshmallows and chocolate sandwiched between graham crackers, is enhanced with chocolate sauce and a double scoop of vanilla ice cream.

The peak times to seek out Comfort are February and August. In February the Great Grilled Cheese meltdown features a different grilled cheese sandwich—grilled Cubano (Swiss, turkey, pork, pickles, and mustard); melted Gorgonzola with pears on baguette—daily. August is Milkshake Madness, when you can go crazy for a huge variety of shakes from chocolate chip cookie to Key lime.

There's another Comfort Diner at 25 West 23rd St, Flatiron (☎212/741-1010).

Grand Central Oyster Bar

As the supply of oysters from beds off Long Island dried up at the end of the nineteenth century, so too did the popularity of the oyster bars lodged in cellars and vaults throughout New York City. But a dependence on oysters from the Chesapeake and other "foreign" waters hindered neither the 1913 opening nor the enduring landmark status of the Grand Central Oyster Bar & Restaurant. Though the words "The Oyster Bar" alone are sufficient, this 400-seat institution is forever linked with the great railroad depot in which it resides. The tiled vaults designed by Rafael Guastavino constitute one of Grand Central Terminal's—and Manhattan's—great architectural treasures.

$10–80

Address Lower level, Grand Central Terminal, 42nd St & Park Ave
☎212/490-6650
Transportation 4,5,6,7,S to 42nd St-Grand Central
Open Mon–Fri 11.30am–9.30pm, Sat noon–9.30pm
Accepts All major credit cards
Reservations Suggested

SEAFOOD

The oyster stew ($9.45) and oyster pan roast ($9.95) are celebrated classics of American cookery, and the daily selection of 30-plus oysters on the half-shell ($1.45–2.75 apiece) remains the best in town—as well as the most common motive for commuters "accidentally" missing the next train back to Connecticut. Yet the oyster platters are admittedly not the novelty they once were now that brasseries all over town feature multi-tiered shellfish extravaganzas. Likewise, the superbly fresh seafood now commonplace at better bistros, seafood restaurants, and local ethnic grills make the Oyster Bar's daily catches seem more expensive and less special than before. For $27.95 it's no longer enough to *serve* swordfish steak. The efforts of a highly skilled chef have to show.

Still, there is no known substitute for grabbing a seat at one of the winding, U-shaped counters and having a bowl of rich, creamy New England clam chowder ($4.75) with biscuits and oyster crackers. From this noble position you can also choose among some splendid sandwiches, notably the grilled tuna with spicy salsa ($9.50) or grilled Asian tuna burger ($10.95), or partake of the famous oyster stew and oyster pan roast. Both dishes are briskly whisked as they bubble up in double boilers so that they're exceptionally creamy at the moment they're poured into a shallow soup dish. The rice pudding ($4.50) and Key lime pie ($5.75) are the dessert equivalents of steadfast old pals.

NEW AMERICAN

Heartbeat

(🍴) Any lactose-intolerant environmentalist with a hefty expense account should hurry along to Heartbeat in a, well, single pulsation of their blood-pumping organ. The posh commissary of the glamorously retro-fitted Hotel W New York is largely organic, mostly non-dairy, and thoroughly original. But even those whose dietary requirements and income are on the average side will admire what chef John Mooney and David Rockwell have come up with. The latter's mid-century modern design is at once striking and warm. Coaster-topped columns encased in a geometric stained-glass mosaic are shaped like the observation towers Philip Johnson designed for the 1964 World's Fair. Eames-era plywood chairs and wheat-straw tabletops are surrounded by walls sheathed in limestone and period fabric.

Lunch $30–75
Dinner $35–80

Address 149 East 49th St, between Lexington & 3rd Aves
☏212/407-2900
Transportation 6 to 51st St
Open Mon–Fri 7am–11am, noon–2.30pm & 6–10pm, Sat 8am–noon & 6–10pm, Sun 8am–noon
Accepts All major credit cards
Reservations Required

The food too is carefully designed, although devoid of nostalgia. The haute-and-healthful menu may start off with a hearty organic vegetable consommé ($11)—the first of several instances in which powdered spices and vegetable juices are substituted for fat. Likewise, the fig-and-mushroom hash matched to the first-rate whole roasted quail appetizer ($11) expels any sense of deprivation. Sliced raw tuna paired with a three-radish salad and wasabe-yuzu dressing ($12) possesses zen-like clarity.

Among possible main courses, Maine lobster with "corn milk succotash" ($28) is a glorified sweetcorn chowder—which is somewhat dispiriting given that it's the lobster you're ostensibly paying for. Steamed black bass is propped over a deceptively deep bowl filled with a saffron artichoke broth ($23). When it comes to Heartbeat's upbeat finales, the menu makes a distinction between "desserts" and "indulgences". The former category includes such low-fat inventions as poached pineapple with green tea granité ($9), goat's milk gelati ($8), and excellent home-made sorbets ($8). The latter—molten chocolate orange cake ($10), white chocolate and coconut mousse with sesame-nut brittle ($10)—are sweet and, as it happens, unearned compensations for prior so-called deprivations.

L'Impero

ITALIAN

(icon) Beyond the gothic uniformity of Tudor City, a planned community west of the UN, the first indication that this is another kind of Italian restaurant is the color scheme: teal blue for the oval-backed chairs; arabica brown (black in daylight) for the fuzzy, tufted banquettes; white for the curtains draped over the walls. The long candle rods clamped to each table, like the surreal display of toilet paper rolls in the chartreuse rest rooms, are the sort of outrageous touches hot designers put in boutique hotels to compensate for lousy plumbing.

Lunch $35–80
Dinner $40–90

Address 45 Tudor City Place, between 42nd & 43rd Sts
☎212/599-5045
Transportation 4,5,6,7,S to Grand Central-42nd St
Open Mon–Thurs noon–2.15pm & 5.30–10.15pm, Fri noon–2.15pm & 5–11.15pm, Sat 5–11.15pm
Accepts All major credit cards
Reservations Suggested

The dining room Vincente Wolf has imagined for Scott Conant's clever yet soulful Italian cuisine is discreetly elegant, save for the 1970s Continental pop issuing from tinny speakers. It's easy to understand why it's been universally praised. The minority opinion is that the place looks like a funeral parlor in an Antonioni film and leaves you every bit as numb.

Unable to build a following at City Eatery, a critically acclaimed flop in the East Village, Conant now finds admirers in this dining-deprived neighborhood for the smallest appetizer details. The bits of pancetta, for example, in the vinaigrette applied to a warm radicchio, baby arugula, and Pecorino Toscano salad ($9) provide a salty kick you reminisce about days later. The polenta that's the starch to a fricassee of wild mushrooms ($10 lunch/$12 dinner) is cooked to the cusp of dissolution. You detect the very last traces of cornmeal grains.

Pastas are sublime, veering from the utter lucidity of house-made spaghetti with tomato and basil ($13/$15) to the fearless luxuriance of braised duck and foie gras agnolotti ($18/$19) or eggplant and taleggio mezzaluna (half-moon pillows) with a lamb shank ragu. As main acts, roasted salmon at lunch ($18) and seared branzino with creamy, rosemary-infused lentils at dinner ($26) balance power and delicacy. But the roasted, tender, deep-flavored, juice-dripping capretto (baby goat; $26/$29) is Conant's tour de force. The wonderful desserts (about $10), specifically the vanilla risotto zeppole or the sesame cannoli, enhance the appeal of the prix-fixe tastings ($42/$49).

Maloney & Porcelli

Whimsical presentation, eccentric Americana, and a name lifted from a downtown law firm make high-rent Maloney & Porcelli resemble an Elks Club for $400-per-hour litigators. Wooden geese fly in a line over the balcony's balustrade, safe from hunters armed only with subpoenas. Fine steaks tagged with potato lollipops as well as seafood, sides, and desserts of Flintstones dimensions are dressed in the fanciful food fashions of corporate chef/partner David Burke. Curious diners can view the show from a counter facing the open kitchen.

Lunch $38–90
Dinner $45–95

Address 37 East 50th St, between Park & Madison Aves

℡212/750-2233

Transportation E,V to 5th Ave; 6 to 51st St

Open Daily 11.45am–11.30pm

Accepts All major credit cards

Reservations Suggested

Among successful starters, twin béchamel-creamed crabcakes with ratatouille ($15) and crisp lobster spring rolls ($15) do not quite elicit the excitement of the filet mignon carpaccio ($9 at lunch/$12 at dinner) or the terrific flat-crusted pizzas ($13). The round white pie topped with Robiolo cheese, truffle oil, and mushroom is so sublime that diners returning from the restroom have been known to follow its scent to the wrong table. Then there's the rectangular red pie of diced tomato and three Italian cheeses, set atop a wooden slab from a wine crate bearing the name of a Grand Cru Bordeaux—an aristocratic platform, like the restaurant itself, for childlike amusement.

With several of the steaks there is—literally and figuratively—no beef. Swordfish marinates for two days before it meets its Portobellos, caramelized onions, lemony sauce, and mushrooms in a fish London broil ($29) while mustard-crusted tuna steak ($29) is sliced into four squares and set in an elegant Japanese context. For a poultry steak, roast boneless breast ($19/$22) is wrapped with dark meat and flavored with thyme and a knockout punch of garlic. Red-meat hankerings are handled by a thick, tasty sirloin ($29/$35) which looks better in the company of stubby fries, or tempura onion rings. Narrowing down the selection of ten desserts ($8) to one is no easy affair. Consensus reduces it to three—chocolate burnout cake, warm apple tart, "drunken donuts" (warm powdered cake donuts with liquored fruit jam)—but you'll have to take it from there.

Marichu

With its location just west of the UN and its status as the city's foremost culinary ambassador from the Basque Country, Marichu could well have been envisaged by chef/co-owner Teresa Barrenechea and her husband Raynold von Samson as a diplomatic mission, or at least a restaurant on one. They instead fashioned a self-confident import which, precisely because it has nothing to prove, proves to be charming, genuine, and special. The candlelit walls are decorated with ceramics and color photos, including one of another New York-Basque connection, the Guggenheim Museum in Bilbao.

Lunch $27–50
Dinner $35–75

Address 342 East 46th St, between 1st & 2nd Aves

☎212/370-1866

Transportation 4,5,6,7,S to 42nd St-Grand Central

Open Mon–Thurs noon–2.30pm & 5.30–10pm, Fri noon–2.30pm & 5.30–11pm, Sat 5.30–11pm, Sun 5.30–9pm

Accepts All major credit cards

Reservations Suggested

BASQUE

The courtyard garden, with its terra-cotta tiling and zigzagging glass canopy, is appropriately spare. Thus nothing comes between your nose and the sizzling, snap-happy gambas (shrimp) al ajillo ($12), whose garlicky component could stop traffic on First Avenue. Other must-try appetizers include the lettuce-wrapped monkfish with béchamel and a sensuous black (squid ink) vinaigrette ($12) as well as the beautifully arranged leaves of endive cradling sharp Cabrales cheese, almonds, and yogurt sauce ($10). Two specials also merit your undivided attention: ajo blanco, a cold soup of almonds, grapes, and olive oil infused with garlic ($8), and the white asparagus served over sweet, olive-oil-immersed piquillo peppers ($14). Befitting the cuisine from Spain's "Region of the Peppers", the piquillos (pimentos) return for the next course, this time stuffed with salt cod and draped with an outstanding, slightly bitter roasted pepper sauce ($18). Among entrees it is second only to the delicate, slow-cooked chipirones (baby squid) en su tinta ($24), with a classic ink sauce centered by a ring of white rice. This is Basque cooking at its most basic and elegant.

The kitchen also excels at grilling; try salty and succulent lamb ribs over scalloped potatoes ($22), tuna steak with a laurel of greens ($24), or filet mignon ($28). The selection of desserts ($7–8) is best represented by the leche frita, three deep-fried squares of eggless milk custard in a honey-like glaze, and tarta de arrese, a custard pie with nantillas (crème anglaise) and raspberry sauce.

Naples 45

🍴 The traditional Neapolitan cooking so close to our moonstruck hearts gets stylishly reworked at this 260-seat, louder-than-a-locomotive lunch factory near Grand Central Terminal. The arcaded ceiling and back bar, with its cool white finish and abstractly floral lighting fixtures, suggest a modern take on the nearby Grand Central Oyster Bar (see p.187). Clubby wooden booths centered on the modish terrazzo hold suits sipping tall pink Napolis—cocktails of Champagne and blood orange purée.

$18–55

Address 200 Park Ave South at 45th St
☎212/972-7001
Transportation 4,5,6,7,S to Grand Central-42nd St
Open Mon–Fri 11am–10pm
Accepts All major credit cards
Reservations For large groups

ITALIAN/PIZZA

To bestow its dough with authenticity, Naples 45 uses a special wet brewer's yeast, a low-gluten durum wheat, and bottled water close in hardness to the H_2O of Napoli. The bakers are less exacting, pulling out pies from the wood-fired, three-door brick oven that are either underbaked as a whole or blackened on one end and raw beige on the other. When baked evenly, the pies are crisp, chewy, and sublime. A drizzle of extra virgin olive oil does wonders for the mozzarella-heavy Margherita, the quattro formaggi (Pecorino Romano, Parmigiano-Reggiano, provolone, mozzarella), and the funghi pie with mushrooms, tomatoes, and mozzarella. Small individual pizzas proportioned for a single meal or shared appetizer cost between $12 and $15. Beautiful and superior ovals measured by the half-meter (serving three to five) go for $24–30.

Appetizers, pastas, and entrees can be as unreliable here as the service. Still, the salads ($7–8 as appetizers, $14–18 as main courses) make for solid lunches, while at dinner there are some chances worth taking: the béchamel-sauced artichoke lasagna ($14.75), or the lemon-roasted chicken audaciously detonated with garlic ($16.95). Yet it's clear that the ambitions of Naples 45's kitchen have diminished the last couple of years. Desserts ($6) such as the seductive fruit and almond tart with zabaglione gelato and a cannoli shell stuffed with orange-scented ricotta ensure an upbeat return to the office.

Pershing Square

Only a homesick pigeon could object to what transpired under the Pershing Square Viaduct extending south from Grand Central Terminal. Between massive granite walls, restaurateur Buzzy O'Keeffe (The River Club, The Water Club) installed a decorative framework of green steel beams and cork bricks which, in their herringbone pattern, evoke the Guastavino tiles in the Grand Central Oyster Bar (see p.187). Cherrywood banquettes and mahogany-and-iron tables enhance the period feel. Meanwhile, a custom-made vestibule of steel, aluminum, and glass leads to a cafe/bakery section and the wooded "Buzz Bar," equipped with a brass foot rail so that commuters can get a leg up under Park Avenue. Still, the most distinct—and least appealing—architectural feat is one of acoustics. Put a dozen diners in the 220-seat dining room, close your eyes, and it will sound like a full house during happy hour.

AMERICAN

Lunch $25–70
Dinner $35–80

Address 90 East 42nd St at Park Ave

☎212/286-9600

Transportation 4,5,6,7,S to 42nd St-Grand Central

Open Mon–Fri 7–10am, 11.30am–3pm & 5–10.30pm, Sat & Sun 8am–3pm & 5–10.30pm

Accepts All major credit cards

Reservations For dinner only

Were Pershing Square a television series, it would be broadcast on HBO, not PBS. Chef Rob Ubhaus's twists and flourishes are aimed at instant gratification rather than long-range enlightenment. The pleasure principle is apparent in the rich French onion soup ($8). Its crusty melted cheese topping is garnished with fried red onions—a frivolous exploit that delights. All efforts to disparage the garlicky "shrimpscargot" ($12) in which shrimp stand in for snails are doomed to failure.

Most main courses are solid: pan-seared Atlantic salmon set against red wine sauce, Vidalia onion risotto, and roasted corn ($20); soft and succulently sweet braised short ribs ($23). Let's thank Buzzy for the chicken pot pie that recalls the great one served at his defunct Cafe at Grand Central. In this rendition, a croissant-wrapped duck leg protrudes through the center of the pastry. You're entitled to study the entire dessert card (all $7)—the cookie plate is fab—prior to selecting the bananas Foster and its coming together of bananas, sugary rum syrup, vanilla ice cream, and pure joy.

The Prime-Burger

The Prime-Burger is a relic to relish on the midtown lunchscape. The circa 1965 coffee shop started as an off-shoot of Hamburger Heaven, a pre-War chain of burger joints. When the HH fleet perished, new proprietors redesigned two of the flagship stores and reopened as The Prime-Burger. This, the last surviving locale, opposite St Patrick's Cathedral, recalls a more optimistic age when urban designers and architects endeavored to satisfy the needs of working people. As an alternative to sitting at the long counter, parties of one have the grander option of occupying one of the 24 box seats collectively known as "the track". Arranged in groupings of six, these large, blond-wood sectionals are divided by wide armrests equipped with high-chair-like trays. What fun!

$5–25

Address 5 East 51st St, between Madison & 5th Aves
℡212/759-4729
Transportation E,V to 5th Ave
Open Mon–Fri 5am–7pm, Sat 6am–5pm
Accepts Cash only
Reservations Not accepted

As forward-thinking as this seating-system was, it's doubtful that the designers thought its appeal would not only last through but also reach a new peak in the twenty-first century. Yet the shop's 1960s modernism, with its groovy lamps and mineral-textured dropped ceiling, is in vogue. Whereas both first-time and longstanding customers used to beg owner Tony DiMiceli to renovate, now they plead with him not to. The mere changing of a spent lightbulb causes a stir. Among the throwbacks painstakingly maintained by DiMiceli and his sons Michael and John include gentlemanly waiters in white jackets and bow ties, a change maker rather than a cash register, and soft, juicy, fresh-tasting hamburgers ($3.65) machine-shaped on the premises with 4oz of—what else— prime meat. The steak fries are cooked to a well-done crisp; the homemade onion rings ($2.95), just scrumptious.

The standard coffee shop fare—challah French toast ($2.35 as a breakfast special), say, or golden chicken-in-a-basket with fries ($9.95)—could fairly be described as reliable. George David has worked the broiler since 1954. At the time of headwaiter Arthur Ward's 1955 arrival, Russell Teal already had five years under his belt as prep man. And Ed Adams has baked his signature apple crumb and sweet potato pies (both $2.95) at this address for more than half a century.

Teodora

🍽 You don't open a restaurant on East 57th and name it after a Byzantine princess without creating expectations of something slick and glitzy. Accordingly, the homey setting and the plethora of knick-knacks that must have been snatched from some grandmother's attic can cause a little confusion. While New York-based Italians in the art, fashion, and wine trades are clearly in their element here, the Americans don't always get it. Italians may be the design kings of the world, but when it

$30–80

Address 141 East 57th St, between 3rd & Lexington Aves
☎212/826-7101
Transportation 4,5,6 to 59th St; N,R,W to Lexington Ave
Open Mon–Sat noon–11pm, Sun noon–10.30pm
Accepts All major credit cards
Reservations Suggested

ITALIAN

comes to dining they could care less about decor if the food is excellent and genuine. No wonder everyone you pass at the bar seems to be conversing in fluent Italian. "That's not true," protests host Salvatore Nasello, insisting his countrymen make up just under a third of the diners. "Thirty percent is a lot of Italians for New York. But without Americans we can close tomorrow."

Should the newyorkese representation ever get as high as Nasello's wishful estimate, Teodora will still speak Italian with the glorious accent of the Emilia-Romagna region for as long as chef-owner Giancarlo Quadalti is preparing piadina romagnola ($12.50). The Ravenna native tops Romagna's semi-crisp, griddle-baked flatbread with Stracchino cheese, broccoli rabe, or salumi (prosciutto, coppa, and salami). The appetizer role of Parmigiano-Reggiano, his region's world-famous cheese, varies from supporting (a mini-lasagna of eggplant, zucchini, and tomato-basil; $9.50) to starring (sformato, a cheese soufflé with porcinis; $11.50).

Teodora's native pasta is tagliatelle alla bolognese ($15.50), a definitive pairing of Emilia-Romagna's preferred pasta shape and ragu. Another can't-miss is the ricotta and-spinach fazzoletto (a raviolo-like triangle; $15.50) with a simple butter and sage sauce. The remarkable fritto misto ($24) is a fried basket of waffled potatoes filled with zucchini, eggplant, calamari, and shrimp. Other fish entrees (from $19.50 for salmon to $28 for whole orato) are dependably fresh. Highlights from the rotated dessert collection ($7) include a splendid millefoglie (like a Napoleon), a whipped-creamy tiramisu, heavenly profiteroles, and runny warm chocolate cake.

Zarela

🍴 The name Zarela is cut out of decorative sheets of tissue paper that hang in banners from one end of this benchmark East Sider to the other. These custom displays of *papel picado*, as that Mexican art of paper-cutting is known, bring fiesta colors and crafts to a very serious dining duplex masquerading as a frolicsome bar. But since 1987, the margarita-ministered merriment has been no match for the combination jab-and-clinch of cooking star Zarela Martinez, a native of Sonora, Mexico. Behind every jab of fiery flavor she loads into her dishes is an underlying warmth. Something smooth or creamy coddles and comforts the area around the burn without diminishing the residual flavors.

Lunch $25–50
Dinner $30–60

Address 953 2nd Ave, between 50th & 51st Sts

☎212/644-6740

Transportation E,V to Lexington Ave; 6 to 51st St

Open Mon–Thurs noon–3pm & 5–11pm, Fri noon–3pm & 5pm–midnight, Sat 5pm–midnight, Sun 5–11pm

Accepts All major credit cards

Reservations Suggested

Forget about the coarsely mashed guacamole ($8.95) serving as your exclusive source of gloppy bliss. The chilaquiles are a creamy, bubbling, molten mass of baked chicken shreds, tortilla strips, sour cream, and tomatilla sauce ($9.95). Try to spoon a small portion of that appetizer from its little casserole and the whole thing slowly oozes out. Same goes for the queso fundido (baked white Cheddar; $8.95) that disarms its pickled jalapenos and spicy chorizo ammunition. Savory spices do the same for Martinez' signature red snapper hash with minced garlic, chiles, scallions, and fresh cilantro ($9.95). A crisp tortilla chip never had a better friend.

The Martinez jab-and-clinch works to best effect in the chiles en nogado ($10.95), a renowned dish from the state of Puebla. A single large poblano chile is stuffed with shredded chicken, chopped dried apricots and prunes, and green olives in a creamy pool of roasted tomato sauce. The chile bites. The sauce soothes. Over and over again. Occasionally she forgoes the spicy sting altogether, as with the tequila-braised half chicken with a mild garnish of olives, raisins, and onions ($14.95). Pastry chef Ed Bonuso's desserts lay it on thick. The Aztec Treasure ($7) is a warm pecan pie with Kahlua and dark chocolate inside and chocolate sauce and vanilla bean ice cream outside.

Midtown West

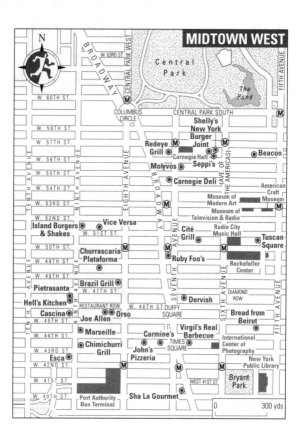

MIDTOWN WEST

N

BROADWAY

W. 63RD ST.

CENTRAL PARK WEST

Central Park

FIFTH AVENUE

The Pond

W. 60TH ST.

COLUMBUS CIRCLE

CENTRAL PARK SOUTH

Shelly's New York Burger Joint

W. 58TH ST.

W. 57TH ST.

Redeye Grill

Carnegie Hall

Beacon

W. 56TH ST.

TENTH AVENUE

NINTH AVENUE

EIGHTH AVENUE

Molyvos

Seppi's

AVE. OF THE AMERICAS

W. 55TH ST.

W. 54TH ST.

BROADWAY

Carnegie Deli

American Craft Museum

W. 53RD ST.

Museum of Modern Art

W. 52ND ST.

Museum of Television & Radio

Island Burgers & Shakes

Vice Versa

W. 51ST ST.

SEVENTH AVENUE

Cité Grill

Radio City Music Hall

W. 50TH ST.

Tuscan Square

W. 49TH ST.

Churrascaria Plataforma

Ruby Foo's

Rockefeller Center

W. 48TH ST.

Pietrasanta

Brazil Grill

DIAMOND ROW

SIXTH AVENUE

FIFTH AVENUE

W. 47TH ST.

RESTAURANT ROW

Hell's Kitchen

Dervish

Bread from Beirut

Cascina

Joe Allen

Orso

W. 46TH ST

DUFFY SQUARE

W. 45TH ST.

Marseille

Carmine's

Virgil's Real Barbecue

International Center of Photography

W. 44TH ST.

Chimichurri Grill

TIMES SQUARE

W. 43RD ST.

Esca

John's Pizzeria

New York Public Library

W. 42ND ST.

W. 41ST ST.

WEST 41ST ST.

Bryant Park

W. 40TH ST.

Port Authority Bus Terminal

Sha La Gourmet

0   300 yds

Beacon

For chef Waldy Malouf, the rotisserie marks a turning point away from fussy fusion food. He relies on that spinning roaster, along with a wood-fired oven and grill, to draw out the essential character of the finest meats, seafood, and vegetables. These rustic ways, as common in Italy and Spain as they are fashionable in California, have rarely been undertaken on such a large scale. With more than 35 foods cooked nightly on the open fire, Beacon's menu possesses the bounty of a Lucullan feast. Oddly, this prodigious output does not prevent the odd diner from asking if there are any specials. (How demanding New

**Lunch $30–80
Dinner $40–85**

Address 25 W 56th St, between 5th & 6th Aves

☎212/332-0500

Transportation F,N,Q,R,W to 57th St; E,V to 5th Ave

Open Mon–Thurs noon–2pm & 5.30–10.30pm, Fri noon–2pm & 5.30–10.30pm, Sat 5.30–10.30pm, Sun 4–9pm

Accepts All major credit cards

Reservations Required

NEW AMERICAN

Yorkers can be.) You might choose to sit a few steps down from the main dining room, where an eight-table section faces the exposed terracotta kitchen. If a view of people is what you're after, try sitting on the perimeter mezzanine. The clubby room with circular pinstriped booths is also nice, though the condom-shaped hanging lamps do take the masculine thing too far.

Listing which of the dishes are perfectly cooked and which are a bit off is a pointless endeavor, presupposing as it does total consistency. But when Beacon beams it is truly a splendid thing. For starters, the roasted artichokes and asparagus ($10) practically explode with flavor. The wood-roasted oysters ($13) are divine, even if the shallots and buttery white wine sauce obscure some of the briny oyster taste.

Main-course standouts include a roasted lobster garnished with curlicues of fennel ($30), its sweet meat wading in a buttery stock enriched with fennel oil and extra virgin olive oil. The knockout veal chop ($32) profits from the grit and pungency of crushed peppercorns. And each serving of the rotisserie-roasted, mole-rubbed suckling pig ($28) contains all the essential parts: leg, loin, shank, and, most crucially, crackling skin. The exceptional dessert lineup is led by the chocolate chocolate chip soufflé ($9) and the caramelized apple pancake ($8). The $19.95 two-course, prix-fixe lunch is a swell deal.

Brazil Grill

(🍴) The bare-faced, full-bellied carnivores who regularly compete in rotisserie steakhouse marathons (see Churrascaria Plataforma; p.207) are apparently too young to remember the archetypal midtown Brazilian chowdowns of yore. Back in the twentieth century Brazilian gluttony was restricted to small eateries where big appetites for garlic chicken, Linguica sausage, salt cod croquettes, and feijoada (the national black bean stew) were both whetted and washed down by multiple caipirinhas (the definitive cocktail of cachaca and lime). Brazil Grill is a likeable throwback to that simpler time, though the portions at this theater district bistro aren't going to feed the Brazilian soccer team. The setting, with harlequin tiling and Dalíesque canvases, is pleasant, providing you don't mind the invisible—not to be confused with unobtrusive—service.

Lunch $25–50
Dinner $25–65

Address 787 8th Ave at 48th St
☎212/307-9449
Transportation C,E to 50th St
Open Daily noon–midnight
Accepts All major credit cards

The shock of not being able to start by attacking an all-you-can-eat buffet is allayed by the tried-and-true appetizers. The fried Linguica sausage ($6.95) either recalls or creates a lasting taste memory. A bite into the bolinhos de bacalhao (salt cod croquettes; $6.95) exposes fresh, steaming-hot but not greasy goodness, as do the variations filled with beef, chicken, or, better still, yuco. And the salada Copacabana with hearts of palm, tomatoes, roasted red peppers, and a lovely house vinaigrette ($6.95) is wonderfully constant.

Many of the grilled meats of the style carved tableside at the churrascarias are featured here as a la carte entrees priced between $10.95 for sausage to $21.95 for filet mignon. But chances are you would be there and not here if that's how you wanted to eat. Better to try one of the seafood specialties ($17.95–18.95), even if those coconut-milk sauces evoke the curries of Southeast Asia more than the casseroles of South America. One sure bet is the outstanding house feijoada ($15.95). The pork-enriched black bean stew is already broth-like, yet additional broth is served to spoon over the rice. Cheese desserts ($4) with condensed milk and guava paste are intensely sweet.

There's another Brazil Grill at 102 MacDougal St, Greenwich Village (☎212/777-7637).

Bread from Beirut

🍴 Breadwinners from the Diamond District, the midtown banks, Rockefeller Center publishing houses, and Broadway theaters converge at this diminutive, corrugated-tin-topped Lebanese eatery/takeout for—what else?—winning breads. The lunch line stretches out the door. Those who rightly insist on having their breads fresh from the cylindrical, colorfully tiled brick oven have two alternatives: they can carry their trays back to the tiny L-shaped dining area bounded by whimsical murals and squeeze into one of eight tables, or they can get a job on this block so that the foil-wrapped breads are still warm when they get back to the office.

$7–20

Address 24 West 45th St, between 5th & 6th Aves

☎212/764-1588

Transportation B,D,F,V to 47th–50th Sts-Rockefeller Center

Open Mon–Fri 9am–9pm, Sat 10am–7pm

Accepts All major credit cards

Reservations Not accepted

MIDDLE EASTERN

Of course not all takeout customers manage to wait that long. For a quick, filling, eat-as-you-walk lunch it's hard to beat the crisp-edged, golf-ball-sized felafel ($4.50) made with chickpeas and fava beans and packed with tahini sauce and pungent pickled turnips in home-baked flatbread that's more like lavosh than a pocket-less pita. Equally tasty and portable is the juicy beef shawarma carved off the spit ($6.50). The beauty of both made-to-order wraps is that their contents are melted together under the weight and heat of a sandwich press. The bright, lemony, mostly parsley tabouleh salad ($5) you must eat sitting down. In an outstanding version of the lentil salad known here as moudardra ($5), the tender brown beans are interspersed with fragrant rice and topped with sweet, crisp, fried onions. The counterman will scoop from under the onions and thus leave them out of your serving, unless you instruct him—twice if necessary—to do otherwise.

Energetic young cooks are continuously sliding out such steaming hot, freshly baked breads as keshik ($5), a chewy yet buttery flatbread heartily stuffed with dried goat cheese, crushed wheat, and sesame seeds, and arayess ($6), a flaky, paper-thin dough folded over ground beef, onions, tomatoes, and pine nuts. Perhaps the best freshly baked Bs-from-B are the flat, pizza-like rounds ($4) that are rubbed with Moroccan olive oil and topped with zaatar, a spice mixture containing sumac, thyme, and sesame seeds.

The Burger Joint

(logo) As a recreation of a cultural icon, the Burger Joint, which opened in the summer of 2002, exceeds exhibits at the Smithsonian and Madame Tussaud's. Beside the soaring atrium of the posh Le Parker Meridien Hotel, in an imperceptible gap between the reception and concierge areas, its secreted entrance ranks somewhere between the 7 1/2th floor in Being John Malkovich and Gate 9 3/4 in Harry Potter. A dark, drab, constricted hallway leads to a neon

$20–40

Address Le Parker Meridien Hotel, 119 West 56th St, between 6th & 7th Aves

☎212/245-5000

Transportation F,N,Q,R,W to 57th St

Open Mon–Sat 11.30am–midnight

Accepts Cash only

Reservations Not accepted

hamburger, the lone indication of what's closeted in the backroom: an unsightly, wood-paneled American greasy spoon that appears to have been transported from a time and place where folks cared nothing about outward appearances. Industrial-sized ketchup cans, shortening containers, and salt canisters are openly displayed above the open kitchen passthrough where orders are placed. A cook blending a too-thick thick shake ($2.50) licks his fingers in full view. Welcome to reality retro.

The firm patties are flame-broiled to order (request medium-rare and you get it or something very close) on a grill that slopes down to let excess grease roll off. Burgers ($4.50) and Cheddar cheeseburgers ($5) are dressed with lettuce, tomato, onion, or pickle in a toasted, generic bun and then wrapped in white butcher paper. Order one with everything and the whole thing merges into a truck-stop classic. Still, for a bare assessment you need to order it plain. Only then can you appreciate—surprise, surprise—what a terrific little sphere of gridiron-sealed chopped meat this is. The opposite is true of the frozen shoestring fries ($1.50). The more junk you put on them, the less objectionable they become. Dessert is restricted to thick, chewy brownies ($1.50) and forlorn donuts.

Beside the cash register, a posting containing the varied letters of a ransom note proclaims the milestone: "uNDeR A BiLLiOn sErVed." Many of those augmenting this impressive statistic are management types in stylish black suits. Crammed into creaky vinyl booths, they watch a TV silently tuned at lunchtime to the Jerry Springer Show. A smoky, authentically odorous soundtrack to that program's daily parade emanates from the grill and its sizzling, grease-dripping burgers.

Carmine's

No New York restaurant cuisine varies as widely in quality, cost, and refinement as Italian. At the high end are temples of truffles and Barolo; at the low end, pizza counters that offer garlic knots and massive tubs of soda to wash down your greasy, cheese-globby slice. Somewhere squashed into the vast middle lies Carmine's, an Italian-American fantasyland that is honest about what it is (unrefined, noisy, gluttonfriendly) and isn't (to be taken too seriously). Mismatched chandeliers crowd the high ceilings, walls are jammed with black-and-white family photographs, and you'll even see a wonderfully passé display of old chianti bottles in wicker baskets.

$25–65

Address 200 West 44th St, between Broadway & 8th Ave
℡212/221-3800
Transportation 1,2,3,7,9,N,Q,R,S,W to 42nd St-Times Square
Open Mon 11.30am–11pm, Tues 11.30am–midnight, Wed 11am–midnight, Thurs–Sat 11.30am–midnight, Sun 11am–11pm
Accepts All major credit cards
Reservations For large groups

ITALIAN

An oversized bread basket will hit your table before you open the menu. Choose carefully: some, like the squares of focaccia with thinly sliced onions or a layer of tangy tomato, basil, and Parmesan, are satisfying; others, like the sesame-seed roll, will merely fill you up. Wine, chosen from a succinct list, is poured into juice glasses. The Etna Rosso from Sicily ($23) makes an ideal complement to the heavily red-sauced menu. All dishes are meant for sharing, including the appetizers. The Caesar salad ($16), with crusty garlic croûtons and optional anchovies straight from the can, serves six adults. Fresh clams on the half-shell ($12/dozen) are perfect for dipping into an uncommonly potent cocktail sauce.

Five types of dried pasta (spaghetti, linguine, angel hair, penne, and rigatoni) are available with a variety of sauces from simple marinara ($18) to vodka ($22). Stray if you must to a massive osso buco special ($35) or a juicy veal saltimbocca ($21) surrounded by buttery prosciutto and redolent of sage. But the real game is a $19 plate of spaghetti and meatballs the size of tennis balls and the weight of cannonballs. The strawberry shortcake ($9)—a pyramid of whipped cream covered with syrupy strawberries atop dense, sugary shortbread—is, like everything else at Carmine's, more than enough for everyone.

There's another Carmine's at 2450 Broadway, Upper West Side (℡212/362-2200).

Carnegie Delicatessen

Reports of this legendary deli's lowered standards are not so much exaggerated as they are tiresome. Although drops in the quality of the food and the consistency of the deli meat appeared to coincide with the passing in 1988 of the great deli king Leo Steiner, it is in all fairness difficult to identify specific things that Leo insisted upon that his successors do not. That the pastrami is no longer cured on the premises could

$12–60

Address 854 7th Ave at 55th St
☎212/757-2245
Transportation B,D,E to 7th Ave;
N,Q,R,W to 57th St
Open Daily 6.30am–4am
Accepts Cash only
Reservations Not accepted

be a factor. Even so, the pastrami and corned beef are good—occasionally superb—if admittedly not, as they once were, the best in New York. And the excellent, golden, crisp-edged, crinkle-cut French fries ($3.95), introduced some five years ago, are infinitely superior to the frozen steak fries served throughout King Leo's reign. Some things stay constant, however: the service staff are as grumpy and unsmiling as ever.

The main draw, and drawback, of the Carnegie, both then and now, is the enormity of the sandwiches. The combination sandwich ($19.95) named after the prior owner, "Leo's Delightin," is a fat, triple-decker, tourist-trapping tower of turkey, corned beef, tongue, coleslaw, and Russian dressing. You can be reasonably certain Leo never touched the darn thing. (Fearful of cholesterol overdose, his daily ration was a roast chicken whose crisp skin was a minefield of garlic.) Its wrist-to-elbow width sustains the misguided but now widespread presumption equating the Jewish deli experience with unspeakable excess.

It's highly recommended that you pay the $3 sharing fee to split with your partner the corned beef sandwich ($11.95), the pastrami sandwich ($11.95), or the combination "Woody Allen" ($14.95). With six extra slices of rye bread, the Woody can easily be divided into four slender sandwiches. In that way, each of you can sample the corned beef, with its glistening beads of oily juices, as well as the peppery, appropriately fatty, and tender to the point of crumbly, pastrami. For dessert, split an order of nut and raisin sourcream rugelach ($5.95), a wedge of splendid New York cheesecake ($6.45), or the shameless combination of the two, the rugelach-crowned cheesecake draped with creamy milk chocolate ($6.95).

Cascina

To speed the gentrification of Hell's Kitchen, the rough-and-tumble district portrayed in West Side Story, property owners adopted the less incendiary name of Clinton. The mixed success of their campaign is apparent inside rustic-chic Cascina, named after co-owner Mikele DeNegri's Cascina Ordolina winery in Piedmont. Italian for "farm estate," the name suits a countrified venue of brick and brushed walls lit by candles and antique brass chandeliers. The young diners who refill the tables emptied by the pre-theater crowd are wrapped in the old-world warmth of the stone-domed, wood-burning brick oven. The ensuing charms confirm the wisdom of their moving to the neighborhood if not their acceptance of its sanitized name. Everyone still calls it Hell's Kitchen.

$21–70

Address 647 9th Ave, between 45th & 46th Sts
☎212/245-4422
Transportation A,C,E to 42nd St
Open Mon–Sat noon–midnight
Accepts All major credit cards

ITALIAN

The charisma exuded by the host seems slicker with each visit. When he persuades lovers to sit at the handsome but very public communal table up front, you suspect he's only trying to make the place look busier to curious passers-by. And when he elicits your response to a failed special like the tepid lasagna ($15), his subsequent expressions of astonishment and regret come across as patronizing. Happily, the opportunities for these are few. The gratis sundried tomato and olive oil dip has you eating well even before the fried calamari ($8.50) and wonderful grilled vegetables ($8) arrive. And the thin pizzas are splendid whether basic (cheesy Margherita; $12.50) or uncommon (sweet chicken sausage with roasted red, green, and yellow peppers; $16).

The best entrees come from that pizza oven, too. The oven-roasted, chianti-sauced veal shank ($18.50) is doubly special because it comes with a creamy risotto perfumed with pure saffron threads. Oven-roasted double pork chop ($18.50), lamb shank ($18.50), chicken in apricot sauce ($16), and whole fish (market price) serve you well. Off the grill comes a fabulous truffle-sauced filet mignon ($22). For dessert, try the sundae of bourbon-like sauce topped with sweet banana and hazelnut ice cream ($7).

There's another Cascina at 281 Bleecker St, West Village (☎212/633-2941)

Chimichurri Grill

Chef Jorge Rodriguez is forever eager to leave his confined workspace. He exits his kitchen more often than his homemade pastas and fat steaks to grab a discreet smoke at the tiny bar, greet first-timers, and share a laugh with old friends. When a host expresses such warmth for his guests it doesn't take much time or effort for them to reciprocate. The reassuring presence of Enrique Pacheco, the gracious waiter with the black vest, quickly transforms the exotic into the familiar. It's a throwback to a pre-1970s generation of small theater-district bistros that first introduced office workers, tourists, and daytrippers to foreign cuisines.

Lunch $18–45
Dinner $30–65

Address 606 9th Ave, between 43rd & 44th Sts

☎212/586-8655

Transportation A,C,E to 42nd St

Open Tues–Thurs noon–4pm & 5–11.30pm, Fri noon–4pm & 5pm–midnight, Sat 4pm–midnight, Sun 3–10.30pm

Accepts All major credit cards

Reservations Suggested

The name comes from the thin green sauce of parsley, oregano, pepper, vinegar, olive oil, and especially garlic that forms the tango rhythm of Argentine cooking. The workhorse condiment may be administered to the plump chorizo appetizer ($8.50) and the incomparably flaky empanadas (two for $8) filled with ground beef, minced olives, and raisins. Excellent appetizer alternatives include the flawlessly grilled baby calamari ($8.50) and the baked polenta ($8.50), a crisp-rimmed round of soft corncake draped with Cabrales cheese.

Due to a US ban on Argentine beef, most of the meat now comes from grass-fed Australian cattle. It's the grass that counts, insists Jorge, not the nationality. He informs anyone who'll listen that his steaks puff out on the grill and cook in half the time without shrinking back to size. No meat lover will shrink back from the hanger steak slathered with warm chimichurri and sided with burnt cauliflower ($22), or the filet mignon plated with Cabrales sauce and polenta fries ($25). Herb-crusted rack of lamb ($25) is luscious to the bone. Among hoofless alternatives are assorted pastas and grilled chicken breast, duck, or Chilean sea bass. The uneven dessert selection ($6–7.50) does feature a wonderful lavender flan and a thin, caramelized apple tart that Rodriguez himself flambés at your table.

Churrascaria Plataforma

Anyone planning a celebration at the Theater District's Brazilian-style rotisserie steakhouse can count on several things. No one will feel rushed. No one will go underfed. And no one will leave before he or she has heard "Feliz Aniversario" sung at least six times. Those repetitions, performed by a bossa nova trio, are appropriate regardless of the occasion, since every diner is fed as if it's their birthday. The salad bar, buffet,

$50–80

Address 316 West 49th St,
between 8th & 9th Aves
☎212/245-0505
Transportation C,E to 50th St
Open Daily noon–midnight
Accepts All major credit cards
Reservations Required

BRAZILIAN/STEAKHOUSE

and endless barbecued meats indulge celebrants of any age who can't get too much of a bad-for-you thing. The arena for these fixed-price excesses ($27.95 for lunch, $39.95 for dinner) is a swank, lofty banquet hall graced with a slate-tiled floor, white leatherette chairs, and brick walls punctuated by mahogany capitals. A circular bandstand divides the bar area from the dining room.

Subtle lighting over the centerpiece salad bar casts a golden glow over the likes of beef carpaccio, sliced ham, octopus salad, stuffed artichokes, and, the most recent addition, sushi. Four silver domes contain such tempting hot dishes as a saffron-scented calamari paella. One salad-bar favorite is tutu de feijao, a delectable mush of red beans, bacon, and yuca flour.

When seated, diners are given a coaster with a red rim ("stop") on one side and a green rim ("go") on the other. By keeping the red side up, diners are telling the waiters who carry around pit-barbecued meats on spits not to carve anything for them. By flipping to green, they signal them to begin the stampede. The mouth-watering variety of rotated meats is as vast as the seasoning is limited. Nearly everything is salty, a bit garlicky, and, in the case of beef, tender and medium-rare. Fattier options—brisket, lamb, skirt steak, fork-tender short ribs, top round dripping with juices—are a cut above. Among other choices are pork sausage and ribs, chicken hearts and thighs, roast beef, flank steak, and turkey wrapped in bacon. Some view the array of side dishes, including decent fried potatoes and plantains, yuca flour, black beans, and addictive fried yuca tots, as mere fillers, threatening their meat-gorging capacity.

Cité Grill

(🍴) Traveling second class has its advantages. Though this, the annex to Cité, may lack some of the breeding of that steakhouse, its informality and lower prices make it one of the better options for relaxed meals near Radio City Music Hall and various Rockefeller Center attractions. The handsome setting, with its Mediterranean tile and vine-engraved L-shaped bar, doesn't make you feel in the least bit slighted, especially since wine lovers may order

$20–80

Address 120 West 51st St, between 6th & 7th Aves
☎212/956-7262
Transportation B,D,F,V to 47th/50th Sts-Rockefeller Center; 1,9 to 50th St; N,R,W to 49th St
Open Daily 11.30am–11pm
Accepts All major credit cards

the $60 Grape Wine Dinner for which Cité is justly lauded. Sign on for that complete dinner and they keep pouring any or all of four specially selected wines until you say stop, or a caring friend says it for you. Before 8pm, when the unlimited pour is uncorked, there are good wines to choose from in the $30–40 range. You can't go wrong matching the full-bodied 1999 St. Joseph Domaine du Chene to red meat for as long as that $39 bottle is available.

The flexibility to choose just about whatever you want for the $46 prix fixe dinner rewards strategic decision-making. There's little reason to start with a sweetcorn chowder with bacon and leeks ($9 a la carte), or any other soupe du jour, when you can have instead the pan-seared crabcake ($16 a la carte) or, better yet, the astonishing lobster cocktail Dijonnaise ($17 a la carte)—no more or less than a whole, firm, and deliciously sweet 1lb, meal-in-itself lobster served cold with a Dijon mustard dressing. Likewise, unless you're mad for sauerkraut, there's little sense in choosing the $17 pastrami Reuben sandwich as a prix fixe main course over the $23 English-cut prime rib or the impeccable pink and uncharacteristically unsmall $27 filet mignon.

Then there's the burger factor. At $12 with chips (or, as a wise substitute, long and slender fries), this chubby, charbroiled, and lean beauty entails no sacrifice. Paired with the lobster cocktail it becomes a surf-and-turf of distinction. Follow that duo with the marble cake and its sidecar of Maker's Mark or banana dolce de leche ice cream ($9) and you truly are living large.

Dervish

Near Times Square, where kilo-watts are counted by the millions, this restaurant's green neon sign hardly seems glaring. Yet few theater displays are so eye-catching as the one that climbs two stories to spell "Dervish." The sign heralds yet another venue to outlast hit-and-run chef Orhan Yegen. He's the talented dervish who opened, guided, and quit two of the best Turkish addresses from the last millennium, Turkish Kitchen and Deniz à la Turk, and two of the best from the new one,

**Lunch $20–40
Dinner $30–55**

Address 146 West 47th St,
between 6th & 7th Aves
☎212/997-0070
Transportation B,D,F,V to 47th-
50th Sts-Rockefeller Center; N,R,W
to 49th St
Open Daily 11.30am–11.30pm
Accepts All major credit cards

TURKISH

Dervish and Beyoglu (see p.247). His challenge here was to convert the retro woodwork, handsome booths, and kitchen at Teatro Grill from Italian to Turkish in two days. While the resulting set-up succeeds in transplanting Turkish dining from the realm of the ethnic eatery to that of a Broadway classic, there is one drawback: the bar section is much live-lier than both the rear and mezzanine dining rooms.

The gap between front and back extends to the menu, in which, quite simply, appetizers rule. Icli kofte ($6.50) are delectably nutty stuffed meatballs enfolded in a cracked wheat crust and tahini dressing. Simi-larly appealing are the soft and sweetly fragrant topik ($5.50)—rolls of kneaded chickpeas and potato stuffed with shallots, pine nuts, and cur-rants. Pristinely pan-fried boregi ($5.50) arrive as golden, feta-cheese cigars hand-rolled in filo, while the grape leaves parceling grilled sar-dines ($7.50) take the edge off their fishiness.

A superior example of cooking en papillote is the brook trout entree baked on a brick stone ($14.50). The dainty fish steams under the cab-bage-leaf wrapping that shields its flavors and juices from the intense heat. You cannot go wrong, either, with whole char-grilled striped bass ($17.50) or the casserole of octopus, mushrooms, garlic, and tomatoes ($14.50). Scooped over a rice pilaf, its pleasures are rhapsodic. Desserts ($5) are delectable. The halvah and the almond pudding boast choice textures, but it's the custardy rice pudding that should have its name in neon. The lunch prix fixe is $13.95; the pre-theater prix fixe, $20.

Esca

The yellow walls, plush fabrics, and centerpiece vegetable/antipasti table are lovely enough, but they are clearly not the esca—Italian for "bait"—that has schools of foodies snapping at the end of the reservations line. Esca's lure is in fact the uncooked bait that the partners behind Babbo, Lupa and Otto (see p.84, p.92 & p.93), superstar chef Mario Batali and restaurateur Joe Bastianich, are dangling. Crudo (Italian for "raw food") is new to New York and much of the world, although the owners insist the raw fish specialty has a widespread and distinguished Italian past. In addition to being a great cook, chef-partner Dave Pasternak is a fanatical weekend angler. In the diner room, host-partner Simon Dean runs a tight ship with too few seats.

Lunch $30–75
Dinner $40–90

Address 402 West 43rd St at 9th Ave

☎212/564-7272

Transportation A,C,E to 42nd St

Open Mon noon–2.30pm & 5–10.30pm, Tues–Sat noon–2.30pm & 5–11.30pm, Sun 4.30–10.30pm

Accepts All major credit cards

Reservations Required

Each individual crudo is proposed as an appetizer ($11–13), much as you would have a single piece of sashimi in a Japanese restaurant. (The comparison also applies to their direct, pronounced flavors.) But it's perhaps better to order a tasting of six ($30 per person) as a first, second, or sole course. After all, this is why you and Esca are here. The exquisitely fresh fish are ingeniously marinated in a variety of spiced, infused, or garnished olive oils. Recent selections on the menu, which changes daily, have included Boston mackerel in Gaeta olive aioli, black bass with toasted pine nuts, Arctic char with pink peppercorns, and hamachi with two fennels.

Before or after the crudo you may have a sensationally clear-cut seafood pasta. Happily, the linguine with clams, hot pepper, and pancetta ($19 lunch/$22 dinner) and spaghetti with fresh mint, chiles, and 1lb of lobster ($22/$24) are available most days. The selection of baked, roasted, fried, pan-seared, or stewed fish entrees is staggering, as the prices can be when it comes to exotic (Columbia River sturgeon; $28) or imported (baked, salt-crusted branzino; $50 for two) selections. No mortal who orders the seductively salty fritto misto ("mixed fry"; $20/$24) covets his neighbor's entree. If panna cotta with caramelized pineapple is the featured dessert ($8), take the esca.

Hell's Kitchen

Is there life in Hell's Kitchen after chef Sue Torres? So far so good. With the in-house promotion to chef of Jorge Pareja, the kitchen has retained, sustained, and maintained the menu's best dishes if not the woman who developed its distinctive slant on modern, regional Mexican cuisine. The margaritas (frozen or on the rocks with fresh-squeezed lime juice and premium tequilas) are as potent and refreshing as ever. The sleekly designed joint starts jumping as early as ever and stays that way all night long. And the one serious hitch is still the same: the reservations policy can lead to long backups for tables at the short bar.

Lunch $18–45
Dinner $25–65

Address 679 9th Ave, between 46th & 47th Sts
☎212/977-1588
Transportation C,E to 50th St
Open Mon 5–11pm, Tues & Wed 11.30am–3.30pm & 5–11pm, Thurs & Fri 11.30am–3.30pm & 5pm–midnight, Sat 5pm–midnight, Sun 5–11pm
Accepts All major credit cards
Reservations Required for pre-theater dining; not accepted at other times

Patience is rewarded by the basket of grilled homemade cornbread with chile-spiked black bean spread. Don't feel constrained by the traditional, three-step eating plan (appetizer, main, sweet). While entrees like duck breast with cranberry mole and sweet potato-chipotle purée ($19) and grilled salmon with fresh corn tamale and salsa de morita ($18) show off the vibrant cooking particular to Hell's Kitchen, its fussiness is shown to better effect in smaller dimensions. It's thus better to structure a dinner around a boatlad of shared appetizers, embarking with the duck confit empanadas ($8)—scrumptious mini-pastry pockets busting at the seams with luscious, sweet-spicy shredded duck. The puddle of fig mole is a clever twist on the classic chile-based sauce. Mini-tacos stuffed with spicy chorizo and apple scotch bonnet salsa ($8) fit snugly into the palm of your hand and can be devoured in three, two, or, for the truly ambitious, one bite.

Cilantro-crusted tuna tostadas ($9) were one of Torres' signatures. Perfectly seared slices of deep, garnet-colored tuna are served on crisp corn tortillas and topped with a lively pineapple salsa and a pretty dollop of guacamole. At the other end of the scale, skip the frisbee-like quesadilla of leaden black bean epazote and goat cheese ($16). Desserts ($6–7) merit your resisting the pressure put on you by the hungry eyes of waiting diners.

211

Island Burgers and Shakes

🍴 Nobody makes a bigger deal about not serving french fries than William Brown, the guilt-ridden proprietor of Island Burgers and Shakes. His menu carries a 114-word explanation of why he doesn't serve them. "We've been hammered on it [not having fries] for years," says Brown. "We had to put an end to it." Strangely, most people would not give a hoot about the fried potato issue had Bill not made such a big deal about it. Diners adore his colorful eatery, which would be the perfect surfers' burger joint if: a) you could fit a board in the narrow shop sideways, and (b) there was a beach anywhere near Hell's Kitchen.

> ## $8–23
>
> **Address** 766 9th Ave, between 51st & 52nd Sts
> ☎212/307-7934
> **Transportation** C,E to 50th St
> **Open** Daily noon–10.30pm
> **Accepts** Cash only
> **Reservations** Not accepted

The burgers ($5.25–9) are fine. An ample amount of satisfactorily fatty beef is spread over such breads as pita, rye, dark rye, Pullman sourdough, sesame bun, and absorbent ciabatta. The last is worth the 50¢ surcharge, especially if you're going heavy on the extra toppings, which seem to number in the hundreds (in fact there are 38 combinations). Contrary to the widely held less-is-more policy regarding New York burgers, Islands' take well to piling-it-on. Burger combos like the "Saratoga" (bacon, Cheddar, horseradish, sour cream) and "Marco's" (pesto, ranch dressing, bacon, Parmesan) are highly recommended (as unappetizing as they may sound, and however you may shudder at the thought of the trial-and-error tastings process Brown must have endured to develop them).

But burgers, however good, are not up to the standard of the grilled chicken sandwiches, also known as churascos ($6.50–8.75). Your choice of extras for these is the same as it is for the burgers, and indeed many of the spicier ones—jalapeno, habanero, Cajun spices—seem to go better with the chicken. Really, everything except the horseradish goes better with the chicken. Considering all the sandwich extras, it's surprising the not-too-thick milk shakes ($3.75) only come in three or, if you're feeling bighearted, four flavors: vanilla, chocolate, strawberry, and black and white (vanilla ice cream and chocolate syrup). That's one fewer than the number of potato chip varieties.

Joe Allen

The theater directory printed on the front page of Joe Allen's menu helps pre-theater diners navigate their route to the appropriate Broadway house. The irony is that most theater-goers already acquainted with this venerable haunt pretty much know where they're going and how to get there. What's truly needed is a map on the cover of *Playbill* leading uninitiated theatergoers to Joe Allen. The brick walls, framed posters (of spectacularly miscast flops), and waiter-playing actors of this long-running, Restaurant Row hit formed

$20–60

Address 326 West 46th St, between 8th & 9th Aves
℡212/581-6464
Transportation A,C,E to 42nd St
Open Mon–Thurs noon–11.45pm, Fri noon–midnight, Sat 11.30am–midnight, Sun 11.30am–11.30pm
Accepts Visa & MasterCard
Reservations Suggested

AMERICAN

the template for theatrical pubs everywhere, among them Joe Allen outposts in London, Miami Beach, and Paris. Certain fixtures cannot be easily reproduced, however; in particular the famous people that regularly occupy its bentwood chairs. If management framed all its credit-card receipts since 1965, it could display one of Broadway's best autograph collections. Better still, we'd discover who was a bigger tipper, Al Pacino or Nathan Lane.

Few would think to copy the second and third pages of the menu with their lists of basic American bistro fare with some contemporary flourishes. The finest of these, a corn leek pancake with smoked salmon and sour cream ($10), works best as a shared appetizer or bar snack, maybe accompanied by a glass of sparkling wine (Mumm Napa is $7). Other good bets include the decent Caesar salad ($7 as a prologue; $12 as the main act) or black bean soup ($6).

Ordering the burger (at $10, the least expensive entree) does not label you as an unemployed actor or bankrupt impresario. It shows only that you recognize quality. A request for the grilled sirloin ($24), on the other hand, could be more easily taken as a faux pas. The kitchen does stage a surefire turkey, as contradictory as that sounds—a roasted breast with country-style cornbread stuffing and cranberry relish ($18)—and there are a couple of sure-ticket sandwiches (both $11): meatloaf on sourdough, and grilled chicken with Cajun mayo and grilled onions on ciabatta. As encores, the upstart hot fudge pudding cake a la mode upstages the immortal banana cream pie (both $7).

PIZZA

John's Pizzeria

Several years ago, a young Belgian tourist boarded a Manhattan-bound A train at the Howard Beach-JFK Airport station, set down his two-ton backpack, and asked a passenger for directions. "Does this train go to John's Pizza?" he asked, only mildly surprised the Transit Authority cartographers had pinpointed Central Park and Yankee Stadium but not Bleecker Street's landmark pizzeria on its subway map. "Will Woody Allen be there tonight?" How joyful he would be today, seated in the newest location of that Village eatery which,

<table>
<tr><td colspan="2">$15–40</td></tr>
<tr><td>Address 260 West 44th St, between 7th & 8th Aves; plus other locations</td></tr>
<tr><td>☎212/391-7560</td></tr>
<tr><td>Transportation 1,2,3,7,9,N,Q,R,S,W to Times Square-42nd St; A,C,E to 42nd St</td></tr>
<tr><td>Open Daily 11.30am–11.30pm</td></tr>
<tr><td>Accepts All major credit cards</td></tr>
<tr><td>Reservations Not accepted</td></tr>
</table>

spectacularly housed in the old Gospel Tabernacle Church in the heart of the theater district, is revered by Broadway's pizza apostles as their Cathedral of St John the Divine. The Belgian zealot, like other locals and foreigners making the same pizza pilgrimage, might not notice, much less care, if John's classic Margherita pie topped only with mozzarella and tomato and baked in a coal-fired oven had slipped a notch or two.

The pizza pies ($11 and up) at the Times Square John's, like that at the other branches, are still pretty good. The 400-plus diners who, during pre-theater hours, vie for seats in the tables and booths below its stained-glass cupola are not knuckleheads. But, sadly, the reputation of this institution far exceeds its performance. The tomato sauce is runny and a tad bland. And the mozzarella, though adequately soft and creamy, needs a sprinkling of grated Romano or Parmigiano *before* the pie is baked. Fortunately, the four brick ovens do still turn out the beautifully charred crusts that have been a hallmark of John's since 1929. When a John's pie is right you have to tear off bitefuls with your teeth. At its best it is crisp, not brittle. Its air pockets compress to the chew. It's irresistible with no more coverage than a drizzle of olive oil.

Desserts ($6) brought in from the Little Pie Company, including a superb ricotta cheesecake and three-berry pie, show a pursuit of excellence and consistency less evident at the pizza stations.

Marseille

(🍴) In 1940–41, New Yorker Varian Fry
secured safe passage to America
for more than 1200 refugees holed up in
Marseille. Had Warner Brothers turned
his exploits into a Humphrey Bogart
movie, its intrigue might have revolved
around a grand cafe in the mold of Fran-
cophile restaurateur Simon Oren's bistro
fantasy. Nancy Mah, a hot designer
whose restaurants resemble Hollywood
movie sets, transformed a corner space
in the Film Center Building into a
beguiling period set suggestive of
French-Mediterranean style and mystery.
With vaguely Moorish arches bending

**Lunch $22–55
Dinner $35–75**

Address 630 9th Ave at 44th St
☏212/333-2323
Transportation A,C,E to 42nd St
Open Mon noon–3pm &
5.15–11pm, Tues–Fri noon–3pm &
5.15–11.30pm, Sat 11am–3pm &
5.15–11.30pm, Sun noon–3pm &
5.15–10pm
Accepts All major credit cards
Reservations Suggested

MEDITERRANEAN

over burgundy banquettes and exquisite Moroccan tiling, the one omission is a Nordic beauty to play the Ingrid Bergman role.

Chef Alex Urena's depiction is likewise loose and romanticized. The
enduring ties between Provence's seaport city and its Mediterranean
neighbors serves as his pretext to merge and modernize French, Spanish,
Italian, and North African flavors. His skilled approach is first reflected in
single-nibble mezze platters cleverly plated in rectangular rows. The fish
mezze ($9) might contain a boquerone (Spanish anchovy) and asparagus
terrine, a brandade croquette, and salmon gravlax. Its meat counterpart
($8) may achieve similar feats for Serrano ham, poached foie gras, and
chorizo. The same artifice imbues superior appetizers like wild mushroom soup with Parmesan foam ($9) and sautéed sweetbreads with
Brussels sprouts and caramelized leeks ($12).

The bouillabaisse ($26) wants to be genuine, but as good as Urena's
fish stew is, its seafood assortment and soup are simply too clean. They've
got no grit. Roasted duck breast ($22), Moroccan seafood burger ($18),
and braised short ribs and beef cheeks with hummus and horseradish jus
($25) are rooted only in the kitchens—Blue Hill (see p.86), Bouley, El
Bulli—listed on Urena's impressive resumé. How the crunchy chocolate
peanut butter tart with celery sorbet ($7) found its way to Marseille is a
mystery. But you'll be glad it did.

Molyvos

With its $34.50 pre-theater menu served one-half block from Carnegie Hall, Molyvos is a superior option for pre-performance dining. Still, it's painful to relegate a visit here to the role of preliminary entertainment. From the food to the decor to the service, few restaurants get it as right as this urbane Greek taverna. With considerable passion, the Livanos family decorated the deep space of terracotta-brushed walls and Mediterranean tiling with vintage photographs, colored bottles, ceramics, and curios. And by dividing the dining area into smaller zones, the effect is at once intimate and expansive, casual and well turned out.

Lunch $30–65
Dinner $35–80

Address 871 7th Ave, between 55th & 56th Sts
☏212/582-7500
Transportation F,N,R,Q,W to 57th St; 1,9,A,B,C,D to 59th St-Columbus Circle
Open Sun–Fri noon–2.30pm & 5–11.30pm, Sat noon–2.30pm & 5pm–12.30am
Accepts All major credit cards
Reservations Suggested

The food is a combination of classic and what top young chefs like Molyvos' Jeff Botsacos like to call "progressive" dishes. The latter are not in this instance fusion or Frenchified inspirations so much as inventive ways to approach, associate, and animate traditional regional ingredients. The menu neither offends old purists nor bores young trendies who, at Molyvos, frequently sit at the same family table. It's tempting to make an entire meal out of mezedes (small plates). Grilled asparagus stands in for gigante beans in a classic combo of exceptionally creamy skordalia (whipped potatoes and garlic) set against unusually crunchy beets ($8.25). The wood-grilled baby octopus with fennel, lemon, and greens ($10.50) is a fragrant standout. The $7.50 charge for the sampler of the customary but hardly ordinary spreads—roasted eggplant, fish roe mousse, cucumber-yogurt—should be as certain a dinner-check fixture as sales tax.

You may choose to zero in on seafood entrees, perhaps a special of pan-seared black bass with fava beans and sautéed wild mushrooms folded into spring onions ($25), steamed salmon wrapped in grape leaves ($19.50), or simply grilled whole fish ($25–30). But grilled baby lamb chops ($23.50) will also delight. Desserts ($7.50), like creamy rice pudding topped with sour cherry preserves and foamed milk or semolina cake saturated with orange-vanilla syrup, epitomize the rare blend of new and old that is Molyvos.

Orso

To best absorb the backstage buzz of this theater district haunt, you need to reserve weeks in advance for a pre-curtain or post-applause table. To reassure yourself that the trattoria of Restaurant Row co-habitant Joe Allen (see p.213) has not actually been buried in a 1980s time capsule, it's better to dine off-peak, between 8pm and 10.30pm. Without the cast of luminaries to blur your starry-eyed vision, Orso reveals itself to be a cozy, tasteful, and densely staffed stomping ground. When, during the pre-theater rush, the waiter who's just uncorked your Montelpulciano recites, "We let you serve your own wine," it's easy to assume that the hurried staff cannot be bothered with refilling glasses. Only during quieter hours can the policy be appreciated as a welcome informality.

$35–80

Address 322 West 46th St, between 8th & 9th Aves
℡212/489-7212
Transportation A,C,E to 42nd St
Open Mon, Tues, Thurs & Fri noon–11.45pm, Sat, Sun & Wed 11.30am–11.45pm
Accepts MasterCard & Visa
Reservations Required

ITALIAN

Sandy walls and pale gray wainscoting give the low, narrow room a bleached-out look. It's as if the sunburst lamps were emitting color-fading UV rays. Fronting the kitchen, four terracotta planters are overstuffed with the crusty breads that will be grooved (but not sliced through) before they and their white bean spread reach your table. Tables are set with colorful Solimene ceramics; the slow revelation of their colorful, vibrant design stems somewhat the sadness of clearing slice by slice one of the crisp, divinely light, thin-crusted pizzas ($14.50). These are typically ordered as a shared appetizer in lieu of or in addition to one of several interesting salads ($8–10).

When Orso first opened, pastas like the ravioli filled with minced salt cod, raisins, and artichokes ($19) or fusilli with porcini, broccoli rabe, hot peppers, and shaved ricotta salata ($17.50) were new and exciting. Now they're merely good. It has become harder, too, to get worked up about the perfectly fine Prosecco sauce for roasted tilapia ($23) or the gorgonzola polenta purée that sits under crumbling pieces of braised chicken ($21). It's no real fault of Orso—perhaps the dishes are simply too familiar. If you prefer your desserts (8.50–9) sweet rather than cloying, take risotto pudding over caramel bread pudding.

Pietrasanta

In review blurbs covering the Italian restaurants around the Theater District and Hell's Kitchen, "great value" generally means cramped and rushed; "rustic" translates as trendy, pricey, and overbooked; and "quaint" is a euphemism for twenty-minute pastas and straw-bottle chiantis. But an entirely separate glossary is required to explain the appeal of affordable, friendly, and hopelessly unfashionable Pietrasanta. In a strange instance of reverse restaurant psychology, the faux marble walls and

$20–55
Address 683 9th Ave at 47th St
☎212/265-9471
Transportation C,E to 50th St
Open Sun & Mon noon–10.30pm, Tues noon–11pm, Wed 11am–11pm, Thurs noon–11pm, Fri noon–midnight, Sat 11.30am–midnight
Accepts All major credit cards

unsightly dropped ceiling manage to entice rather than ward off hungry, pre-theater passers-by. The assumption is that if a place as unconcerned with appearances as Pietrasanta is crowded, it has to be for the food, value, and service. In this instance at least, the assumption is correct.

Nary a table goes without the homemade mozzarella, either fresh with roasted peppers ($6.95), pan-fried ($5.95) within the spinach fettuccine alla pietrasanta (with zucchini, peas, and a tomato cream sauce; $13.95), or melted atop a pizza ($10.95). The pizzas, though decent, are hard to classify, falling as they do somewhere between a classic New York pie and a more generic variety. The extra zip of the Gorgonzola and grilled eggplant pie has the edge over the flatter-tasting Margherita. Grilled eggplant also brings allure to the baked bread topped with olive and tomato ($6.50).

If you're going to have a homemade pasta (that's a given) and a cream sauce (debatable), the pre-eminent pairing is the gnocchi with wild mushrooms ($10.95). Alternatives can be overproduced or basically too rich, as is true of the farfalle with salmon, basil, and sage ($15.95). But any inclination to favor simpler main-course options is challenged by the giddy pleasure of sautéed chicken breast with pancetta, smoked salmon, and a pink vodka sauce ($15.95)—a dish once accurately praised by a kind waitress, a third-year student of Pietrasanta's reverse psychology, as "weird and misleadingly good." Otherwise, the variations on veal scaloppine ($14.95–16.95) are sure bets, as is the grilled and commendably straightforward salmon ($19.95).

Redeye Grill

Redeye is a high-flying brasserie ideally suited for anytime, any-appetite, any-way-you-are suppers. It has partially supplanted Petrossian, the Carnegie Deli (p.204) and the defunct Russian Tea Room as the haven around Carnegie Hall for late-night smoked fish. Its pastrami smoked salmon club ($16.95) takes on two Carnegie Deli titans—pastrami and smoked salmon—in a single, overstuffed bagel. Decadent seafood platters and muraled columns painted with lascivious New York fantasies seem inspired by another legendary haunt,

$30–85

Address 890 7th Ave, between 56th & 57th Sts
☏212/541-9000
Transportation F,N,Q,R,W to 57th St
Open Mon–Wed
11.30am–11.30pm, Thurs–Sat
11.30am–12.30am, Sun
11am–11pm
Accepts All major credit cards
Reservations Suggested

AMERICAN/SEAFOOD

Paris' La Coupole. The intelligentsia can go ahead and debate the symbolism in the mural of three nudes romping atop the Chrysler Building with a toy globe. We're hungry.

Appetizers assembled at the "Dancing Shrimp" carpaccio/sushi/salad bar include nine kinds of smoked fish ($11–14), none more dazzling than the smoked sturgeon drizzled with white truffle oil. That sturgeon can get to be an expensive habit. Sashimi and smoked fish are combined in four irresistible maki rolls ($11.95–12.75), one juxtaposing jalapeno, smoked salmon, and yellowfin tuna. The grilled shrimp and chorizo quesadilla ($9.95) and the popped rock shrimp with a hot pineapple sauce ($13.50) are surefire picks.

The kitchen is especially adept at keeping grilled fish moist and tender. Each fish entree, ranging from $21.95 for Atlantic salmon to $24.95 for Gulf red snapper, comes with a stuffed baked potato, a vegetable, and a trio of sauces: tomato-basil, lemon pesto, and green herb. Lobster comes many ways, including within a cioppino (Ligurian fish stew; $32.50) also stocked with Alaska king crab, mussels, and shrimp. If you don't feel like fish, the steaks, chops, and main-course salads (some of them smoked fish extravaganzas), are huge. Atop a dessert tray, a scoop of Crisco-simulated cream and a whole, unpeeled banana stand as a representation of the truly outstanding banana cream pie ($8.95). The strawberry shortcake and the warm apple pie (both $8.95) are great too, despite their whimsical displays—some people are here more for the whimsy than the food in any case. There's live jazz most nights after 9pm.

PAN-ASIAN

Ruby Foo's

(icon) R-U-B-Y F-O-O'-S is a block-let-tered blockbuster heralding a new Broadway adaptation of an old Hollywood fantasy of a Chinese dining palace. More than fifty years ago, the restaurateur Ruby Foo opened Chinese joints in Boston, Miami, and New York, and today the name awakens a sentimental longing for a notorious, palatial icon that exists only in our collective imagination. In a spectacular, 300-seat, 7000-square-foot interior distinguished by mah-jong-tiled

$30–75

Address 1626 Broadway at 49th St
(T)212/489-5600
Transportation 1,9 to 50th St;
N,R,W to 49th St
Open Sun–Wed 11.30am–midnight,
Thurs–Sat 11.30am–1am
Accepts All major credit cards
Reservations Suggested

walls, dynastic statues on lacquered displays, and magnificent, orange-glass lanterns with hanging tassels, designer Nancy Mah surpassed anything Fu Manchu-creator Sax Rohmer or Charlie Chan-author Earl Derr Biggers might have envisioned.

Opened in 2000, the self-defined "dim sum and sushi palace," like the year-older original on the Upper West Side (2182 Broadway; (T)212/724-6700), exhibits its executive producer's amazing knack for knowing what and how a particular demographic of New York wants to eat. Stephen Hanson (Atlantic Grill and Ocean Grill; see p.246 and p.275) figured he'd run up checks faster with sushi and Chinese-Thai-Malaysian-Japanese "dim sum" than with straight Chinese. You can find better and cheaper interpretations of yellowtail-scallion maki ($8.50) and steamed vegetable dumplings ($5.95) elsewhere, but not together in a tourist magnet as singularly entertaining and convenient to the theater district as this.

Waitresses rightly counsel you to eat tapas-style, sharing such appetizers as toothsome teriyaki-sesame sea bass with wakame seaweed salad ($7.95); tamarind-glazed baby back ribs ($7.95); delectably puffy wedges of goat cheese tempura with greens and a tart-spicy sesame-chile dressing ($8.50), and a side of soft tofu cubes with a hot, chile-spiced garlic sauce ($4.95). From "main plates," wok-fried jumbo shrimp with pepper lime sauce and coconut sticky rice ($19.50) is exactly the kind of scrumptious junk you want to be eating here. Same for the ingenious dessert sampler ($7.50), a bento box of chocolate cake, cherry sundae, and sushi-shaped morsels (wasabi marzipan, for example) to dip in chocolate sauce.

Seppi's

🍴 What is Seppi's doing with a name like Seppi's? And why is Seppi's doing whatever it's doing with the name Seppi's at the Parker Meridien Hotel? Such questions are unavoidable when you choose an Italian name and Carnegie Hall/City Center location for a SoHo-styled French bistro. Yet the moniker and address suit a fish-out-of-water restaurant that maintains an island of late-night, downtown cool in a sea of midtown uptightness. The stamped tin walls, black-and-white leather booths, slate-board menus, butcher-paper-topped

Lunch $25–75
Dinner $35–80

Address 123 West 56th St, between 6th & 7th Aves
☎212/708-7444
Transportation F,N,Q,R,W to 57th St
Open Mon–Fri 11.30am–4.30pm & 5.30pm–1.45am, Sat 5pm–1.45am, Sun 10.30am–1.45am
Accepts All major credit cards
Reservations Suggested

FRENCH

tables, and informal service certainly suit a spin-off of the perennially popular SoHo bistro Raoul's. Seppi's is named after the father of brothers Serge and Guy Raoul.

While the bulk of Seppi's menu is classic French prepared with flair, chef/co-owner Claude Alain Souilliard honors his partners' Italian heritage with several dishes, most notably a melt-in-your-mouth osso buco with saffron risotto ($25). For starters, a mint-accented celery root remoulade cradled in endive leaf enlivens lamb pâté ($8). Escargot in buttery garlic sauce ($9) reaches the table piping hot in its baking dish. Among entrees, the shiitake-stuffed baby chicken ($20) is sawed in half to give you a peek at the juicy filling, while succulent duck breast ($24) is advantageously plated with a sweet potato gratin, and a black-pepper-corn-slathered steak au poivre ($26) comes with first-rate frites. In a stellar fish dish, two grilled daurade fillets are propped over cumin-dusted root vegetables on a plate painted red with a beet-and-sumac sauce ($24)—the last vestiges of Seppi's Middle Eastern period.

Downtown dessert impulses and excesses ($7–15) are as uninhibited as ever. A chestnut napoleon is layered with the densest chestnut cream imaginable and garnished with a sticky-sweet fig sauce. Crème caramel is flanked by two big balls of ultra-rich whipped cream. And both chocolate options—warm, nearly flourless cake and a Black Forest tower—possess a shameless degree of cocoa pleasure.

AMERICAN

Sha La Gourmet

(🍴) Wholesome, homey food on Broadway, just steps away from 42nd Street? Sounds highly unlikely, which is why denizens of the theater and garment districts treasure this little shop, which from the outside looks no different from so many other takeout shops that clutter Manhattan. It is, for sure, mainly a sandwich, salad, and hot-table business, sending luncheon orders to the fashion showrooms and shops on the surrounding streets. The difference here is

$6–20
Address 1435 Broadway, between 40th & 41st Sts
☎212/869-9414
Transportation 1,2,3,7,9,N,Q,R,S,W to 42nd St-Times Square
Open Mon–Fri 6am–6pm
Accepts Cash only
Reservations Not accepted

Abe and Vera, the owners. They run Sha La as a personal canteen, with five tables for two set against the wall opposite the food cases. Of course no one will mind if you pull up a third chair. You can't miss Abe. He is generally sitting at his desk at the back of the long, narrow storefront, often eating his own food. A good sign.

Vera, presiding over the hot table, knows most of her customers by name. To one she will recommend the vegetable burgers ($6.50 for a platter) that "just came out of the fryer." To another, she'll say "the brisket [$6.50 for a platter] is particularly good today." Vera knows who dotes on her creamy macaroni and cheese ($4); who habitually takes a slab of the moist baked salmon ($9); who likes turkey meatloaf ($7); who orders corned beef ($5) only when the meat is fatty; and who is willing to chance a new creation. There is always hot, freshly roasted turkey breast with a crust of rosemary—for sandwiches ($6.50) or to be customized into a plate with salad and/or vegetables ($8).

Further down the line is the cold station, where Sha La's manager, Salim, supervises the sandwich and salad making. On any kind of bread, including lavosh wraps, you can have freshly cooked strips of chicken breast dressed with nothing but Hellmann's mayonnaise and diced celery ($5.95), or shrimp salad, cold cuts, or cheeses. Besides green salad, there are several bean and grain salads, tomato and onion, and cucumber with dill. Don't ignore the bakery counter as you leave. Stop for an espresso or soft-serve ice cream, and some of the best cakes, pastries, and cookies in midtown.

Shelly's New York

If restaurants could be evaluated by how successfully they indulge their owners' whims, Shelly Fireman's flights of fancy (Redeye Grill, see p.219) would hover in the four-star stratosphere. This brasserie firmly establishes the Bronx native as Manhattan's crown prince of upper-crust cravings. Local kids of advancing age recognize Shelly's as the birthday-bash venue their parents could neither afford nor endure. The one-time Automat and, most recently, Motown Café has been transformed into a four-story funhouse emblazoned with what teenagers, current and former, consider to be great art. Peter Max abstracts adorn the walls behind the dining room's comfy banquettes and half-moon booths. A circular mural painted by Red Grooms shows a motley ensemble of voracious New York characters.

Lunch $30–70
Dinner $40–80

Address 104 West 57th St, between 6th & 7th Aves
☎212/245-2422
Transportation F,N,Q,R to 57th St
Open Mon–Thurs
11.30am–11.30pm, Fri & Sat
11.30am–12.30am, Sun
11am–10.30pm
Accepts All major credit cards
Reservations Suggested

AMERICAN/SEAFOOD

The kitchen pampers grownups with longstanding, deep-rooted aversions to the word "no." Among its many fat-enriched highlights is a thick and exceptionally buttery New England clam chowder ($7) and, as starters or sides, gooey, crusty, ham-fortified macaroni and cheese ($8) and the creamiest of creamed spinaches ($7). There are tiered platters ($65/$122) displaying lobster, jumbo shrimp, Alaskan king crab legs, oysters, and stone crabs over ice. The sweet and meaty stone crabs, air-freighted up from Florida, may be ordered a la carte for a small fortune—$23–41/lb. Entrees include 30oz and 50oz porterhouse steaks ($39/$65). Good, leaner options include sesame-seared salmon ($20) and miso-glazed Chilean sea bass ($24). The showstopper dessert is a large glass bowl containing ice cream, chocolate ganache, cookie crumbs, a massive dollop of whipped cream, and a jumbo wooden spoon for mixing and mashing them together. It can be ordered as part of the $35-per-person sharing deal, which includes an oyster platter or seafood salad and the porterhouse.

The best thing about brunch (entrees $12–24) at Shelly's is the breakfast pantry, with its zucchini cheese mini-muffins and crispy puff-pastry palmiers. The chocolate chocolate-chip French toast ($13) is marvelously frivolous, and the banana cream pie is outstanding.

Tuscan Square

(🍴) No one need ever again schlep all the way over to Italy to enjoy the untold riches of Florence and Siena and their surrounding vineyards, olive groves, and marble quarries. Today the Tuscan countryside has been assembled in a midtown food mall. The mogul behind this Planet Tuscany is restaurateur Pino Luongo (Le Madri, Coco Pazzo). Here his core business expands from wines and prepared foods to include clothing, table linens, and beauty products. It's one-stop shopping for Tuscan totebags, tagliolini, towels, and toothpaste. But as easy as it is to ridicule this theme park, there's no

**Lunch $15–70
Dinner $35–85**

Address 16 West 51st St at Rockefeller Plaza
☎212/977-7777
Transportation B,D,F,V to 47th-50th Sts-Rockefeller Center; E to 5th Ave
Open Mon–Fri 11.30am–3.30pm & 5–10pm, Sat noon–3.30pm & 5–10pm
Accepts All major credit cards

denying the good taste of Luongo and his team. Nearly every inch of the two-level, 12,000-square-foot space has style. The casual 120-seat restaurant is squeezed in behind a grand, curving staircase leading down to the marketplace, gourmet takeout counter, and open kitchen below. And if you like what you're eating or, better still, what you're spilling it on, you can buy practically all of it on your way out.

The marketplace centers on a handsome salad bar where bottles of extra virgin olive oil hang on an iron rod and swing down like foozball men to give your salad a kick. There's a brick pizza oven and a pasta station where fresh ravioli is cut from long sheets, and an eating counter where video terminals allow you to watch your lunch being prepared. No one is sticking pinkies into saucepans here! The marketplace's weekend lunch options are handier and less expensive than the restaurant's. Pizzas are $9.50 and up, while lunch boxes with two of the following—soup, fruit, pasta salad, antipasto plate, half-sandwich—cost just $10.

At the restaurant, prix fixe lunches and dinners have been replaced with an a la carte menu. The flexibility better suits the needs of Rockefeller Center office workers, shoppers, and tourists. A grilled squid and radicchio lunch plate ($10) or, at dinner, the penne with sausage, sun-dried tomatoes, fresh ricotta, and tomato sauce ($15) is often enough. And the 32oz rib-eye ($38) is patently more than enough—except, maybe, for the gourmands with the guts to order it.

Vice Versa

The Italians have marched into Paris, or at least the theater district's version of it. Years from today, Franco Lazzari, Daniele Kucera, and Stefano Terzi, all alumni of Central Park South's San Domenico, may be remembered as the brave rivoluzionari who infiltrated the north side of West 51st Street's 300 block and ended decades of dominance by pre-theater escargots and after-the-curtain chocolate mousses. And quite apart from breaking the Gallic time warp, Vice Versa's lasting contribution may be affordable sophistication. Superior in quality, comfort, and service to the pasta cafes on Ninth Avenue and more economical than established favorites like Orso (see p.217), Vice Versa fills an important gap.

Lunch $25–55
Dinner $40–75

Address 325 West 51st St, between 8th & 9th Aves
☎212/399-9291
Transportation C,E to 50th St
Open Mon–Fri noon–2.30pm & 5–11pm, Sat 5–11pm
Accepts All major credit cards
Reservations Suggested

ITALIAN

The dining room is sleek and stylishly understated, and the Italian cooking is rustic, flavor-focused, and of the moment. Chef Terzi borrows from all the right places: tonnato (tuna sauce) from Sicily, duck ragu from Tuscany, warm flourless chocolate cake from NYC. His antipasti collection is led by the pan-fried tortino (pie) of artichokes and calamari loosely bound by flour and garlic ($11.50). Other pleasing starters include a semolina flan with taleggio cheese and mushrooms ($12.50) and a green lentil soup advantageously corrupted with pancetta ($8.50).

As befits a San Domenico veteran, Terzi prepares three sensational pastas: long twists of strozzapreti ("strangled priest") tangle with a fabulously chunky duck ragu laced with carrots, fennel, and black olives ($13.50). The ravioli-like casoncelli are stuffed with ground veal and, for a hint of sweetness, amaretto cookies, and then topped with brown butter, sage, and Parmigiano ($14). Spinach tagliatelle take on the sweetest possible mussels, Manila clams, scallops, and tomato ($13.50). One meat dish of comparable quality is the thick veal medallions bronzed to perfection and plated with a dreamy Parmigiano cream sauce ($23.50). When it comes to desserts ($6–7.50), you'll be safe with tiramisu and pear tart. But who cares for security when red currant-sauced espresso semifreddo and a devilishly creamy pistachio panna cotta with apricot sauce have broken the French frontier?

Virgil's Real Barbecue

The 10,000-mile fact-finding tour that took the founders of Virgil's to 100 barbecue joints from Tennessee to Texas was surely one heck of a road trip, but it may not have been the wisest way to formulate a recipe. The best regional styles don't always travel easily across a county, let alone a country, and don't take well to amalgamation: smoked ham from Maryland, beef brisket from Texas, mustard sauce from South Carolina. Such give and take, however commendable, ultimately comes off as a phony and noncommittal. In the end, the crucial piece of Virgil's geography is Times Square. You won't find any place accommodating larger groups with bigger food and finer brews for more moderate prices in a better party atmosphere any closer to the crossroads of the world.

$20–65

Address 152 West 44th St, between Broadway & 6th Ave
℡212/921-9494
Transportation 1,2,3,7,N,Q,R,S,W to Times Square-42nd St; B,D,F,V to 42nd St
Open Sun & Mon 11.30am–11pm, Tues–Sat 11.30am–midnight
Accepts All major credit cards

The two-level space is a handsome shrine to American barbecue, with photos on the walls and a map delineating the owners' favorite BBQ joints printed on the placemats. (Out of modesty or, more likely, honesty, they've excluded their own.) Make no mistake, Virgil's favorably fatty, beautifully crusted, hickory-, oak- and fruitwood-smoked meat that falls off those ribs ($19.95) is tender and smoky, almost too smoky. It's darn decent barbecue and clearly preferable to the dry and tough brisket ($17). The pig-out portions both of the entrees and the sides (good potato salad, fries, beans) that come with them push your digestive capacity to the breaking point.

You'll do fine if you stick with appetizers and sandwiches. The crisp, cornmeal-coated, scallion-specked hush puppies with maple butter are great ($5.95), and the loopy buttermilk onion rings with creamy blue cheese dip ($6.50) are pretty good if delivered fresh from the frying hopper. Pulled pork on a sesame seed bun ($10.50) is gently spicy and smoky and can be easily doused to taste with Memphis hot sauce. With desserts ($5.95) you need to choose carefully. The fluffy peanut butter pie is exactly what you want it to be, whereas the gooey, cloying pecan pie and doubly dense chocolate cheese pie are unyielding.

Murray Hill and Kips Bay

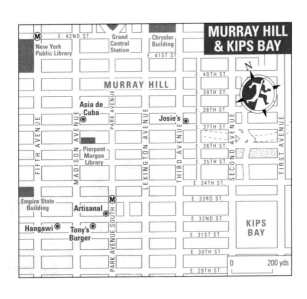

Artisanal

🍴 Who would have thought the combined stench of 200-plus different cheeses could lure capacity crowds to one of Manhattan's notoriously cursed restaurant spaces? Terrance Brennan, that's who. The chef of the acclaimed Mediterranean restaurant Picholine made his fromagerie the centerpiece attraction at what became, seemingly seconds after its spring 2001 opening, one of New York's most bustling brasseries. Adam Tihany's Deco design bestows jazz age romance upon aged Gouda, Berkshire blue, Colston Bassett Stilton, and—

Lunch $18–70
Dinner $32–80

Address 2 Park Ave at 32nd St
☎212/725-8585
Transportation 6 to 33rd St
Open Mon–Thurs 11.45am–11pm,
Fri 11.45am–midnight, Sat
11.30am–midnight, Sun
11.30am–11pm
Accepts All major credit cards
Reservations Required

would you believe it?—fondue. The upbeat mood for the 160 diners seated on cane chairs and banquettes is set by vintage posters, moderne lighting fixtures, and, underfoot, the black, gold, and burgundy syncopation of the geometric tiles.

Brennan takes fondue to the limit, with seven varieties (among them Stilton with Sauternes and Fontina with white truffle oil) and, to supplement the bread cubes, six "baigneuses" (beef tips, potatoes, kielbasa, etc). These first-rate fondues almost surmount the intrinsic fondue problem—diminishing returns, where the second dip never tastes as good as the first. Even so, it's best to relegate the fondues to the bar. If you must get an early cheese fix, order the sensational, three-fromage French onion soup ($8.50) or a basket of gougères (cheese puffs; $6/$9).

If you choose to ignore cheese altogether you can still have a truly great meal. The moules marinière ($9.50) or the garlicky escargot pastries ($10.50) are particularly good. Though limp frites detract from the steak options, the brasserie fare, with its French-Mediterranean accents, can be exceptional: pan-crisped skate with a blood orange butter sauce ($17.50), say, or venison steak au poivre with a grain of squash and prune ($25). As for the delectably crisp yet succulent chicken cooked under a brick ($19.50)—you could sample thirty cheeses at Artisanal and still leave talking about this one dish. If concluding with a cheese plate at America's greatest cheese restaurant is not already a no-brainer, the bland desserts make it so.

Asia de Cuba

Better to surrender to the seductions of a glamorous hotspot like the Morgans Hotel's Asia de Cuba than fight them. Leave the rational considerations—do you get your money's worth? Are there dishes you'd go back for? Would you enjoy the coffee-lacquered duck as much if you tried it at a Polynesian supper club in Piscataway?—to the spoilsports. Designer Philippe Starck and dining impresario Jeffrey Chowdorow have devised a stylish platform for some very amusing "Chino-Latino" experiments. The 50ft marble slab that slashes the center of this balconied exhibition hall

$40–90

Address 237 Madison Ave, between 37th & 38th Sts
℡212/726-7755
Transportation 7 to 5th Ave; 4,5,6 to 42nd St-Grand Central
Open Mon–Thurs noon–3pm & 5.30–11pm, Fri noon–3pm & 5.30pm–midnight, Sat 5.30pm–midnight, Sun 5.30–11pm
Accepts All major credit cards
Reservations Required

is less a two-sided communal dining counter than a fashion runway. With leatherette chairs and crescent-shaped booths surrounded by white curtains, it's either Starck's vision of heaven or merely a way station on the steep ascent. Waiters in Maoist jackets bring you technicolor cocktails, repeatedly change your grease-absorbing napkins, and rightly advise you that all servings are sized to be shared family-style.

The menu does not divide the two cultures in the same way as the Cuban-Chinese eateries of Upper Broadway (see Flor de Mayo; p.271). The fusion here has no trade barriers, dealing freely in wonton chips and plantain crisps, Asian mushrooms and Caribbean spices. The standout starter is Thai beef salad with seared rounds of beef carpaccio, oranges, avocado, crisp curls of twice-baked coconut, and a lightly creamed chipotle dressing ($18). Fried calamari salad is a trove of tiny ringlets buried in chicory, banana, and chayote ($17.50), while the excess of the foie gras empanada ($25) is only to be applauded.

Entrees should be shared and shared just once. The lacquered duck with a blood orange vinaigrette ($29 for half a duck) is initially yummy, but has limited staying power. Succulent, grilled, mojito-glazed rib steak tingles with a sake- and foie gras-enriched mango sauce ($42). Cuban-spiced roast chicken ($28) is about as straightforward as it gets. Among desserts (about $10), surrender if you must to the guava mousse in a chocolate tuile or the towering chocolate coconut layer cake.

Hangawi

Usually when you are advised to dine on the late side, it's to correspond with the time when the energy and noise levels of some stylish haunt are nearing their peak. Here, the advantage of reserving for 9pm or after is just the opposite. The zen-like tranquility of this vegetarian shrine, with its low tables, colorful seat cushions, New Age folk music, antique artifacts, heavy ceramics, and framework of wood, stone, and copper, is defeated by the dinner-hour din. True balance between yin and yang or, in Korean, um and yang, is not achieved until the crowd thins and the clamor fades. Only when you can hear the patter of the servers' slippered feet against the wood-planked walkway does Hangawi begin to feel like the remote, peaceful, mountain retreat it was so meticulously designed to resemble.

**Lunch $14–60
Dinner $30–65**

Address 12 East 32nd St, between Madison & 5th Aves
☎212/213-0077
Transportation 6 to 33rd St
Open Mon–Thurs noon–3pm & 5–10.30pm, Fri noon–3pm & 5–11pm, Sat 1–11pm, Sun 1–10pm
Accepts All major credit cards
Reservations Suggested

KOREAN/VEGETARIAN

Chef Steven Chung's menu can be appreciated at any hour, providing your inseam is 36 inches or less (legroom is minimal) and you're wearing the appropriate hosiery (shoes must be checked at the entrance). The most comprehensive introduction to his cuisine, with its emphasis on carrots, radishes, root grains, potatoes, and tofu, are the multi-course, prix fixe lunches ($19.95/$24.95/$34.95) and dinners ($29.95/$34.95). A la carte ordering, however, gives you more flexibility. Either way, few diners skip one soothing porridge ($3.95) or another, in such clear-flavored varieties as pumpkin or delicious black sesame. Eschew the spoon and instead pick up the bowl: the rice-thickened texture seduces your upper lip as the hot soup slides in under. Among the other appetizers, all of them elegantly assembled, are skewers of oyster mushrooms and scallions ($8.95), and a crunchy salad with bean paste, lemon dressing, and the gently bitter perfume of shredded ginseng root ($8.85).

Among main-course stone rice bowls ($19.95), the stuffed eggplant variety is superb. The kimchee wraps ($15.95) are a must, if only to watch the server secure the kimchee stuffing into the fragile, potato-vermicelli pancakes. For dessert, the gelatinous tofu puddings (lemon or chocolate) are okay for what they are.

Josie's

Rare is the restaurant that can delight both a carnivorous Capricorn and the leaf-loving Libra he or she is meeting. But at Josie's, a loud playroom sleekly designed in the style of vintage diner, chef/owner/juice maven Louis Lanza satisfies dietetically mismatched couples with what he calls "conscious cuisine." In conscious English, this means that all dishes are certified organic and dairy-free without his resorting to serious deprivation. The Latin- and Asian-accented contemporary American food is worth every certified bite—as the sexy singles slurping the sangria of the day (pineapple-cantaloupe-grape, pear-apple-citrus) by the liter ($17) will attest.

Lunch $15–40
Dinner $22–50

Address 565 3rd Ave at 37th St
℡212/490-1558
Transportation 6 to 33rd St; 4,5,7 to 42nd St-Grand Central
Open Mon–Thurs noon–11pm, Thurs & Fri noon–midnight, Sat 11.30am–midnight, Sun 11.30am–10pm
Accepts All major credit cards
Reservations Recommended

You might begin by sharing such creative small plates as ginger-grilled calamari with feisty pineapple-red pepper salsa ($8), nori "sushi" rolls stuffed with brown rice, Portobellos, and steamed spinach ($6.75), and pan-seared spicy black soy bean dumplings with mango miso sauce ($7). Main courses are divided into thematic sections. "Earth Friendly" (100 percent vegetarian) options include roasted "meatloaf" with rosemary jus ($12). Made from lentils, wild rice, red beans, mixed veggies, and seitan, this savory loaf has no off-taste or mushiness to offend meat eaters. Under "Ravioli & Pasta," the sweet potato ravioli with Gulf shrimp, sweetcorn, and roasted peppers in a white wine leek sauce is stellar ($15). Stir-fries are fairly ho-hum compared to sesame seared tofu ($13), grilled teriyaki chicken ($14), and lemongrass-curry shrimp ($16).

The "Market Seafood" section boasts a world-class tuna burger ($19) as imposing as its red meat counterpart ($11). The dairy-free, wheat-free pies ($6.50) are not chalky or cement-like, as such things often are. Deep-dish, three-berry ginger pie topped with a butterless walnut-oat crumble is the perfect thing to end a (virtually) guilt-free meal. (Let's not count that third liter of sangria.)

There's another Josie's at 300 Amsterdam Ave, Upper West Side (℡212/769-1212).

Tony's Burger

Forget the four tables at this drab greasy spoon near the Empire State Building. To absorb the Tony's experience you must plant yourself on one of the nine stools covered in worn black leatherette, lean your forearms on the lunch counter topped with marble floor tiles, and watch the skilled short-order cook and his burgers sweat under the sizzling heat. Above his confined work space, a range hood traps a good 95 percent of the greasy smoke emanating from the grill and griddle. The remainder infuses every inch of space above belt level with what only urban romantics would term "ambiance." Some regulars know to do separate laundry loads for clothes worn at Tony's. Others have taken to twice shampooing their hair and eyebrows at the earliest opportunity.

$4–15
Address 34 East 32nd St, between Park & Madison Aves
☎212/779-7191
Transportation 6 to 33rd St
Open Mon–Fri 7am–7.30pm, Sat 7am–4pm, Sun 8am–noon
Accepts Cash only
Reservations Not accepted

HAMBURGERS

The Tony's burger is champ in the sphere of wide, flat patties which know no color gradations between deep-red rare and well-done gray. The soaking-wet surface of a cooked, 6oz burger, its toasted sesame-seed bun left open, is marked with charred dashes like a highway divided by dotted lines. It's a thing of beauty. A basic burger with iceberg, tomato slices, and pickle is $4.40; a deluxe with a thimble of coleslaw and a heap of frozen (but good for their type) fries, $5.70. You'd do best to spring for the bacon burger or bacon cheeseburger deluxe ($6.50/$6.95). Each comes with six or seven strips of crisp-edged but neither brittle nor curled bacon. With the layered bacon as thick as the burger pattie itself, the chew is extraordinary.

The subject of bacon brings to mind Tony's other superlative sandwich, the BLT ($3.75), its bacon strips flattened with an iron as they cook. In this instance it might be preferable to sit at the table. You don't really want to see just how much mayo is spread over the toast. Also worth a look are pocketless pita sandwiches like the tuna melt ($4.95). At breakfast, it is possible to order eggs with a side of gyromeat in place of bacon. But no one you know and admire would do that.

Uptown

Harlem

Amy Ruth's

(🍴) When, during summers spent on
his family farm in Alabama, Carl
Redding was warned that cooking was
for girls, the Harlem native did not heed
his grandfather's advice. Strangely, he
preferred cooking and tasting alongside
his maternal grandmother to cleaning the
pigpen and picking cotton (hello?). It may
be a vestige of granddaddy's thinking
that influenced the naming of this wonderful Southern-style cafe. True, it's likely
Redding first thought of pasting a sepia
portrait of Amy Ruth Bass throughout his restaurant as a loving tribute to
his grandmother, who died in 1987. Many of the recipes are hers. But
surely he knew the restaurant's feminine persona would help him compete with Sylvia's, the doyenne of Harlem restaurants (see p.241). It isn't
girls we think feed us better than boys; it's the mothers of their mothers.

$8–35

Address 113 West 116th St,
between Lenox & 7th Aves

☎212/280-8779

Transportation 2,3 to 116th St

Open Sun–Thurs 7.30am–11pm, Fri
& Sat 24hr

Accepts All major credit cards

Reservations Not accepted

SOUTHERN

To offset its homespun image, Amy Ruth's incorporates touches of
refinement, sometimes to comic effect. When the manager scurries over
to prevent people from seating themselves at one of many unoccupied
marble tables, the waitresses roll their eyes. And when an eatery that
serves Sanka instead of brewed decaf pushes bottled water instead of
NYC H$_2$O, it's the diners who do a double take. The atmosphere is otherwise classy, easy-going, and popular with the politicians, religious
leaders, and dignitaries who have dishes named after them. Redding sure
knows how to play the name game.

Whenever a restaurant serves waffles throughout the day and—on
weekends—the night, the message is clear: order them. These golden,
deep-grooved, fluffy but not bubbly waffles ($4.95) are served with a
variety of co-stars—the "Rev. Al Sharpton" comes with fried or smothered chicken ($8.50)—but never without pure maple syrup. Should you,
acting against your best interests, want to consider something else, the
salmon croquettes ($7.50) and corned beef hash ($7) are swell breakfast
items accompanied by eggs, hot grits, and warm biscuits. The fisherman's
platter ($15.95) boasts a generous assortment of fried jumbo shrimp,
crabcakes, catfish fingers, and, like all entrees, a choice of two sides (fried
okra and candied yams are good). The only dessert superior to sweet
potato pie ($2.75) is—what else?—the w-a-f-f-l-e-s.

Bayou

(🍴) The most admirable of Bayou's many qualities happens also to be the one most likely to disappoint a first-time diner's expectations: the second-floor bistro does not rely on any of the Prud-homme-proportioned excesses, Emeril-emulating histrionics, or party-time razzle-dazzle non-Louisianans have come to associate with Cajun restaurants. Not from the kitchen, where chef Anthony Bob-bitt executes a small, classic repertoire with contemporary restraint and savoir faire. And nowhere in the bar and dining room, a brick-walled, tin-ceiling number which,

Lunch $16–35
Dinner $25–50

Address 308 Lenox Ave, between
125th & 126th Sts
☎212/426-3800
Transportation 2,3 to 125th St
Open Mon–Thurs 11.30am–4pm &
6–10pm, Fri 11.30am–4pm &
6–11pm, Sat 6–11pm, Sun
noon–7.30pm
Accepts All major credit cards

softly illuminated by antique-style lamps and sconces, emits the amber and creamy glow of a vintage sepia print. Old black-and-white photos are in fact the only decorative indication of Bayou's regional bent. Why, there's not so much as a single Mardi Gras bead on the entire premises!

Two appetizers are so good it's hard to imagine a Bayou dinner without them: One is fried oysters coated with coarse cornmeal, advantageously set over sautéed greens, and topped with melted Brie ($10.95); the other, sautéed chicken livers (and quite a few of them) posed on herbed toasts and coated for double crispness with a Port wine demiglace and sesame seeds ($7.95). The thinnish turtle soup underscored with horseradish and pepper ($5.50/$6.50) comes in third; the trio of greasy and flimsy crabcakes with roasted tomato salsa ($12.95), a distant fourth. Among entrees, the two-inch-thick double-cut grilled pork loin chop with a green peppercorn demi-glace, spring onions, and mashed yams ($17.95) is a juicy knockout. The cornmeal-battered catfish fillets, fresh, firm, flaky, and scrumptious, are served with golden hushpuppies, chunky remoulade, and excellent fries ($15.95).

Bobbitt's controlled touch does unfortunately sap some badly needed energy and spice from the crawfish étouffée ($14.95), in this instance a rather bland and pale rendition of the traditional Cajun stew that should be anything but. Conversely, the desserts ($6.50) are every bit as cloying as you may hope—or fear. Your approval of the bourbon-sauced bread pudding, the peach cobbler, and the delectably smooth caramel custard will be relative to the size of your sweet tooth.

Sylvia's

🍴 It was more grit than grits that got Sylvia Woods her start in the food service industry a half-century ago. The South Carolina farm girl who had never set foot in a restaurant lied about her work experience to land a waitressing job at a Harlem lunch counter. She was found out on the first minute of her first shift. When the boss asked for a coffee, she pulled the wrong lever and put the cup—and herself—in hot water. The boss was impressed. "He told me, 'If you have that much nerve, I'm gonna teach you,

Lunch $11–40
Dinner $15–50

Address 328 Lenox Ave, between 126th & 127th Sts
☎212/996-0660
Transportation 2,3 to 125th St
Open Mon–Fri 11am–10.30pm, Sat 8am–10.30pm, Sun 11am–8pm
Accepts All major credit cards
Reservations For large groups

SOUTHERN

I'm gonna make you the best waitress,'" recalls Woods. Eight years later, she and her husband, Herbert Woods, bought the eight-stool eatery, expanded the menu of Southern down-home cooking (the description "soul food" was coined a few years later), and changed the name from Johnson's to Sylvia's. A legend was born.

The publication of a Sylvia's cookbook in 1992 was initially looked upon as the most significant disclosure of classified documents since the Pentagon Papers. But home cooks soon learned what many long-standing diners already knew: it's the woman who made those sweet, spicy, tangy spare ribs ($12.95) and gravy-smothered chicken ($10.55) famous and not the other way around. Sure, the collard greens ($2.50) were solid, especially before the kitchen surrendered to nutritional correctness by replacing the pork skins and bacon drippings in that classic side dish with smoked turkey wings. Certainly, the candied yams ($2.50) and sweet potato pie ($3.50) have always been terrific. But personal warmth and not recipes have established Woods as the toast and taste of Harlem for 40 years. When the Queen of Soul Food says she likes to rub shoulders with her customers, be they politicians, movie stars, neighborhood regulars, or Japanese tourists, she means it in the literal sense.

Another quality that makes fried catfish ($11.95) and twin smothered pork chops ($12.95) taste better is the on-site music. Saxophonist Lonnie Youngblood plays on Saturday afternoons, while the sweet voices of Ruth and Clay Simpson animate the rousing Sunday gospel brunch.

Upper East Side

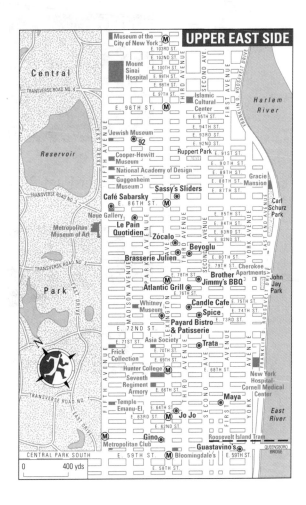

UPPER EAST SIDE

Museum of the
City of New York

Mount
Sinai Hospital

E. 103RD ST.
E. 102ND ST.
E. 100TH ST.
E. 99TH ST.
E. 98TH ST.
E. 97TH ST.

Central

TRANSVERSE ROAD NO. 4

Islamic
Cultural
Center

E. 96TH ST.
E. 95TH ST.
E. 94TH ST.
E. 93RD ST.
E. 92ND ST.

Harlem
River

Jewish Museum
92

Cooper-Hewitt
Museum

National Academy of Design
Guggenheim
Museum

Ruppert Park

E. 91ST ST.
E. 90TH ST.
E. 89TH ST.
E. 88TH ST.
E. 87TH ST.

Reservoir

TRANSVERSE ROAD NO. 3

Sassy's Sliders

Gracie
Mansion

Café Sabarsky

E. 86TH ST.

Neue Gallery

Metropolitan
Museum of Art

Le Pain
Quotidien

E. 85TH ST.
E. 84TH ST.
E. 83RD ST.
E. 82ND ST.

Carl
Schurz
Park

Zócalo

Beyoglu

TRANSVERSE ROAD NO. 2

Brasserie Julien

E. 80TH ST.
E. 79TH ST.

Park

Brother
Jimmy's BBQ

Cherokee
Apartments

Atlantic Grill

E. 78TH ST.
E. 76TH ST.

John
Jay
Park

Whitney
Museum

Candle Cafe

E. 75TH ST.

Spice

E. 74TH ST.
E. 73RD ST.

Payard Bistro
& Patisserie

E. 72ND ST.

Asia Society

Trata

E. 71ST ST.
E. 70TH ST.
E. 69TH ST.

Frick
Collection

Hunter College

New York
Hospital-
Cornell Medical
Center

Seventh
Regiment
Armory

E. 68TH ST.
E. 66TH ST.

TRANSVERSE ROAD NO. 1

Temple
Emanu-El

E. 64TH ST.

Maya

East
River

Jo Jo

E. 63RD ST.
E. 62ND ST.

Gino

Metropolitan Club

Roosevelt Island Tram

Guastavino's

QUEENSBORO
BRIDGE

CENTRAL PARK SOUTH

E. 59TH ST.

Bloomingdale's

E. 59TH ST.

E. 58TH ST.

0   400 yds

FIFTH AVENUE · MADISON AVENUE · PARK AVENUE · LEXINGTON AVENUE · THIRD AVENUE · SECOND AVENUE · FIRST AVENUE · YORK AVENUE · EAST END AVENUE · FRANKLIN D. ROOSEVELT DRIVE

For the post-preppy neurotics of the Upper East Side's well-heeled Carnegie Hill district, lunches and dinners at 92 have become their equivalent of eating in. The rapid routinizing of so polished and not-exactly-cheap a restaurant in Woody Allen's backyard was no accident. By furnishing family-friendly 92 with burgundy banquettes and Art Moderne woodwork and hardware, owner Ken Aretsky essentially dressed up his everyday diner-with-counter like a swank brasserie-with-bar so his clientele could dress it right back down. If anything, the undertaking is too successful. With interlopers from distant zip codes stopping by after visits to the nearby Cooper-Hewitt, Guggenheim, and Jewish Museums and prices down from a year ago, nowadays locals must suffer the indignity of needing to make a reservation to dine at home.

Lunch $20–65 Dinner $25–75	
Address	45 East 92nd St at Madison Ave
☎	212/828-5300
Transportation	6 to 96th St
Open	Mon–Thurs 11.30am–10pm, Fri & Sat 11.30am–10.30pm, Sun 10am–10pm
Accepts	All major credit cards
Reservations	Suggested

AMERICAN

The first edible brought to the table is a baguette in a wax paper bag bearing the trademark designer-logo of Carnegie Hill resident Eli Zabar. It's a perfect touch. In these parts, the Eli's Bread logo is as sure an emblem of good breeding today as the polo-shirt alligator was some twenty years ago. Starters like fried calamari ($8), solid Caesar salad ($8), and a sweet French onion soup ($9) are neither memorable nor uninteresting, which is to say they're just right for 92's needs. As is often the case with old TV shows, it's the predictable things that hold up best to repeat viewing.

The easy pleasure of bacon-wrapped meatloaf ($18) notwithstanding, the top daily entree is pan-roasted chicken ($16) with the crisp, golden coating of the finest roast duck. If you can take the high salt quotient it's a keeper. The pretty lean steakburger ($9.50 at lunch, $13 at dinner with the works) begets thick, beautiful fries; the homemade-mayo-slathered lobster roll ($23), the crunchy shoestring variety. Exercises in ice cream excess—banana split ($6), root beer float ($5), hot fudge sundae ($7)—bring it all home.

SEAFOOD

Atlantic Grill

(🍴) Replicating his successful formula at Ocean Grill (see p.275), owner Stephen Hanson created this large, stylishly appealing fish house with a menu to match. Factor in smooth service and prices as low as anyone visiting this high-rent location could hope for and it's easy to understand why the place became so wildly popular so quickly with so broad a cross section of East Siders. True, few dishes live up to the promise offered by the handsome, wood-and-chrome-detailed bar lined with Jacques-Henri Lartigue's dreamy photos of the French Riviera. Yes, nothing you put fork to is as fabulous as the studded ecru chairs and brown-velour Hollywood booths in the main dining room. And yes, no appetizer welcomes you as enticingly as the caned chairs and long banquettes in the tiled oyster bar room. But the kitchen does most things quite well and a few things extremely well, and that is apparently well enough.

| **Lunch $28–50** |
| **Dinner $35–75** |

Address 1341 3rd Ave, between 76th & 77th Sts
☎212/988-9200
Transportation 6 to 77th St
Open Mon–Thurs 11.30am–4pm & 5pm–midnight, Fri & Sat 11.30am–4pm & 5pm–12.30am, Sun 10.30am–4pm & 5pm–midnight
Accepts All major credit cards
Reservations Required

So what if you wouldn't travel here exclusively for the decent sushi maki rolls ($6.50–8.95) and the sushi and sashimi platters ($21.50–31). It's nice to have them available in a restaurant that can also launch your meal with a chopped salad with cucumber, feta, capers, tomato, roasted peppers, onions, and chickpeas ($8.50). On the East Side, great chopped salads like this are a widespread obsession. The sesame-crusted lobster roll ($8.95) with two dips—the citrus soy sauce is nicest—is also outstanding.

Often the fashionably treated New American seafood entrees ($18–21.95)—mustard-glazed halibut, couscous-crusted swordfish, teriyaki Chilean sea bass—are executed with too much restraint. But the buttery, herb-crusted salmon with mushy risotto ($18.50) is a happy exception. Moreover, two sides, a spring-roll-like vegetable strudel and horseradish mashed potatoes, are simply amazing. Come dessert time there's no regretting the warm, crunchy-almond-topped apple crisp with honey cinnamon ice cream ($6) and, for sheer frivolity, the caramelized banana ice cream tower with toasted marshmallow sauce and hot fudge ($6.50).

Beyoglu

Nowhere is the no-brainer of New York-based Turkish dining—go heavy on the appetizers—more valid than at Beyoglu, a duplex bistro named after a once cosmopolitan district in Istanbul. With its lunch and dinner menus structured tapas-style around assorted mezzes or small plates there is really no serious alternative. Not so when deciding where to sit. The mood within the main-floor dining area, with its brocaded

$15–45

Address 1431 3rd Ave at 81st St
☎212/650-0850
Transportation 6 to 77th St; 4,5 to 86th St
Open Daily noon–midnight
Accepts All major credit cards
Reservations Suggested

French doors, light-shaping sconces, and cartoonish floral wall motif, is playful yet dressier than the low prices—mezzes are $3.50–6.50—would at first indicate. The beautiful upper level is another sort of fairy tale, decorated as it is with old fabrics, photos, divans, and tables suggestive of Beyoglu in its early twentieth-century heyday. You're almost surprised they're pouring Coca-Cola over ice cubes but not absinthe over sugar cubes.

The excellent mezze selection was designed by Organ Yegen, the hit-and-run chef (see Dervish, p.209) who in this instance did not even stick around for dinner. The face of Beyoglu now belongs to George, the young, charming, and exceedingly friendly general manager. If you want to know more about the arnavut cigeri (pan-fried calf's liver with raw onions and parsley) or the zeytinyagli ispanak (spinach sautéed in olive oil with shallots and dill), George is the guy to ask. If, however, you're worried about catching a movie after dinner, don't dare even ask him the hour, as the response may cover notions of time in Turkish theater, soccer, and politics. Whatever your plans, do not skip the whipped yet intense tarama, the mujver (zucchini pancakes), the mashed eggplant salad, and peanut-butter thick hummus (maybe the best in Manhattan). The grid-marked rounds of house-baked Turkish bread, only vaguely akin to pita as we know it, are outstanding.

Four or five daily specials ($12.50) are offered as main courses. The iskander kebab, with thin slices of spit-carved lamb and beef and toasted bread cubes in a yogurt-creamy garlic sauce, isn't bad. But as long as you've survived the upstairs/downstairs dilemma, better to stick to the mezzes and, for dessert, the custardy, grain-free rice pudding.

Brasserie Julien

(🍴) Accomplished French chef Philippe
Feret runs his and his wife Cecilia's
neighborhood brasserie with the unremit-
ting perfectionism of a home
improvement fanatic. He is always taking
on an interior design project, be it creating stained-glass panels for a backbar
of hand-finished woods, gilding the classical capitals of the tall columns, or
crafting an Art Deco partition for the open
kitchen doorway to match the elevator
doors of the Chrysler Building. The

$28–75

Address 1422 3rd Ave, between
80th & 81st Sts
℡212/744-6327
Transportation 6 to 77th St
Open Sun–Thurs 5.30pm–midnight,
Fri & Sat 5.30pm–2am
Accepts All major credit cards
Reservations Suggested

upshot is an informal yet plush backdrop for a suitor who wants to
romance an existing love interest or, on weekend nights especially, meet a
new one either at the bar or the innovative chef's table reserved for communal, family-style dining. A jazz duo plays on Fridays and Saturdays.

Feret's continuous menu-tinkering mostly entails adapting French classics for American tastes. He is far less concerned with dazzling technique
and fussy presentation, though he is capable of both, than setting down
lots of likeable food. The homemade pâté ($9.50) and marinated smoked
herring with potatoes ($11) are both served à volonté, meaning diners
can have as much of these two appetizers as they want. You could easily
make an entire meal with repeated servings of the herring and potato
salad. But no one with an eye on a main course will require seconds of
the copious salads ($7.50–10.50), the foie gras terrine ($14.50), or the
pastis-flambéed escargots with garlic parsley butter ($12).

Entrees may lack for finesse but never size. Whatever free space there is
on a 12oz veal chop plate ($26) is occupied by a duxelle of wild mush-
rooms and a cheese gratin. Moroccan chicken bisteeya ($19.50), a
sweet-and-savory filo pie, is accompanied by a high pile of mesclun
greens. Grilled striped bass ($22), flambéed in pastis and stacked high
over green and white asparagus, fennel, sun-dried tomato, and black
olives, is a long-distance delight. Fondues, amply portioned for two—
cheese ($34), beef ($40), seafood ($40), vegetable ($20), or chocolate
($16)—are fabulous for late-night sharing and romancing. There's more
for chocolate lovers in the hot-sauced profiteroles and the molten-cen-
tered Valrhona chocolate cake with pistachio sauce and vanilla ice cream
(both $8).

Brother Jimmy's BBQ

The fact that Carolinian Manhattanites are routinely critical of the hickory-smoked ribs at Brother Jimmy's should not be immediately interpreted as an indictment of their quality and authenticity. Kvetching about local translations of foods from back home is an immutable consequence of moving to the world's great melting pot. It's one way transplanted New Yorkers of diverse origins convey their ethnic pride. Though it's unlikely that the BBQ is as good here as at the famed North Carolina joints it was

$11–45

Address 1485 2nd Ave, between
77th & 78th Sts; plus other locations
☎212/288-0999
Transportation 6 to 77th St
Open Mon 5pm–midnight,
Tues–Thurs noon–midnight, Fri &
Sat noon–1am, Sun noon–midnight
Accepts All major credit cards
Reservations Not accepted

inspired by, the slow-smoked, vinegary-sauced, tart-and-tangy ribs are pretty darn tootin' good. Furthermore, it's a good bet that some of the postgraduate regulars are wearing Duke Blue Devils, Wake Forest Demon Deacons, or University of North Carolina Tar Heel boxer shorts under their beer-stained jeans.

Brother Jimmy's is above all an endurance challenge. For the frat-party refugees, it's a raucous marathon of boozing, scarfing, and belching. For everyone else, it's a test of just how much of that boozing, scarfing, and belching they can stand. Some synchronize their visit with the quiet lull between happy hour and televised basketball games that begins at around 7.16pm and concludes at 7.35pm. Others ask to sit in the side dining room away from the bar. This room too is cluttered with the odd collectibles—vintage soda pop bottles, old BBQ menus, rabbit seed sacks—that give Jimmy's make-believe shack its southern character.

The meaty ribs ($17.50 with two sides) come three ways: northern (with a sweet glaze), southern (spicy and with a sour ting), or, best of all, the deep and complex, 21-spice dry rub (spicy and, as the description implies, no sauce). Don't fret about missing the moist marinade. A squeeze bottle of runny, spicy, and wickedly tart sauce is at the ready. Other options to look at are the pulled pork sandwich ($7.95), the BBQ half-chicken ($12.50), and assorted finger foods/starters: stuffed jalapenos, Buffalo wings, hush puppies, fried onion "straws" (a single $5.50 order feeds five). To finish, the warm pecan pie has just the right proportions of nutty crunch and sweet gooeyness.

Café Sabarsky

🍴 The short stroll from the entrance of the Neue Gallery New York to the elegant staircase leading up to its galleries of early twentieth-century German and Austrian art can be negotiated in anywhere from seven seconds to four hours. In fact, some people never make it to the staircase. Without paying admission they detour to Café Sabarsky, take possession of an Adolf Loos black bentwood chair and a white marble table,

$18–55

Address 1048 5th Ave at 86th St
☏212/288-0665
Transportation 4,5,6 to 86th St
Open Mon & Wed 9am–6pm,
Thurs–Sun 9am–9pm
Accepts All major credit cards
Reservations Not accepted

pull out the necessary reading or writing materials, and nurse a kleiner brauner (espresso) until the lights beneath the Josef Hoffmann sconces are extinguished. Art collector Ronald Lauder opened the Neue Gallery in 2000 and named the in-house cafe in memory of its co-founder, the art dealer and curator Serge Sabarsky.

Café Sabarsky is housed in the beautifully restored drawing room of a Fifth Avenue mansion dating from 1914. Furnished with reproductions of classic pieces from the Viennese Secessionist and Arts and Crafts movements, it is an elegant evocation of a grand Viennese coffeehouse without the tobacco smoke and intellectual fire. But passions are stirred by the soups, sandwiches, and pastries (and, it must be added, the clueless service). The Austro-Hungarian menu of Kurt Gutenbrunner, chef-owner of the superlative Austrian bistro Wallsé (see p.172), sets a new standard for museum cafes.

Open-face rye bread sandwiches like ham with grated horseradish and chives ($10.50) and liverwurst dabbed with minced onion confit ($10.50) are so good you almost have to slow yourself down to fully appreciate their individual parts. The rich and creamy chestnut soup ($10) has stimulated discussion groups. The quality of the entrees justifies their prices. The boiled beef with creamed spinach and potatoes ($25) is every bit the standout here as it is as Wallsé. You can also come in at any time to enjoy one of Gutenbrunner's splendid Viennese tortes or a kaffee mitt schlag ($5). Oh, and the galleries are said to be great too.

Candle Café

The rosy-cheeked, East Side thirty-somethings sitting at the dark-wood tables come with the territory. But few past experiences in the organic-vegan dining realm prepare you for the mass of folks crowding the sidewalk, or the booze that awaits them. Unlike most eateries of its ilk, the sleek and casual Candle Café has a liquor license and serves a thoughtful, modest selection of organic and sulfite-free wines and organic beers. The organic Samuel Smith lager is a smooth and balanced reward for waiting it out.

$12–45

Address 1307 3rd Ave, between 74th & 75th Sts
☏212/472-0970
Transportation 6 to 77th St
Open Mon–Sat 11.30am–10.30pm, Sun 11.30am–9.30pm
Accepts All major credit cards
Reservations For large groups

AUSTRIAN

Start with a plate of edamame ($6.50), the steamed, sea-salted soybeans that have become a favorite healthful snack addiction. Since service can be slow and there's no breadbasket, these little pods—and a Sam Smith lager or two—will tide you over until your food arrives. Appetizers are hit or miss, with Asian dumplings ($7.95) falling into the latter category. The bright green spinach envelopes, though pretty, are doughy and filled with an insipid vegetable mixture. The Caesar salad ($6.95), with crisp piles of romaine and a creamy, caper-accented dressing, hits the mark. The south-of-the-border seitan sandwich ($10.95) is a between-the-bread feast. A multigrain hero is stuffed with chile-rubbed grilled seitan and smoky-sweet caramelized onions and then slathered with spicy vegan chipotle mayo. A gigantic slab of tempeh lasagna ($12.95) layered with spinach-herb tofu ricotta, tomato sauce, and soy mozzarella is as good as it is huge. One sizeable treat to look out for is the grilled seitan burrito ($14.95)—a spinach tortilla packed with yellow Basmati rice, steamed greens, and navy beans, embellished with tofu sour cream, pico de gallo, guacamole, and ranchero sauce.

Dairy-free desserts are massive, too, and happily so. The cocoa-coated double layer chocolate cake ($5.25) is one rich, gooey, duplex slice of devil's food heaven. Alternatively, you could turn to the fruit drinks, smoothies, and soy protein shakes that fall under the category of "Fruition Nutrition." The apple Betty ($5.50), with apple, pear, banana, and cinnamon, takes America's classic dessert and lets you suck it through a straw.

Gino

🍴 Central casting could find Italian character actors to fill the roles of the bow-tied waiters. The costume guy could outfit them in the signature gray jackets with red cuffs. The set designer could re-create everything from the red, zebra-print wallpaper to the warped, fluorescent-lit wall panels. A Neapolitan chef could be found to prepare a red sauce of comparable quality. And still you would not have Gino. They simply don't make 'em like this anymore and they couldn't if they tried. The clatter, energy, and swagger of this circa 1945 haunt and

Lunch $25–65
Dinner $30–75

Address 780 Lexington Ave, between 60th & 61st Sts
☎212/758-4466
Transportation 6,N,R,W to Lexington Ave-59th St; F to Lexington Ave-63rd St
Open Daily noon–10.30pm
Accepts Cash only
Reservations Not accepted

former Rat Pack hangout benefit from renewable sources of energy: regulars bring their kids and friends who bring their kids and friends and so on.

Do not try to slip Mario or Sal a few bucks and expect to get quickly seated. They won't take money from just anyone. If you don't care to wait at the bar, you have perhaps three options: 1) come very early, maybe after a shopping jaunt to nearby Bloomingdale's; 2) shower a regular with gifts from Bloomingdale's and come in later with him or her; or 3) return often enough (say three times a week for five years) to merit the VIP treatment.

The grub, like the service, is agreeably gruff and habit-forming. No-nonsense appetizers like the watery chopped salad ($9.50) and the piping hot clams oreganato ($8.75) are not so much served to you as they are shoved at you. It's as much a part of the show as keeping secret the contents of the house sauce (lightly creamed tomato) that goes out with good gnocchi ($13.50) and paglia e fieno (a $13.95 weave of egg—"straw"—and spinach—"hay.") Linguine with clams ($14.75) has all the clams you need in a sauce great for dunking that mediocre Italian bread, while broiled chicken "Gino" ($15.95) is indiscriminately slathered with chopped garlic (you decide if that's a good thing). Veal parmigiano ($17.95) is appealing, the cheese, sauce, and breading clinging to the tender meat. The pleasing cheesecake ($3.95) and tiramisu ($3.95) notwithstanding, the thick and soused zabaglione ($4.95) is a must. It's too big by half for its tall glass dish.

Guastavino's

Opened on February 14, 2000, Sir
Terence Conran's Valentine to New
York was named for Rafael Guastavino,
the Catalan architect who designed the
tile vaulting for the Grand Central Oyster
Bar (see p.187), and the soffit soaring over
the restaurant and beneath the Queens-
borough Bridge. Once occupied by the
produce vendors of Bridgemarket, the
arcaded space languished as a storage
facility until investors led by London's lord
of home design and restaurant development leased a 25,000-square-foot share
for the 300-seat brasserie and the
dressier, 100-seat Club Guastavino. The
tile vaults, limestone walls, and 40ft
columns that support them were left bare
to dwarf the sleekly sculpted fixtures, both
in furniture and flesh, of the sexy, loud, elongated bar.

ITALIAN

$22–80

Address 409 East 59th St, between
York & 1st Aves
℡212/980-2455
Transportation N,R,W to Lexington
Ave; 4,5,6 to 59th St
Open Mon–Thurs 11.30am–2.15pm
& 5.30–10pm, Thurs & Fri
11.30am–2.15pm & 5.30–11.30pm,
Fri 11.30am–2.15pm & 5.30–9pm,
Sat 11.30am–3.15pm &
5.30–11.30pm, Sun
11.30am–3.15pm & 5.30–10pm
Accepts All major credit cards
Reservations Suggested

The disappointment of downstairs dining is that the overhead mezzanine—where you'll find Club Guastavino—cuts off the view and
expanse of the arcades. Consolation comes with the knowledge that the
brasserie shares with its upscale companion the same executive chef,
Daniel Orr, a small-town Indiana boy who made his New York name at
the venerable French restaurant La Grenouille. His history suits a menu
that blends sophistication with family values in such appetizers as Portobello stuffy (a vegetarian riff on Rhode Island stuffed clams; $9);
flatbread topped with red onion confit, arugula, blue cheese, and walnuts
($8); and chicken soup with one great matzoh ball ($7.50).

Of low-end main courses, fried scrod ($14), a Monday blue plate spe-
cial, acquires a batter of Brooklyn ale to go with hand-cut fries. The
center-cut pork chop ($26) spends quality time in a bourbon and mus-
tard marinade before it acquires its oven-roasted glaze. And the LBJ
Texas beef brisket ($16.25) is prepared with the tangy barbecue sauce of
the ex-president's legendary pitmaster, Walter Jetton. For a Louisiana
finish, there's the burnt vanilla ice cream ($7.25), a New Orleans hybrid
of British Trinity cream and French crème brûlée.

Upper East Side

Jo Jo

🍴 Jo Jo is short for Jean-Georges Vongerichten as well as the name of the townhouse duplex where, beginning in 1991, he blazed a new East Side trail for worldly and wily French cuisine. Although the Alsatian had already substituted vegetable juices and herb-infused oils and vinaigrettes for creamy sauces and heavy meat stocks at a luxurious midtowner called Lafayette, it was in this snug and, for a while at least, reasonably priced bistro that he pioneered his penchant for spare, flavor-concentrated dishes with Asian intonation. The same minimalism is not true of the million-dollar, 2001 makeover. Velours, silks, and brocades in reds, oranges, and plums outfit its rooms like those of a Belle Époque bordello. Waitresses are dressed in lacy black slips.

Lunch $30–90
Dinner $45–100

Address 160 East 64th St, between Lexington & 3rd Aves
☎212/223-5656
Transportation F,N,R,W to Lexington Ave; 4,5 to 59th St; 6 to 68th St
Open Sun–Thurs noon–2.30pm & 5.30–10pm, Fri & Sat noon–2.30pm & 5.30–11pm
Accepts All major credit cards
Reservations Required

Only on the East Side, where the two economic classes are old money and new money, is it not a stretch to term an establishment with a $35 entree a "bistro." Still, the sensational $20 prix fixe lunch and $35 pre-theater dinner give bargain access to world-class cuisine. Chef de cuisine Ron Gallo directs a team that turns out distinctive dishes which get better the better you know them. Two longstanding starters are Peekytoe crabmeat with cumin crisps, mustard tarragon butter, and diced mango ($14), and faintly sweet, orange-dusted shrimp ($14). Pumpkin and mascarpone ravioli with fried sage and brown butter ($10) are a temporary show.

With entrees, Jean-Georges augured the trend whereby side attractions command as much attention as star ingredients. In one take on duck breast ($26), the accompaniments are a honeyed, gingered shallot confit and a filo-pouch of ground duck leg and foie gras. Pepper-crusted venison ($29) is impeccable, yet it's the poire au lard, a hash of pear and bacon, that you will tell your grandchildren about. Jo Jo also set off the national craze for warm, underbaked chocolate cake. Though divine as ever, better to get in on the ground—or second—floor with the banana brioche flan with caramel ice cream or the warm tarte Tatin with spiced cider ice cream (both $9).

Maya

(YI) This East Sider Mexican has the look and lineage of greatness. At two prior restaurants (Savann and Savann East), chef-owner Richard Sandoval, the 1992 winner of Mexico's National Toque D'Oro, possessed an uncommon understanding of the contemporary cooking that mid-range diners want and the price they are willing (long waits, squeezed tables) and not willing ($15 appetizers, $20-plus entrees) to pay in order to get it. At Maya he's gone for shorter waits, well-spaced tables, and bigger checks. In a comfortable dining

$35–75

Address 1191 1st Ave, between 64th & 65th Sts
℡212/585-1818
Transportation F to Lexington Ave-63rd St; 6 to 68th St
Open Sun & Mon 5–10pm, Tues–Thurs 5–11pm, Fri & Sat 5–11.30pm
Accepts All major credit cards
Reservations Suggested

FRENCH

room, Mayan masks are bordered by blue frames painted onto coral-colored walls. Earthenware, candlesticks, and the volcanic-rock mortars called molcajetes (for guacamole) were commissioned from renowned silver designer Emilia Castillo. How you feel about the guacamole service will define how you feel about Maya and its somewhat polished take on Mexican food. Rather than serve the dip directly in its native mixing bowl, they place it in a silver cup propped inside. Some see this as bringing uptown elegance to south-of-the-border tradition; others see a pricey ($9.50) order of guacamole.

Fortunately, not all appetizers are so confined. The chile relleno ($11.50), a stuffed and roasted poblano pepper cushioned with superb black bean purée, is bursting with shrimp, scallops, and calamari that spill out into a cilantro oil salsa. The tamal al chipotle ($8.50), a moist tamale filled with shredded chicken, is diagonally striped with delightfully smoky chipotle sauce and crema fresca.

Main courses feature impressive architecture and color, sometimes at the expense of the star ingredients. You remember the tampiquena ($23.95) more for its poblano-peppered potato gratin and mole poblano enchilada than its filet mignon. Choose instead the grilled shrimp with a goat cheese-stuffed roasted Anaheim chile ($22.95) and the steak chilaquiles ($22.50) layered with sliced tortillas, black bean purée, crema fresca, and Manchego cheese. The okay desserts ($6.50) may be as simple as a rich flan or as dramatic as sweet bananas flambéed with tequila.

Upper East Side

Le Pain Quotidien

Despite the flourishing presence of five additional locations in Manhattan and another 24 stores in Belgium alone, it is hard to believe that the Pain Quotidien just two blocks from the Metropolitan Museum of Art is not the only one of its kind. Its long wooded communal table, aged floorboards, sienna walls, country-style antiques, and rustic baskets of freshly baked breads and rolls are not the stuff of which food chains are usually made. Somehow, Alain Coumont, who opened the Brussels flagship in

$14–35

Address 1131 Madison Ave between 84th & 85th Sts; plus other locations
℡212/327-4900
Transportation 6 to 86th St
Open Mon–Fri 7.30am–7pm, Sat & Sun 8am–7pm
Accepts All major credit cards
Reservations Not accepted

1990, has managed to duplicate his cafe/bakery without sacrificing its local charm. Quite the contrary. Le Pain Quotidien is the un-Starbucks, a gathering place that, like a skilled painter who adores his subject, both absorbs and greatly enriches the collective character and color of the surroundings.

Little actual cooking is done on the premises, excepting a soupe du jour ($4.95/$6.95). What the kitchen knows how to do best is assemble superior ingredients on tartines (open-faced sandwiches), in beautiful salads, and atop charcuterie platters and cheeseboards. Several sandwiches are habit-forming, among them a thick-cut pleasantly salty jambon de Paris (cooked pressed ham) with three separate fine mustards ($7.95); Scottish smoked salmon with fresh dill ($12.75); and the subtle combo of ricotta, radishes, and scallions ($7.75) that ought to be a rite of spring. Among the platters there is no surer way to transform a thirty-minute lunch into a picnic than the assiette toscane (Tuscan platter; $11.50) from which ricotta, pesto, black olive tapenade (that's Provençal, but no one would dare send it back), sundried tomatoes, prosciutto, and Parmesan may be spread atop a long sliced baguette.

Served with butter and jam, slabs of the fabulous breads ($2.95)—baguette, wheat levain, peasant rye, walnut, five-grain—are a natural for French-style breakfasts with a café au lait ($2.50) for dunking or, during museum breaks, with a Belgian hot chocolate ($3.25). The flaky croissant and brioche (both $2.95) are among the best in town, but it's the pain au chocolat ($2.95) of which there can be no other.

Payard Bistro & Patisserie

To meet the public's growing appetite for homey desserts, many top pastry chefs are turning to grandparents rather than grand masters for inspiration. Fruit crumbles and bread puddings abound. François Payard has long been following his grandfather's example—the distinction being that his papi ran a celebrated pastry shop on the French Riviera. Forget cozy and quaint. Payard the patisserie is a boutique on the level of FAO Schwarz and Tiffany, its precious toys—chocolates, pastries, candies, cakes, breads—tantalizingly displayed in look-but-don't-touch showcases. The goodies even shape the decoration of the mezzanine bistro. Croissant forms are molded into classical friezes. Blown-glass globe lights are shaped like cream puffs. How fortunate for Payard that his pastries are world-class. Anything less would be a spectacular letdown.

Lunch $25–75
Dinner $45–80

Address 1032 Lexington Ave, between 73rd & 74th Sts
℗212/717-5252
Transportation 6 to 77th St
Open Mon–Thurs noon–10.30pm, Fri & Sat noon–11pm
Accepts All major credit cards
Reservations Required

BELGIAN

With the dot-encircled "P" logo imprinted everywhere but on the toilet paper, it was initially difficult for the bistro's chef, Philippe Bertineau, to make a name—or even an initial—for himself. His first appetizers were too fussy and intricate, as if he were trying to match the stylized precision of the pastries. But he soon made the transition to rustic and robust, instilling Payard with the soul if not the humility of a bistro. There is no comfier kick-off to a winter dinner than celery root, chestnut, and mushroom soup ($7) or a twice-baked upside down cheese soufflé with Parmesan sauce and truffle oil ($12).

It didn't take long for several entrees to become signature dishes. If Monsieur B erased the braised lamb shank ($28) or four-peppercorn-sauced sirloin ($29) from the menu there'd be hell to pay. There was practically a riot when he replaced the halibut that enriched the bouillabaisse ($26) with Chilean sea bass. The $34 pre-theater prix fixe, with seatings at 5.45pm and 6pm, makes the prices more palatable. And the lunchtime croque monsieur ($12 with a seasonal salad and herb vinaigrette) is hardly a lesser pleasure. Try any signature dessert (about $9), from the warm banana tart and white chocolate mousse combination to the passion fruit gratin, and a dot-encircled P will be forever emblazoned on your heart.

Sassy's Sliders

Naming the three colloquialisms for the bite-size burgers of the pre-McDonald's era—belly bombers, belly busters, and sliders—is no problem. But explaining the origin of those terms is a difficult task valiantly undertaken by Sassy's co-owner Michael Ronis. "It was called a slider for the way it slid down your throat," he explains, "and actually for how it slid out the other way, too." The same goes for the other terms, which accurately describe an attack by these deliberately greasy burgers on our systems. The pioneer who first launched this digestive assault on America was J. Walter Anderson. In 1916 he divided unwieldy amounts of ground meat into smaller patties, mashed in shredded onions, seared them quickly on both sides, and thus invented what soon became the White Castle belly bomber. Exhibiting a flash of genius, he placed freshly baked buns atop the puny patties as they cooked to absorb the beef flavor, the onions, and, yes, the grease.

$4-12
Address 1530 3rd Ave, between 86th & 87th Sts
☎212/828-6900
Transportation 6 to 86th St
Open Sun–Thurs 11.30am–10pm, Fri 11.30am–11pm, Sat 11.30am–midnight, Sun noon–10pm
Accepts Cash only
Reservations Not accepted

Sassy's revives the spirit of belly-busting burger joints put to pasture by the big franchises. (White Castle is still around, but it long ago stopped making quality sliders, partly due to its substituting frozen meat for fresh.) Sassy's 99¢ sliders are made with freshly ground beef, turkey, or, in the veggie version, grated carrots, zucchini, Chinese cabbage, soy, and pickles. Like silver dollar pancakes, these sliders somehow taste different to their larger forebears, possibly because they're a hoot to gobble down. The skinny fries ($1.79/$2.09) are dandy; the sweet potato fries ($2.09/$2.59), uncharacteristically crisp. An $18.99 combo with fifteen burgers and three large fries easily feeds five children or one inebriated undergraduate.

Situated seconds away from several multiplexes, this reasonably fast food outlet is ideal for a quick snack before or after a screening. The brightly lit joint's curvy blue Formica counters, enamel-like white wall panels, and cheery menu graphics represent an inviting, 1950s celebration of J. Walter Anderson's easy-in/easy-out legacy. But the absence of public restrooms on the premises can be somewhat less amusing.

Spice

With the advent and spawning of Spice (there are branches in the Village and Chelsea), Thai food finally attains the junky status of face-stuffing Chinese takeout. But order this cheap chow to go and you're missing half the noisy, stinky, crispy fun. In a loud, funky, post-industrial cafe redolent of soy sauce, the twisted legs of a spidery lighting fixture point low-wattage bulbs toward stainless-steel tables and a cement floor. For self-respecting diners concerned with outward appearances and inward consumptions, the cool, dark and somewhat austere setting provides stylish cover for an hour of spicy, sweet, sour, salty, greasy, and near-instant gratification.

Lunch $10–20
Dinner $18–40

Address 1411 2nd Ave, between 73rd & 74th Sts; plus other locations
☎212/988-5348
Transportation 6 to 77th St
Open Daily 11.30am–11pm
Accepts MasterCard & Visa
Reservations Not accepted

Constructing a meal without fried foods is possible. You could conceivably start with steamed vegetable dumplings ($4) and move on to a credible steamed fish with vegetables, ginger, and black beans ($16). But such a noble act would require skipping all the compulsory appetizers: crisp, hot spring rolls packed with carrot, cabbage, and vermicelli ($4); ground shrimp and crab fritters with sweet-and-sour dip ($4); Thai crêpes filled with shredded chicken, peanuts, and sweet chile sauce ($5); fabulously crunchy calamari ($5). Even the imaginative Caesar salad ($3) with miso ginger dressing owes its appeal to fried wonton croûtons.

Likewise, big portions of noodles are nobody's idea of spa cuisine. The peanut-packed pad Thai ($8) and broad "drunk man" noodles with basil and shrimp ($8) satisfy the all-important junk quotient with a doggy bag's worth to spare. For theatrical excess, you can't improve upon the crispy duck ($13), a vertical sphere with broccoli, celery, carrot, baby corn, pineapple chunks, Thai basil, and fresh ginger piled over fatty slices of duck breast—that is, of course, unless you want to spoon it over a side of "six o'clock" fried rice with chile, onion, and basil. Dessert brings the dinner full circle: sweet banana is rolled in a spring roll wrapper and cooked to order in hot oil ($3). See now why it may be better to enjoy this good-and-greasy stuff within the obscurity of Spice, where the delicious guilt is shared, than do takeout and risk going public.

Trata

THAI

It would be all too easy to fall in love with Trata, as you might an alluring companion with Aegean-blue eyes, on the first dinner date. This hit spin-off of the Greek seafood house Milos duplicates its model's market-style, you-pick-it/we-grill-it system, only it doesn't require you to raid your savings to pay for it. Sadly, Trata's handsome informality notwithstanding, it is almost as easy to become disillusioned on the second date. The trouble is, when you

$30–65

Address 1331 2nd Ave, between 70th & 71st Sts
℡212/535-3800
Transportation 6 to 68th St
Open Sun–Thurs 5–11pm, Fri & Sat 5pm–midnight
Accepts All major credit cards
Reservations Required

see an ice chest of trophy fish displayed in the middle of a restaurant named after a Greek fishing boat and decorated with photos of Greek fishing villages, anything less than consummately cooked seafood can bring about distress. Luckily, the happy memory of several winsome appetizers ultimately wins over conflicted diners.

Smooth, bread-thickened taramasalata (fish roe dip; $6.75) and top-notch tzatziki (yogurt and cucumber dip; $6.75) are indispensable starters. To that duo you should add a golden triangle of saganaki (fried kefalograviera cheese; $8.50), a crabcake ($15.50) so packed with crab-meat it barely holds together, tender grilled octopus ($11.95), and fresh, imported, flawlessly grilled sardines ($9.50). The entree list is dominated by whole fish hand-picked from the display and grilled to order. Mostly seasoned with capers, lemon, and olive oil, the daily catches are priced by the pound (up to $28) and may include such Mediterranean imports as the delicate loup de mer or the versatile royal dorade. Loup de mer could be singled out for the tautness and brilliance of its gray-silver skin; royal dorade for the brightness and color of its eyes and the firmness of its flesh.

The kitchen does not do as well with alternative main courses, whose ubiquitous mix of veggies makes things seem repetitive. For a sweet finish there is an enormous wedge of good baklava ($6.50). And two desserts will have you falling in love with Trata all over again: an ultra-rich and creamy Greek yogurt with Greek honey ($6.75) and delectably warm loukoumades (fried honey balls; $7).

Zócalo

The fixation on authenticity that dogs most commentary on Mexican food is worn out, be it from the Mexicophile who resents seeing one of the world's great cuisines reduced to cheesy slop, or the tequila-toting tourist who gets off a plane from Mexico and alerts every passing motorist on the Van Wyck Expressway that the Mexican food up here is nothing like it is down there. But who among us can really tell what is authentic anymore? Every Mexican restaurant has a style and regional focus totally different from the next. Zócalo's regional feel is unmistakably Upper East Side, from the front bar holding fifty tequilas to the cozy middle room and the comfortable, stucco-walled rear dining room painted to match the color of the blood orange margaritas. Service is solicitous, even on frenzied weekend nights.

$35–75

Address 174 East 82nd St, between Lexington & 3rd Aves
☎212/717-7772
Transportation 4,5,6 to 86th St
Open Mon–Thurs 6–11pm, Fri & Sat 6–11.30pm, Sun 5.30–10.30pm
Accepts All major credit cards
Reservations Suggested

GREEK

The food is robust and stylish without overreaching for refinement. Chomp on warm, freshly fried tortilla chips and smoky chipotle salsa while you choose. You can forget the usual chicken stuffing for flautas. Zócalo's are rolled over braised short ribs and sided with guacamole and charred tomato salsa ($7.50). When crab comes into play in a full-plate-sized quesadilla ($8.95), the fresh lump crabmeat is found both inside and outside the tortillas. And sautéed calamari acquires Spanish chorizo, white beans, piquillo peppers, *and* grilled bread ($9.50).

Tampiqueña, a chile-rubbed grilled hanger steak with a wine-cured goat cheese quesadilla, guacamole, rice, and beans ($22.50), is just the beginning of the beefy excitement. Should the unbelievable roast garlic-and jalapeno-stuffed rib steak ($28.95) with chimichurri sauce and smashed potatoes be on the menu, you're in luck. As for fish, tacos red snapper over banana leaves with coconut rice has a pleasantly sour passion fruit sauce ($24) that's not the least bit cloying, and the grilled mahi mahi tacos ($21) are terrific. The must-have dessert is a smooth and rich vanilla flan with fresh berries and caramel sauce ($6.50).

There's another Zócalo in Grand Central Terminal, Midtown East (☎212/687-5666).

Upper West Side

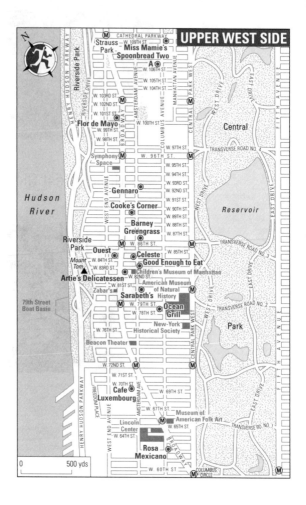

A

(🍴) Finding the funky fusion café known as A (as in the A train) buried in a Morningside Heights barrio rather than, say, the 18th arrondissement of Paris is something of a miracle, albeit a rather condensed one. In a storefront too narrow for a multi-lettered name, a few French-speaking dreamers of Caribbean and Senegalese origin have installed a 24-seat hybrid with truly Bohemian tastes. The stainless-steel

$18–35

Address 947 Columbus Ave, between 106th & 107th Sts
☎212/531-1643
Transportation B,C,1,9 to 110th St
Open Tues–Sat 6–11pm
Accepts Cash only
Reservations Not accepted

equipment in the thumb-sized kitchenette is arranged vertically so that the burners are stacked above twin compact ovens at eye level. In a dining area rumbling with world house music, say a techno version of Gershwin's Summertime, the whitewashed brick walls are covered with large subway maps, one of which appears to be a shower curtain.

The repertoire is limited to an A-list of five appetizers ($6–8) and four entrees (all $10). The starter that best reflects the menu's crosscultural aspirations consists of wood-smoked mussels served escargot-style in a black butter sauce cut with cilantro and chile. The succulent moules are nevertheless upstaged by the study in green, an olive-oil-marinated and grilled avocado in which the pit is replaced by a fluffy, mousse-like stuffing of spinach, roasted red peppers, and mushrooms. The rustic process of presenting main-course casseroles in a hallowed bread bowl is evolving. Previously, the featured stew was a peppery, vegan cassoulet with sweet peas and seitan in a coconut soy cream sauce. More recently it's been a five-mushroom ragout in the same curry. If either is available during your visit, order it. As an alternative, you can expect some French take on Jamaican jerk; either a duck confit leg or wood-smoked chicken.

With no license to sell alcohol, A invites diners to bring their own beer or wine. Some Columbia students do most of their drinking prior to dinner at Delbar, the Jamaican beer-and-punch bar next door. You can give your name to the host and he'll come fetch you at Delbar when your wood-framed table is ready.

Artie's Delicatessen

🍴 Red neon letters set against a gleaming-white, enamel-like back-drop spell out the ultimate tribute to a late restaurateur and, less conspicu-ously, a near forgotten New York institution. Artie's represents the unreal-ized dream of Artie Cutler, co-creator of, among other Manhattan successes, Carmine's (see p.203) and Virgil's Real

$10–35

Address 2290 Broadway at 83rd St
☎212/579-5959
Transportation 1,9 to 86th St
Open Daily 9am–11pm
Accepts All major credit cards

Barbecue (see p.226), to open a Jewish deli. Its pastrami is made from a secret formula bought at a close-out auction by one of Cutler's surviving partners, Jeffrey Bank. The uncertain quality of the recipe, said to have been used by the deli Schmulke Bernstein, a lost Lower East Side land-mark, is almost beside the point. The very existence of a recipe, any recipe, indicates that Artie's is curing its own pastrami, a rarity nowa-days. That alone would have made its honoree proud.

With solid Eastern European Jewish (non-kosher) cooking from chef/co-owner Chris Metz, Artie's has become a valuable neighborhood resource with the obligatory hanging salamis, frankfurter grill, and appe-tizing display case. The Formica tables, mirrored walls, snug booths and globe lights are the modest trappings of a retro coffee shop.

Thin, peppery, deep-pink slices of house-cured pastrami are piled high on rye bread ($7.75). The sandwich is best when carved fresh out of the steamer; it's worth insisting your pastrami be warm. The corned beef sandwich ($7.50) is a tender compromise between juicy and lean, and the terrific hot brisket of beef sandwich ($7.50) is gratifyingly undry, meaning that the meat does not need to be doused in gravy, lathered with mustard, or detonated with horseradish. A pot of tender flanken ($13.95), the boiled beef dish that is the Jewish version of short ribs, is combined with hearty mushroom barley soup. Chicken in the pot ($12.95) contains smooth hunks of white and dark meat, lightly salted chicken soup, and terrific matzoh balls of the floater (soft and light) rather than sinker (firm and dense) variety. Satisfying sides on top of the gratis coleslaw (great!) and smallish, uncrunchy pickles include golden French fries ($2.95) and semi-smooth chopped liver ($4.95). Home-made chocolate rugelach ($3.95) and diner-style rice pudding ($2.95) get the dessert nods over ordinary cheesecake ($3.95).

Barney Greengrass

The last remnants of wallpaper depicting New Orleans' French Quarter are now taped to the walls of the drab Barney Greengrass dining room. Third-generation owner Gary Greengrass wisely has no intention of papering over the homely and incongruous covering before he has to. Likewise, the wood-grained Formica tables and wainscoting are not going anywhere anytime soon. These homely, fluorescent-lit fittings are

$9–25

Address 541 Amsterdam Ave, between 86th & 87th Sts
℡212/724-4707
Transportation 1,9,B,C to 86th St
Open Tues–Fri 8.30am–4pm, Sat & Sun 8.30am–5pm
Accepts All major credit cards
Reservations Not accepted

so closely associated with "The Sturgeon King" that the devoted throng waiting outside for a weekend table could easily turn into an angry mob were any renovations proposed. Tellingly, when the second Barney Greengrass opened in Beverly Hills in the 1990s, it was outfitted with sleek, stylish decor—and employees. For the anti-snob snobs (forgive them their acronym) of the Upper West Side, it's an unsettling harbinger of what could happen here if Gary did not hold the line.

The furnishings inside the adjacent retail deli date back to 1929. Behind vintage marble counters, a wide array of high-quality, premium-priced goods are stocked in white-enamel, black-trimmed Art Deco cabinets, shelving, and refrigerator cases. On weekends, diner-style chairs and tables are set up on its terrazzo floors to increase seating capacity. Still, the buttery, thinly sliced, oil-glistening Nova Scotia smoked salmon somehow tastes better in the New Orleans room. It may be ordered as a single-person appetizer sandwich ($10 including cream cheese and a bagel) or within spectacular, two-to-three-person smoked fish platters—Nova solo ($21), Nova and smoked whitefish ($23.50), Nova and world-class smoked sturgeon ($29.50)—including two bagels, cream cheese, black olives, sliced tomatoes, sliced onions, and coleslaw. Another Nova specialty is the "LEO" scramble of lox (smoked salmon), eggs, and onions ($12).

Among non-fish selections, the coarse-textured chopped chicken liver ($6.75 with rye bread or a bagel) is deservedly legendary. Whatever their order, a few discerning Greengrass regulars ask to have the large, bready, and bloated bagels sliced in thirds rather than halves. The three-piece bagel happens to be a perfect fit for the three-slice Nova appetizer.

Cafe Luxembourg

In a dining guide organized by location, it's natural for many of the restaurants to be singled out for the way they reflect the personality of their surroundings. This bistro is extraordinary for the extent to which its character differs from that of a neighborhood disparaged for its dearth of both fine and hip dining. It's surprising that the U.S. Postal Service will even deliver mail addressed to Cafe Luxembourg within the Upper West Side's 10023 zip code. The food itself is

Lunch $20–65
Dinner $30–80

Address 200 West 70th St, between Amsterdam & West End Aves
☎212/873-7411
Transportation 1,2,3,9 to 72nd St
Open Daily 9am–midnight
Accepts All major credit cards
Reservations Required

somewhat overpriced and sometimes less than wonderful. But the glamor radiated by this very downtownish translation of 1930s Montparnasse is a two-decades-old constant. The fantasy of Cafe Luxembourg is depicted in its own Brassai-like postcard of three plump, naked women standing against the zinc bar. The reality comes alive in a beige-tiled room of caned chairs, terrazzo flooring, arched windows, and Deco blinds whose soft, tawny lighting flatters the complexion of smartly attired New Yorkers, some of whom work at nearby Lincoln Center and ABC News.

It's always fashionably correct to order dinner from the "brasserie" menu no matter the depth of your pockets. It features a commendable lobster roll ($16) and smoked salmon sandwich ($13.50) as well as the thick, juice-dripping Luxemburger ($14 with amazing fries). The $38.50 prix fixe is peculiar, as you'd pay no more if you chose its best selections—cornmeal-crusted oysters with saffron aioli ($9.75) and lightly crisped, succulent, herb-roasted free-range chicken with sautéed spinach and creamy mashed potatoes ($18.95)—a la carte. A solid alternative is the horseradish-crusted salmon with sautéed spinach, beet sauce, and fava beans ($23).

Among lunch and brunch enticements there is an excellent and crusty BLT sandwich made with smoked Danish bacon and arugula ($10 with fries or salad), a superb salade Niçoise made-to-order with fresh tuna, and the same Luxemburger and desserts (about $8)—crème brûlée, German chocolate cake, lemon tart—that you find in the un-West Side-like evening.

Celeste

🍴 "The tiny tables are too closely spaced." "There's always a wait." "You can't eat Roman-style fried artichokes every night." "It's difficult to say *no* to the insistent cheese guy." There end the convincing arguments against the Neapolitan-nuanced spinoff of Teodora (see p.195). The exposed brick walls and homespun keepsakes are a good fit for this stretch of Amsterdam Ave., reflecting as they do a Mediterranean variation of Good Enough to Eat (see p.273), the country cafe that first defined the immediate area's folksy character. Still, it's not rustic blue dish towels filling the 60-seater. Rather, it's the confidence chef/co-owner Giancarlo Quadalti shows in the sophistication of his clientele. He dazzles them with simple goodness and low prices rather than affectation or mammoth portions.

> **$20–50**
>
> **Address** 502 Amsterdam Ave, between 84th & 85th Sts
> ☎212/874-4559
> **Transportation** 1,9,B,C to 86th St
> **Open** Mon–Fri 5–11pm, Sat & Sun noon–3.30pm & 5–11pm
> **Accepts** Cash only
> **Reservations** Not accepted

ITALIAN/PIZZA

The salad pairing carpaccio-thin slices of baby artichoke with oversize shavings of Parmesan ($8) introduces Quadalti's approach. It's simple, visually plain, and unforgettable. The same can be said of such antipasti as the balls of mozzarella di bufala ($9.50) and the marinated tuna combined with a tomato bread salad ($8). The thin, soft-crusted pizzas ($10–12), though much improved, remain less than the sum of their exquisite but inadequately integrated parts.

Pastas ($9–9.50) are breathtakingly spare, especially homemade ones like flattened, spinach-and-ricotta filled raviolini with butter and sage or featherweight potato gnocchi with tomato and basil. Dry ones—spaghetti with white clams; tagliatelle with shrimp, cabbage, and Pecorino (sheep's milk cheese)—are toothsome, too. And space must be cleared for the fritto misto (mixed fry) with calamari, shrimp, and red mullets ($9.50). Fish and meat entrees (mostly $15) are agreeable yet discretionary. But reject a cheese plate ($10–30) in favor of a tart or a creamy gelato (most desserts are $5.50) and you essentially slap the face of Carmine, the commuting co-owner who always returns from Italy with a suitcase of choice Pecorinos. To tease the cheese guy, you might thank him for transporting the incredibly creamy mascarpone that goes into Celeste's extraordinary tiramisu. "The mascarpone isn't mine," he concedes. "I don't think it would travel all that well."

Cooke's Corner

The name doesn't sound any better after you hear the story behind it. Chef James Yacyshyn and his wife Maggie Long met Brian Cooke on a cruise to Antarctica and later named their restaurant after the cartoon that the British writer had penned for the London Daily Mail. (Lucky thing Charles Engelhard wasn't the cartoonist they befriended, or the bistro might be called "Absolute Tripe.") Copper-colored silk curtains at the storefront window and

$25–75

Address 618 Amsterdam Ave at 90th St

☎212/712-2872

Transportation 1,2,B,C to 86th St

Open Mon–Thurs 5–10pm, Fri & Sat noon–11pm, Sun noon–9.30pm

Accepts All major credit cards

Reservations Suggested

beige leatherette banquettes behind the tightly spaced, oak-inlaid tables were meant to import a downtown modern feel. But Cooke's Corner works better if you place it firmly in its Upper West Side context and praise it as a casual, scaled-down alternative to neighborhood phenomenon Ouest (see p.276).

Local residents Yacyshyn and Long were frustrated by the dearth of dining options in these parts in the late 1990s, and decided to open a place where they themselves would want to eat. (Perhaps it would have been easier to move?) Though ethnic and theme eateries flourished, not many local kitchens were then devoted to the straightforward, contemporary American cooking thriving elsewhere in the city. Today, starters like sizzling tiger shrimp in garlic ($9), house-cured gravlax with mustard dill sauce ($7), and a trio of crisp goat cheese cakes with a salad of endive, tomato, black olive, and garlic croûtons ($7) would stand out in any precinct. Yacyshyn knows the flavor associations he's after and won't allow himself—or his diners—to get distracted.

Servers rightly push the "four-hour" braised beef with red wine and shallot sauce and spätzle ($15). The time-softened meat is their resonant response to Ouest's braised short ribs, while the braised lamb shank with cumin ($18) is a direct challenge to Ouest's signature dish. But if there's crooning to be done, why not for the maple-glazed, pan-seared salmon and mélange of steamed greens ($15) that answers to no one? The maple treatment adds just the right measure of sticky sweetness. The $18 prix fixe, served between 5pm and 7pm, is a steal. Both the short ribs and the salmon are among its selections.

Flor de Mayo

No one could possibly confuse this budget eatery with the chic fusion restaurant Asia de Cuba (see p.230), even though their personalities are split along the same cultural lines. Still, when this lunchtime stalwart moved to its present location more than ten years ago, the polished parquet floor and oak-trimmed laminate signaled a major upgrading of a fading cheap-eats genre. And after the premises — but happily not the prices — were renovated in fall 2002,

Lunch $8–35
Dinner $12–35

Address 2651 Broadway, between
100th & 101st Sts
☎212/663-5520
Transportation 1 to 103rd St
Open Daily noon–midnight
Accepts All major credit cards
Reservations Not accepted

CHINESE/LATINO

old regulars feared the trusty home of $4.95 lunch specials had been converted into yet another brick-walled bistro. Flor de Mayo also differs from most of the remaining cheap "China-Latina" joints — unlike the Cuban-Chinese who had twice fled Communist revolutions, Flor de Mayo's owners immigrated from Peru.

At dinner, many don't even bother to open the menu, much less pay attention to its Chinese half. They request such Cuban standbys as ropa vieja (shredded beef; $8.15), picadillo (chopped beef; $7.75), or unexpectedly moist pernil asado (roast ham; $8.15). All are served with sweet plantains and a steaming-hot heap of rice (white or yellow). Pink or black beans ($1.20) you order on the side. The dry-spiced but not spicy pollo a la brasa is one of the best rotisserie birds ($6.50 for a half-chicken). You apply the heat yourself by dunking bites of chicken into a Peruvian dip of minced onions, chile, lime juice, and vinegar. Whatever you order, you will need an avocado and lemon side salad ($3.50).

The Chinese food is actually far better than most give it credit for. Ask for sautéed bok choy ($6.75), even when ordering Cuban (there's not much greenery in that neighborhood), and choose if you want it cooked with garlic or ginger and scallions. Of the Hong Kong specials, king do gai ($8.95) delights as much for the sweet-and-sour dipping sauce you can spoon over the rice as for the crisp and moist fried chicken nuggets. And nostalgic hankerings for greasy roast pork lo mein and shrimp chow mein ($9.95) are indulged in a New York minute.

There's another Flor de Mayo at 484 Amsterdam Ave, Upper West Side (☎212/787-3388).

Gennaro

Gennaro Picone needs a wake-up call. As the man behind an Italian restaurant that makes nearly every published short list of affordable places to eat, the Sicilian immigrant is something of a living legend on the Upper West Side. True, nobody has been seen kissing his ring. But there are probably devout diners who would throw their raincoats over a puddle he was about to step in if it got them a table pronto. All that said, the price of dining-on-the-cheap at Gennaro is climbing. The waits of up to an hour

$20–40

Address 665 Amsterdam Ave, between 92nd & 93rd Sts
℡212/665-5348
Transportation 1,2,3,9,B,C to 96th St
Open Sun–Thurs 5–10.30pm, Fri & Sat 5–11pm
Accepts All major credit cards
Reservations Not accepted

are part of the deal. People expect it. But the slapdash and arrogant treatment you're apt to experience once seated is deplorable. During one recent visit, a busboy asked permission to move a table and chairs a few feet to open up a clogged service lane. Three minutes later, a waiter dragged the table back to clear the narrow path the prior action had closed off. Voicing their frustration got the hapless diners only a shrug, a smirk, and a tepid ricotta and spinach tortellini in a lukewarm butter and sage sauce.

So why the nightly lines? Are these folks masochists? Is treating-'em-bad-and-making-'em-like-it part of the successful formula? Well, they certainly don't come for the terracotta tiling, unvarnished wainscoting, and decorative ceramics. Brisk Mediterranean flavors and the accomplished, though at times sloppy, Italian cooking is the draw. Indeed, it's hard to hold a grudge and also manage the antipasto della casa ($21.95), a captivating collection of hot and cold vegetables, prosciutto, mozzarella, shellfish, and other rotated specialties. As alternatives, the $8.50 alliances of potato and Portobello (in a tart) and grilled calamari and couscous (Sicilian-style, with pine nuts and raisins) are advantageous ones.

The fine pastas ($8.50–9.95) and roast Cornish hen ($12.95) notwithstanding, the second most compelling reason for tolerating random table shifts is the tender braised lamb shank in a rich red wine sauce. The first is the $14.95 that you'll pay for it. The tiramisu ($5.25) you can live without.

Good Enough to Eat

AMERICAN

On weekend mornings the cow-bell chimes hanging over the doorway ring at 9am. At 9.08am it is already too late. All the unvarnished wood tables are filled and a line of young families, students, and assorted combinations of chirpy early risers and the morning-after mopers they've dragged out of bed is already forming next to the fence that surrounds the small sidewalk terrace. Soon the wait to be seated and sipping java will exceed an hour, defeating the whole point behind the rural wallhangings, recurring cow motif, homespun pies and cakes, and understated name: to transport the quaint, and presumably serene, charms of a small-town breakfast nook to the Upper West Side. Still, even if you can drive to the country in the time it now takes to get a brunch-time table, the schmoozing, eavesdropping, and people-watching out here in the heart of Seinfeld country is certainly more diverting than it is on the Long Island Expressway.

Breakfast $10–15
Lunch $18–30
Dinner $18–55

Address 483 Amsterdam Ave, between 83rd & 84th Sts
℗212/496-0163
Transportation B,C to 81st St; 1,9 to 86th St
Open Mon–Thurs 8am– 4pm & 5.30–10.30pm, Sat 9am–4pm & 5.30–11pm, Sun 9am–4pm & 5.30–10pm
Accepts All major credit cards
Reservations Not accepted

Good Enough to Eat appreciates that burnt toast does not a great day begin. That when your fluffy but not airy flour-grain pancakes are both topped and filled with blueberries ($8.75), only good things can come after. Patience has no better reward than the "Lumber Jack" ($8.50), a plate of two plain pancakes, two scrambled eggs, and two thick, desirably chewy strips of outstanding slab bacon. Eggs are special too, perhaps loosely scrambled with red onion, chopped tomato, and dill ($5.50); in overstuffed omelettes ($7.75–9) or soaked into homemade cinnamon-swirl bread for French toast ($8.75). A warm biscuit with strawberry butter accompanies all egg dishes. Oddly, the waffles ($7.50–9.50) don't cut it.

Lunch and dinner comforts are more iffy. The buttermilk onion rings ($4.75 as starter or side) and the main course, four-cheese macaroni and cheese ($10.75), are splendid. But the veggieburger ($10.50) crumbles apart, the BBQ chicken sandwich ($10.50) is all sauce, and the pizzas ($12.50–13.50) are barely GETE. With the rustic pies (apple, blueberry, pecan, lemon meringue) and cakes ($5–5.50) it's almost impossible to go wrong.

SOUTHERN

Miss Mamie's Spoonbread Two

Formica meets gingham at this countrified urban diner where northerners get to sip lemonade from mason jars and order up down-home food. What fun! The restaurant grew out of *Spoonbread and Strawberry Wine*, a family memoir written by sisters Carole and Norma Darden that traced their African-American ancestry largely through home-grown formulas for cosmetics, medicines, and Southern cooking. Norma, formerly a successful Wilhemina

$16–35
Address 366 West 110th St at Columbus Ave
☎212/865-6744
Transportation 1,9,B,C to 110th St
Open Mon–Thurs noon–10pm, Fri noon–11pm, Sat 10.30am–11pm, Sun 10.30am–10pm
Accepts All major credit cards

fashion model who did not know the difference between sautéeing and pan-frying, used the book's recipes as the basis first for a catering company, Spoonbread, and then for this restaurant named after her mother (as well as a Harlem spin-off, Miss Maude's, honoring her aunt). The ruffled strawberry curtains and red-and-white checkerboard floor were patterned after Mamie Jean Sampson Darden's kitchen in Alabama.

One peek at the ample-times-two portions tells you this is no place for a present-day or future Wilhemina model to nourish her willowy assets. Two practices do put a lid on the caloric and cholesterol overloads, however. Firstly, the collard greens are fortified with smoked turkey wings instead of pork fat. Secondly, there is, thank heavens, no foreplay. Without appetizers to trouble with, diners get hot and heavy in a hurry with falling-off-the-bone BBQ ribs stuck to a gooey sauce of honey and molasses ($12.95); long-simmered short ribs dripping with tangy, cayenne-revved juices ($14.95); gravy-smothered chicken ($10.95); and splendid fried chicken ($10.95) and well-seasoned fried Louisiana catfish ($12.95) that both benefit from frequent oil changes. All orders come with cornbread and a choice of two sides.

Sensational desserts (mostly $3.95) are large. Some of the cream pies don't appear to have been cut or sliced. Rather, each portion is transferred to a plate in one big blob. Both the coconut cake and the sweet, creamy, banana pudding will have you running out—check that, lumbering out—to find the Darden cookbook and copy the recipes.

Ocean Grill

With its ocean liner styling, of-the-moment seafood and raw bar selections, and prime location opposite the American Museum of Natural History, the Ocean Grill has many things going for it. Trend-surfing owner Steve Hanson (Ruby Foo's, see p.220, and Atlantic Grill, p.246, as well as Blue Water Grill, Isabella's, and Park Avalon) runs a noisy neighborhood cruise. Service is energetic; prices, fair.

Beyond the suspended silk beachball that lights the foyer is a long dining room with coffered ceiling, hardwood floor, leatherette booths, banquettes, and a porthole view of the kitchen. In another, clubby dining room, an undulating, 1950s chandelier illuminates a busy gallery of seashore photos. One night you might sit beneath a beach shot of Brigitte Bardot. Another time, it may be Marilyn Monroe filling a swimsuit.

The "ocean" theme is sometimes carried a bit too far in dishes as salty as the Atlantic. But though seasoning may be a little off, most of the food is at least pretty good and some of it is really rather special. There are two large salads good enough to make regulars out of anyone. You could devote Tuesdays to the classic Caesar with Parmesan croûtons ($7.50); Thursdays, to the gorgeous Green Market salad with roasted corn, beets, asparagus, red pepper, cucumbers, and crumbled goat cheese ($8.50). The thin lobster bisque ($6.50) and heavy steamed shrimp dumplings ($7.95) are appetizer alternatives. Among entrees, a thick slab of wood-grilled yellowfin tuna ($18.50) is far superior to the same high-quality fish in a pepper-crusted version ($18.50). Still, what's reinvigorated Ocean and its diners are the elaborate specials ($18–26), among them tuna with nutty black Thai rice, shiitakes, and sea urchin, or butter-poached lobster with taro purée and confiture of ginger and lemon. Desserts like the caramelized banana ice cream tower ($6.50) and the Granny Smith apple dome ($6) form the skyline of the Hanson empire.

Lunch $20–50
Dinner $30–65

Address 384 Columbus Ave, between 78th & 79th Sts
☎212/579-2300
Transportation 1,9 to 79th St; B,C to 81st St
Open Mon 11.30am–4pm & 5–11pm, Tues–Thurs 11.30am–4pm & 5–11.30pm, Fri & Sat 11.30am–4pm & 5.30pm–midnight, Sun 10.30am–4pm & 5–11pm
Accepts All major credit cards
Reservations Suggested

275

Ouest

Named for the direction of the setting sun and pronounced as it is translated, Ouest thrives in a part of town where not long ago sophisticated restaurants were as scarce as right-wing Republicans. Quite why the cultured, prosperous Upper Ouest Side had failed to adequately support the few influential chefs it had attracted remains a mystery. More apparent are the factors that enabled this particular breakthrough. When you pass from the squeeze of the

$40–85

Address 2315 Broadway at 84th St
☎212/580-8700
Transportation 1,2 to 86th St
Open Mon–Thurs 5–11pm, Fri &
Sat 5pm–midnight, Sun
10.30am–2pm & 5–10pm
Accepts All major credit cards
Reservations Required

tapered bar to the dark-wooded expanse of the high-ceilinged dining room, the effect is of a hip, trendy, noisemaker. But the large, red-and-orange lampshades and comfy crescent-shaped red leather booths befit a restaurant that is ultimately as bourgeois as its core diners. The distinction is that co-owner Tom Valenti, perhaps the least glamorous of New York's celebrity chefs, projects the same hippie-lefty image that many a self-deceiving Upper West Sider still sees when he looks in the bathroom mirror.

Valenti's cooking is robust in both content and technique. Most plates give the impression of depth and volume, even when portions are stingy (see: short ribs). He may be the only chef who can turn a sweet-pea broth ($9 as a special) into a star turn, while turning even the nutritionally correct on to a truffled omelette soufflé with cream-enriched mousseline sauce ($10).

Limiting your signature dish to specials status is cruel. Choosing Mondays and Tuesdays as the days to release those braised lamb shanks ($26) from slow-cooking captivity shows pure chutzpah. But Valenti has responded to his diners' frustrations by combining two of his best entrees, braised short ribs and filet mignon, into a sensational daily combo ($32). Another lush distraction is the duck ragoût with potato gnocchi and Parmesan ($23). The $26 pre-theater (Mon–Fri 5–6.30pm) prix fixe is unbeatable. Among desserts, the mascarpone tart with cranberry compote ($9) and creamy lemon chiboust ($8) are so satisfying you might think you're seeing a lot more of you in the mirror the next morning.

Rosa Mexicano

(🍴) The opening in 2000 of a second Rosa Mexicano had devotees of the East Side favorite (1063 1st Ave, Midtown East; ☎212/753-7407) hoping for the best and fearing the worst. Would its arrival bring dependable dining to a food-cursed part of town? Or would the offshoot be a disappointment that managed only to drain valuable resources from the original? Most of those hopes and only a few of those fears have been realized: this snazzy Rosa belongs near the top of the city charts in the categories of "Best Mexican" and "Best Near Lincoln Center." Designer David Rockwell played to the weaknesses of a difficult two-story space. Against the constrictive main wall he installed a striking 30ft, blue-tile water wall that serves as the diving cliff for 240 white figurines. The staircase alongside this abstract Acapulco is composed of terrazzo slabs matched to the hues of the belt-woven chairs. Windows facing the State Theater add continuity and splendor to the upper level.

Lunch $25–50
Dinner $40–75

Address 61 Columbus Ave at 62nd St

☎212/977-7700

Transportation 1,9,A,B,C,D to 59th St-Columbus Circle

Open Mon noon–3pm & 5–11pm, Tues–Fri noon–3pm & 5pm–midnight, Sat 11.30am–3pm & 5pm–midnight, Sun 11.30am–3pm & 5–11pm

Accepts All major credit cards

Reservations Suggested

MEXICAN

The menu, a 40/60 mix of new and established dishes, is supervised by Roberto Santebanez. With this position must come the acceptance that his most accomplished appetizers will invariably play second avocado to the guacamole ($14 for two) prepared tableside and served with chips, silver-dollar corn tortillas, and, ideally, a frozen pomegranate margarita. Still, it is starters like hongos ($8), a garlicky sauté of meaty wild mushrooms propped over a polenta-like mush, and the desirably chewy chicken ravioli wading in a shallow pool of smoky poblano pepper sauce and melted manchego that distinguish this from other moderate-to-upscale Mexican eateries.

Perhaps the best of the platillos principales is the mixióte de cordero (chile-rubbed lamb shank; $22). Staged within the rumpled round rim of its open parchment casing, the smoky lamb juices are deeply flavored. Another kind of roasted chile flavor, this one dark, heavy, and spicy, imbues every tender bite of the braised chilayo (pork loin; $20). Good dessert options ($7–8) include a chocolate mousse pastry on a chocolate-peanut pedestal.

Sarabeth's

🍴 Pretty, pricey Sarabeth's is a mid-block fantasy world bursting at its wainscoted seams with not only city folk but also suburbanites who drive into town merely to be transported back out to some country cottage in either of the two Englands—New or old. Were Martha Stewart and Laura Ashley contemporaries, you could see them fitting in just fine here, admiring the sheaves of wheat and jam jars displayed in the centerpiece hutch. Soon they'd get around to the serious business at hand: sitting down with Sarabeth Levine and devising interesting new ways to enjoy poppyseeds. If, embold-

$15–60

Address 423 Amsterdam Ave, between 80th & 81st Sts; plus other locations
☎212/496-6280
Transportation 1,9 to 79th St; B,C to 81st St
Open Mon–Fri 8am–10.30pm, Sat 8am–4pm & 5.30–10.30pm, Sun 8am–4pm & 5.30–9.30pm
Accepts All major credit cards
Reservations For dinner only

ened by each other's company, they felt like being wicked, they could order the "green and white" (scrambled eggs with scallions and cream cheese; $8), the lemon ricotta pancakes with berries and warm pure maple syrup ($9) or any of the delightful breakfast items as late as 4pm.

Not since the Great Depression has New York witnessed such long lines of people waiting for bowls of oatmeal as outside this leader on the breakfast and brunch circuit. The most seasoned cynic could not, however, fault the quality of the homemade jams, omelets, muffins, and, yes, oatmeal. The porridges (from $4.25 for the "Baby Bear" bowl to $5.50 for "Big Bad Wolf") are at once creamy and granular, with honey, fresh cream, bananas, raisins, and wheatberries among the accessories. The Goldie Lox ($9.50), a scramble of smoked salmon and cream cheese, is an egg thing that some Upper Westsiders see more often than their spouses. Jams and breakfast breads, all available for carryout, deserve their fame.

The cuteness peaks at lunch, most notably with the crisp-edged, moist-centered polenta logs ($4), arranged like the megaliths of Stonehenge, and the salad of poached salmon, corn, tomato, and chopped lettuce ($13) set out in perfect bands of pink, yellow, red and green. Still, their composition, like that of the smoked mozzarella sandwich ($10.50), the Virginia ham and Vermont Cheddar club-style sandwich ($11.75), and the soupy chicken pot pie with a puff-pastry lid ($14) are undeniably first-rate.

Brooklyn

Bay Ridge and Bensonhurst

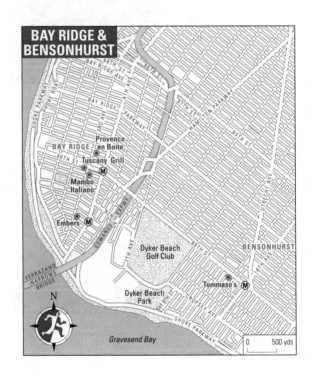

BAY RIDGE & BENSONHURST

BAY RIDGE AVE

BAY RIDGE AVE

86TH ST

86TH ST

SHORE ROAD

SHORE PARKWAY

3RD AVE

4TH AVE

7TH AVE

BAY RIDGE PARKWAY

HAMILTON PARKWAY

65TH ST

UTRECHT AVE

BAY RIDGE

Provence
en Boite

Tuscany Grill Ⓜ

86TH ST

Mambo
Italiano

Embers Ⓜ

GOWANUS EXPWY

2ND AVE

Dyker Beach
Golf Club

86TH ST

BENSONHURST

7TH AVE

VERRAZANO
NARROWS
BRIDGE

Dyker Beach
Park

BAY ST

CROPSEY AVE

Tommaso's Ⓜ

SHORE PARKWAY

Gravesend Bay

N

0   500 yds

Embers

You almost have to leave Brooklyn entirely to get to the borough's "other" steakhouse. Situated at the end of the R subway line and near the approach to the Verrazano Narrow Bridge, Embers is cherished as the working-man's Peter Luger's in that its location and prices are miles south of that famous Brooklyn steakhouse. You don't need to look far to figure out how owner Louis Rocanelli can charge as little as $32.95 for a 60oz T-bone steak-for-two. He owns the butcher shop next door and probably gives himself a good bulk price on those well-aged Brooklyn hunks. But only an Arthur Andersen accountant could see a profit in selling a Ruffino Chianti Classico 1997 Ducale Riserva Gold for $54 when other restaurants are getting $75–85 for the same bottle. Whatever the explanation, you can be reasonably sure Rocanelli's wine supplier does not wait as long as ordinary mortals do for a Saturday night table.

Lunch $15–30
Dinner $30–60

Address 9519 3rd Ave, between 95th & 96th Sts
☏718/745-3700
Transportation R to 95th St
Open Mon–Fri noon–2.45pm & 5–10.30pm, Sat noon–2pm & 4.30–11.30pm, Sun 2–9.30pm
Accepts MasterCard & Visa
Reservations Not accepted

Stereotypes about the gaudy fashions of Embers' regulars are sustained by the odd diner dressed for a hot date in gold jewelry and designer jogging suit. That said, workout garb is not that ridiculous in view of the cramped conditions both at the bar and in the two dining rooms, and the physical exertion required when taking on a steak. Besides, the marble wallpaper and suspended acoustic ceiling are hardly the decorative counterparts of a smart, black leather blazer.

The menu is shorter than it appears. Much shorter. You basically want to concern yourself with three superb, absurdly affordable steaks (in order of preference): the juicy T-bone (a 32-ouncer is $22.95), the New York sirloin ($18.95), and the filet mignon ($19.95). They're the reason you're here. The rest is window dressing. Even the potato choice is a charade. While the potato pie—smashed potato with grated Parmesan, prosciutto bits, and butter—is justifiably revered and an absolute must, the frozen fries are a joke. The fine frutti di mare (cold seafood salad appetizer; $8.95) is the single exception to the steak-only rule. Ordering any dessert once is a mistake. Ordering one twice is a crime.

Mambo Italiano

To your left, in a caricaturist's mural of Italian movie stars, native daughter Marisa Tomei asks Joe Pesci whether he can mambo. Overhead, a signora's long-dried undergarments dangle from a clothesline. To your right, Patricio, a tenor who happens to be your co-waiter, serenades your table with a Neapolitan love song as he fills your glasses with Chianti. So goes your introduction to the mondo of Mambo Italiano,

$30–65

Address 8803 3rd Ave at 88th St
☎718/833-4432
Transportation R to 86th St
Open Mon–Thurs noon–11pm, Fri & Sat noon–midnight, Sun 2–10pm
Accepts All major credit cards
Reservations Suggested

a campy, hand-clapping, family-forging, diet-destroying dining destination that's ideal for bachelor—or bachelorette—parties, birthday celebrations, and other boisterous bashes. Besides the crooning servers, nightly entertainment is provided by the likes of Johnny Lala, who does a great Al Green, and Jeannie, a red-headed Aretha.

Mambo Italiano differs from other singing restaurants in that the place actually has a kitchen. While the food will please Brooklyn sophisticates, plates are large enough to stretch even the most voracious diners to their limits. Family-style platters portioned and priced for two people can feed at least three. Appetizers include cleanly fried calamari with spicy red sauce ($17.95), an imposing cold antipasto ($18.95), and an all-encompassing frutta di mare ($18.95) with cold shrimp, calamari, and scungili (a cousin of conch) marinated in olive oil, garlic, and lemon juice.

Mambo's pastas are stirring illustrations of creativity and overkill. Fettuccine Mambo ($27.95) piles shrimp, lobster, scallops, peas, artichokes, and a creamy tomato sauce over its pasta. But this is child's play in relation to the shameless glut of the special lobster Stoli for two ($45.95)—two lobsters with pink vodka lobster sauce, shrimp, and fusilli pasta. And then there are the veal, chicken, and steak entrees, including a 32oz porterhouse topped with sautéed onions and mushrooms ($39.95). Best advice for dessert ($19.95), after ogling a cart topped with the likes of chocolate cheesecake, tiramisu, and a napoleon, is to take two shorts and one long: an espresso and a walk on the short side, and then a nap on the long.

Provence en Boîte

The name Provence en Boîte—
"canned Provence"—features two
out of three French passions brought to
Bay Ridge's main dining strip by
charming hosts Leslie and Jean-Jacques
Bernat. The shelves in their endearing
bistro/pastry shop are crowded with vintage *boîtes*, meaning "tins" or "cans," for
such old-time Gallic groceries as Aigue-
belle cocoa and Maggi bouillon cubes.
Hung beneath those shelves and draped
over the tables are fabrics and table-

Lunch $12–35
Dinner $27–60

Address 8303 3rd Ave, between
83rd & 84th Sts
☎718/759-1515
Transportation R to 86th St
Open Sun–Thurs 7.30am–11pm, Fri
& Sat 7.30am–midnight
Accepts All major credit cards

FRENCH

cloths in Provençal colors and patterns. The third Bernat
passion—pastries—may not be present in the name, but they are promi-
nently arranged in a display case just inside the front door so that they
are the first, last, and most lasting images of a breakfast, lunch, dinner,
brunch, or between-meals visit.

The pre-dessert cooking is two-thirds provençal and one-third classic
French. The former is best represented by escargots à la Provençale
($10.50), a traditional preparation in which the snails are sautéed with
chopped mushrooms, parsley, and garlic and simmered with white wine
to create a richly flavored but not thickened sauce. Classic French flavors find expression in the French onion soup ($7.50), admirable less for
the diluted soup than the crusty cheese topping, and the tartiflettes savo-
yardes ($8), a cheese-topped potato gratin. Entree highlights include
herb-roasted chicken smothered in mushroom sauce and paired with
good frites ($15), a small salmon fillet with a lightly sour sorrel cream
sauce prepared according to the recipe of Pierre and Jean Troisgros
($16.50), and a pretty good bouillabaisse of shrimp, mussels, scallops,
monkfish, and haddock in a pale, fennel-scented broth with rouille-
smeared toasts afloat ($19.75).

Jean-Jacques Bernat is a pastry chef by trade, a fact made plainly
obvious by his delectable, camera-ready pastries ($3.75). The apricot tart,
chocolate-mousse-filled porcupine, and hazelnut nougat praline pastry
figure among the best options. But Bernat is proudest of his Lafayette, a
triumph whose integral parts—almond dacquoise, chocolate mousse,
fresh raspberries—may be drawn out by a glass of dessert wine like
Muscat Beaume de Venise or Muscat de Rivesaltes (both $5).

Tommaso's

Tommaso Verdillo doesn't look like the Brooklyn treasure he is any more than his renovated, kitsch-congested dining room resembles a multi-starred restaurant. You simply don't expect to be serenaded with the finest Italian food, wines, and arias by a guy dressed for a trip to the Laundromat. But Verdillo's casual garb, the old family photos, and the standup piano make more sense once you think of this as his

$35–75

Address 1464 86th St, between
14th & 15th Aves
☎718/236-9883
Transportation W to 18th Ave
Open Tues–Sun noon–midnight
Accepts All major credit cards
Reservations Suggested

home and not his place of business. This requires some imagination, as few domiciles have 14,000 bottles of wine in their basement. Though a diner's checks, aspirations, and body weight may be fattened somewhat by the likes of foie gras gently sautéed with bittersweet caramelized orange peel $13.95), there is no compromise in opting for the most basic Southern Italian dishes that also pepper the menu. As Verdillo likes to say when comparing a $20 and $200 wine: "They're both excellently made. There are just different things going on."

Not that he is above snobbery. He regarded requests for his $20 prix fixe dinners as social blunders and eventually took them off the menu. Now there's no choice but to start with such appetizers as the stuffed artichokes ($8.50) and deep-fried mozzarella in carrozza ($6.50). Two cannelloni preparations display unusual finesse and each merit serious consideration: frutti di mare (seafood-stuffed) with crab sauce ($14.95) and veal-and-Swiss-chard-filled in a heady leek, mushroom, and veal sauce ($14.95).

As for entrees, succumbing to the breast of veal stuffed with spinach, ground veal, raisins, pine nuts, and bread ($16.95) is almost like being adopted into an extended family. It's challenged in scope only by the osso buco ($23.95), a veal shank braised to tender perfection and portioned by the cubic acre (half a shank per order). Other alluring possibilities include calf's liver sautéed with onions, figs, and pancetta ($17.95) as well as a cassoulet ($17.95) given an Italian accent with its use of cannellini beans. Settling upon one of two outstanding desserts—semifreddo topped with chocolate sauce ($5.50) or vanilla coconut flan ($4.50)—assures a creamy, melt-in-your-mouth finish.

Tuscany Grill

Festive lights are strung from the outside of this Bay Ridge trattoria. The Verrazzano-Narrows looms in the distance, a twinkling if steely stand-in for the Ponte Vecchio. Inside, John Conforti, perched at the bar, warmly greets all-comers. Throughout the evening, he casually makes his way from farmhouse table to farmhouse table between the deliberately distressed walls of the softly lit dining room, chatting with regulars and first-timers alike. His wife Marny is mostly confined to the kitchen, turning out her partially Tuscan, wholeheartedly rendered Italian cuisine which, together with seamless service and copious portions, packs the house even on weeknights.

$30–70

Address 8620 3rd Ave, between 86th & 87th Sts

☎718/921-5633

Transportation R to 86th St

Open Mon–Thurs 5–10pm, Fri & Sat 5–11pm, Sun 4–9pm

Accepts All major credit cards

Reservations Required

Marny previously cooked at Al Forno in Providence, Rhode Island, and it was she who introduced Brooklyn to that restaurant's claim to fame: wood-grilled pizza. Cooked over an open fire, Marny's extremely thin, light, crisp-crusted grilled pizzas ($12 and up) pose not a question of if, but only how, and when. Shared appetizer? Entree? Side dish? Cheese course? Combinations ranging from the standard Margherita—tomato, mozzarella, basil—to gorgonzola, roasted peppers, and onions are all sparingly topped so that the dressings neither soften nor overwhelm the crust. A pizza appetizer may be supplemented with the rustic salad of warm red cabbage ($9) or, if you're not opposed to bread-on-bread, bruschetta ($6) with a mix of ripe tomatoes, fresh basil, and fine extra virgin olive oil heaped onto grilled Tuscan bread.

Pasta comes in first-course half-portions or as a sizeable entree. Tripolini Toscana ($8.50/$14) is a robust bowl of bow-ties, fresh tomatoes, radicchio, grilled sausage, and black olives. Grilled chicken filled with herbed goat cheese and served over spinach alongside rosemary potatoes ($18) is a hearty invention, playing the perfectly charred and crisped skin against the succulent meat and oozing cheese. Other laudable entrees include a trio of sausages from Faicco's Pork Stores (the Brooklyn branch is on 11th Ave) served with sautéed bitter greens and garlic mashed potatoes ($17), and balsamic-glazed oven-roasted pork tenderloin. As a coda, the wild berry tart ($6.50) bears a scrumptious overflow of sweet, tangy fruit.

Brooklyn Heights, Dumbo
& Downtown Brooklyn

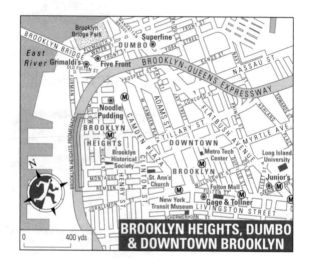

BROOKLYN HEIGHTS, DUMBO & DOWNTOWN BROOKLYN

Five Front

An accurate description of Five Front hardly suggests that of a genuine restaurant. It instead suggests an impossible request from a demanding location scout seeking an idealized setting for a pivotal movie scene: "Hey kid, find me a lighthearted, understated, romantic, kid-friendly, pubby-bistro sort of place in a historic Brooklyn townhouse with brick walls and pressed tin on the ceiling and staircase. It has to be near the warehouse lofts of DUMBO and the brownstones of Brooklyn Heights and within a Marion Jones leap of the Brooklyn Bridge. It should have a bar, preferably something long and glossy, two cozy dining rooms, and a secluded, spacious garden. And, oh yeah, it's gotta serve rustic, Italian-inspired American food *and* a big-time burger. Get back to me in an hour, will ya, with five options."

Obviously there is but one so-qualified candidate, just as there is only a single Five Front appetizer to consider, the short rib dumplings in a veal demi-glace ($8). So outstanding are the translucent skin, melted beef filling, and rich, sticky reduction of these half-moons that the lone alternative to ordering them as a starter would be to order them as a main course. That scenario might open with the elegant, no-nonsense salad of crisp, baby Bibb lettuce with roasted garlic and a Dijon vinaigrette ($5). The San Vito lo Capo couscous ($15) turns a routine school night into a Sicilian festival. Chef Paul Vicino turns clams, mussels, shrimp, scallops, and monkfish in a garlicky, parsley-potent fish broth all spooned over *kous kous*, as the semolina grains are known in the Tapani area of Sicily. Leaning more to the north is the slow-braised lamb shank with crisp-edged polenta ($16).

Closer to home, chicken potpie ($15) is capped with a pastry disk and filled with choice strips of chicken breast, al dente haricots verts, and fresh thyme. The burger ($9) is distinguished by its fried-onion topping and hard roll. The warm banana bread pudding cake ($7) isn't what you'd call a dessert; rather, it's a grand finale.

$18–50

Address 5 Front St, between Old Fulton & Dock Sts

☏718/625-5559

Transportation A,C to High St; F to York St; 2,3 to Clark St

Open Mon 5.30–11pm, Wed & Thurs noon–3pm &5.30–11pm, Fri noon–3pm & 5.30pm–midnight, Sat 11am–4pm & 5.30pm–midnight, Sun 11am–4pm & 5.30–11pm

Accepts All major credit cards

NEW AMERICAN

AMERICAN

Gage & Tollner

When Charles Gage opened his restaurant in 1879, Brooklyn was still an independent municipality of roughly 600,000 inhabitants, the third largest city in the US. When he moved it to its current address in 1882, the Brooklyn Bridge was still a year away from opening. Now, the entrance to the exquisitely restored Gage & Tollner is a direct passage to that glorious time and place. The solid mahogany tables, bentwood chairs, velvet brocade, and gaslit chandeliers of cut glass reflected in long rows of arched mirrors distinguish with Victorian elegance the first restaurant interior to be designated a landmark by the city Brooklyn joined in 1898. Yet this

Lunch $22–70
Dinner $32–80

Address 372 Fulton St at Red Hook Lane & Smith St

☎718/875-5181

Transportation M,N,R to Lawrence St; 2,3 to Hoyt St; A,C,F to Jay St-Boro Hall

Open Mon–Thurs 11.30am–3.30pm & 5–10pm, Fri 11.30am–3.30pm & 5–11pm, Sat 3.30–11pm

Accepts All major credit cards

Reservations Suggested

is no museum, even if the mannered, uniformed servers do recall a long-lost era. A magnet for business and political lunches by day, at night the restaurant attracts an effervescent, well-dressed, and diverse crowd from the surrounding communities.

The menu spoils any lingering illusion of time travel with words like "balsamic" and "lemongrass." But it does feature some of the throwback seafoods and chops that once defined grand New York dining. The kitchen performs faithful covers of the venerable southern-style dishes of his legendary predecessor Edna Lewis. Among them are crabmeat Virginia ($12.95), a potato galette with spinach and fresh, spicy, crabmeat; outstanding Maryland she-crab soup or lobster bisque (both sherry-creamed and $6.50); and clam bellies ($11.95 appetizer; $19.95 entree), breaded and broiled Ipswich clams fitted with buttered vegetables into unrelated Cherrystone shells before you slurp those soft, sweet babies down.

Among entrees, grilled salmon ($18.95) is close to perfect, nicely set up with mashed potatoes and a mustard dill sauce. A pat of not quite melted butter compensates for the sporadic dryness of mammoth steaks ($24.95 for a sirloin; $29.95 for a T-bone) as do rotated sauces for veal chops ($29.95). You're better taken care of with a grilled whole fish like orata ($22.95). The dual chocolate mousse ($6.50) is the cake to pluck from the fine dessert cart.

Grimaldi's

It isn't for tiring that Brooklyn's pizza-loving romantics get weak at the knees while waiting in line at Grimaldi's. The pizzeria is perched at the foot of the Brooklyn Bridge, affording a breathtaking view of the Brooklyn waterfront and the Lower Manhattan skyline. Hearts are further stirred by the old Sinatra recordings spilling out the door, accompanied by both the Nelson Riddle Orchestra and the waft of garlic emanating from the brick oven. Inside, an entire wall is covered with photos of Ol' Blue Eyes. Oh, baby, this is how pizza was meant to be.

$6–25

Address 19 Old Fulton St, between Front & Water Sts

☎718/858-4300

Transportation A,C to High St; F to York St; 2,3 to Clark St

Open Mon–Thurs 11.30am–11pm, Fri 11.30am–midnight, Sat noon–midnight, Sun noon–11pm

Accepts Cash only

Reservations Not accepted

PIZZA

Once seated, the only thing that can come between you and your pizza is the antipasto ($10) of mozzarella, salami, Sicilian olives, and roasted peppers. Better to skip it entirely and have those sweet roasted peppers atop your pie, either a six-slice small ($12 and up) or eight-slice large ($14 and up), both baked and spottily charred in the coal-fired oven. The result is a delicately chewy and divinely thin crust save for the outer rim, whose air bubbles are so large it looks as though the pizza has sprouted mushrooms (such pockets should probably be deflated by the baker). The pizza is crisp enough to support its thin layers of milky mozzarella and zesty plum tomato sauce, but not so stiff as to prevent easy folding of each slice, according to the native practice.

The best additional toppings are the crumbled fennel sausage ($2) and extra grated cheese ($2). Avoid the anchovies (for some bizarre reason they're served with capers—and you get more capers per portion than the anchovies themselves) and see if you can get them to put the fresh basil on the pie *after* it is baked. The blackened, shriveled basil has the pungent aroma of marijuana—presumably not what you want on a masterpizza such as this. For some, the overstuffed cannoli is a perfect dessert. For others, the departing view of lower Manhattan is sweet enough.

Junior's

The black shopping bag of Barney's New York invariably carries gifts of style and distinction. A mere glimpse of the egg-blue bag trademarked by Tiffany makes women quiver with anticipation. But no gift bag will excite a knowing and cholesterol-indifferent dinner host more than the orange-striped white bag imprinted with the oval logo of Junior's. It typically holds New York's most famous cheesecake and an emotional reminder of Brooklyn's landmark and still flourishing bakery/coffee shop/restaurant/deli.

$10–60

Address 386 Flatbush Ave at DeKalb Ave

☎718/852-5257

Transportation M,N,Q,R,W to DeKalb Ave; 2,3 to Nevins St

Open Sun–Wed 6.30am–12.30am, Thurs 6.30am–1am, Fri & Sat 6.30am–2am

Accepts All major credit cards

Reservations Not accepted

Mediocrity, the pitfall of wearing so many hats, does not escape Junior's. Those who opt for ambitious seafood platters, barbecue dishes, or Italian specials are gluttons for disappointment. Those who stick to a narrow rotation of old standards leave happy. Breakfast is close to a sure thing, as all eggs and omelets ($4.95–8.50) come with a prodigious assortment of rugelach, mini-Danish, and rolls. Similarly, no lunch or dinner is served without a setup of pickles and coleslaw. Nothing bests the broiled steakburger ($6.50–9.25)—a 10oz mound of ground meat oozing juices with every squeeze. Citing the hot open roast beef sandwich ($10.25) as a standout may be a surprise even to the waiters, who are unaccustomed to taking orders for the large platter of rare, beautifully pink meat. Lastly, the combination sandwich pairing lean and prim corned beef with fatty and depraved pastrami ($9.25) makes perfect sense.

So just how good is that famed cheesecake? It can be difficult to know what to make of the thin, cursory layer of spongy crust that now serves as its graham-cracker foundation. Each wedge ($4.50–5.25) is not so much a cake as it is several inches of blended cream cheese topped with nuts and fruit. And, as it happens, that turns out to be a very good thing. The egg cream ($2.50) is stirred in a measuring glass showing exactly how much milk, chocolate syrup, and seltzer to pour into it. You can buy egg cream kit and take it to a loved one in a striped plastic bag.

There's another Junior's in the lower level dining concourse, Grand Central Terminal, Midtown East (☎212/983-5257).

Noodle Pudding

There's never been a name posted outside this establishment, and for good reason. An Italian restaurant that never has and apparently never will serve noodle pudding cannot possibly in good conscience flaunt the name "Noodle Pudding." It's painful even to write those words atop this review. The Brooklyn Heights trattoria is so-called because the proprietor answers to the family name of Migliaccio and is known to his Jewish friends as Mr Kugel. *Migliaccio* is Italian for *kugel*, you see, which is Yiddish for a baked pudding often made with noodles. Neither Antonio Migliaccio nor his restaurant is Jewish. But his family did prepare its namesake dish Neapolitan-style (recipe: fettuccine, eggs, butter, milk, ricotta, raisins, sugar, and vanilla all baked until golden) back on the island of Ischia in his native Campania. "It's a sin to throw out leftover pasta," he recalls. "So we made noodle pudding."

It is also a sin, Mr Kugel, not to serve your migliaccio di Ischia at a low-priced, otherwise unassuming neighborhood restaurant called Noodle Pudding. Diners take home only warm memories of your fried calamari ($8.50) and sliced Portobellos served over mixed greens ($6). They like the way your lamb Bolognese clings to the rigatoni ($9.50) and how your crusty slices of grilled lamb ($16) deliver their rosemary scent. They're also impressed with the Reagan-era price of your grilled filet mignon and the option of having it in two sizes ($14.75 and $22). They adore too your veal Milanese with arugula and mozzarella, though it's not always possible to tell how hot, cold, or tepid each ingredient should be. They're even mildly amused to learn that bread pudding ($5) has surpassed tiramisu and seasonal fruit tarts in popularity and is now your signature dessert. Good for you!

Nevertheless, no one will fully appreciate the modest elegance of the spare and comfortable dining room you decorated, the romantic sounds of the Italian and French music you play, or the beautiful view out the wrought-iron picture window you built until the family dish is added to the dessert menu. It's either that, Signore Kugel, or a name change.

$25–60

Address 38 Henry St, between Cranberry & Middagh Sts
☏718/625-3737
Transportation A,C to High St; 1,2 to Clark St
Open Tues–Thurs 5.30–10.30pm, Fri & Sat 5.30–11pm, Sun 5–10pm
Accepts Cash only
Reservations For large groups

ITALIAN

NEW AMERICAN

Superfine

Superfine is the sort of haunt you expect to find in burgeoning urban art colonies. Created inside the brick shell of an old auto-parts depot, this emphatically unpolished restaurant/bar/lounge/art space reflects the (re)building boom in the Brooklyn warehouse district dubbed DUMBO—Down Under the Manhattan Bridge Overpass. The locals love Superfine because it embodies the bohemian, do-it-yourself ethos even the million-dollar loft owners among them

Lunch $12–30
Dinner $22–45

Address 126 Front St at Pearl St
℡718/243-9005
Transportation F to York St
Open Tues–Fri 11.30am–3pm &
6–11pm, Sat 6–11pm, Sun
11am–3pm & 6–10pm
Accepts All major credit cards

pretend to live by. Visitors are properly thrilled to climb the loading ramp that cuts between the split-level bar and lounge (love that tangerine-colored pool table!), be seated opposite the all-stainless-steel open kitchen, and grab an authentic, post-industrial taste of DUMBO. In chef Laura Taylor's hands that means seasonal contemporary American brasserie fare presented in the offhand manner of an off-campus coffeehouse.

There are no printed menus and no clear demarcation between appetizers and entrees; the specials and unspecials are instead magic-markered on and just as quickly dry-erased from the whiteboard that tours a dining platform composed of diamond-perforated steel sheets scattered with mix-and-match dinette tables. The selection is determined as much by supply, meaning Greenmarket availability, as demand. Still, the chances of your feeling cheated out of a prized dish are slim; the standouts—tender, faintly bitter grilled calamari with watercress and aioli dip ($8); juicy, pan-braised pork chop with roasted vegetables ($14); a rare roast beef sandwich with chive cream cheese and watercress ($9)—are rerun as often as *Friends*. Moreover, anything that comes with the crisp, matchstick fries "antiqued" in hot oil to a deep, amber demi-gloss is a sure crowd-pleaser.

Stop in often enough and you'll likely get a crack at the good, if not superfine, steamed mussels with roasted tomato and garlic ($11), pepper-glazed steak au poivre ($20), and grilled polenta with a wild mushroom and crumbled sausage ragu ($15). The most tempting $6 dessert is the blanco y negro (cinnamon ice milk and espresso cream), though it lacks the richness of the chocolate nut torte and the gratification of the chocolate cookie ice cream sandwich.

Carroll Gardens, Cobble Hill & Boerum Hill

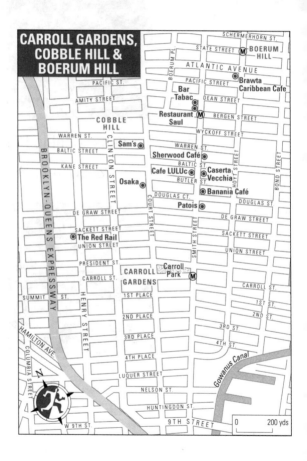

CARROLL GARDENS,
COBBLE HILL &
BOERUM HILL

SCHERMERHORN ST.

STATE STREET Ⓜ BOERUM HILL

ATLANTIC AVENUE

PACIFIC STREET ● Brawta Caribbean Cafe

PACIFIC ST.

AMITY STREET

Bar Tabac ◉

DEAN STREET

COBBLE HILL

Restaurant Saul ◉ Ⓜ BERGEN STREET

WYCKOFF STREET

WARREN ST. Sam's ◉

WARREN STREET

BALTIC STREET Sherwood Café ◉

BALTIC ST. Caserta Vecchia ◉

KANE STREET Cafe LULUc ◉

BUTLER

Osaka ◉ ● Banania Café

DOUGLAS CT. DOUGLAS ST.

Patois ◉

DE GRAW STREET

DE GRAW STREET

SACKETT STREET

◉ The Red Rail SACKETT STREET

UNION STREET

UNION STREET

PRESIDENT ST.

CARROLL Carroll Park

CARROLL ST. GARDENS Ⓜ

CARROLL ST.

1ST PLACE 1ST ST.

2ND PLACE 2ND ST.

3RD PLACE 3RD ST.

4TH ST.

4TH PLACE

LUQUER STREET

NELSON ST.

Gowanus Canal

HUNTINGDON ST.

9TH STREET 9TH STREET

BROOKLYN-QUEENS EXPRESSWAY

SUMMIT ST.

HENRY STREET

HAMILTON AVE.

COLUMBIA STREET

W 9TH ST

N

0   200 yds

BOERUM PL.

CLINTON STREET

COURT STREET

SMITH STREET

HOYT ST.

BOND STREET

Banania Café

In retrospect, it was probably not the most brilliant idea to name the place after a French brand of cocoa powder made with banana flour and closely associated since 1915 with its caricature logo of a smiling Senegalese infantryman in a red fez. The use of that advertising image, though racially insensitive to some, reflected only the noble intention of a new kid on the block to be as welcoming to young children as a mug of hot Ovaltine on a Sunday morning in January. To warm the hearts of their parents it took something more. Copper sheeting installed as wainscoting casts a soft amber glow over the tin-ceilinged room of paper-clothed, candlelit tables, while chef-owner Danforth Houle's Mediterranean and Asian flourishes distinguish Banania from other budget bistros nearby, Houle's own Cafe LULUc (see p.302) among them. The outcome, somewhat ironic given the cramped conditions and frequently brusque service, is the most grownup, romantic, family-friendly (especially for brunch), and, to many, refreshingly unhip French bistro of the Smith Street lot.

$22–50

Address 241 Smith St at Douglass St
☎718/237-9100
Transportation F,G to Carroll St
Open Mon–Thurs 5.30–11pm, Fri & Sat 5.30–11.30pm, Sun 10am–4pm & 5–10.30pm
Accepts Cash only
Reservations Not accepted

FRENCH

If Houle's cooking can be faulted, it's for being too ambitious, which can make it difficult to execute the menu with consistency. It's nice that he wants to do something a little different with escargots ($6.50) besides the usual garlic and butter. But the lemon juice makes them too tart. Moroccan spiced calamari with frisée ($7) are more successful, however, and the cornmeal-crusted oysters with celery root purée ($6) offer a becoming play of flavor and textures.

Among main courses, the overproduced vegetable Wellington ($13) resembling a giant, browned empanada filled with roasted tomatoes, garlic, spinach, and melted goat cheese is frivolous fun. Who cares if the first bite is ten times more pleasurable than the last? You can also get a darn good steak frites for $16. And the Provençal-style, pan-roasted cod with black olive potato purée ($13.50) is a winner. The dessert to try at least once is the fried banana ravioli in chocolate sauce ($5)—an unobjectionable tribute to the namesake Banania.

Bar Tabac

The faded fantasies (Jules in the East Village, Café Noir in SoHo) that Georges Forgeois pieced together out of old furnishings, advertisements, and collectibles were convincing because he managed to leave each effort one vintage Dubonnet ashtray short of theme-restaurant sentimentality. That knack for knowing when to quit failed him when he moved to Brooklyn's bistro-dotted Smith Street. Forgeois filled his exquisitely ripened period piece with every trite trapping in his retro bistro treasure trove. The old mirrors, aperitif placards, and illuminated red "carotte" (the lozenge-shaped signpost seen outside all French bar-tabacs) mounted on the tobacco-stained walls would have been sufficient. But Forgeois couldn't help himself, and went ahead and parked a vintage scooter and old foozball inside the restaurant.

$25–55

Address 128 Smith St at Dean St
☎718/923-0918
Transportation F,G to Bergen St
Open Mon–Tues 11.30am–1am, Wed & Thurs 11.30am–2am, Fri 11.30am–3am, Sat 11am–3am, Sun 10am–1am
Accepts AmEx
Reservations Suggested

The phoniness is happily lost on locals delighted to have this breezy brunch spot and easy-going late-night haunt in their midst. And Bar Tabac does exhibit some originality where it counts most: in the kitchen. A selection of ten grilled brochettes grouped under the heading "Bistro Bites" suggests new possibilities for aperitif nibbling, tapas-style dining, or wee-hours munching. At $5 a pop for everything from marinated beef to Burgundy snails to pastis-and-parsley-buttered-mushrooms-on-a-stick, they're pretty much irresistible.

Good standards like onion soup gratinée ($5) and warm goat cheese salad with beets, frisée, and raspberry walnut vinaigrette ($7.50) pave the way for a more conventional meal with French sauce and soul. While a New York strip admirably fulfils the steak-frite duties ($16.50), seasonal comforts—in winter, expect the likes of beef bourguignon ($15.50) and braised lamb shank ($15.50)—go deeper to the bone. Others may find no reason to wander from the steamed mussels with white wine, shallots, and, to the side, gilded frites ($11). The French wine list describes bottles by their place of origin but not their producers and vintages. This would be acceptable were the choice limited to carafe-style table wines. But with ten bottles at more than $35, it's arguable that Georges Forgeois chose the wrong place in which to hold back.

Brawta Caribbean Cafe

$18–40

Address 347 Atlantic Ave at Hoyt St

☎718/855-5515

Transportation A,C,G to Hoyt-Schermerhorn; 1,2 to Hoyt St

Open Sun & Mon noon–10.30pm, Tues–Thurs noon–11pm, Fri & Sat noon–11.30pm

Accepts All major credit cards

Reservations Not accepted

The thing to do upon entering Brawta is to follow your nose and ears but not immediately your eyes. Up front, the sterile stainless-steel open kitchen, along with the young Brooklyn professionals waiting for their carry-out orders, do nothing to evoke the superb little West Indian restaurant this is. But follow the unmistakeable reggae rhythms of Bob Marley to the color-splashed, candlelit cafe just to the rear and that unflattering first impression vanishes like Jamaican punch on a sweltering summer's day. To accompany the soundtrack, Marley's image is deeply carved into each of the round, glass-covered tabletops. Look up and there he is again, portrayed in one of the oil paintings hung over the L-shaped banquette.

Hospitable servers help first-timers surrender to the relaxed island mood and pace. The tropical fruit drinks are a major component of the Brawta—"something extra" in the native patois—experience. The fruit punch ($4) is a rich, resonant, honey-sweetened mix of strawberries, mango, pineapple, papaya, and banana. The invigorating pine-ade ($3), blending tart pineapple and spicy ginger, is a perfect foil for an appetizer or snack of beef patties ($2)—soft, peppery ground beef encased in a flaky pastry. As starter or side dish, macaroni and cheese ($4) is distinguished by shredded carrots and sweet red peppers.

Beware the deviously surreptitious heat within the unmatched main course, jerk chicken ($9.50). Marinated overnight in pimento, hot pepper, onions, thyme, and, naturally, secret spices before being slowly cooked (at Brawta, even the grilling is unhurried), the fall-off-the-bone tender meat releases an atomic burn not fully felt until the ninth bite. Bodies are also subjected to an unexpected crescendo of flesh-reddening heat by the shrimp sautéed with broccoli and carrots and bathed in a coconut curry sauce ($15). All entrees are served with a large side of chopped cabbage steamed with green peas, carrots, corn, and onions. From the "Sweet Tings" menu, the moist bread pudding ($4) is a revelation, made with pineapple and creamy, lip-smacking rum sauce.

301

Cafe LULUc

FRENCH

(🍴) The younger, hipper, stunted sibling of Banania Cafe (see p.299) reduces the economy bistro to the bare essentials: whitewashed walls, tin ceiling, red banquettes, pine floorboards, short menu, eye-level mirrors, and fast waiters who snub French arrogance rather than their diners. Space is so tight at this teensy-weensy place that you may end up sitting on top of someone at the next table—not necessarily an unpleasant notion considering the attractive crowd. Singles can make a more conventional introduction for themselves at the tiny bar or, better still, out on the the sidewalk, which is crowded with folks waiting—or merely pretending to wait—for a coveted table. (Show up before 7pm to avoid a delay.) During weekend brunch, baby-stroller gridlock thwarts such socializing beneath a sign that originally read "Cafe LULU." After a Fort Greene restaurant called Loulou protested, the "c" was painted on, echoing the co-owner's first name, Jean-Luc.

Lunch $11–35
Dinner $18–45

Address 214 Smith St, between Butler & Baltic Sts
☎718/625-3815
Transportation F,G to Bergen St
Open Sun–Thurs 7.30am–midnight, Fri & Sat 7.30am–2am
Accepts Cash only
Reservations For large groups

Frogs' legs à la meunière ($7.50), pan-roasted with lemon, butter, and parsley, may seem a ridiculous notion for so modest an eatery, but the meat is tender and plump and there is enough of it on this starter for a main course. Still, orders for the nice salad of cold roasted beets tossed with Granny Smith apples and a soothing goat cheese dressing ($7) outnumber those for grenouilles by about ten to one. Some don't bother with an appetizer at all, going straight to the very good, if a little too lean, burger ($7.50, $8.50 with cheese) served over a rich brioche bun with superbly crisp, salty fries.

LULUc somehow manages a convincing grilled hanger steak with caramelized shallot sauce and frites for $12.50. The homey, fairly juicy grilled pork chop with thyme-scented wine gravy ($15) is outfitted with a frisée salad and always fashionable garlic mashed potatoes. The astonishingly good pistachio-crusted baked cod ($14) comes with asparagus and mashed potatoes that are this time infused with basil. While all the desserts look special, flaky-crusted, beautifully caramelized tarte tatin ($5) tastes especially so.

Caserta Vecchia

🍴 If the complimentary bruschetta topped with fresh tomato and basil doesn't instantly win you over, the B&W print of Maddalena Carusone, the Amelia Earhart of New York pizza bakers, might. It's among the 1950s family photos that decorate the walls and menu covers of the restaurant/pizzeria opened by her daughter, Lina D'Amato, and her nephew, Alfonso Carusone, in the fall of 2002. And if that bit of history doesn't strike a chord, consider that Alfonso, a third-generation pizzaiollo from Caserta in the Campania region of southern Italy, was employed at Gemelli's when that restaurant was destroyed in the 9/11 attacks. Still not sold, you unsentimental fool you? Then for heaven sakes try the pizza.

Lunch $10–50
Dinner $15–45

Address 221 Smith St, between Baltic & Butler Sts
☎718/624-7549
Transportation F,G to Bergen St
Open Tues–Thurs noon–10.30pm, Fri & Sat noon–11pm, Sun noon–10.30pm
Accepts All major credit cards
Reservations Not accepted

ITALIAN/PIZZA

The Neapolitan-style pies the ever vigilant Carusone withdraws from his crackling brick oven are objects of delicacy and desire. To fully appreciate their thin, puffy-ended, feathery yet resilient crusts you need to sample one with nothing but olive oil, salt, and rosemary. Carusone bakes this very thing whenever there's a vacancy in the oven and sends it out, gratis, in small slices. Most of the 17 pizza varieties (from the $8.50 Margherita to the $13.50 Campagnola—Mozzarella, cherry tomatoes, prosciutto, arugula) are blanketed with San Marzano tomatoes and Fior di Latte, the dry, dense, imported cow's milk mozzarella Carusone prefers it to its buffalo counterpart because it doesn't become runny. Though New Yorkers are not generally taught to regard ooziness as a bad thing in a pizza cheese, these pies make a solid case for one that holds the production together.

Chef Francesco Pennachio, Naples born and raised, handles intricate (a baby octopus carpaccio that looks to have been shaved from a slab of Carrera terrazzo; $7.50) and basic (spaghetti with cherry tomatoes and basil; $7) with equal aplomb. Be sure to take notice of his paccheri (like rigatoni that's been ironed smooth) with a meat ragu ($11) and grilled Cornish game hen marinated in rosemary, garlic, and white wine ($14.50). Good tiramisu ($5) is the lone everyday homemade dessert. But occasionally Pennachio toys with a panna cotta that should be adopted into the Carusone family.

Carroll Gardens, Cobble Hill & Boerum Hill

Osaka

Just as guys called Tiny are rarely mistaken for jockeys, eateries named after giant metropolises seldom accommodate the population of a single brownstone. The oversized ambition suits a clever sushi joint, named after a city known as "the kitchen of Japan", which aspires to be both better than and equal to a trusty neighborhood restaurant. Osaka safeguards the honored status of a local favorite through its friendly feel and improvised informality. The clientele consists largely of drop-ins from the Cobble Hill Cinemas. But much of the food, cooked or raw, is too good to be dismissed by destination diners, and the decor—circular metallic place mats, blond-wood benches, washi-lined panels suspended below halogen fixtures—is stylish enough to welcome wayfarers from foreign zip codes.

Lunch $11–30
Dinner $18–50

Address 272 Court St, between Butler & Douglass Sts
☎718/643-0044
Transportation F,G to Bergen St
Open Sun–Thurs 11.30am–3pm & 5–10.30pm, Fri & Sat 11.30am–3pm & 5–11pm
Accepts MasterCard & Visa
Reservations Not accepted

The three-man sushi crew is headed by Kenny Li, a craftsman with a knack for reptilian-looking rolls. The spicy Osaka roll ($7.95), with extra-crisp salmon skin, fine strands of crab, and ground seaweed salad, is a long scorpion wrapped in wide swirls of green (avocado) and orange (flying fish roe). The sweet dragon roll ($9.95), containing eel and wondrously thin slices of ripe avocado, is a cucumber-tailed monster breathing cool flames of ginger. The rice-heavy black pepper roll ($6.95) is an inside-out sensation of tuna, avocado, and a spicy special sauce. No roll, however, can surpass the complex pleasures of the salmon skin salad ($5.50)—a leaf-lined glass bowl of candied salmon skin countered by a mildly spicy salad of cucumber, seaweed, and sesame seeds. Panko-crusted tempura, ordered as an hors d'oeuvre ($4.95) or main course ($10.95–14.95), revitalizes the tired, often soggy standard.

There are a few wrong notes. Teriyaki shrimp ($11.95) may be sweet and snappy, but the sauce is thick and gooey. Chewy meat in the beef sukiyaki ($13.95) detracts from the exquisite arrangement of glass noodles, gently cooked vegetables, and fragrant broth. Fried banana with honey sauce ($3.50) would be a hit in any locality. But tempura (fried) ice cream, with a hardened crust that breaks off its frozen filling, should be categorized as a NIMBY (Not In My Back Yard) dessert.

Patois

(🍴) Many years from now, walking tours of historic Brooklyn will no doubt stop at this, the cozy fin-de-siècle bistro where chef Alan Harding and partners Jim and Paul Mamary ignited the Smith Street restaurant boom. We can practically hear the guide recalling service so friendly it was hokey. How when the recorded voice of the late French songstress Barbara met the hot-garlicky scent of the buttery spinach-cushioned escargots in mid-air, the effect was of some make-believe Paris occupied by Brooklynites. Peeking inside, tour groups will see the red banquettes, missile-shaped lamps, and old tin ceiling, and wonder how the premises could date from the late 1990s and not some fifty years earlier. The guide will explain all about retro fashions and the ensuing dining renaissance during the first decade of the twenty-first century.

$27–60

Address 255 Smith St, between Douglass & DeGraw Sts
☎718/855-1535
Transportation F,G to Carroll St
Open Tues–Thurs 6–10.30pm, Fri & Sat 6–11.30pm, Sun 11am–3pm & 5–10pm
Accepts All major credit cards
Reservations For large groups

FRENCH/AMERICAN

Thankfully, back in the present, we can taste the appetizers for ourselves. Tangy mussels steamed with garlic and tomatoes in white wine ($7). Thick split pea soup with pancetta crisps and croûtons ($7). Homemade country pâté with cornichons ($7.50). Grilled vegetable terrine with goat cheese ($7). Rustic, piping hot entrees are presented as integrated ensembles rather than as main courses with two accompaniments. There are at least four standouts. Superbly succulent roast chicken au poivre ($14), luscious to the bone, is perfectly matched with wilted, peppercorn-dotted greens, and lumpy mashed potatoes. Grilled salmon is integrated into a couscous lentil salad ($14). Coq au vin is assembled with spring rather than winter veggies ($13). And the vegetable casserole assembles basil polenta, roast tomatoes, and buffalo mozzarella.

Desserts ($5–6), among them crème brûlée, bread pudding, chocolate mousse, fruit clafoutis, and a rotation of tarts (walnut, lemon, chocolate), are uneven. Under the umbrella of $12 Sunday brunch, the eggs Patois (essentially a Florentine with a Dijon hollandaise) and reputable challah French toast may be a secondary consideration to the all-you-can-drink mimosas. It would be interesting to hear what the tour guide had to say about that particular ritual.

AMERICAN

The Red Rail

You won't find steep hills, dense fogs, or Tony Bennett's heart on the streets of Carroll Gardens. Yet approaching the deceptively familiar Red Rail neon sign, the atmosphere is so suggestive of San Francisco that you can practically feel the heaviness in your tired thighs, the misty sky, and Anthony Benedetto's signature lament. The neighborhood blend of bedrock Italians and freshly rooted bourgeois bohemian Brooklynites—BoBoBros—echoes the changing demographics of North Beach, the San Francisco enclave that gave New York Joe

Brunch $14–20
Dinner $20–40

Address 502 Henry St at Sackett St
☎718/875-1283
Transportation F,G to Carroll St
Open Mon–Thurs 5.30–10.30pm,
Fri & Sat 9.30am–3.30pm &
5.30–11pm, Sun 9.30am–3.30pm &
5.30–10pm
Accepts Cash only
Reservations Not accepted

DiMaggio. The laid-back mood inside this sentimental luncheonette, coupled with its taste for tofu and grits, goat cheese and Monterey Jack, Formica tables and old plastic radios, transports you to northern California quicker than American Airlines. Still not convinced? The Red Rail offers valet stroller parking, a kid-friendly amenity that's a natural extension of the easygoing, sweetheart service. This is the kind of place that when you can't decide between the goat cheese salad and the Caesar, warmhearted waitresses will passionately debate the merits of each as if their rent money—no small amount in these parts—were riding on your decision.

The crackling home-fried potatoes offer reason enough to brave the sizeable crowds that show up for weekend brunch ($10 prix fixe). But you might as well enjoy too the solid burrito stuffed with eggs, vegetarian chili, and Jack cheese, or any of the superb sandwiches on bread baked by Brooklyn legend Paul Cammareri. The triple-decker Portobello club sandwich ($8), with bacon, roasted pepper, and pesto mayo, is stacked between thick slices cut from a Pullman loaf. The Sacramento cheese-steak sandwich squeezes a real steak, goops of melted cheese, mushrooms, and clandestine hot pepper into a garlic-slathered ciabatta roll.

Dinner, though less consistent, is improving, as demonstrated by the spicy roast pork chop with sweet potato risotto ($14), the pressed half chicken with green beans and savory bread pudding ($11), and the sirloin steak au poivre ($16). Desserts ($6) are homemade—and maybe they shouldn't be.

Restaurant Saul

The alternately challenging and modest designs of Saul and Lisa Bolton are in perfect sync with a community that is thrilled about but also a little fearful of its gentrification and accompanying explosion of new restaurants. Tin ceiling tiles, stamped with a retro motif, constitute a blend of both the quaint and newly resourceful Brooklyn. One exposed brick wall has a varnished sheen; the other, left untreated, is without luster. Saul the chef also wants his short, cloth-bound menu both ways. The high-quality ingredients and meticulous preparation distinguish a cooking alumnus of Bouley and Le Bernardin. But the sweet excesses, as well as the prevalence of devilishly good mashed potatoes, reflect the personal tastes of a self-indulgent home cook. If he likes crème anglaise *and* caramel sauce poured around a superb warm apple tart that requires neither, that's how it is to be served. It's not for nothing that Saul gives the place his first name.

$35–70

Address 140 Smith St, between Bergen & Dean Sts

℡718/935-9844

Transportation F to Bergen St

Open Mon & Wed–Sat 5.30–11pm, Sun 11am–3pm & 5.30–10.30pm

Accepts All major credit cards

Reservations Suggested

NEW AMERICAN

Dinner begins with a gratis amuse-bouche, ideally the Pecorino-dusted wild mushroom soup sipped from a sake cup. Its pointed saltiness makes for a consummate tickler. If you're doubly lucky, the steamed mussels in a white wine broth gently seasoned with tarragon will then make a guest appearance as the special appetizer of the day ($11). The best nightly starter is the duck confit ($10), as much for the Gorgonzola-stuffed poached pear as for the crisp, succulent, beautifully bronzed, sufficiently fatty duck. The bacon and onion tartlet ($10), with fromage blanc standing in for an eggy, quiche-like filling, inspires lasting loyalties. But the hamachi tuna tartare ($11), handsomely plated with spicy avocado purée, is saturated to disadvantage in almost syrup-sweet soy sauce. This forfeits the feel of the tuna.

Sweet main courses like juicy grilled pork chop with broccoli rabe, potato purée, and gingered plums ($22), and the pan-roasted chicken breasts with baby leeks, wild mushrooms, and potato cake ($20) benefit enormously from the piping hot dishes on which they are served. For closers ($6–8), the lemon custard soufflé and the frilly baked Alaska mated with a chocolate cookie are yummy.

PIZZA/ITALIAN

Sam's

In the heart of Brooklyn's bistro boom and in a classic neighborhood beset by surges of gentrification and Manhattanization, how nice it is to have a homely but oh-so-homey joint to fall back on. When the new and prosperous locals see the wine list at this old Italian place for the first time, they might easily assume its prices—$11 to $17— are per glass rather than per bottle. Those with young children soon come to cherish the low ceiling, wood paneling, plastic-covered and kid-friendly tables, and the florescent-burning time warp those dated fixtures represent. Where's the fun in moving to Brooklyn without the opportunity to drink a cheap red out of a juice glass and slurp large platefuls of red-sauce-smothered, fifteen-minute spaghetti at a moment's notice?

$10–45

Address 238 Court St at Baltic St
℡718/596-3458
Transportation F,G to Bergen St
Open Daily 11am–11pm
Accepts Cash only
Reservations For large groups

Sentimentality aside, there are two very good reasons to include Sam's on your essential dining list. The first is pizza. Walk through the front dining room to the rear of the back one and you will reach a trapezoidal opening offering a peek into the kitchen—and history. Inside is a free-standing pizza oven made of Philadelphia brick that was installed at this address, like Sam's itself, in 1930. The old man who's been baking pizzas here for over fifteen years is named Mario, but if you call out "Sam" he will turn his head and say, "What?" The crusts he bakes in that oven are phenomenal. Thin in the middle, a little puffy on the ends, crisp but not hard, delectable to the chew, nice bend. It would be great with just olive oil, but Mario/Sam loads them with runny, unspiced tomato sauce and divinely oozy mozzarella. A large, eight-slice pie is $15; a single slice, $5 (no kidding). Any additional toppings or, for that matter, Italian appetizers and entrees are too dicey to endorse. The $6.50 antipasto is hapless.

The second great thing about Sam's is the Italian (ricotta) cheesecake ($3.25). Dusted with powdered sugar, the crunchy, soaking-wet wedge may look forlorn, but that's how it's supposed to be. This is one of the greatest ugly cheesecakes of them all.

Sherwood Café

Sherwood Café is an apt name for such a fairy tale of a restaurant. An impressive antique crystal chandelier fills the room with dancing light produced by the kind of flicker bulbs you find at 99¢ stores. A shabby six-foot-tall Madonna and Child acts as the room's centerpiece. You almost forget that baby Jesus is missing his left arm as your attention is stolen by the non-rotating disco ball hung in the right corner of the room. It appears as though each fixture is trying to out-kitsch the next. Every item with a

$18–40

Address 195 Smith St, between Baltic & Warren Sts

☎718/596-1609

Transportation F,G to Bergen St
Open Mon–Thurs 4pm–midnight, Fri 4pm–1am, Sat 11am–1am, Sun 11am–midnight

Accepts Cash only
Reservations For large groups

little orange sticker on it is actually for sale. Now if only the patrons would do some buying and relieve some of the clutter. Cobble Hill's slacker-bohemian counterpart to cafe society sits for many moody hours drinking cafés au lait and espressos, only to be interrupted by their most feared vision of their future selves: yuppie mommies and daddies trying to negotiate their fully accessorized, twin-engine baby strollers through the overcrowded dining room.

As the waiter seats you, he'll probably ask if you'd like a coffee. When in Rome—or France—that is to say, Brooklyn—why not skip the java and have a $5 glass of the house red (Côtes du Rhône) or white (Chardonnay). The rillettes ($5) comprise a hearty portion of very good shredded goose pâté served with a garnish of cornichons, pickled pearl onions, and olives. It's great spread on the crusty French (or Brooklyn?) bread. Or try one of the large cheese planchons ($13), samplers of French (decidedly not Brooklyn) cheese that are great for sharing.

The open-faced croque monsieur ($8.50) is a ham and Swiss sandwich loaded with rich béchamel sauce and thoughtfully served with a mesclun salad. For even heartier fare, try the roasted free-range chicken ($12.50) served with garlicky string beans and incredibly rich mashed potatoes. After cutting into the crisp, perfectly browned chicken skin, a cloud of trapped steam escapes, screaming praise of the luscious meat below. For dessert, put a buy order on the chocolate cake decked out with fresh raspberries and real whipped cream ($5).

Coney Island, Brighton Beach, Sheepshead Bay & Homecrest

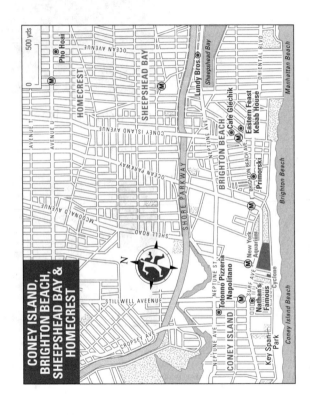

CONEY ISLAND, BRIGHTON BEACH, SHEEPSHEAD BAY & HOMECREST

0   500 yds

HOMECREST

Pho Hoai

OCEAN AVENUE

SHEEPSHEAD BAY

AVENUE U

AVENUE U

CONEY ISLAND AVENUE

OCEAN PARKWAY

Lundy Bros.

Sheepshead Bay

SHELL ROAD

McDONALD AVENUE

SHORE PARKWAY

NEPTUNE AVE

BRIGHTON BEACH

Café Glechik

BRIGHTON BEACH AVE

Eastern Feast

Kebab House

Primorski

ORIENTAL BLVD

Manhattan Beach

STILLWELL AVEENUE

CROPSEY AVE

NEPTUNE AVE

Totonno Pizzeria

Napolitano

NEPTUNE AVE

SURF AVE

New York

Aquarium

Nathan's

Famous

Key Span

Park

Cyclone

CONEY ISLAND

Coney Island Beach

Brighton Beach

N

Cafe Glechik

You need to take a deep breath before stepping from the dark gray of Coney Island Avenue into the blinding whiteness of Cafe Glechik. Though just a block from the Russian shops, markets, and nightclubs of bustling Brighton Beach Avenue, this rustic eatery seems a world apart from an ethnic enclave that is itself a world apart. The scene between walls adorned with traditional, hand-embroidered white linens and blouses does not appear any less exotic once

$8–35

Address 3159 Coney Island Ave, between Brighton Beach & Oceanview Aves
☎718/616-0494
Transportation Q to Brighton Beach
Open Daily 11am–11pm
Accepts Cash only
Reservations Not accepted

your narrowing pupils have adjusted to the snug storefront's bright light. Nearly every square foot of the animated dining floor is covered with tables, every square inch of which is covered with pots, crocks, pans, bowls, clay casseroles, and plates, every millimeter of which is heaped with foods not immediately recognizable to even the most cosmopolitan American. Explanations in broken English don't help all that much. What the heck is "green borscht" anyway? As New York eating adventures go, Cafe Glechik is one amazing ride.

And is it cheap! A big hearty bowl of that mildly sour green borscht, stocked with rice, chopped hard-boiled eggs, and sorrel (the green part), is $4. The steaming hot, dill-seasoned, curative chicken soup loaded with chewy, mini-pelemyi (dumplings) is just $4.50. And the pot of country-style mushroom, barley, and bean soup provides a meal for $6.50. Round one of your meal should also involve herring and potato ($4), smoked mackerel ($4), and vareniki, which are large, half-moon dumplings filled with potato, cabbage, or meat and served in a large crock ($4–4.50 for an order of 25).

The prospect of entrees may have you phoning friends for reinforcements. This is more than you and your dinner companions bargained for. Stuffed cabbage packed with minced pork and carrots ($7.50) is substantial enough even without the swathe of sour cream. The beef stew in-a-pot sweetly enriched with prunes ($9.50) is a challenge for two to knock off. And that's not factoring in the salty, garlicky, dill-flecked new potatoes swimming in butter. For dessert, the vareniki return, this time with bubbling farmer cheese and a sour cherry-jam sauce.

Eastern Feast Kebab House

The magnificent domes and minarets of Samarkand depicted in the large murals are echoed in the tapered patterns of the artificial brick-work. The pink-patterned stonework cast onto the laminate tables is yet another humble indication of cultural pride. And the new tin ceiling and exposed ventilation duct are the trimmings of an eatery firmly planted in modern-day Brooklyn. Still, the most prominent and noble dis-

$7–25
Address 1003 Brighton Beach Ave at Coney Island Ave
☎718/934-9608
Transportation Q to Brighton Beach
Open Daily noon–11pm
Accepts Cash only
Reservations Not accepted

play of Eastern Feast's identity past and present is both in the glass display cases up front and atop the large charcoal grill in the window. Speared onto metal skewers that make the ordinary wooden ones look like toothpicks, the lamb, beef, pork, and chicken kebabs look fit for a man—a very large man—who would be king. When the wind is blowing in from the south and the grill is fully engaged, the charcoal smoke travels all the way up the boardwalk to entice French and German tourists as well as resident Russian sunbathers with the smells they associate with summer vacations by the Black Sea.

Once you're drawn in, it isn't only the kebabs that demand attention. A wonderful combination plate ($8) may be assembled from such cold appetizers as finely grated carrots sharpened with lemon and black pepper; firm white beans with crunchy red onions; assorted pickled vegetables; pepper-red couscous; hummus; eggplant caviar, or babaganoush. Alone they are just $3. Among soups there is the option of Ubeki lagman ($6), with lamb chunks, vegetables, and thick homemade noodles in a meat borscht, and the Russian alternative of a meaty hot borscht ($4). The cheburekas ($2), parsley-spiced meat turnovers, are best when still fresh and not subjected to a microwave reheat.

Kebabs may be ordered as single skewers ($3.50 with a pedestrian salad and rice or fries) or as part of a two-skewer platter ($10). Although some diners take on two and even three kebabs, even one constitutes a hard night's work for most people. Forget the paprika-dusted chicken version and stick to the tender, juicy, charred chunks—actually, they would have to be cut in four to be called chunks—of lamb.

Lundy Bros

(🍴) Ask a dozen Kings County kibitzers for the inside dope on the circa 1995 Lundy's and you're liable to hear the same refrain. "The food stinks," they groan. "Except maybe the biscuits, the steamers, the Boston chowder. And the crabcakes. And the fries. And the rice pudding." Imagine what they'd say if they actually liked the place? That's not to poke fun at sentimentalists who see the futility of trying to relive their most cherished memories from the original Lundy's, which closed in the late-1970s. Nor to downplay the unpardonable seriousness of frequent service lapses and overcooked lobsters. But it sure is swell

**Lunch $20–50
Dinner $25–75**

Address 1901 Emmons Ave at Ocean Ave
☎718/743-0022
Transportation Q to Sheepshead Bay
Open Mon–Wed 11.30am–3.30pm & 5–9pm, Thurs 11.30am–3.30pm & 5–10pm, Fri & Sat 11.30am–3.30pm & 5–11pm, Sun 11am–2pm & 3–9pm
Accepts All major credit cards
Reservations Suggested

SEAFOOD

to re-encounter the stucco archways, stained-glass windows, and iron-railed stairway of this great Mediterranean villa on Sheepshead Bay.

The updated menu faithfully preserves a few essentials, namely the Southern biscuits, the steamers, and special "Shore Dinners." Baked with White Lily flour, the biscuits, when served warm (if they're not, send them back), are as good as the originals. Immigrants who can no longer take their kids to see the Dodgers at Ebbets Field can at least give them a Brooklyn welcome to America through Lundy's biscuits. Meaty steamers accompany the Deluxe Shore Dinner, along with a cup of creamy clam chowder (forget the thin, Brooklyn red version), a half-steamed lobster, a piece of fish, two sides (you probably want creamed spinach and the long, bronzed deli fries), dessert, and coffee for $26.95.

Fried fish—calamari ($7.95 as an appetizer), shrimp ($18.95), diver sea scallops ($19.95), flounder ($16.95), a fisherman's platter containing all four ($21.95)—are better than mediocre grilled or broiled choices ($16–22). The thin-crusted pizzas ($7.95–11.95), linguine with white clam sauce ($15.95), and chopped steak ($10.95) are all pretty good. Enormous desserts ($5.95–7.95) don't merit blowing your monthly calorie budget in a single night. You might share the blueberry pie four ways.

The Manhattan Lundy's, opened in 2001, is pretty much a disaster. It's at 205 West 50th St, Midtown West (☎212/586-0022).

Nathan's Famous

(🍴) The sentimental strollers along the Coney Island boardwalk all have the same fantasy. They close their eyes for a moment, then reopen them to see the world's playground in its heyday. Suddenly, all the vanished arcades, rides, funhouses, and restaurants are back. A Brooklyn kid flips his last nickel in the air. If it lands heads, he uses it to buy a subway token; tails, he grabs yet another frankfurter at Nathan's and walks home. The pinch that awakes everyone from this nostalgic dream is the $2 subway

$3–15

Address 1310 Surf Ave at Stillwell Ave
℡718/946-2202
Transportation F,Q,W to Coney Island-Stillwell Ave
Open Sun–Thurs 8am–1am, Fri & Sat 8am–2am
Accepts Cash only
Reservations Not accepted

fare, the $2.25 price of a frankfurter, and, alas, the disappearance through age, neglect, or vandalism of most of Coney's storied attractions. Still, there is reason for optimism. The opening in 2001 of a minor league baseball stadium, KeySpan Park, has revitalized the area. Nathan's has for the first time set up outdoor picnic tables for on-site munching. And nothing short of a happy ending to Hamlet could match the timeless thrill from the first explosive bite of a juicy, garlicky, naturally encased Nathan's frank.

The traditionalists who claim the franks are better at the original emporium than at the franchises are not romantic fools. The snappy casing and luscious spices may be the same, but there's no way to duplicate the surroundings. Location affects how things taste and it's silly to think otherwise. It's why the very red wine you adored at a Parisian brasserie doesn't taste the same at home. In the instance of Nathan's, the ocean breeze that whistles down from the boardwalk, the classic neon signs above the landmark, and the dexterity of the pros who work the grills are factors that cannot be duplicated. Even the Nathan's franks served during Brooklyn Cyclones games inside KeySpan Park taste different. Perhaps it's because they're about double the price. Or maybe it's that classic "baseball" taste—another factor that's impossible to explain.

Franks get lonely without an order of crisp-edged, golden-brown, crinkle-cut, half-moon French fries ($1.75 and up). They're fried in corn oil, usually very hot, and rarely soggy. Other items rate well below the franks and the fries.

Pho Hoai

The delighted diners from a distant Q-train depot regarded a pause between courses as a welcome chance to rewind their appetites. Anthony, the assistant manager of Pho Hoai, was happily surprised to catch their chopsticks in the resting position, and seized the moment to satisfy his curiosity. "How," he asked, "does our food compare to Chinatown?" That query was the only thing the Vietnamese eatery and its capable staff got wrong all evening. The question

Lunch $7–25
Dinner $10–35

Address 1906 Ave U, between East 19th & East 20th Sts
☎718/616-1233
Transportation Q to Ave U
Open Daily 10.30am–10.30pm
Accepts MasterCard & Visa
Reservations Not accepted

should have been, "How does Chinatown's food compare to ours?" The superiority of this informal, utilitarian neighborhood eatery is probably due to the fact that it is geared towards the Vietnamese students who live nearby and seem to care as much about what they eat as how they look.

The crunchy, ungreasy cha gio (Vietnamese spring rolls; $3.50) and the thin layer of clean-tasting oil on the fried crab plate ($8.95) prove that anything fried merits consideration. The joy of those crabs ranges from the sweet meat tucked into the top shell to the last tasty bits of fried onion and scallion. Even these are surpassed by the so nuoc dua ($6.95), incomparably meaty mussels wrongly translated on the menu as clams. The sweet, spicy, and buttery components of the mussel broth epitomize a kind of balanced ensemble cooking that eludes other Southeast Asian kitchens. The same harmony is even apparent in fresh, nicely cut squid sautéed with lemongrass, onions, crunchy green pepper, and spicy red chile sauce ($6.95).

While powerful hits of lemongrass, chile, or cilantro can provide great action, it is also a thrill when delicate flavors are drawn out but not drowned out by the dominant notes. Such is the case with table-grilled beef ($12.95), barbecued shrimp on sugar cane ($10.95), beef fondue (thin slices of raw meat that you cook in broth at the table; $12.95), and seventeen varieties of rice noodle beef soup ($4.25–5.25). Each big bowl is a meal in itself. Forgo dessert and close instead with a hot or iced coffee with sweet condensed milk.

Coney Island, Brighton Beach.......

Primorski

Faced with stiff competition from the glitzier nightclubs in and around Brighton Beach, Primorski endures as the affordable and now quaint option for Russian-style banquets with a Georgian-Jewish slant. Its ballroom is flanked by illuminated, painted-glass wall plaques bearing colorful seascapes and the scripted word *Primorski* — "by the water." On a bandstand sheathed in sheets of reflective yellow plastic, three vocalists and one keyboardist play Russian, American, and Continental pop deep into the night. Only the food is more relentlessly entertaining.

Lunch $9–30
Dinner $25–65

Address 282 Brighton Beach Ave, between Brighton 2nd & Brighton 3rd Sts

☎718/891-3111

Transportation Q to Brighton Beach

Open Mon–Thurs 11am–5pm & 7pm–midnight, Fri 11am–5pm & 7pm–2am, Sat 11am–4pm & 7pm–2am, Sun 11am–4pm & 7pm–1am

Accepts All major credit cards

The customary way to eat at Brooklyn's Russian nightclubs is from a pre-set banquet menu. Primorski's prix fixe (from $25 per person on weeknights to $35 on weekends) includes overlapping onslaughts of warm yeasty flatbread, hot appetizers, pickled vegetables, smoked fish platters, cold vegetable salads, cold cuts, Russian crêpes, several hot entrees, assorted shashlik, fresh fruit, desserts, coffee or tea, bottomless soft drinks, and one bottle (per five diners) of Kremlovskya vodka. For anyone unfamiliar with the cuisine, the advantage of the banquet is that there's no difficulty communicating with the waiters and you get to try many things without any nasty surprises when the bill comes. The disadvantage is that you probably don't want all that food, and that the superb appetizers fill you up long before the shashlik arrives. Mind you, nothing about those mediocre kebabs will have you regretting any initial lack of restraint.

Should you choose from the extremely inexpensive a la carte menu, the starters you don't want to miss are the potato dumplings with grilled onions ($3.90), the basturma (thinly sliced dried beef; $3.90), the gefilte fish (Primorski's version of the Jewish poached fishcakes are pâté-like; $5), eggplant caviar ($2.50), and khachapuri (a warm, lightly salty, fabulously flaky, and gently crusty Georgian cheese bread; $3). If entrees are still relevant, consider the wonderful stuffed cabbage ($6.25) or stuffed grape leaves ($6.75) instead of the grilled meats. Daily soup-and-entree lunch specials are $5.99, vodka not included.

Totonno Pizzeria Napolitano

All eyes were on Joel Ciminieri's hands as he slid out what appeared still to be New York's finest pizza from the old brick oven. He pretended not to notice when his wife Louise, known to the cognoscenti as Cookie, inspected the pie's underside and noticed a tiny pop hole. Through coded messages perfected only through years of happily married life, Cookie gave Joel a look that said, "what the heck is this?" He glared back paragraphs about

$7–30

Address 1524 Neptune Ave, between 80th & 81st Sts
☎718/372-8606
Transportation F,Q,W to Coney Island-Stillwell Ave
Open Wed–Sun noon–8.30pm
Accepts Cash only
Reservations Not accepted

PIZZA

the joys of working alone. Indeed, the greatest challenge then for Joel and now for his son and successor Lawrence is not in sustaining a 75-plus-year tradition. Rather, it's getting their pizzas past the very tough Cookie who is respectively the niece and granddaughter of the legendary pizzaiollos Jerry Pero and Anthony "Totonno" Pero.

The original shop (the Upper East Side satellite, 1544 2nd Ave, ☎212/327-2800, lacks the same quality control) is hidden among auto-repair lots in a rundown residential area far removed from the Coney Island beach and boardwalk. Only a screen door separates you from the aromas and emotions of 1924. Not much has changed inside the tin-and-wood, table-service eatery since then, except that some of the yellowed newspaper clippings heralding war and baseball victories have been replaced by glowing framed reviews.

The pizza ($15.70 and up for a large pie) is elemental. Nothing to it, as Lawrence says. Just good handmade mozzarella, imported tomatoes, and a coal oven. Yet there is magic in the hands of a baker who turns out a crust as thin, chewy, crisp, and lightly charred as his. Furthermore, something supernatural happens when the tomatoes and cheese melt under the volcanic heat of that oven. Interestingly, the true flavor of the classic, New York-style Margherita is not tomato. It's the salty tang acquired from a dusting of Pecorino Romano. Extra toppings (sausage, pepperoni, anchovies, etc) are minimal, as they should be. Instead of doctoring this pizza, the best policy would be to strip it down. Requesting a red pie (no Mozzarella) or a white pie (no tomato) garners a nod of approval from Cookie.

Fort Greene & Clinton Hill

**FORT GREENE &
CLINTON HILL**

NASSAU STREET

BROOKLYN-QUEENS EXPRESSWAY

EDWARDS ST
PORTLAND ST
ASHLAND PLACE

MYRTLE AVENUE

WASHINGTON PARK
CARLTON AVENUE
ADELPHI STREET
CLERMONT AVE
VANDERBILT AVE
WAVERLY AVENUE
CLINTON AVENUE
WASHINGTON AVENUE
JAMES PLACE
WILLOUGHBY AVE
DEKALB AVE

Pratt
Institute

CLIFTON PLACE

Fort Greene
Park

CLINTON
HILL

AVENUE

Long Island
University

Chez
Oskar

GRAND
CAMBRIDGE
AVENUE
PLACE

CUMBERLAND ST
OXFORD ST
SOUTH PORTLAND
LAFAYETTE
GREENE AVENUE

Ⓜ

A Table

FORT GREENE

GATES AVENUE

Locanda
Vini & Olii

S. ELLIOT PLACE
FORT GREENE PLACE

Ⓜ

FULTON STREET

Thomas Beisl
LIVINGSTON ST.
ASHLAND PLACE
FLATBUSH

PORTLAND AVE

STATE ST
NEVIS STREET
ST

Ⓜ

Brooklyn
Academy
of Music

AVENUE

ATLANTIC AVENUE

PACIFIC STREET

3RD AVENUE

PACIFIC
STREET

DEAN STREET

DEAN STREET

N

0   400 yds

À Table

First-time diners from distant precincts who pop in before or after a performance at the Brooklyn Academy of Music would be wrong to imagine that the corner of Lafayette and Adelphi was always like this. With its high wooden ceiling, plaster of Paris walls, old communal tables, and 8ft winged "A" (part of a vintage advertisement), the circa 1999 restaurant looks old enough to be its own grandfather. Given the current fashion for French retro throughout Brooklyn's burgeoning communities, that in itself is hardly unusual. But the absurdly

Lunch $12–35
Dinner $28–65

Address 178 Lafayette Ave at Adelphi St

☎718/935-9121

Transportation G to Fulton St; A,C to Lafayette Ave

Open Sun–Thurs 8am–11pm, Fri & Sat 8am–11.30pm

Accepts All major credit cards

Reservations For large groups

FRENCH

friendly À Table doesn't feel much like a new old bistro either. When a waiter practically sits down at your table while taking an order, you have the feeling he and others before him have done this for decades. When one of the many kids who come in for brunch pulls out a plaything from the toy box, you could easily assume—incorrectly—that his or her smiling parents are reliving a memory from their Fort Greene childhoods.

Chef-owner Jean-Baptiste Caillet, formerly manager at Balthazar (see p.124), pays no mind to trendiness, fuss, or presentation. Good eating is what matters. The baby spinach, sliced avocado, and pine nut salad is an unwieldy heap drizzled with lemon vinaigrette ($9). Likewise, ham, saucisson, country pâté, and garlic sausage are hastily arranged on the abundant charcuterie platter ($10). Small wonder then that monkfish, universally recognized for its ugliness, has become the signature entree. It is served Provençal-style with black olives, pistou, cherry tomatoes, sautéed mushrooms, and potato purée. The next best options are steaks—shell steak au poivre with very good frites ($20) or hanger steak with shallot sauce and a potato gratin ($17).

The wine list features 27 wines under $28. The 2000 Cuvée de Bois-fleury from the Pouilly Fumé producer Alain Caibourdin is fruity, mineral-like, and great value at $28. The 1999 Madiran from Chateau Barrejat ($24) is lush with red fruits. A glass of Sauternes or Banyuls may accompany the oozy flourless chocolate cake ($5), depending on whether you're matching the pistachios that flavor the ice cream, the strawberry garnish, or the chocolate itself.

Chez Oskar

FRENCH

(🍴) In a jazzy, 17-foot-long mural above a row of red banquettes, painter Charlotta Janssen has portrayed Chez Oskar as an idealized French colonial cafe packed with bohemians, hipsters, refugees, and black marketeers. If you were exiled to Casablanca and desperate for a forged exit visa granting passage to America, this is exactly the sort of place you'd come to get it. All that's missing from Chez Oskar is a guy named Oskar. The original proprietor was Charles Sorel, a Parisian who worked as a waiter at three Manhattan bistros and

Lunch $15–35
Dinner $25–60

Address 211 Dekalb Ave at Adelphi St

☎718/852-6250

Transportation C to Lafayette Ave; G to Fulton St

Open Mon–Thurs 11.30am–midnight, Fri & Sat 11.30am–1am, Sun 10.30am–midnight

Accepts All major credit cards

named his first place after the son of his partner. He asked Janssen to fashion a casual and comfortable haunt appropriate for a quiet coffee, a noisy supper, or anything in between. At first she was only responsible for the oval lightshades and blue, gold, and burgundy patinas of this classic corner space with its wood casement windows, terracotta-tiled floor, and stamped-tin ceiling. Now, as the new owner, she's in charge of everything.

Always regard the words "fresh tuna in the Niçoise" as an indicator of good things to come. That $12.50 salad as well as the $8.50 citrus salad reveal a kitchen with a true bistro soul that doesn't bother with pretty presentation. The chef's concern is with getting as much and as many of his favorite foods on a single plate as possible. For openers there's no topping the mussels marinière ($10) with plenty of onions, fresh tomatoes, and white wine broth to sop up with crusty bread from Sullivan Bakery. But the garlic-laden, Burgundy-style escargots ($7.50) come awfully close.

Of the entrees, the roast monkfish ($15) arrives as a bouillabaisse-inspired Provençal festival with rouille, potatoes, and saffron fish broth. The sirloin steak au poivre ($19), with its back-kicking peppercorns and decent fries, is, like a true friend, always there for you, even while the braised lamb shank ($18) vies for your undivided affection. Then there's the Dijon-sauced roast chicken ($14), which is as juicy as you have the right to expect. By dessert time, only the homemade crème caramel ($6) will prevent you from taking an early exit visa.

Locanda Vini & Olii

🍴 *Locanda* suggests an old Italian inn and the promise of a good meal and a good bed. *Vini & Olii* harkens back to stores that carried wines, olive oils, and produce from local growers. Taken together and today, Locanda Vini & Olii is more than a place of business based on old-world hospitality. It is the libretto for a labor of love staged inside Lewis Drug Store, a 130-year-old Brooklyn pharmacy set among the handsome brick and limestone houses of the nascent Clinton Hill district. Meticulously

$25–65

Address 129 Gates Ave at Cambridge Place
☎718/622-9202
Transportation C to Clinton-Washington Aves
Open Tues–Thurs 6–10.30pm, Fri & Sat 6–11.30pm, Sun 6–10pm
Accepts MasterCard & Visa
Reservations Suggested

ITALIAN

restoring the stunning mahogany woodwork down to every last apothecary display case, drawer, and compartment, Catherine de Zagon Louy and husband François Louy now dispense rustic Tuscan remedies and Italian liquid cure-alls for all kinds of chronic New York ailments.

With chef Michele Baldacci in the kitchen, the goal, according to the Louys, is to assemble the foods a Tuscan housewife might prepare for guests. Everything from the heart and home, even when traveling outside the region for inspiration. The quality of the food is not quite as high as you want it to be given that the place is so beautiful and the people are so nice. The cooking is a little uneven and the baking can be bland. That said, you can have a wonderful time passing around such shared plates as the cheeseboard ($9.75), the charcuterie platter ($11.50) and its seafood counterpart (octopus soppressata and tuna salami; $12), and the crostini ($7.75–12.50), along with such appetizers as sardines in a sweet-and-sour marinade ($8.75) and wild boar carpaccio ($9.75).

The great second-act aria is the chestnut lasagnette ($9.75), white ribbons of pasta with chickpeas and a Luganega pork sausage ragu. It's just one of several pastas, along with marvelously chewy tagliatelle with porcini ($9.75) and melt-in-the-mouth eggplant ravioli with tomatoes ($10), that upstage the meat and fish entrees. The wine list, pasted on a bottle, proposes well-chosen reds—the 2001 Virzi from Sadafora ($25), a Sicilian blend of Nero d'Avola and Syrah, is recommended—at low markups.

Thomas Beisl

AUSTRIAN

(🍴) Thomas is for owner Thomas Ferlesch, the onetime wunderkind who, as chef at the departed Vienna '79, earned four stars in a now yellowed New York Times review. Beisl is for the Viennese term for bistro. And Thomas Beisl is for the patrons, performers, and paperpushers from the Brooklyn Academy of Music—across Lafayette Ave—who seek a versatile spot to meet and eat before, after, or instead of the spectacle. It can be difficult to distinguish the artists from the ticketholders, who, like tennis fans, often dress like the virtuosi they're paying to see. But look closely and you'll identify

Lunch $10–50
Dinner $20–60

Address 25 Lafayette Ave, between Ashland Place & St. Felix St
℡718/222-5800
Transportation 2,3,4,5 to Atlantic Ave; M,N,R,W to Pacific St; G to Fulton St; C to Lafayette Ave
Open Mon–Fri 4pm–midnight, Sat & Sun 11am–midnight
Accepts AmEx
Reservations Suggested

the dancers by their nimbly expressed aversion to the buttery sauces, fatty charcuterie, and creamy desserts central to the Viennese tradition. Most others with their backs against the gray-black banquettes and their feet on the geometric terrazzo adore the fare and the venue for it, a darkwood beisl with Beaux Arts moldings and vintage mirrors and placards.

Mr. Berger, the dapper and proficient host, makes a persuasive pitch for the Schiele cocktail—a chartreuse-colored concoction of elderberry syrup, woodruff, champagne, and gelatin. But you might pass directly to the Austrian brews and wines that pair so well with the batter-fried mushrooms ($6), the large endive, pear, and gorgonzola salad ($7), the coarsely diced salmon tartare ($7), and the chicken liver terrine, a forceful and, at $6, affordable foie gras wannabe.

Ferlesch rotates several outstanding entrees, including a long-simmered sauerbrauten with sliced potato dumplings browned in butter ($16); a roast chicken ($14), with rosemary tucked beneath the skin that's as marvelously crisp, golden and succulent as that of roast duck; and a short rib pot au feu ($16) that releases the comforting vapors of cabbage the instant you lift the lid off its Le Creuset stewpot. Time or appetite might dictate stopping at the bar for a burger on a ciabatta bun ($8), a Portobello, goat cheese, and roasted pepper panini ($8), or a knockout dessert: the farmer's cheese strudel ($5) doused with hot vanilla custard sauce, perhaps, or the schlag-crested linzertorte ($5).

Park Slope

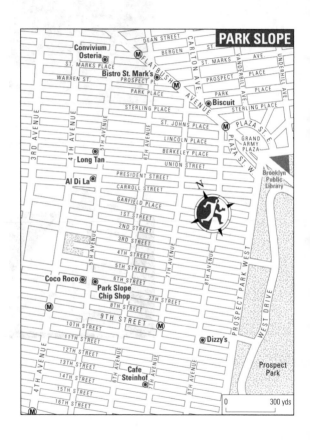

PARK SLOPE

DEAN STREET
BERGEN ST.
Convivium Osteria
ST. MARKS PLACE
ST. MARKS AVE.
Bistro St. Mark's
WARREN ST.
PROSPECT PLACE
PARK PLACE
PARK PLACE
STERLING PLACE
Biscuit
STERLING PLACE
ST. JOHNS PLACE
PLAZA ST. E.
LINCOLN PLACE
GRAND ARMY PLAZA
Long Tan
BERKELEY PLACE
PLAZA ST. W.
UNION STREET
Al Di La
PRESIDENT STREET
Brooklyn Public Library
CARROLL STREET
GARFIELD PLACE
1ST STREET
N
2ND STREET
3RD STREET
4TH STREET
5TH STREET
Coco Roco
6TH STREET
Park Slope Chip Shop
7TH STREET
8TH STREET
9TH STREET
10TH STREET
Dizzy's
11TH STREET
12TH STREET
PROSPECT PARK WEST
13TH STREET
WEST DRIVE
Cafe Steinhof
14TH STREET
15TH STREET
Prospect Park
16TH STREET

3RD AVENUE
4TH AVENUE
5TH AVENUE
6TH AVENUE
7TH AVENUE
8TH AVENUE

FLATBUSH AVENUE
CARLTON AVENUE
UNDERHILL AVE.
VANDERBILT AVE.

0   300 yds

Al Di La

The last thing on your mind when dining in Al Di La is *l'al di la*—"the life beyond." For what mortal can train his thoughts on the afterlife while the dizzying aroma of sage-scented garlic soup is in the air and the broth's silky finish is lingering on the palate? What living soul can obsess about destiny with spoon-shaped, gnocchi-like malfatti constructed of Swiss chard, Ricotta, and Parmigiano-Reggiano in play? And what true New Yorker can utter even one sentence in the future tense before Mrs Di Rosa's meatballs have been polished off? By suspending a Murano blown-glass chandelier from the varnished tin ceiling of an old Brooklyn storefront, Italian-born cooking teacher Emiliano Coppa and American chef Anna Klinger (formerly of Lespinasse and the Union Square Cafe, p.80) have fashioned an enchanting marriage of Venetian and Brooklynese design. Theirs is a neighborhood place superior to 99 percent of all destination restaurants.

$25–50

Address 248 5th Ave at Carroll St
☏718/783-4565
Transportation M,N,R to Union St
Open Mon, Wed & Thurs
6–10.30pm, Fri & Sat 6–11pm, Sun
6–10pm
Accepts MasterCard, Visa
Reservations Not accepted

ITALIAN

Some of the rotated dishes on the hand-printed menu used to be listed only in Italian, requiring explanations from Coppa. This was fortunate, as he is a gracious host whose soft voice and accent could make canned peas sound irresistible. People have been known to ask him twice what the "malfatti" ($11) are, just to hear him repeat his description of the Swiss chard and ricotta gnocchi that have become Klinger's signature pasta. Typical of the fine antipasti options are mussels steamed in white wine with grilled bread, shallots, garlic, and tomato ($8.50); and a nice pairing of baccalà mantecato (salt cod whisked with oil in the manner of a mayonnaise) and grilled polenta cake ($8).

Among main courses, the braised beef cheeks ($18.50) are so tender and unctuous they may have begun to cook even before the lease for Al Di La was signed. Marinated and grilled whole orata fish ($17) is stuffed with lemon confit and served with roasted fingerling potatoes. Sliced hanger steak served with balsamic-tossed arugula ($15) is sensational. Desserts (all $6), never Al Di La's strong suit, encompass a chocolate hazelnut ice cream, a ricotta tart, and a warm pear cake with bittersweet chocolate chips.

Biscuit

Customer fidelity is earned but not entirely encouraged at Biscuit, a wainscoted storefront symbolically adorned with old rolling pins and meat cleavers on the Prospect Heights side of Flatbush Avenue. The rickety old school chairs are not meant to support the weight of grownups who subsist on radish sprouts, much less those who scarf down fatty pork ribs, double-dipped fried chicken, potato salad, cheese grits, chile-powdered fries, and pecan pie a la mode with any regularity. An individual of said inclination would have to pull over a second of the eight ragtag tables just to

Lunch $10–50
Dinner $8–30

Address 367 Flatbush Ave, between 7th Ave & Sterling Place
☏718/398-2227
Transportation Q to 7th Ave; 2,3 to Grand Army Plaza
Open Mon–Thurs 11am–11pm, Fri 11am–midnight, Sat 10am–midnight, Sun 10am–10pm
Accepts Cash only
Reservations Not accepted

find a place to set down his or her Diet Coke. Nonetheless, would-be regulars might look at the bright side of these limitations: the distance from the counter where orders are placed to the dining area is not so much a stroll as it is a half-turn.

Chef/co-owner Joshua Cohen prepares barbecued pork three ways. His ribs ($8 for an already imposing half rack which, like the $15 full rack, comes with two sides) are tender, pleasantly gooey, and deeper to the bone than you expect; the pulled pork ($6.50 for a 6oz serving, $11.50 for a 12oz), a gratifying pile of buttery and intermittently crusty strips and crisp-edged shards. But it's the messy Mr. Brown sandwich ($5.50) composed of dark, caramelized pulled pork from the outer portion of the pork butt that has diners whooping with delight. The eight-spiced, tomato-based house barbecue—and basting—sauce has just enough tang and sting. Try too the mustard sauce and the vinegary, gut-penetrating Carolina-style sauce, if only as condiments.

Chicken ($5.50 for a quarter, $7.50 for a half) is served either with barbecue sauce or in a twice-dipped fried version for exceptional crispness. The buttermilk biscuits remain the requisite side attraction ($3, the same price as all the standard sides), even though co-owner/baker Maio Martinez has removed the lard from their batter. Best among her desserts (mostly $3.75) is the Devil's Advocate Cake—a devil's food cake with peanut buttercream and no apparent argument against it.

Bistro St Mark's

🍴 Park Slope may have been seeking in a bistro what many of us look for in a mate: an appearance that is contemporary and attractive, with a down-to-earth nature underneath it all. The sleekly modern and mirrored Bistro St Mark's, with its comfy banquettes and neighborly ways, is exactly that. Finding true love is nevertheless a tricky business. Some locals find the place too noisy; its service, too slow. But most are grateful to have a restaurant that understands them and takes time to listen.

Lunch $15–45
Dinner $30–65

Address 76 St Mark's Ave, between 6th & Flatbush Aves
☎718/857-8600
Transportation 1,2,4 to Bergen St
Open Mon 5.30–11pm, Tues–Thurs noon–11pm, Fri noon–midnight, Sat 9am–midnight, Sun 9am–10pm
Accepts All major credit cards
Reservations Suggested

Chef Johannes Sanzin cooks for a community that's predominantly liberal in politics but conservative about food. His menu reads as sophisticated and fussy, but the dishes it outlines ultimately come across as accessible. He truly knows how to work that trendy/down-to-earth thing, especially when it comes to appetizers. Jalapeno-infused scallop carpaccio ($9) has more of a spicy tickle than burn. In the lemon–cilantro accompaniment for grilled sardines ($9), each flavor is distinct but none overpowers. The mushroom salad with fresh herbs and Asian pears ($8) startles mostly by its freshness. And caramelized sea scallops with pasta and tomato cilantro sauce ($9) is a short story with the depth of a novel.

Seasonal main courses are firmly in the bistro mold. The relationships between meats/fish and their sides are splendid; witness the leg of lamb with cherry tomatoes and flageolet beans ($20), the thyme-crusted tuna with a marinated fennel salad and a soy ginger vinaigrette ($20), and the monkfish medallions with two olive sauces and pistachio oil ($18). Even pastries manage to be at once fashionable and grounded. The coffee and almond semifreddo with crushed pistachios ($6) fools you into thinking it's either exotic or traditional. Neither is quite right. The pairing of yogurt ice cream with Grand Marnier-marinated strawberry ($7) replays familiar flavor associations. And the volcanic chocolate soufflé with fine vanilla ice cream ($7) is among the best of its kind.

Cafe Steinhof

(¶) The late actress Hildegard Knef was hailed by critics as "the thinking man's Marlene Dietrich" and described by Ella Fitzgerald as "the greatest singer in the world without a voice." That solves the mystery of the haunting beauty in that old movie poster and eliminates the only distraction to keep you from loving Cafe Steinhof. Few would dare call this the thinking man's Wallsé (see p.172) or Café Sabarsky (p.250). It's not half as serious or expensive as those Manhattan eateries. But

$20–45

Address 422 7th Ave at 14th St
☎718/369-7776
Transportation F to 7th Ave
Open Mon 5–11pm, Tues–Thurs 11am–4pm & 5–11pm, Fri & Sat 11am–4pm & 5pm–midnight, Sun 11am–4pm & 5–11pm
Accepts All major credit cards
Reservations Not accepted

Paul Goebert's pub-like spinoff from—and survivor of—Max & Moritz, his recently closed bistro, appeals to every segment of the Park Slope populace. Brick walls, bench-style mahogany banquettes, and Austrian-German memorabilia transport this Park Slope corner to Vienna's Bermuda Dreieck. You'll soon believe it once you've established a rapport with such house draughts as Jever (an Austrian pilsner), Gosser (an Austrian lager), and Schneider Weisse (a German wheat beer).

Within Steinhof the friendly pub is a pretty good little bistro welcoming to children and other beings who do not drink alcohol. That said, those who drop in on a Monday night are in for a surprise. Sure, we're all used to seeing early-week spaghetti promos or chicken-wing giveaways. But only here does *montag nacht* turn into a rockin' $5 goulash party. As an alternative to beef there's also all-you-can eat fillet of smoked trout—not typically the stuff of stuff-a-thons.

The daily menu lists both snacks and more substantial satisfactions. The assorted cheese and charcuterie plate ($9) ably fills both needs. Or you could start with the terrific smoked trout and potato salad appetizer before moving on to such meats as the split and grilled bratwurst ($9), the agreeably pink and unusually moist smoked pork loin ($12), or tender sauerbraten with red cabbage purée ($12). The mushroom fricassée with bread dumplings ($9) makes a nice meatless alternative, as do three dynamite desserts (all $5.50): apple bread pudding, linzertorte, and chocolate crêpes.

Coco Roco

The price of co-ops in Park Slope is affected by the quality of the nearby public schools. But it's surprising that a large premium is not put on any real estate within delivery reach of Coco Roco. It's not that anyone minds dining elbow-to-elbow with the diverse mix of Brooklyn couples, families, and work buddies. The votive-lit brown paper bags add a touch of romance to an informal space of brush-painted walls, exposed brick, and folkloric decoration. But when you're waiting twenty minutes to place an order

$10–50

Address 392 5th Ave, between 6th & 7th Sts

☎718/965-3376

Transportation F to 4th Ave; M,N,R to 9th St

Open Sun–Thurs noon–10.30pm, Fri & Sat noon–11.30pm

Accepts All major credit cards

Reservations For large groups

PERUVIAN

that may take thirty minutes to reach your table, the prospect of glistening rotisserie chicken dropped off at your doorstep is an enticing one. In addition, becoming familiar with pollo a la brasa is crucial to any child's education and thus could very easily fall into the realm of homework.

Coco Roco does many things well besides chicken. Peruvian standards like papa rellena (meat-stuffed potato pies; $6.50), papa a la huancaina (boiled potatoes in spicy cheese sauce; $6), and the Lima barbecue addiction anticuchos (skewered beef heart; $6.95) are first-rate. Fresh seafood runs hot (fried squid, steamed mussels, grilled octopus) and cold (eight ceviches). Standouts from the cevicheria ($10.95-15.95) include a bracing cocktail of mussels, shrimp, squid, red snapper, cancha (toasted corn), and sweet potato in a spicy lime marinade, and a red snapper with only papaya ginger juice as backup.

The fact that some mains seem Manhattanized—potato-crusted red snapper ($13.95), say, or grilled salmon with couscous-styled quinoa ($12.95)—is not such a bad thing. Neither is the Argentine lean of the charred sirloin slathered with scallion-powered chimichurri ($13.95). No breath mint can conquer its alliance of scallion and garlic. But it's still a cause for celebration that the chicken spins in a window-front rotisserie kept apart from the cosmopolitan kitchen. It's served in halves ($4.95), whole ($8), or shredded into a thick baguette sandwich with ripe avocado and jalapeno mayo ($5.50). Each dessert ($5) is sweeter than the next. Gummy bread pudding is sauced with tres leches, while banana fritters come with amazing tropical fruit ice creams.

Park Slope

Convivium Osteria

(🍴) The Brooklyn address is a cunning disguise. Convivium Osteria is the sort of family-run inn you dream of coming across on a journey through the Mediterranean countryside. Mom and pop live above a cozy dining room festooned in farmhouse rustic. The lower-level tapas lounge takes after an Iberian wine cellar connected to a charming patio and moonlit garden. More enchanting still, the dizzying aromas throughout recall three-quarters of the owners' origins. Carlo Pulixi was born in Sardinia and raised in Rome. Michelle Pulixi is of Portuguese and Irish descent. Accordingly, the robust cooking incorporates Portuguese, Sardinian, and Roman specialties with great finesse and care. The missing 25 percent of their combined heritage? As of this writing there's been no evidence of an Irish stew.

$30–75

Address 68 5th Ave, between Bergen St & St Mark's Ave
☎718/857-1833
Transportation 2,3,4 to Bergen St; B,M,N,R,W to Pacific St
Open Mon–Thurs 6–10.30pm, Fri & Sat 6–11.30pm, Sun noon–10pm
Accepts AmEx
Reservations Suggested

Any permutation of appetizers turns into an immersion course in classic Mediterranean flavors. From land there's Roman-style artichokes dressed with olive oil, mint, and garlic ($10), and a refreshing salad of fennel, orange, red onion, and olives ($7.50). All salads are fabulous. From the sea there's grilled baby octopus with a chopped celery salad and black olives ($11), charred Portuguese sardines ($9), roasted prawns with sea salt ($16.50), and soft and puffy, milk-soaked, batter-fried salt cod fillets ($9).

The salt cod returns for the second act, most impressively in the casserole with sherry, green olives, onion, and mashed potatoes ($18). The Pulixis' devotion to salt cod, rare by New York standards, is matched by their diners' unexpectedly positive response to it. The widespread appeal of the seafood stew ($18), on the other hand, packed as it is with prawns, mussels, clams, and monkfish in a tomato cilantro white wine broth, is hardly a shock. And only the spice-averse put up a fight against the grilled baby chicken with the Portuguese hot pepper sauce piri-piri ($16). Pappardelle with a savory, Roman-style oxtail ragu that contains tomato, cinnamon, nutmeg, and chocolate ($13) is joyfully hearty. Chocolate returns in the more traditional role of melt-in-your-mouth cake. And panna cotta with berry compote or apple pie with vanilla custard cream won't disappoint. Desserts go for $6 to $8.

Dizzy's

(🍴) If you can navigate the hodge-podge menu—"Would you like a side of cheese fries with your Oriental grilled chicken salad, madam?"—you'll quickly discover that finding a good meal at Dizzy's is an effortless pursuit. A true new-old neighborhood joint, the diner stands as a vibrantly colored testament to yuppified Park Slope. Regulars pile in, meal after meal, to order chocolate-stuffed French toast ($7.50) for dinner or a traditional grilled cheese sandwich ($5.95) for a mid-afternoon snack. The fluorescent green and yellow walls and fire-engine-red banquets imbue the busy premises—and premise—with whimsy. Crisp linen tablecloths, flickering candles, and bud vases filled with delicate flowers soften their edges.

$12–40

Address 511 9th St at 8th Ave
☏718/499-1966
Transportation F to 7th Ave
Open Mon–Thurs 7am–10pm, Fri 7am–11pm, Sat 9am–4pm & 6–11pm, Sun 9am–4pm & 6–10pm
Accepts Cash only
Reservations Not accepted

To get things off to a fine start, try a sake cocktail in three forms (all $5): sake Bloody Mary, sake margarita or sake cosmopolitan. For beverage therapy of the nostalgic kind, try instead an old-fashioned Brooklyn chocolate egg cream ($3.25; $4.50 turns it into an ice cream soda) or a thick, rich, chocolate shake ($4.50)—just the thing to wash down an order of ultra-spicy but amazingly un-messy Buffalo wings ($6.95). This gentrified version of classic Buffalo wings is not dripping with toxic-orange butter sauce. A shrewd choice for shared appetizer or main course is the macaroni and cheese ($7.45). Served with a noncomformist Caesar salad, this hearty bowl of rigatoni swims in a soupy sauce made from five cheeses. The entire bowl is then topped with Rice Crispies and broiled to create a real juvenile joyride. More cheesy fun is to had with the "Our Way" grilled sandwich made with Cheddar and bacon ($7.95 with fries and homemade coleslaw).

Substantial burgers ($8.95) deposit eight ounces of charbroiled ground sirloin on a very good brioche roll. Be careful not to order too many additional toppings. At a dollar apiece, you could easily end up with an expensive jawbreaker. Also, beware of the cranberry chutney, which overpowers the turkey and smoked bacon on the roast turkey club ($8.95). Ask your well-meaning but easily distracted waiter either to go easy on the chutney or put it on the side. If you still have some digestive capacity in reserve, gaze over to the dependable dessert case.

Long Tan

THAI

The great thing about this new sort of Thai place for a new sort of Brooklyn is its versatility. With four distinct environments—bar, lounge, patio, and dining room—you can spend an entire Saturday evening in one place and still feel as though you've made the Fifth Avenue rounds. The cement-floored dining room itself is divided by an open kitchen sided by a counter and a row of red-padded stools shaped like flattened lollipops. It also happens that each eating area is subdivided by successions of wood-block booths attractively back-lit with Japanese-paper sconces. And those tables themselves are effectively split between those who favor green tea martinis and those who prefer ginger-kamikazes.

$20–45
Address 196 5th Ave, between Union & Berkeley Sts
☎718/622-8444
Transportation M,N,R to Union St
Open Mon–Thurs 5.30pm–midnight, Fri & Sat 5.30pm–2am, Sun 11.30am–4pm & 5.30pm–midnight
Accepts MasterCard & Visa
Reservations For large groups

Long Tan only opened in 2001 and already chef Jeff Hardinger is treated like a rock star asked to play the same couple of hits over and over again. An old hand at pan-Asian pop, the alum of Ruby Foo's (see p.220) has put together a balanced menu of noodle dishes, curries, salads, and appetizers. But requests keep coming back to the kitchen for his crispy little squid rings with chile sauce ($6) and pan-seared duck breast ($13). The great appeal of the latter is not lost on the servers. Ask a waiter near the end of his shift where the rest room is located and he's liable to answer "pan-seared duck breast." Sliced on the bias and offset by sautéed bok choy, the crisp-skinned, tamarind duck is tart, tender, and sweetly succulent.

Good alternatives abound. Among appetizers, the tasty crab and mango summer roll ($5) is cut like a sushi maki into five bite-sized coils striped with colored mayo squiggles. Poached squid ($5) boasts a nice lime-drizzled toss of tomato, greens, and carrots. Among mains, the rice noodles with stir-fried vegetables ($8) and lamb chunks with a richly spiced coconut curry ($9) both prove good value. And crusty, pan-roasted salmon ($13) with a salad of julienned raw papaya, pepper, and leeks is just splendid. Finally, the sticky rice pudding ($6) and fudge-like chocolate cake ($6) are merely okay; the caramelized banana ($6), pale and syrupy.

Park Slope Chip Shop

When British expat Chris Sell said the only thing he missed from home was proper fish and chips, it's small wonder he moved to New York in the first place. But this slight to his motherland — and perhaps also his mother — turned into a boon for fellow expats, anglophiles, and nutritionally incorrect Brooklynites. It led him to open this amusing, kid-friendly, and, in a manner of speaking, healthy showcase for Britain's national dish. Of course "healthy" here refers to the size of the portions and not the nutritional benefits of, to take one

$15–35

Address 383 5th Ave, between 6th & 7th Sts

℗718/832-7701

Transportation F to 4th Ave; M,N,R to 9th St

Open Mon–Wed noon–10pm, Thurs & Fri noon–11pm, Sat 11am–11pm, Sun 11am–10pm

Accepts Cash only

Reservations Not accepted

BRITISH

example, the chip butty — salted chips (for the uninitiated, these are french fries, not potato chips), vinegar, and ketchup sandwiched between slices of buttered bread ($5).

Sell's recipe for fish and chips was inspired by his favorite chippie in London, the dearly departed Upper Street Fish Shop. While we don't dare compare the results to that Islington legend, the battered cod is jolly good and the chips are, as the menu maintains, bloody lovely. The crust is crisped to a golden-brown shell thick enough to conceal the superbly moist fish. The chips, sliced with an imported cutter to the regulation size of twelve millimeters, are hot, unsoggy, and, by design, not crisp. The $9 pairing can be bought to stay or to go, the latter wrapped in a sheet from the New York Times.

It turns out Sell's sentimental longings do not stop at fish and chips. The whimsical shop is furnished with imported wood dining tables and adorned with boyhood posters (Beatles, James Bond, Pink Floyd) and tacky royal memorabilia. The selection of English draughts ($5) is outstanding. Better still, they're poured into an imperial pint, which is four ounces larger than am American one And he and his compatriot waitstaff proudly serve shepherd's pie ($9), bangers and mash (sausages and mashed potatoes; $9), Welsh rarebit (baked cheese toast; $4), and mushy peas, a traditional accompaniment whose best application, according to American opinion, is as a substitute for baseboard. It would probably be best if Sell's enthusiasms stopped at dessert. The crumbles and rice puddings are drowned in runny custard.

Sunset Park

SUNSET PARK

Greenwood Cemetery

Sunset Park

Tacos Matamoros

Ocean Palace

Maimonides Medical Centre

Jade Plaza

GOWANUS EXPRESSWAY

FORT HAMILTON PARKWAY

N

0   300 yds

Jade Plaza

(🍴) As the boundaries of Manhattan's Chinatown slipped deep into Little Italy and the Lower East Side, new immigrants from the southern provinces of China looked east. Today, more than 60,000 Chinese make their homes and run more than 500 businesses in Brooklyn's Sunset Park. Development along a fifteen-block stretch of Eighth Avenue, the community's commercial center, has included a plethora of food markets and restaurants, each of them more pros-

Lunch $12–25
Dinner $20–55

Address 6022 8th Ave, between
60th & 61st Sts
☎718/492-6888
Transportation N to 8th Ave
Open Daily 8am–11.30pm
Accepts MasterCard & Visa
Reservations Not accepted

perous than the last. Jade Plaza represents the summit of Sunset Park glitz, an enormous, carpeted banquet hall bearing three symbolic displays of opulence: a framed art piece posing shark fins against a violet backdrop; a glass display case of fine Cognacs; and two enormous tanks filled with live fish and prawns. The message is clear: Brooklynites need not cross the East River for an opulent, banquet-style Chinese dinner.

Stepping into Jade Plaza at 11am on a weekend is one of the great thrills in the contemporary Brooklyn dining experience. Upwards of 200 diners are here for dim sum ($2–5 per item) to rival any in Manhattan's Chinatown. Har gow—the shrimp dumplings that are the test of any dim sum—contain large pieces of fresh shrimp beneath their delicate, translucent skins. The rice noodles, too, pan-fried to order at the roving carts, are outstanding.

The English-language dinner menu lists routine dishes and too few of the seafood specialties that distinguish the kitchen. (You can get a peek at that mysterious warren through an open door on 60th Street.) For non-Chinese diners, ordering is therefore a frustrating negotiation, involving gestures and jabs at dishes on neighboring tables. You'll be tempted by the bird's nest of woven taro filled with glistening scallops, shrimp, and conch rimmed with Chinese vegetables ($22.95) and the monstrous, salt-baked Dungeness crab (roughly $20/lb) with its crisp, glistening, chile-spiced, salt-encrusted body, and its sweet, meaty interior. Steamed whole fish (carp, bass, cod; $12–16/lb), topped with slivered scallions and fresh cilantro, rests in a ginger broth so good that you'll want to continually spoon it over the fish, as if basting, or even directly into your mouth like a soup.

Ocean Palace

The popularity of this glittery, two-floor Cantonese restaurant and banquet hall within Brooklyn's Chinese community comes in waves. Some new place opens to great fanfare in Sunset Park, everyone flocks over to try it, then sooner or later they return to trusty, hospitable, user-friendly Ocean Palace until the next big thing is ballyhooed in the Chinese newspapers. Actually, it's not all that different from the city's fickle restaurant scene at large. Ocean Palace may also fall victim to another vagary of the public taste. New Yorkers seem to love new eateries that look old but not old eateries that look new.

Lunch $8–45
Dinner $15–45

Address 5421 8th Ave, between 54th & 55th Sts
☎718/871-8080
Transportation N to 8th Ave
Open Daily 8am–11.30pm
Accepts All major credit cards
Reservations For large groups

Fortunately, there are always enough diners who care only about good food and good value to keep Ocean Palace running at high tide. You can come in at any hour and be assured of getting superb, dim-sum-quality dumplings (all $2 for four)—steamed mixed vegetables, steamed shrimp (har gow), or even deep-fried pork—as well as the highest quality lacquered-style roast meats—duck ($6.50), pork ($6.50), quail ($11.95), and suckling pig ($9.50). And you are almost sure to hear a pitch for the egg-white-battered jumbo shrimp topped with a citrusy, mayonnaise-like sauce and scattered with honey-sesame walnuts ($16.95). Though repeatedly described as "the number one" dish both here and at the second Ocean Palace (1414 Ave U, Homecrest; ☎718/376-3838), you may find you care little for the soft, puffy batter or the whipped sauce.

A far superior, if less novel, jumbo shrimp preparation is with black beans and crunchy Chinese broccoli ($13.95). Among other time-tested bets to come back for are braised whole sea bass with vegetables, bean curd, and ginger scallion broth (market price; $15–20); and hyper-tenderized steak with black pepper sauce ($12.95). The Peking duck service ($19.95 for a whole on weekdays, $25 on weekends) with pancakes rather than buns is fine, but they're stingy with the scallions. Ocean Palace is receptive to special requests. For example, instead of a side of bok choy ($6.95) and another of pan-fried noodles ($6.95), you could have them combine the two into a combo ($7.50 or thereabouts) that provides enough for three.

Tacos Matamoros

It would be a mistake to judge Tacos Matamoros by its minimal comforts and humble accoutrements. Instead, take your reading by peering into the open kitchen, where tortillas are being warmed on the griddle, and cooks are busy chopping cilantro and onions and carving up huge slabs of meat. With the accommodating and efficient waitresses and Sunset Park locals speaking only Spanish, it's exactly the sort of authentic scene you would hope to encounter on a Mexican road trip.

$5–25

Address 4503 5th Ave, between 45th & 46th Sts
℡718/871-7627
Transportation N,R to 45th St
Open Daily 8am–1am
Accepts Cash only
Reservations Not accepted

MEXICAN

At just a buck (that's half the going rate), each taco consists of a double layer of soft corn tortillas folded over the deliciously moist meat of your choice, along with chopped onions and cilantro. Once you've ordered, a bowl of hot sauce and a plate of lime wedges arrive at your table. The carnitas tacos are an inspired mix of fatty, juicy, crackling-crisp pork bits sure to enthrall those with no compunction about consuming such scrappy, cholesterol-loaded meats. Queasy diners are apt to prefer the cabeza taco, at least until they learn that the tasty, marinated beef comes from the cow's head parts. The pork taco boasts marvelously tender strips of meat. If your budget allows an increase of 50¢, that pork is at its best cooked in a mole sauce, hidden in a pocket of rice, reddened by a fiery chile sauce, and wrapped in a corn husk—namely in the dish called rojos y mole tamale.

The traditional posole stew ($5) contains a substantial hunk of superbly tender pork, an abundance of whole garlic cloves, and a dollop of creamy hominy all submerged in and slowly infiltrated by a pork broth. Garnished with the chopped onion and cilantro, it's absolute satisfaction. The chiles rellenos ($8)—cheese-stuffed Poblano peppers—are splendid, too, though just occasionally the filling is not fully melted. The rice that accompanies entrees like sizzling steak fajitas ($8) and plump burritos ($5) is moist and fluffy; the refried beans, utterly creamy. Sticky-sweet fruit shakes may be too sugary to sip with dinner, but the mango-papaya variety ($2.50) makes an excellent finish.

Williamsburg & Greenpoint

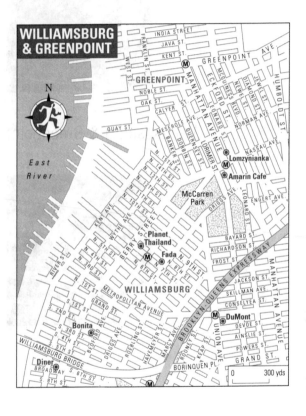

WILLIAMSBURG & GREENPOINT

INDIA STREET
JAVA ST
KENT ST
GREENPOINT AVE
GREENPOINT
NOBLE ST
OAK ST
CALYER ST
QUAY ST

FRANKLIN ST
WEST ST
MANHATTAN AVENUE

MESEROLE AVE
DOBBIN ST
GUERNSEY ST
LORIMER ST
ECKFORD ST
McGUINNESS BLVD
NEWEL ST
DIAMOND ST
JEWEL ST
HUMBOLDT ST
NORMAN AVE
NASSAU AVE

Lomzynianka
Amarin Cafe

LEONARD ST
ENGERT AVE

McCarren Park

DRIGGS AVE

N 15TH ST
N 14TH ST
N 13TH ST
N 12TH ST
N 11TH ST
N 10TH ST
N 9TH ST
N 8TH ST
N 7TH ST
N 6TH ST
N 5TH ST
N 4TH ST
N 3RD ST
N 2ND ST
N 1ST ST

BAYARD ST
RICHARDSON ST
FROST ST

Planet Thailand
Fada

East River

KENT AVE
WYTHE AVE
BERRY ST
BEDFORD AVE

WILLIAMSBURG

METROPOLITAN AVENUE
GRAND ST
S 1ST ST
S 2ND ST
S 3RD ST
Bonita
S 4TH ST
S 5TH ST
BEDFORD
DRIGGS AVE
ROEBLING ST
HAVEMEYER ST
MARCY AVE

JACKSON ST
SKILLMAN AVE
CONSELYEA ST

DuMont
DEVOE ST
AINSLIE ST
POWERS ST
GRAND ST

RIVER ST

WILLIAMSBURG BRIDGE
Diner
BROADWAY
S 6TH ST
S 8TH ST

BROOKLYN QUEENS EXPRESSWAY
MANHATTAN AVENUE
ROOMEY ST
KEAP ST
UNION AVE
BORINQUEN PL

0   300 yds

Amarin Cafe

The young bohemians may take some responsibility for the climbing rents in Greenpoint, but they have little to do with the clang that hits you over the head upon entering their favorite Thai luncheonette. Conversation is in fact laid-back and low-key. Rather, the racket is made by the cooks as they jiggle their woks over gas burners turned up to the max. The constant rattle establishes the rhythm of this modest eatery and the rapid rate at which you get served. When the chef in the open, behind-the-counter kitchen transfers a steaming pad Thai from wok to plate, it is garnished with bean sprouts and fresh cilantro by one woman and delivered to the table by another in a matter of seconds.

$10–30

Address 617 Manhattan Ave, between Driggs & Nassau Aves
☎718/349-2788
Transportation G to Nassau Ave
Open Sun–Thurs 11am–10.30pm, Fri & Sat 11am–11pm
Accepts Cash only
Reservations Not accepted

THAI

Appetizers are greatly enhanced by this speedy delivery. The crisp, tightly wrapped Thai spring rolls ($2.95) arrive too hot to handle, as tempted as you will be to do so. They're served with the same syrupy chile garlic sauce that accompanies the superbly crisp, bordering-on-crunchy fried calamari ($3.75). Delectable fried wontons stuffed with chicken, potato, and onion ($3.25) are endowed with a cool cucumber dip. Those who prefer to stay clear of the frying oil can opt for one of three salads ($4.95–7.25)—easily mistaken for main courses.

The joy of the pad Thai—shrimp ($6.50), chicken ($5.95), or mixed vegetable ($5.95)—is not only its two levels of heat, as key as their hot chiles and hot serving temperature are. The coarsely chopped scallions found in most of the noodle and rice dishes act as flavor activators, their fresh, pungent crunch setting off the entire ensemble of co-ingredients. Broad spicy noodles with chicken or beef ($6.25) put forward an inspired mix of sweet (brown bean sauce) and spicy-pungent (chile and onions). On the meatless side, describing the auspicious mix of sautéed veggies teamed with tofu ($6.25) as al dente would be imprecise. They're downright chunky. Dessert is up close and personal. Order a crème brûlée ($2.75) and the vanilla custard is sugared and torched in full view. Impressive stuff, though its caramelized lid could be crispier.

Bonita

(🍴) Turns out the servers at Diner (see p.349) were not eating the same bistro fare they were pushing on paying customers. For staff meals, Oaxacan cook Jose Gonzalez was slinging Mexican street food that had his co-workers shoving aside the superb mussels and steak frites. This phenomenon did not escape the attention of co-owners Mark Firth and Andrew Tarlow, who moved Gonzalez into a vacated rice-and-beans joint a few blocks away and, not waiting to take down the "Comidas Criollas" sign out front, opened Bonita. Though spruced up with subway-like wall mosaics, bentwood chairs, and Frida Kahlo lookalikes to wait on vintage-clothed post-adolescents and unkempt lawyer types in carpenter's clothes, the joint is essentially a standard luncheonette where, if you plant your butt on a leatherette stool at the marble counter, everything cooks before your eyes. This means that thin, brittle, homemade tortilla chips are no more than five seconds out of the deep hot oil by the time they reach your—ouch!—fingers.

| Lunch $10–50 |
| Dinner $12–40 |

Address 338 Bedford Ave, between South 2nd & 3rd Sts
☎718/384-9500
Transportation L to Bedford Ave; J,M,Z to Marcy Ave
Open Daily 11am-midnight
Accepts All major credit cars
Reservations Not accepted

Make sure you get an order of guacamole ($5) to go with those chips. Bonita's version is at once smooth and chunky—this will make total sense once you've dipped into it, with ample doses of salt, lime, and onion. You also want the Mexican corn on the cob dusted with Parmesan cheese and rubbed with chile mayo ($3) and the fabulous fried calamari ($6.50) coyly mixed with fried onion—there's no hint of this ingenious stroke on the menu—and served with cilantro dip. Throw in the main course soft tacos (pork, chicken, steak, or, better still, flaky fish fillet; $6–6.50), and it's easy to understand why the waitstaff at Diner had such a low turnover prior to Gonzalez's transfer.

The lunch-dinner menu is rounded out by a good mushroom fajita ($8), though it lacks the sizzle of meat variations, chiles rellenos ($9.50), and rotisserie half chicken ($9.50). Brunch should be stellar, given that Gonzalez did brunch at Diner and has good ideas for French toast, pancakes, and egg things with Mexican sweet or spicy slants. Regrettably, the execution has been sloppy.

Diner

(🍽) Diner appears to subsist in a no-man's-land of vacant trash-strewn lots and warehouses gloomily shadowed by the trestle of the Williamsburg Bridge. The dining car itself has long been concealed beneath a ruinous resurfacing sadly typical of the neighborhood's tin-siding and brick-facing saboteurs. But step inside and you encounter a great American classic bursting with martini-swilling geeks and mussel-slurping Manhattan exiles. The diner now occu-

| **Lunch $10–30** |
| **Dinner $15–60** |

Address 85 Broadway at Berry St
☏718/486-3077
Transportation J,M,Z to Marcy Ave
Open Sun–Thurs 11am–midnight,
Fri & Sat 11am–1am
Accepts MasterCard & Visa
Reservations Not accepted

AMERICAN

pied by Diner is a 1920s model with the barreled roof, long granite counter, and hardwood interior typical of the pre-Art Deco period of diner design. The six vintage booths beside the windows are always in great demand and worth waiting up to thirty minutes for. The rear dining pen, though fun and funky, has none of the movement and exhilaration of the mosaic-filled main room.

The original at this site, The Broadway Diner, no doubt served up a hamburger and fries (what diner didn't?), but it was surely nothing like the outsized fare served here today. The twenty-first-century burger ($8) at the hip, bistrofied Diner that stands in its place is a fat, rounded, blackened, juicy mass of loosely packed, none-too-lean beef slipped into a seeded bun with lettuce, tomato, and raw onion. You'll come across grapefruits smaller and drier. The long fries ($3) are sliced and bronzed in the manner of the great Jewish deli fries of yore. Sized between frites and steak fries, they merit being called french fried potatoes, with added emphasis on *potatoes*. Other mainstays include the steamed mussels ($11), the hanger steak ($15), and enormous rib-eye ($17).

Co-owner Andrew Tarlow worked at Odeon (see p.183) where he absorbed their lots-of-good-food-on-a-plate, to-heck-with-presentation philosophy. Servers recite the list of specials to diners while simultaneously scribbling on the butcher paper that covers their tables. It's a nice touch. An off-menu meal might start with grilled crostini of roasted red peppers, anchovies, shaved Parmesan, and olive oil ($7.50); continue to tapenade-topped tortilla Española with wilted escarole ($12.50), and conclude with chocolate bread pudding and whipped cream ($5.50).

DuMont

(W) Nature has spoiled the storefront ruse of Colin Devlin, formerly a bartender at Balthazar (see p.124). For the opening of DuMont he installed an old awning, once a prop for the movie *Godfather II*, bearing a telephone number, a trade ("paints and blinds"), and, most disorienting of all, a street number ("241") that had nothing to do with his bistro or its address. This led hundreds of con-fused first-timers to conclude they'd lost their way. Perhaps it was they and not a violent windstorm that tore the awning down. Regardless, the rest of Devlin's found objects are happily intact. The pressed-tin walls, beehive mosaic floor, L-shaped dark wood bar, and wooden restroom doors with frosted glass panels bring old Brooklyn charm to this former plumbing store. Red banquettes that could have been salvaged from a 1960s Pontiac provide funky cushioning for the mostly young, shabby-chic diners. And commonality between the served and the servers, recently extended to a 60-seat garden, translates into a carefree vibe that is less Manhattan than Berkeley.

Lunch $10–25
Dinner $15–45

Address 432 Union Ave, between Metropolitan Ave & Devoe St

☎718/486-7717

Transportation L to Lorimer St

Open Daily 11am–3pm & 6–11pm

Accepts MasterCard & Visa

Reservations Not accepted

Appropriate, then, that co-chefs Chris Wei and Stephanie Sugawara were co-workers at Chez Panisse in Berkeley. Their low-priced menu is deliberately brief, with just a couple of appetizers, entrees, and desserts augmented by nightly specials. Your choice is essentially between some-thing basic like the solid burger with good fries ($8.50) and something a little more daring, like the truly special special of pan-roasted red snapper topped with salsa verde and balanced on a warm salad with sautéed mushrooms and crispy potatoes ($14.50). While the DuMont salad ($7.50) with pickled haricots verts, radishes, pecans, crumbled blue cheese, bacon lardons, and balsamic vinaigrette is the logical appetizer, there's something to be said for sharing the macaroni and cheese ($9). Its radiatori are uniquely qualified to trap the bacon bits and gooey Gruyère, white Cheddar, and Parmesan cheeses. The steak frites cost just $19. Well-chosen wines are $19–27.

Weekend brunch dishes ($4–8) include baked eggs with tomato, andouille sausage, and white beans; brioche French toast with sautéed apples; a Gruyère-and-egg scramble; and a pressed ham-and-cheese sandwich.

Fada

Around Marseille, the locals refer to a revolutionary apartment complex designed by the legendary French architect Le Corbusier as Maison du Fada —"House of the Crazy." At first glance there is nothing terribly unusual, much less *fada*, about the corner establishment so-named by Pascal Jatteaux, a Marseillais, and Romain Brisson, who's from St-Rémy-de-Provence. It's merely another one of those disarming, new old-

Lunch $10–35
Dinner $25–55

Address 530 Driggs Ave, at North 8th St
☎718/388-6607
Transportation L to Bedford Ave
Open Sun–Thurs 8am–midnight, Fri & Sat 8am–1am
Accepts AmEx

FRENCH

looking bistros blossoming throughout new old-looking Brooklyn. You know the setup. Banquettes and bentwood chairs. Subdued lighting. Surfaces brushed with a custom paint color akin to ochre after it's been exposed to 70 years of tobacco smoke. Antique mirrors and vintage placards hung on exposed brick walls. Happily, the provençale focus sets Fada apart. And Jatteaux and Brisson, if not already *fada*, are driving themselves to that end with their attempts to serve an authentic *bouillabaisse marseillaise* without access to most of the requisite Mediterranean fish.

There's French onion soup ($5), naturally, but better you start with the baked escargots with garlic and spinach ($6). A spoonful of pastis adds a Marseille accent to sautéed calamari served with warm potatoes ($6). Mixed platters like the Provençale, which includes tapenade and ratatouille, and the charcuterie plate ($13), are great as shared appetizers or anytime wine accompaniments. Among main courses there's steak frites ($15), naturally, with a little tin pail of excellent fries. The filet mignon ($17) is another bargain. But neither is in the same class as the traditional *aïoli garni* ($14) composed of beautifully arranged tomatoes, carrots, haricots verts, artichoke hearts, hard-boiled eggs, mushrooms, salt cod, and the thick, creamy, garlic-powered mayo that gives the dish its name.

The bouillabaisse ($28), made with monkfish, rougets, and an impressive assortment of replacement fish, is steadily improving. Maddeningly, it's only served on Tuesday nights and not every one at that. Every excuse short of stormy weather along the Marseille coastline has been offered to explain its absence. You know what the desserts ($5) are without asking: crème brûlée, tarte Tatin, a warm chocolate something. Consider instead the enticing cheese plate ($13).

Lomzynianka

The humble hominess of Lomzynianka gratifies both the working-class, immigrant Polish families and the fashionably thrifty East Village émigrés-with-trust-funds who live side-by-side in the trendily déclassé neighborhood of Greenpoint. Painted landscapes of Colonial-era Americana are hung on the faux-brick walls beside a stuffed deer festooned with a floral garland. In one corner of the narrow room is a tribute to the most famous Pole of our time, Pope John Paul II. The tables are tightly spaced, each covered with a mauve tablecloth and a thick protective plastic cover a la grandma. Somehow, the owners managed to find small lamps in exactly the same shade of mauve as the tablecloths. The boiled pierogi are just about the only other things that match on the entire premises.

$7–20

Address 646 Manhattan Ave, between Nassau & Norman Aves
℡718/389-9439
Transportation G to Nassau Ave
Open Daily noon–9 pm
Accepts Cash only
Reservations Not accepted

Order a cherry-flavored Polish soda ($1) in two varieties, red or white, and the friendly waiter will pour you a tall glass straight from a two-liter bottle pulled out of the fridge. Every entree includes a mixed salad plate loaded with sweet sauerkraut, vinegary shredded red cabbage, and a nicely balanced coleslaw. Red borscht is served three ways: as a drink ($1—let's write that out, one dollar), as a bowl of hearty, chunky beet-based vegetable soup filled with potatoes and white beans ($1.50) or as a dumpling vegetable soup ($2). Deep-brown potato pancakes already larger and puffier than those you find elsewhere come five to a $3.50 order.

Fluffy-textured veal balls in creamy dill sauce ($4.50) are served alongside mashed potatoes without discernible butter or cream. Don't despair. The plain spuds are profoundly improved simply by using your fork to sweep the dill sauce into them. The $5.50 "Polish Platter" is the ultimate in bargain samplers. It encompasses stuffed cabbage—tender layers of wilted cabbage encasing a veal and rice mixture similar to that of the veal balls; bigos—the traditional hunter's stew of stringy meats and sauerkraut in a glistening gravy; intensely flavored if overcooked (and dried out) kielbasa; and three doughy pierogi. For dessert or brunch, blueberry blintzes ($3.50) baked to order with a generous topping of stewed blueberries arrive as soft, delicately rolled crêpes with sweet cheese oozing out the sides.

Planet Thailand

**Lunch $9–25
Dinner $15–45**

Address 141 North 7th St, between
Bedford Ave & Berry St
☎718/599-5758
Transportation L to Bedford Ave
Open Sun–Thurs 11.30am–1am, Fri
& Sat 11.30am–2am
Accepts Cash only
Reservations For large groups

THAI/JAPANESE

Good, cheap chow built a name for this arty Thai luncheonette. But it was the loss of that name through a trademark dispute with Planet Hollywood that made the rechristened "Plan-Eat Thailand" famous. In 1999, the fortunes of these adversaries took some unexpected turns. As the celebrity-backed bully announced bankruptcy proceedings, the underdog was moving to a large, two-winged industrial loft around the corner from its original, coffee-shop-like digs. And though no identifying sign was posted anywhere, the pre-litigation name was printed on the menus. The new Planet Thailand can be entered from metal-and-glass entrances on both North Seventh and Berry Streets. The latticed garage door on North Seventh opens to an immense assembly plant that, with its cafe tables, arcing counter, and partly open kitchen, constitutes the Thai sector. Up a few stairs from a funky bar inlaid with colored beer bottles is artist John Kessler's cleverly mechanized fountain. The Berry Street entrance leads to an equally large Japanese section equipped with a sushi bar and hibachi bar. But while it's easy to applaud the retro spirit behind the hibachi grill and the chef's parody of Benihana dexterity, those Japanese dishes aren't really so great. Whether seated in Japan or Thailand, it is wisest to choose from the Thai menu.

Ideal places to start: fresh spring rolls with apricot sauce ($3.25), spicy smothered chicken wings ($4.25), and anything answering to a word search for squid—fried ($3.95), grilled ($3.50), or tossed in a spicy salad ($3.75). Grilled beef ($4.75), like most beef options, is unremarkable. Of the several low-priced entrees, you'll do fine with shrimp curry in sweet, spicy, and fabulously silky coconut sauce ($7.95), sautéed frogs legs with basil and chile ($8.25), or sliced chicken with basil, onion, and pepper ($6.95).

Still, the great Planet Thailand constant is its pad Thai: shrimp ($6.95), chicken ($5.25), or vegetable ($5.50). The steaming-hot noodles are woven with bean sprouts, scallion, Thai spices, and large egg pieces. The Frenchified desserts don't really work—the ginger crème brûlée's caramelized topping is massacred—so it's best to have ice cream.

Queens

Astoria and Long Island City

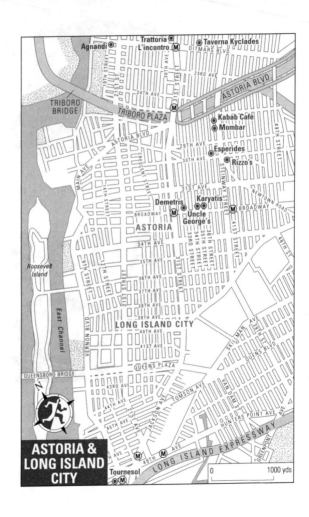

ASTORIA &
LONG ISLAND
CITY

Agnandi

It is a good ten-minute walk from the elevated subway and the nearest commercial district to Agnandi—"something viewed from afar." But the distance traveled cannot be measured in time or blocks. Hostess Maria Lambrianidis has fashioned a snug taverna that is more personal in its tastes than a mother's dining room or a teenager's bedroom. Old B&W stills show Melina Mercouri, Aliki Vouyouklaki, and other movie idols in the romantic scenes you wish to remember them by, even if you

$18–55

Address 19-06 Ditmars Blvd at 19th St

☏718/545-4554

Transportation N,W to Ditmars Blvd

Open Mon–Fri 3pm–midnight, Sat & Sun 1pm–midnight

Accepts All major credit cards

Reservations Reservations suggested

GREEK

don't recognize them or their roles. Likewise, you don't need to be Greek to appreciate the homespun table linens brought over from Greece and protected with cheap, transparent plastic. What isn't so clear, as you watch this pampering diva work the folksy dining room, alternately welcoming, advising, serving, gossiping, flirting, and reminiscing, is whether she's more a product of the family house or the movie house.

The attention of all newcomers is rightly directed to the "Tastes of Constantinople," nine appetizers linked to the Greek community in the Turkish city renamed Istanbul. Sissy, the chef, was born and raised there. The finest of her hometown treats are the pastroumali ($7)–flaky, filo-wrapped sandwiches of thinly sliced cured beef (pastourma) and cheese, and baccalao skordalia ($7)–crisp and golden salt cod beignets with garlic-powered potato dip. You'll have to travel to Mykonos and beyond, though, for the fabulously fragile, dill-specked zucchini croquettes ($7.50) and the grilled and stuffed calamari ($8.50) exploding with the flavors compacted in their tomato, basil, and salty feta filling.

No dinner should pass without your crowing for the rooster with tomatoes and pasta ($13.50). The seasoned braising liquid is reduced so that the tomato both clings to and melds together the cock and the hilopites (tiny pasta squares) finished off with grated, fast-melting kefalo-gravieri cheese. Take notice, too, of the grilled salmon with lemon and olive oil or, if you don't mind recurring ingredients, Spetsiotiso sauce (tomato, onion, feta, dill). Meat entrees (from $9.50 for chicken souvlaki to $19.50 for grilled T-bone) and desserts are, in comparison to Maria and her menu, rather predictable.

Demetris

The market-style seafood grills that rule Astoria's Greek dining scene certainly feed us better and more healthily than the kitschy tavernas that once characterized this Hellenic enclave. But even so, many people lament the loss of those plate-smashing, bazouki-playing, table-dancing, ouzo-guzzling, moussaka-scarfing feasts of times past. For them, no eatery bridges the gap between sophistication found and innocence lost better than Demetris. (The former Syros

**Lunch $10–45
Dinner $25–60**

Address 32-11 Broadway, between 32nd & 33rd Sts
☎718/278-1877
Transportation N,W to Broadway
Open Daily noon–midnight
Accepts All major credit cards
Reservations Suggested

was renamed in 2001 after its new owner, gyro and pita-bread tycoon Demetris Astin.) The iced fish case and thick-barred grills just inside the window assure us that fresh whole fish and blazing charcoal are at the ready. But the weekday keyboardist and weekend bazouki-led band that perform in the glass-roofed, vine-strewn, blue-and-white patio sustain a festive atmosphere. And the Adriatic murals, nautical ornamention, and Greek-key friezes are hopelessly sentimental.

There's nothing sappy, however, about the fresh cold dips and charred pita that start the banquet. The creamy tsaksiki (yogurt with cucumber), tangy taramasalata (fluffed fish roe), unapologetically bitter melitzanosalata (puréed eggplant), and forceful skordalia (whipped potato and garlic) included in the pikilia antipasto ($8.95) are all vividly rendered. The surest return, though, to Greek salad days is—predictably—the Greek salad ($5.75) topped with fistfuls of crumbled feta (though you do want to keep the waiter away from the oil, vinegar, and lemon). The spanakopita ($5.50) is another wonderful throwback, though the delicate filo layers of this home-baked spinach pie are superior to the greasy ones we used to know.

If personal growth and increasing girth preclude a béchamel-enriched return to moussaka and pastitsio, chargrilled whole fish ($18–25 with two sides) is the way to go. Hankerings for something behind the times and over the top *can* be satiated by the Demetris combination special ($25). But those who can polish off its broiled scallops, lobster tail, and sole, its jumbo shrimp and clams with crabmeat stuffing, *and* its side oval of potatoes, should not be too quick to gloat. There's still the cinnamon baked apple and honeyed pastries (both served gratis) to conquer.

Esperides

Esperides strikes just the right balance between homey taverna and elegant restaurant. While its terracotta tiles, teak chairs, blue cloth napkins, and concealed blue neon are dressier than anything at the nearby tavernas, its $10.95–14.95 dinner specials, including an outstanding, full-bodied avgolemono (egg, lemon, and chicken) soup make it sufficiently casual and affordable for large family dinners. Owners Gregory and Steve Soldatos, veterans of the diner

Lunch $20–30
Dinner $25–70

Address 37-01 30th Ave at 37th St
☎718/545-1494
Transportation N to 30th Ave; R,G
to Steinway St
Open Daily noon–midnight
Accepts All major credit cards
Reservations Accepted

GREEK

trade, know how to please a diverse clientele. They've hired Greek hotel chef Constantinos Athens to do grilled fish and meats for the simple-is-best crowd, more elaborately prepared and sauced dishes for fussier appetites, and baked standards for moussaka/pastitsio traditionalists. Vigilant waiters help you navigate the varied menu by giving useful advice. Instead of the usual noncommittal nonsense ("everything our chef does is fabulous"), they'll talk you out of a mediocre selection (the undrinkable house red) and into a winner (an $18 bottle of the Greek white Kouras).

A yea-or-nay on taramasalata, however, is not required as the fish roe spread is served as a complimentary snack. The value of this gesture goes beyond the savings of $4.25. It frees up an appetizer slot for knife-surrendering grilled octopus ($9.80), lightly fried zucchini disks ($6.25), delectable saganaki (hot fried triangles of kefalotiri cheese; $6.25), and grilled halloumi (the salty Cypriot cheese; $5.95). A superb follow-up to mezze overload is decently grilled or broiled fish—whole red snapper ($22.50 for a $1\frac{1}{2}$ pounder) or fillet of sole ($14.95). Anything heavier would fill up valuable digestive capacity ordinarily reserved for desserts. Those with expandable storage space may relish the silky fillet of salmon with leeks and lemony cream sauce ($15.95), the grilled red mullet fillets with lightly creamed wine sauce ($15.95), and the juicy, lemon-scented roast piglet ($14.95). Steaks and chops ($15.95–21.95) reflect the Greek preference for oversizing and, to many tastes, overcooking.

For dessert, ground walnut cake ($3.50) is so moist you can practically suck out the honey with a straw. Order too the creamy, sharp-flavored sheep's milk yogurt with honey ($3.50).

EGYPTIAN

Kabab Café

Playing board games. Gossiping with and listening to the troubles of young diners. Smoking his long-tubed hookah (water pipe). These are a few of the things Ali El Sayed would rather do than cook. Ask the jolly Egyptian about Rita Abatzi and Rosa Ashkenazi, the two women (and old loves?) whose framed photos hang on the back wall and he will sit down and tell you about these star vocalists of 1930s rebetika music while your fellow diners (fifeen at most) are kept waiting for their kofta kebabs, veg-

Lunch $8–30
Dinner $15–40

Address 25-12 Steinway St, near Astoria Blvd
℡718/728-9858
Transportation N to Astoria Blvd; G,R to Steinway St
Open Tues–Sun 1–11pm
Accepts Cash only
Reservations Not accepted

etable tarts, and hibiscus teas. No one complains. Such interludes are vital to a tiny, ragged, bric-a-brac dive with its own special rhythms. When the duets of Louis Armstrong and Ella Fitzgerald are playing on the hi-fi, the sizzling iron pans provide an accompaniment as sure and easy as a brush over a snare drum.

Despite its name, Kabab Café's true specialty is felafel. The reason is twofold. Firstly, it is prepared in the original Egyptian style with crushed and soaked green fava beans rather than the now common (at least in New York) chickpeas. Secondly, the balls are pan-fried in clean, shallow oil while most others are deep-fried in dubious oil. The result is hot, fresh, lightly spiced felafel cooked to a dark brown crisp. They're available as an appetizer ($5), in a pita sandwich ($3.50), on a platter ($8), or as part of the best option of all, a fabulous mezze with hummus, babaganoush, fava beans, and sliced fruit ($10 plus $4 for each additional person).

Ali also insists on being taken seriously for his more elaborate Egyptian cooking. He has a friendly rivalry with the chef at nearby Mombar (see p.366), who happens to be his brother. When you order a seafood special ($14–18), perhaps a pan-roasted whole red snapper buried under hacked vegetables, coarsely chopped garlic, cumin, and zatar (a Middle Eastern spice mix of sumac, thyme, and sesames), Ali brings the pan to the table. Holding the handle in one hand and tongs in the other, he fillets the whole fish on the spot. He's quite an act.

Karyatis

The neoclassical decor at Karyatis does not lie. The moderate prices do. In an argil-toned space thankfully devoid of glitz—and, for once, Aegean blue and white—Greek wall reliefs lifting scenes from the Parthenon are set in illuminated wall recesses. They, like the dried flowers, sculptured sconces, and shallow dishes of red peppercorn-dotted Peloponnese olive oil, indicate an establishment of good taste—surely *the* destination in Astoria for finer Greek cuisine.

**Lunch $25–55
Dinner $30–65**

Address 35-03 Broadway, between
35th & 36th Sts
☏718/204-0666
Transportation N to Broadway; G,R
to Steinway St
Open Daily noon–midnight
Accepts All major credit cards

GREEK

Conversely, the prices—entrees mostly in the mid-teens—offer no clue of how good and consistent this restaurant is when host Costa "Charlie" Tzivelekis is directing the show. Karyatis refers to the Karyatides, the six stone maidens who support the roof of the Erechtheum in ancient Athens. Here, the two replicas displayed on the rear wall uphold, albeit symbolically, chef Panos Seretis' accomplishment.

The pikilia ($10.95 small/$14.95 large) assembles all the obligatory cold spreads on one exquisitely arranged platter. With its distinctively fluffy taramasalata (fish roe dip) and smoky melitzanosalata (eggplant dip), the ensemble is the highlight of the meal. Still, you shouldn't neglect the more uncommon hot appetizers like the grilled sepia (cuttlefish; $11.95), with twice the flavor of the usual frozen calamari, or the crisp, golden croquettes of eggplant cooked with kefalograviera, the Greek version of Gruyère ($7.95).

Main courses also pose a quandary between trite but trusty items and less familiar fare. Select the moussaka ($13.95) or a grilled whole fish (about $15) and you won't go home in a funk. But why not experience the delectable moist shellfish in the seafood giouvetsi ($21), a Greek cross between paella and risotto with orzo in place of rice, or the armaki karyatis ($17.95), whose pristine lamb slices and veggies suggest a lamb pot au feu. The closing dinner dilemma is: should you stay or should you go? Stay for a pastry, say the kadaifi ($5), a nutty, shredded-wheat-like tuft. If you're after a honeyed dessert, go instead to a nearby cafe.

Mombar

(II) The eccentric design of this out-
wardly anonymous restaurant on
Astoria's main Middle Eastern shopping
strip is not, as you might imagine, the
work of a starving artist paid in hummus
and babaganoush by a bighearted
restaurateur. The multiple collages of
found fabric, furniture, and building materials were pieced together by Moustafa
Rahman, the Gaudí of Egyptian cooking.
His marble floor is a patterned mosaic of
brick-sized fragments in pink, gray, tan,

$25–65
Address 25-22 Steinway St, between 25th Ave & Astoria Blvd
☎718/726-2356
Transportation N,W to Astoria Blvd; G, R to Steinway St
Open Tues–Sun 5pm–midnight
Accepts Cash only
Reservations Accepted

and black. A wooden pantry/curio case protrudes from the open-kitchen
counter like a mud-brick home from the slopes of an Egyptian village.
Colorful inlays turn each tabletop into a distinct work of art.

The restaurant is named for a mixed Egyptian sausage by a chef who
has found religion in the artful mixing of disparate ingredients. The
menu exhibits the same level of accomplishment as well as what outer-
borough residents call "Manhattan prices" to prove it. Too costly for
many locals, Mombar is packed on weekends but still struggles for a
school-night audience. All dinner roads lead from the Sahara mix ($8), a
circular mezze of first-rate hummus, foul (slow-cooked fava bean purée),
intense babaganoush, and fresh fruit slices arranged around half-moon
pita chips. An outstanding spread regrettably missing from that mix is
be-sara ($7), a fava bean purée combined with molokhiya (an essential
Egyptian leafy vegetable), cilantro, and a garnish of grilled onions.

An array of Middle Eastern and North African spices generously
infuse main courses, some of which come with pyramids of rice. (You'll
find more Ancient Egyptian imagery on the kitschy glassware.) Such
permanent dishes as rabbit stew thickened with molokhiya greens ($18),
molasses-glazed duck breast ($19), and sayadia (baked shrimp, mussels,
and calamari; $18) are listed on the menu mostly to guide first-time and
cautious diners. But a quick look around tells you the chef doesn't care
much for convention. He prefers that you and he conjure up
impromptu specials based on your tastes, his talents and moods, and
what looked best to him during that day's forage through local markets.
This close and varied collaboration between diners and chef produces
Mombar's greatest collage of all.

Rizzo's

🍴 Sicilian pizza partisans generally prefer square slices to Neapolitan triangles because they're thicker and breadier. Some no doubt crave the hardened corners of these pan-baked pies. Still, the local version of sfincione, as the thick pizza of Palermo is known, is best appreciated as a platform for zesty tomato sauce. Even the cheese cognoscenti agree. Sicilian pizza, says Luigi Di Palo of Di Palo's cheese store in Little Italy, is "a thick piece of bread topped with sauce and maybe some

$4–9

Address 30-13 Steinway St, between 30th & 31st Aves

☎718/721-9862

Transportation N,W to 30th Ave; R,V to Steinway St

Open Mon–Sat 11am–9pm, Sun noon–7pm

Accepts Cash only

Reservations Not accepted

PIZZA

cheese." And nowhere are those squares better than at this tomato-lover's paradise. As long as the name "Rizzo's" burns in yellow neon with the green-lit "Fine Pizza" close behind there is hope for New York pizza-lovers who demand a good-quality tomato sauce to go with molten mozzarella, grated Romano and Parmesan, and a resilient crust.

Thinner and lighter than a typical Sicilian, Rizzo's singular crust is the compact format for a thick layer of chunky sauce made from whole tomatoes. Joe Rizzo learned the classic recipe not in his native Sicily, but at Pizza Amore, a defunct chain of pizzerias. Rizzo's faux marble booths, fluorescent-blue wall menu, and $1.75 slice price are obviously not as old as the small shop, which opened in 1959. But the family pride, personable service, and old-world quality are treasured relics from another time.

The most dramatic change in the pizzeria's history was in the mid-1990s when Dave Rizzo finally convinced his dad to let him develop a Neapolitan alternative. "When my father opened, pizza was still a relatively new ethnic food," explains Rizzo. "Everybody was willing to try whatever you had. Now young people know pizza and they expect it to be round." Dave's triangular slices accomplish for Neapolitan pizza what his father's squares did for Sicilian: the easy-chew crust is thinner, lighter, and more of one delicate piece than its counterparts and, yep, there's more tomato sauce. The triangle has developed a loyal following, not all of them that young. The cognoscenti, Dave Rizzo among them, request a quick reheat to make their triangles crispier.

Taverna Kyclades

Contrary to stereotypes, Kyclades is not one of those folksy ethnic outposts where proud immigrants welcome you with open arms and old-country hospitality and show you faded snapshots of a family reunion held in a remote village. Rather, this is a cute little place where someone who hasn't smiled since 1997 throws a couple of menus your way and then comes back anywhere between one and twenty minutes later to take your order. Those who

Lunch $14–50
Dinner $20–60

Address 33-07 Ditmars Blvd,
between 33rd & 35th Sts
☎718/545-8666
Transportation N,W to Ditmars Blvd
Open Daily noon–11pm
Accepts All major credit cards
Reservations Not accepted

land an outdoor table either beside the watermelon stand or under the billboard advertising cooperative apartments hardly mind being ignored and left alone. Some even encourage it. Should they hang out all night draining one bottle of retsina after another, this disturbs only those waiting for their tables.

The Greek seafood dishes are dependably market-fresh, beginning with the appetizers—tender grilled octopus ($10.50), fried calamari ($7.95), fried smelts ($8.95), and grilled or fried sardines ($7.95). With them it's customary to pass around $4 plates of the traditional spreads—taramasalata (here the fish roe is extra fluffy and salty), skordalia (cold potato purée with almost enough garlic to choke you), and tzatziki (yogurt with cucumber). This onslaught of food could set you to wondering if orectika, the Greek word for appetizers, actually means appetite killers. Once they've been eaten up, the only thing preventing you from eighty-sixing the entrees is your inability to flag down a waiter.

Grilled whole fish, such as striped bass, red snapper, or porgy (market price from $17–22 per person) are what Kyclades does best. The prevailing and perhaps accurate condescension around these parts is that the grilled and likely overcooked salmon steak ($13.95), grilled swordfish ($17.50), and sizeable swordfish kebab ($15.95) are only requested by those terrified of fish bones. Faux pas or not, no one regrets ordering the fish steaks and, for that matter, those composed of lamb and beef. At $14.95 for succulent char-grilled lamb chops and $16.50 for a T-bone too large for its plate, each served with maybe two pounds of lemon potatoes, they're solid buys. But be careful: both come on the bone.

Tournesol

With its whitewashed tin ceiling, globe lights, pine-planked floor, red banquettes, and anaglypta-decorated walls, Tournesol bears a close resemblance to Brooklyn's Cafe LULUc (p.302). Is it possible the entrepreneurial Frenchmen behind these startups are using the same make-your-own-bistro kit? Owner Pascal Escriout, formerly the maitre d' at Artisanal (see p.229), at least distinguishes the first such bistro-on-a-shoestring in Queens by encouraging his chef to venture beyond the narrow steak-frites formula. Considering that Tournesol—"sunflower"—is a single subway stop from Grand Central, the incredibly low prices are attractive to Manhattanites, too.

**Lunch $12–40
Dinner $25–50**

Address 50-12 Vernon Blvd, between 50th & 51st Aves
℡718/472-4355
Transportation 7 to Vernon Blvd-Jackson Ave
Open Mon 5–10pm, Tues–Fri 11.30am–3pm & 5.30–11.30pm, Sat & Sun 11am–3.30pm & 5.30–11.30pm
Accepts Amex
Reservations Not accepted

FRENCH

At eight bucks, the terrine of foie gras with Muscat wine is the most expensive *and* underpriced appetizer. Given the cost and quality, it's hard to make a convincing argument for any alternative. Still, the frisée salad with diced bacon lardons and poached egg ($6.50) is just fine for what it is. The beef carpaccio with cepe (like porcini) oil ($7) is fresh and elegant. And the calamari, lightly floured and pan-fried with pimientos and beets ($7), is a welcome change from the usual fried ringlets.

To make his menu distinctive, chef Christophe Morvan is sometimes a tad too ambitious. But considering the prices, it would be churlish to quibble (although we're doing it anyway) about the excessive sweetness of the crisp-edged skate with red cabbage and mango sauce ($14) or a mound of saffron risotto overshadowed by the parmesan disk that tops it and the mussels that encircle it ($16). These flaws are easily pardoned. Enjoying either dish requires little effort. As alternatives, there's the low-risk option of bacon-wrapped monkfish with eggplant and vegetables ($15) or the absolute certainty of crusty sliced hanger steak and golden frites ($13 lunch, $15 dinner). The molten-centered chocolate dome ($5) is the dessert you want.

Trattoria L'Incontro

The pizza oven was not installed in the center of Trattoria L'Incontro's dining room to augment the central heating system. That may be the only way it has not been put to practical use. In addition to its pizza-baking, fish-roasting, and meat-roasting chores, the brick igloo accommodates the sauté pans, saucepans, and casseroles denied space in the kitchen's convection oven while serving as the ultimate restaurant come-on. Like a real estate agent who bakes a loaf of bread in a co-op just before prospective buyers arrive, chef-owner Rocco Sacramone relies on the spellbinding, burning-wood fumes to ensnare unsuspecting passers-by. And once exposed to the charms of this spacious trattoria brightened by vineyard murals and hearty cooking, they invariably come back with their families or their dates.

$25–75
Address 21-76 31st St, between Ditmars Blvd & 21st Ave
☎718/721-3532
Transportation N,W to Ditmars Blvd
Open Sun,Tues, Wed & Thurs noon–10pm, Fri & Sat noon–11pm
Accepts All major credit cards
Reservations Suggested

Rocco and his mother/co-chef Tina are from Abruzzi, but you won't find much evidence of the abruzzese fondness for chile. Even the red sauce paired with the excellent fried calamari ($7.95) is tame unless you request otherwise. The pleasures of grilled sardines ($9.95) and grilled octopus ($9.95), the latter paired with a balsamic vinaigrette, as well as the grilled escarole with white beans, olive oil, and lemon ($7.95), are certainly not lost on Astoria's still sizeable Greek community. The addition of grated Asiago adds a hospitable, half-sweet/half-sharp bite to the San Marzano tomatoes, fresh basil, and mozzarella atop the golden, firm-crusted Margherita pizza ($5.95).

With several local places for simply grilled fish and meats already flourishing, the Sacramones' impulse to do more than just lean on their centerpiece pizza oven is understandable. Fortunately, the excesses in pastas and main courses are minor. A splash of wine sauce does little harm to the oven-roasted whole orata seasoned with parsley, rosemary, and garlic ($22.95). And the veal chop stuffed with spinach, prosciutto, and Fontina ($25.95) is enticing, if not quite a convincing argument against the basic grilled veal chop. The notorious chocolate pizza ($8.95) is not truly a pizza and not purely chocolate. It's a crisp dessert panini of Nutella-filled pizza dough as well as a surefire temptation that real estate agents should know about.

Uncle George's

As resourceful and resilient as New Yorkers can be, the thought of living in a city without a 24/7 resource for fresh taramasalata, that fluffy and creamy fish roe spread, is too frightening to contemplate. That's why the Landmarks Preservation Commission should confer protection upon the cheap-eats champion Uncle George's. Spartan both in decor and by origin, the glass-enclosed cafe-restaurant may be architecturally

$8–35

Address 33-19 Broadway at 34th St

☎718/626-0593

Transportation N,W to Broadway

Open Daily 24hr

Accepts Cash only

Reservations Not accepted

GREEK

indistinguishable from most corner coffee shops. But surely some kind of official status is merited by so valuable an institution. While budget-minded students, couples, and families came by during the afternoon and early evening, the true beneficiaries of Uncle George's round-the-clock home cooking and hospitality are the hard-working men (restaurant workers, cabbies, etc) or hard-clubbing men and women of Astoria for whom 9-to-5 means only the short odds on a racehorse.

The Greek grub is not by anyone's estimation outstanding. But most dishes are pretty good, the portions are enormous, and the prices appear to predate the advent of color television. For starters, check out these rates: $2.50 for taramasalata, skordalia (garlic potato dip), or tzatziki (yogurt-cucumber dip). Or $6 for a large Greek salad with too much feta cheese (who's complaining?). And $6 for a plate of saganaki (salty, golden slices of fried kasseri cheese) that two can easily divvy up. Stuffed grape leaves big enough for three will set you back $7.

The best main courses come from the rotisserie, which is in the front of the restaurant: crisp-skinned roast half-chicken ($5.50), barbecued baby lamb ($12), or kokoretsi ($11). Whether you enjoy the succulent kokoretsi may depend on you not knowing about all the lamb organ meats with which it is prepared. If you've already read that sentence it's probably too late. The best fish alternatives are the grilled red snapper and fried red mullets (both $13). Or you can plod through the roast lamb with orzo ($8.50), the gloppy pastitsio ($8), and the ubiquitous side dish, lemon potatoes. For dessert, it's best to decamp to one of the nearby Greek pastry shops such as Omonia (32-20 Broadway) which, sadly, is closed between 3am and 8am.

Flushing

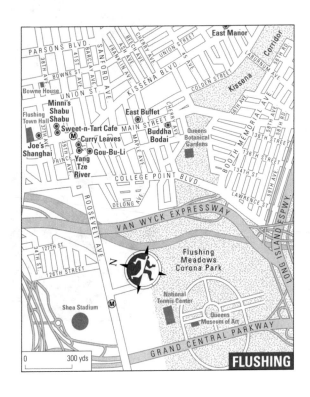

FLUSHING

Buddha Bodai

(🍴) In a strip mall beside the Queens Botanical Gardens, Flushing's resident Indian Hindus, observant Jews, vegetarian and lactose-intolerant Christians, Chinese, Korean, and Thai Buddhists and likely a fair number of atheists, agnostics, and secular humanists, too, are united in their adulation for chef Michael Wong. He's a culinary celebrity and master illusionist who puts only tofu, wheat gluten, mushrooms, and

Lunch $6–30
Dinner $15–30

Address 42-96 Main St at Cherry Ave
☎718/939-1188
Transportation 7 to Main St
Open Daily 11am–11pm
Accepts MasterCard & Visa

VEGETARIAN/CHINESE/KOSHER

other vegetables into his magic hat and pulls out sliced fish with Chinese vegetables ($9.95), General Tsao's chicken ($12.95), and lamb with mixed vegetables and garlic sauce ($12.95). So skilled is Wong's meatless trickery that rather than exhibit his delicious deceptions under artful lighting or muted spots, the carpeted dining room's floodlit glare is about 4000 watts too bright. Looking cool or hiding crow's feet would be the least of your reasons for wearing sunglasses throughout dinner.

Basically, this is a very good and inexpensive vegetarian, dairy-free Chinese family restaurant. Most start with the house special assorted appetizer ($12.95), a Shanghai-style, mostly cold sampler of vegetarian mock duck with shiitake mushrooms, crispy duck, bean curd chicken, and crunchy orange vegetables. These should be supplemented with a six-piece order of thin-skinned vegetable dumplings (steamed or pan-fried; $3.95). Kids love too the fold-your-own moo shu pancakes ($6.95).

It isn't only the absence of meats and dairy that puts Wong to the test. In his Buddhist cooking tradition, main courses must make do without the hits of garlic, onion, and scallions that might rouse sexual desire and disrupt meditation. He nevertheless produces such high-impact delights as ground vegetarian chicken wrapped in a crisp lettuce leaf ($9.95), meaty portobellos with an au poivre-like black pepper sauce ($10.95), chewy steak with Chinese broccoli ($12.95), and sautéed wide rice noodles with shreds of imitation beef ($7.95). You might imagine that the display of dry goods sold in the front of the restaurant would shed light on some of Wong's tricks. But it contains only organic radish seeds, abzuki beans, barley flakes, fenugreek, preserved black beans, and the like. You'll see few people buying.

Curry Leaves

(Y) The narrow restaurants on the north side of 40th Road in Flushing's Chinatown are folded into the streetscape like the pleated bellows of an accordion. To locate Curry Leaves you might have to resort to trying every door between numbers 129 and 141, crying out "roti canai" (the Indian-style crêpe) until someone answers back: "to stay or to go?" Beyond the recessed and pinched entranceway, the room widens

$9–35
Address 135-31 40th Rd, between Main & Prince Sts
☎718/762-9313
Transportation 7 to Main St
Open Daily 11am–11pm
Accepts Cash only
Reservations Not accepted

into a pleasant enough dining area with glass-topped, floral tablecloths and, for a tropical effect, balsa-wood siding. Of course no one is here to look at furniture. The draw is the cheap, fresh, abundant, and spicy Malaysian chow.

The selections and prices are so similar to those at Manhattan Malaysian restaurants like Nyonya and Penang (see p.104 and p.130) that, when you place their takeout menus on top of one another and hold them up to the light, even the misspellings line up. Here the food is distinguished by the bold application of belachan, the dried, salty, fermented shrimp paste adored by Asian diners whose tolerance for its pungency is higher than a typical Westerner's. You first pick up its taste in rojak ($5.25), where it cuts into the sweetened soy sauce dressing a chunky salad of jicama, green mango, and cucumber. The belachan's influence is less apparent in achat ($2.95), a piquant pickled vegetable dish sprinkled with sesame seeds and chopped peanuts. The roti canai ($2) have large chunks of chicken in the curry dip.

Fish head curry ($14.95) rewards anyone with the courage to order it. It's a cross between a gumbo and a Thai seafood curry, with tomatoes, okra, eggplant, green beans, and fish pieces in a scintillating, golden, coconut fish broth. The fusion turns Chinese-Indian in mee goreng ($4.75), a stir-fried toss of smoky, wok-seared egg noodles with squid sauce, tofu, bean sprouts, and shrimp. Chile chicken ($14.95), which we know is Indian-style only because the menu says it is, comes as a whole, dark-and-crunchy-skinned bird atop a mild chile sauce. With dessert comes the refreshing discovery of chendal ($2), a shaved-ice confection with red beans, chewy jujubes, bean noodles, and coconut milk.

East Buffet

The mother of all New York City's Chinese buffets, East Buffet is the ideal family or big-group restaurant for those who don't know what they want until they see it, and maybe not even then. Seven head chefs are required to oversee the kitchens that supply and continually replenish the sprawling buffet with separate stations for sushi, dim sum, soups, noodles, Peking duck, raw oysters, American/Western hot foods, Asian barbecue (Korean short ribs) and satay (chicken, beef), along with dessert soups, pastries, and fruits. With clean, comfortably spaced dining areas that seat up to 400 people, the operation occupies the entire second floor of a glitzy shopping mall in a residential stretch near Flushing's Chinatown.

Lunch $12–30
Dinner $25–40

Address 42-07 Main St, between Maple & Franklin Aves
☎718/353-6333
Transportation 7 to Main St
Open Sun–Thurs 11.30am–3pm & 5–11pm, Fri & Sat 11.30am–3pm & 5pm–midnight
Accepts MasterCard & Visa
Reservations Not accepted

CHINESE

The college students are hardly alone in their determination to eat as much food for as little as possible. To that end, the best time to go is during weekday lunches when the buffet is just $9.99 ($6.99 for kids aged 3–10). But the selection expands and improves at night, especially on weekend evenings, when the dinner buffet goes up from $19.99 ($10.99 for kids) to $23.99 ($13.99 for kids). Value-motivated diners can stuff themselves on high-cost specialties like stir-fried lobster with ginger and scallions, Dungeness crabs, shark's fin soup, lacquered roast squab (very good!) and, from the carving board, Peking duck and beautiful prime rib. Should anyone be looking for us, we too can usually be found at the carving board (getting the duck and their steam buns while hot makes a big difference) or waiting for the next batches of lobster and crabs.

Be sure to plan a stop at the dim sum bar, especially for the translucent casing and firm shrimp filling of the har gow. Other items to check out elsewhere include the winter melon seafood soup, the grilled cuttlefish, and such tong shi (sweet dessert soups) as white fungus with almonds and papaya, mung bean, coconut taro, and tapioca. Do not expend a single calorie of your total ingestion on anything Italian (lasagna, fettuccine alfredo).

CHINESE

East Manor

If all-you-can-eat buffet restaurants rank in the Top Ten of outer-borough dining no-nos, gaudy catering halls, especially wedding factories with the word "Manor" in their title, cannot be far behind. The latter are best kept for invitation-only affairs to which you have mercifully been snubbed. As such, the great danger of visiting East Manor, the glitzy and inordinately lavish offshoot of East Buffet (see p.375), is that the myriad

$25–40

Address 46-45 Kissena Blvd at Laburnum Ave
℡718/888-8998
Transportation 7 to Main St
Open Daily 4.30pm–midnight
Accepts MasterCard & Visa
Reservations Not accepted

pleasures of its Chinese buffet spreads can easily lead you to disregard the tenets so vital to successful New York restaurant navigation. To avoid a return to steam-table torment and reheat hell, remember that East Manor is the exception to those hard-and-fast rules.

What makes East Manor so special is its incredible setup for the interactive dining experience known as Chinese hot pot or, in Japanese, shabu-shabu. At each table, a large, two-sided pot filled with a light chicken broth is set over a portable gas burner. Diners repeatedly visit the long buffet tables, choose from their extensive and continually replenished selection of raw seafood, raw meat, and raw vegetables and then cook it all themselves in the simmering broth. A variety of condiments and sauces is available for spicing and dipping. Rare is the opportunity when you can both cook and eat lobster, prawns, blue crabs, snow peas, spinach, watercress, black mushrooms, lamb, beef, chicken, pork, and even goose intestine at the same time and table. Kids love it—the concept that is, not the goose intestine.

The $19.95 weekend adult price is remarkable in that it also includes full and free access to the sushi bar (not bad), the dumpling and dim sum bar (surprisingly good), the Peking duck carving station (excellent), the fruit and dessert bar (stick to the former), and a nightly selection of cooked entrees (of varying quality) that might include Mandarin-glazed salmon, grilled mushrooms, baked scallops, and Korean-style barbecued short ribs. The ninety-minute time limit on tables is rarely imposed. Besides, most groups are ready to throw in the white napkin after an hour of mad, blissful gorging.

Gou-Bu-Li

(🍴) The legend of the little dog with the great buns flourishes at sixty Gou-Bu-Li restaurants in China and in one neon-lit eatery in Queens, New York. Gou-Zu, a master of bo zu (stuffed steamed buns), is said to have received the pivotal food review of his career more than 140 years ago from the Dowager, Mother of the Emperor. Her blurb—"eating them can extend one's life"—is inscribed next to a painting that hangs in

$11–35

Address 135-28 40th Rd, between
Main & Prince Sts
☎718/886-2121
Transportation 7 to Main St
Open Daily 8.30am–10.30pm
Accepts Cash only
Reservations Not accepted

the original Gou-Bu-Li shop in the northeastern Chinese city of Tianjin. Following that rave, the ambitious Gou-Zu had no time to socialize. People started to call him Gou-Bu-Li—"Gou-Zu not social." The name, and the buns, stuck.

The masters who skillfully shape the bo zu at this Flushing franchise were trained at company headquarters. Each bun is sealed with the uniform pleat that is a bo zu master's signature. The Dowager's enthusiasm for the buns is justified by the unusual texture of their bready skins. They manage to be chewy yet soft, resilient yet delicate. While some eighty varieties are prepared in China, only six are re-created in Flushing: minced mixed vegetables, pork (with scallion, ginger, soy sauce, and sesame oil), lamb, red bean, beef, and cabbage pork. A bamboo steamer filled with eight plump, teetering bo zu ($4.50–5.25) is accompanied by a small bowl of cilantro-scented beef broth.

The fried noodles and noodle soups are unique to the Queens Gou-Bu-Li. Working from big blocks of paste, the noodle chefs adroitly shave strands of wheat noodles into giant woks of boiling water. The shaved noodles are used in soups with beef, pork, chicken, vegetables, or seafood (all $4.50). But you should go for the pan-fried noodles ($5.25 for pork; $5.95 for seafood) for a better appreciation of their remarkably chewy texture. Sized somewhere between linguine and fettuccine, these jagged-cut, chewy noodles expand the realm of pasta possibilities to untold heights. (It would have been interesting to know what the Dowager thought of them.) Unfortunately, Gou-Bu-Li has not been able to thrive on dumplings and noodles alone. And most attempts to extend the menu have fallen short.

Joe's Shanghai

🍴 No man is more responsible for the Shanghai uprising of the last decade than Joe Si, who opened this, the first of four Joe's Shanghais, in May 1995. Although his kitchen made a strong case for the sweet, bold-flavored cuisine of Jiangsu province as a timely alternative to the spicy sameness of Hunan and Szechuan or the subtlety of Cantonese, Joe's empire was effectively built on a single item: shao lung bao—steamed pork or crab-and-pork dumplings filled with scalding hot meat juices barely restrained by a flimsy casing. And although much of the cooking now seems as worn out as the carpeting, the shao lung bao remain unequalled.

$12–45
Address 136-21 37th Ave, between Main & Union Sts; plus other locations
☏718/539-3838
Transportation 7 to Main St
Open Sun–Thurs 11am–11pm, Fri & Sat 11am–midnight
Accepts Cash only
Reservations Not accepted

The surest indicator of quality is the long wait for an order of eight dumplings (crab-and-pork $6.75; pork $4.50). That's because all table orders (as opposed to takeout) are prepared to order—a lofty claim supported by the composition of the soup dumplings, so called because the jellied fat stuffed inside them liquefies when steamed. Poke inside one of the crab-and-pork variety and you will find there is separation between the soft, moist crab and the harder, drier pork. Had they been refrigerated, the two would be congealed. The surge of fresh flavors is astonishing. Diner beware: attack the dumpling too quickly and your mouth will be burned by the hot juice. Start by putting the dumpling in a plastic spoon, top it with fresh soy sauce and shaved ginger, nibble a tiny hole in the wrapper, and then suck out a little of the liquid. The rest will spill into the spoon.

Other appetizers to ponder are the pan-fried, potsticker-like pork dumplings ($4.60) and such traditional cold dishes as smoked fish ($6.45), spicy pickled cabbage ($6.60), and mock vegetarian duck (in fact bean curd; $6.45). You could then go on to the likes of Shanghai pan-fried noodles (pork, beef, chicken, or vegetable; all $8.60); crispy yellowfish fingers battered in dry seaweed ($15.95); flabby pork shoulder braised in sweetened soy sauce ($14.60); the crusty and enormous pork meatballs known as Lion's Head ($13.50), and a braised whole fish ($14.95).

Minni's Shabu Shabu

Japanese by name and inspiration only, Minni's specializes in the one-pot, tabletop dining that's all the rage in Asian communities throughout the world. The Day-Glo soft drinks, cheery servers, and stylish young clientele spread over four bright, spanking clean, sleekly designed, taxi-yellow floors belong in a Far Eastern cartoon. At first glance, it's not immediately apparent where the puffs of steam rising from the tables are

$11–25

Address 136-17 38th Ave, between Main & Union Sts
℗718/762-6277
Transportation 7 to Main St
Open Daily 11.30am–2am
Accepts All major credit cards
Reservations Not accepted

coming from. The stainless-steel pots are inserted through round openings in the laminate tabletops, where they come to rest atop hidden electrical heating elements. With the lip of the sunken pot at table level, diners have leverage when dropping and lifting foods from the clear chicken broth.

The illustrated placemat menu enumerates 25 dinner platters, ranging from a quartet of chicken and flawlessly curled pork, beef, and lamb ($9) to a fresh seafood combo ($12.95) of oysters, sliced fish, Manila clams, shrimp, squid, cuttlefish, and sea scallops. All such platters come with a plate of Chinese cabbage and greens, golden mushrooms, soft tofu, tofu skin, tempura, corn, vermicelli, fish balls, taro, and rice cake. Free access to the self-service sauce bar lets you flavor your broth and spice up your cooked ingredients with custom mixtures made from several sauces (soy, BBQ, peanut, fermented red bean, sweet-and-spicy, leek) as well as chopped cilantro, scallions, chiles, and garlic. Once back at the table, you may cook foods in any order you please, although starting with veggies will create a more flavorsome broth in which to prepare the best items—oysters, crabs ($2 apiece), and steamer-like clams. The broth is not merely a cooking liquid; it evolves into an interesting soup, depending on your cheffing skills. Remember that simmering times vary from about fifteen seconds for carpaccio-thin meat slices to the fifteen minutes it takes to hard-boil an egg.

Teriyaki-marinated squid and sliced Taiwanese sausage (both $2.50) are the best, if ultimately skippable, hibachi-style BBQ selections. Cold drinks include thick, non-dairy fruit smoothies (mango, star fruit, passionfruit), and Taiwanese iced tea with black, tapioca-like sago pearls.

Sweet-n-Tart Cafe

It's much too easy to overlook the savory dishes that turn this modern and lighthearted Chinese dessert cafe into a legitimate breakfast, lunch, and dinner destination. The rice dough for the juicy pan-fried dumplings ($4.35) achieves an elusive balance between delicacy and durability. The smooth congees (rice porridges; $2–7.95) are neither runny nor too thick. The noodle soup with shrimp and watercress dumpling makes a terrific little $4.25 meal. And you'd be hard-pressed to choose between the pleasures of rice steamed in a bamboo log with Chinese sausage and taro ($5.50) or rice steamed in lotus leaf with dried scallop and shrimp ($9.75). Turning towards the open kitchen and giving a thumbs-up to the noodle cooks would at least let them know their efforts are appreciated.

$6–25

Address 136-11 38th Ave, near Main St
☎718/661-3380
Transportation 7 to Main St
Open Daily 9am–midnight
Accepts Cash only
Reservations Not accepted

Sweet-n-Tart's name and fame comes from its assortment of tong shui ("dessert soup"). Balancing the Yin and Yang of our bodies, these eighteen hot and fifteen cold dessert soups are believed to be extremely nourishing, and even curative. Yet it is the affordability and accessibility of the tong shui and not their medicinal qualities that draw the ABCs—American-born Chinese—to Sweet-n-Tart. For instance, although the black sesame paste soup ($2.50) is said to restore color to white hair, it would probably take several gallons of it to turn Steve Martin into a redhead. The quantity of silky, pudding-like milk with ginger juice ($3) required to greatly improve one's complexion might also make him obese. Rather, the fun in these little white bowls is in the variety of flavors, colors, and combinations, from the exotic (snow fungi, quail eggs, lotus seed) to the familiar (almond, walnut, tapioca). Even the deceptively ordinary pear with almond tong shui ($4.25) is a study in elegance, its dots of shaved almond floating over the clear soup like petals in a pond.

The post-dessert dessert menu is reason alone to drop by, maybe after dinner elsewhere. There are fabulous fruit shakes ($3.75), mango, watermelon, and kiwi among them, and mysterious ice creams ($2–4) mixed with fruit, red beans, Chinese Jell-o, and tapioca-like sago pearls.

There's another Sweet-n-Tart Cafe at 76 Mott St, Chinatown (☎212/334-8088).

Yang Tze River

When people have to wait for a table, it's usually best they be kept out of sight. The spectacle of restless and ravenous standees—as you surely would be if compelled to hang beside Yang Tze River's dumpling station without so much as a nibble—can make seated diners feel rushed and anxious. Yet here, the nightly line that pushes into the dining room animates it with a palpable energy that inspires diner, waiter,

$8–40

Address 135-21 40th Rd, between Main & Prince Sts

℡718/353-8500

Transportation 7 to Main St
Open Daily 11am–midnight
Accepts Cash only
Reservations Not accepted

and chef Zhu Ping alike. Furthermore, the continuous supply of diners to refill the tables assures a steady supply of fresh foods to restock the kitchen. The Buffalo fish you're eating one night was probably still swimming the day before.

Groups are shuffled into cozy booths or seated around square tables that expand into larger round ones. Green murals portray the springtime splendor of the restaurant's namesake river. The Shanghai-style dinner begins with the customary cold appetizers (mostly $3.95), although there is nothing routine about Zhu's elegant assortment. Here you will find finely shredded bean curd bound to golden mushrooms and fresh cilantro; a nutty toss of bean curd and salty vegetables analogous to a Chinese tabouleh; and a mix of chicken, shrimp, and veggies in a gelatinous web of green bean sheets. From there it's on to—finally!—the dumplings, most assuredly the flavorful shao lung bao ($5.75) packed with dreamy quantities of crab meat, and the ethereal steamed vegetable dumplings ($5.25) filled with water chestnuts, carrots, black mushrooms, cabbage, bean curd, cellophane noodles, and various greens too microscopic to identify.

The good-value, $16.95 combination dinners, which include rice, soup, and a choice of three dishes, make it possible to eat family-style without dining as part of one. Still, it's better to round up a large group and share such chef's specialties as crispy duck ($8.95); Buffalo fish fillets immersed in a stupendous spicy red bean meat sauce ($6.95); and the brilliant if esoteric braised sea cucumber dotted with shrimp roe in a lush Shanghai "red" soy sauce reduced to the color and thickness of a Mexican mole ($19.95).

Woodside & Jackson Heights

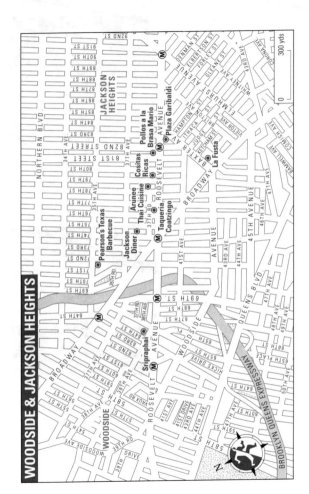

WOODSIDE & JACKSON HEIGHTS

JACKSON HEIGHTS

WOODSIDE

NORTHERN BLVD

92ND ST
91ST ST
90TH ST
89TH ST
88TH ST
87TH ST
86TH ST
85TH ST
84TH ST
83RD ST

34TH AVE
82ND STREET
81ST STREET
80TH ST
79TH ST
78TH ST
77TH ST
76TH ST
75TH ST
74TH ST
73RD ST
72ND ST
71ST ST
70TH ST
69TH ST
64TH ST

35TH AVE
34TH AVE
45TH RD

Pearson's Texas
Barbecue

Pollos a la
Brasa Mario
Cositas
Ricas

Arunee
Thai Cuisine

Jackson
Diner

37TH AVE

Taqueria
Coatzingo

ROOSEVELT AVENUE

BROADWAY

La Fusta

Plaza Garibaldi

PENMAN ST
ELBERTSON ST
FORLEY ST
GLEAN ST

ELMHURST AVENUE

HAMPTON ST
ITHACA ST
JUDGE ST
KETCHAM ST

VICTOR AVE
WHITNEY AVE
43RD AVE

BROADWAY

BAXTER

BROADWAY

41ST ST

41ST AVE

43RD AVE
44TH AVE
45TH AVE
46TH AVE

43RD AVE
44TH AVE
45TH AVE

QUEENS BLVD

HICKS DRIVE
65TH PL

46TH AVE
47TH AVE
48TH AVE
49TH AVE
50TH AVE

47TH AVE
48TH AVE

BRAMHALL AVE
COM-SIAL AVE

CORNISH AVE
43RD AVE

45TH AVENUE

46TH AVE

64TH ST
65TH PLACE
65TH ST

69TH ST

37TH RD
38TH AVE

39TH AVE
40TH AVE
41ST AVE
41ST DRIVE
44TH AVE

Sripraphai

ROOSEVELT AVENUE

HICKS DRIVE

65TH ST
64TH ST
60TH ST
58TH ST

BROADWAY

55TH ST
54TH ST

58TH ST
60TH ST
61ST ST
62ND ST
63RD ST

ROOSEVELT AVE

39TH AVE

38TH AVE
58TH ST

WOODSIDE AVE

39TH DRIVE

BROOKLYN QUEENS EXPRESSWAY

N

0   300 yds

Arunee Thai Cuisine

(🍴) The countrified Arunee is ideally suited to leisurely gatherings of families and friends. Beyond a vestibule sheathed in blond wood and strewn with plastic flowers to suggest a tropical hut is a proud but sober ethnic restaurant whose pale wainscoting, paintings of Bangkok's floating markets, faded photographs, and Thai artifacts give it a wonderfully dated quality. The tin-plated menu covers are engraved with an image of Buddha. Standing metal soup bowls shaped like springform pans are set over gas burners to keep their contents warm. And appetizers and entrees are presented in jade-green ceramic serving dishes by obliging waitresses.

$7–45

Address 37-68 79th St, between 37th & Roosevelt Aves

☏718/205-5559

Transportation 7 to 82nd St

Open Mon–Fri 11am–10.30pm, Sat & Sun noon–10.30pm

Accepts Cash only

Reservations Not accepted

Given that Thai diners are in the majority, you might think it a faux pas to order such generic standards as satay sticks (beef, pork, or chicken; $5.95), spicy beef salad ($8.95), or pad Thai ($6.95). They wouldn't agree. The beef is like candy, the pad Thai qualifies as a shrimp dish, and the marinade for the satay is so good you can easily do without the peanut goop. Venturing into less familiar territory, the chile-fired chicken soup ($3.75/$7.50) hits you on all sides with accents of lemongrass, coconut, and galangal. Crisp chicken wings with a stuffing (think egg roll) of pork, cellophane noodles, and onions ($4.50) served in a ceramic boat with sweet-sour chile dip are endlessly fascinating. If a French prodigy nailed down the stuffed wing thing he could create an international stir.

Anyone uneasy about ordering the whole steamed red snapper ($19.95 for a specimen that feeds three) ought to grow out of that fish-bone phobia here and now. Cooked with mixed veggies and a preserved plum sauce, each bite offers an exhilarating attack of sweet, salty, spicy, and pungent notes. Then allow yourself the untroubled amusement of guay tieow kie mao ($5.95)—essentially fettuccine and meat sauce. But be wary of all-in-one dishes like sizzling seafood ($9.95) with squid, shrimp, crab leg, mussels, and mixed vegetables, which end up being unfocused and messy. The dessert to see, and taste, is sangkhayo fakthong ($2.50), a coconut custard in a hollowed pumpkin shell.

Cositas Ricas

Dario Franco built his first proto-type eatery by doing one thing well: rotisserie chicken (see Pollos a la Brasa Mario, p.393). For Cositas Ricas he could carry seven business cards, one for each activity: bakery, coffee shop, soda fountain, ice cream parlor, steak-house, country kitchen, family restaurant. In other words, it's a Queens diner, an observation quickly confirmed by the vinyl booths, green neon lighting, and a glass-enclosed sidewalk cafe. The major

$8–35

Address 79-19 Roosevelt Ave at 80th St
☏718/478-1500
Transportation 7 to 82nd St
Open Sun–Thurs 7am–2am, Fri–Sat 7am–4am
Accepts All major credit cards
Reservations Not accepted

distinction is that the language is Spanish, the accent is Colombian, and the waitresses are clad in knitted headscarves, cream-colored sports shorts, and leggings. Also, a close inspection of the croissants, donuts, and pastries displayed under the red neon sign *panadería* ("bakery") reveals them to be about twice their usual size.

You don't need to understand Spanish to hear what to order. The sizzling grill and whizzing blenders are in overdrive from early morning to even earlier morning, turning out succulent steaks and, to go with them, tropical fruit milkshakes. The extremely salty Romanian skirt steak comes swimming in fatty juices and is served with a country-style plate salad, rice, and fried yucca ($14.95). The equally sopping and nicely blackened palomilla (thin, top round steak) comes on a $9.50 platter with baby shrimp in salsa Diana (spicy meat sauce), rice, salad, and an arepa (corn cake). Despite the goofy appeal of these platters, you're better off with just a steak and a side of fried potato balls. The arepas rellenas (stuffed corn cakes), though, are sensational sandwiches: steaming hot, lightly gritty, and stuffed with spicy chorizo ($4.75), chopped beef ($4.75), and, best of all, chicken and tangy guacamole ($5.50).

The top-notch milkshakes ($3.50), among them mango, banana, and papaya, are poured from colorful plastic pitchers. The 33-percent-full pitcher is then left at the table so you can pour a refill, recalling the old New York soda fountains where steel canisters invariably contained enough for a glass and a half. Technicolor gelati are not especially good. But the pudding, with its crunchy, crystalline topping, is a marvel of rich density. A three-inch wedge is enough for six.

La Fusta

(🍴) The first thing that quadruple-bypass patients see upon their release from Elmhurst Hospital is the storefront of this great Argentine parrillada (grill). Nothing like a fat juicy steak after open-heart surgery, is there? To make matters worse, La Fusta caters to its sizeable lunch trade from the hospital it faces by cutting 20 percent off its already low prices. That brings down the cost of such cholesterol heavyweights as grilled sweetbreads to $8.50. If it's any consolation to those who succumb to

$20–55

Address 80-32 Baxter Ave,
between Broadway & Ketchum St
☎718/429-8222
Transportation 7 to 82nd St; R,V to
Elmhurst Ave
Open Mon–Fri 11am–11pm, Sat
noon–1am, Sun 1–11pm
Accepts All major credit cards
Reservations Suggested

temptation, La Fusta's beef is grass-fed, which means it's less fatty, and presumably lower in bad cholesterol, than its grain-fed counterparts. What's more, it's hard to imagine a less stressful venue for red-meat gorging. Opened in 1973, La Fusta—Spanish for "riding whip"—is a folksy place with jockey caps and photos of champion thoroughbreds hanging on the half-timbered walls.

No newfangled empanadas in these parts. The choice is limited to juicy ground beef ($2.50) and shredded chicken ($2.50), both fillings enriched with chopped egg and chopped green olives. These terrific half-moon pies look nothing alike. The hard, crisp, bubbly pastry of the beef empanada is the result of frying. The chicken empanada is baked and as a result has a much softer and lighter casing. Two other appetizers to consider are the "grilled" (actually it's baked) provolone sprinkled with dry oregano ($5), and the avocado and watercress salad for two ($9.50).

The front-running cut of beef is the juicy, two-inch-thick, extremely tasty grilled shell steak ($19.80 with potatoes). A medium-rare rendition cuts beautifully, its inside a vivid pink with some deep redness towards the center. It, like all steaks, can and should be slathered with superbly thin, garlic-concentrated chimichurri sauce, the condiment of chopped parsley, olive oil, and vinegar. Several meat alternatives may be compared in the mixed grill for two ($28.50), an inspired sampler containing rib steak, succulent skirt steak, beef tripe, sweetbreads, plump chorizo, and outstanding blood sausage. Unfortunately, both the fried and mashed potatoes are dreadful. Dolce de leche dessert crêpes ($4.80), torched for a caramelized effect, are sweeter than you could possibly imagine.

INDIAN

Jackson Diner

Cheap-eats champions who fondly recall the original Jackson Diner, probably the first 1950s Formica-and-chrome Queens coffee shop to serve lamb vindaloo, approached its 1998 move with trepidation. The downside of a beloved eatery's success and subsequent expansion is too often higher prices and inferior food. Happily, the cartoonish, leaf-shaped fixtures suspended from the high ceiling of the whimsically designed, family-friendly new space have had little negative impact. Even before the appetizers arrive, the traditional trio of condiments attests to Jackson Diner's enduring reputation as one of the city's best inexpensive Indian restaurants and outer-borough dining adventures.

Lunch $9–15
Dinner $18–35

Address 37-47 74th St, between 37th & Roosevelt Aves
☎718/672-1232
Transportation 7 to 74th St-Broadway; E,F,R,V to Roosevelt Ave-Jackson Heights
Open Sun–Thurs 11.30am–10pm, Fri & Sat 11.30am–10.30pm
Accepts Cash only
Reservations Not accepted

Most dinners start with golden pakora (fritters; $3.50), coconut-battered chicken malabar ($6.95), or the pea and potato turnovers that most people recognize as samosas ($3.50). Better to defy convention by sharing an entree as an appetizer. If, for example, you put the Kasmiri kebab ($11.95) next to any starter, it's guaranteed that the charred log of cheese-dipped, egg-washed chicken breast and its pile of grilled onions would vanish first. So why not build your entire dinner around entrees? The black lentils and red kidney beans in the ginger- and cilantro-spiced dal makhani ($8.95) are splendidly al dente. Compared to the soupy or gloppy renditions dished up elsewhere it's a godsend. The dosas (vegetable pancakes; $6.50–7.95) seem to stretch from 74th Street to Roosevelt Avenue. The eggplant purée baingan bhurta ($9.95) is rich in flavor and composition, while chicken, lamb, and goat dishes (all $11.50) cooked in the tandoor oven or the kadhai (Indian wok) are dependable.

Praise for the breads comes with one clarification or, rather, unclarification. Ask for them "dry." They will otherwise arrive slathered in ghee (clarified butter). This suggestion is not made only on nutritional grounds. The nan and paratha ($2.50–3.50) simply taste better without the grease. This review does not apply to the $6.95 lunch buffet, which is always a chancy proposition.

Pearson's Texas Barbecue

First-timers who hunt down Pearson's Texas Barbecue to a remote block of Dominican, Indian, and Middle Eastern shops in Jackson Heights are certain they've lost their way, very much like Robert Pearson himself. He is the Cockney hairdresser who moved from Texas to Connecticut to show the Yanks how to do barbecue. His first joint, Stick to Your Ribs, drew devotees from as far away as New York. Pearson eventually followed some of them home, opening a second, counter-service locale in Queens and then a restaurant on the Upper West Side that was doomed from the start. Later he sold out to his partner, Ellen Goldberg, who moved the business to the back of an Irish saloon, Legends Bar, and changed its name from Stick to Your Ribs to Pearson's Texas Barbecue.

$10–30

Address 71-04 35th Ave, between 71st & 72nd Sts

☏718/779-7715

Transportation 7 to 74th St-Broadway; E,F,R,V to Roosevelt Ave-Jackson Heights

Open Wed 5.30–9pm, Thurs noon–9pm, Fri noon–10pm, Sat 2–10pm, Sun 2–8pm

Accepts Cash only

Reservations Not accepted

BARBECUE

As long as Goldberg was up for a name change, she might have instead called the barbecue joint Stick to Your Brisket, after the specialty that best rewards all those who've made it this far. That barbecued beef is carved to order from a hunk of point-cut brisket sitting on the cutting board, its luscious-looking meat dripping with fatty juices. The brisket is sold by the pound ($14) or as a sandwich ($6.75) on an almost crusty Portuguese roll that does a heck of a better job keeping the barbecue sauce and fatty juices off your fingers than the soft sandwich breads and buns you find down south. Pearson's also does right by tender, smoky, barbecued pork ribs ($14.50 per lb, figuring that to be four or five large ribs), pulled barbecue pork ($13 per lb; $6.25 as a sandwich), and pulled barbecued chicken ($13 per lb; $6.25 as a sandwich).

Sides—fries, onion rings, pork beans, coleslaw—are uniformly unremarkable. The tomato-based, lightly sour, thinner-than-ketchup barbecue sauce comes in four Texas-style grades: mild, medium, hot, and mean. Pearson himself used to describe the mean as being "far too hot for humans." Diners may prepare their own custom blends at the self-service sauce bar.

MEXICAN

Plaza Garibaldi

(🍴) It was a quiet Sunday night, the jukebox was blaring, young women were swing-dancing between the tables, and the men were draining one Corona after another. What, you might wonder, would Plaza Garibaldi be like on a Saturday night? Returning six nights later, you'd find it filled with kids, teenagers, older couples, extended families—all Spanish-speaking. Early on, though, the mariachi band starts setting up, the bar is half-empty. Things don't really pick up until other restaurants

$8–40

Address 82-12 Roosevelt Ave, between 82nd St & Baxter Ave
☏718/651-9722
Transportation 7 to 82nd St-Jackson Heights
Open Mon–Thurs 9am–2am, Fri–Sun 9am–4am
Accepts All major credit cards
Reservations Not accepted

begin to close and their staff finally clock off for the night. Plaza Garibaldi is the casual Jackson Heights eatery where many of the Mexicans who prepare American, Italian, and French food by day and night go to eat their native cooking. And once you've sampled the food, especially the garlicky steaks, and experienced the cheery, colorful atmosphere, it's easy to understand why.

Plaza Garibaldi prepares satisfying soft tacos at the going rate of $2 apiece. But with taco stands, trucks, and dives on every block of Roosevelt Avenue serving as good if not better versions, they seem pointless. Better to start with something oozy, either the enormous nachos plates ($4.25–9) or the wonderful pots of salty, spicy, queso fundido (cheese fondue) studded with diced chorizo and served with warm homemade tortilla chips ($4.50). Then you want to address the steaks, shell or skirt, all blackened to a crisp yet dripping with juices—the most succulent piece of medium-well done beef you'll ever put fork and knife to. Steaks come unadorned or dressed to the max, but always with rice and beans. The bistec mixto puebla ($13.50) consists of skirt chunks sautéed on a hot griddle with fairly hot poblanos and onions, while bistec ranchero ($12) is smothered in tomato sauce and japapenos.

Along with the main ingredients (chicken $9.50, beef $10.50, shrimp $12), accessories, and stack of warm tortillas, the sizzling fajitas are loaded with more onions, mushrooms, and bell peppers than you can imagine. They can easily be shared; the heavenly flan ($2.50), never.

There's another Plaza Garibaldi at 102-16 Roosevelt Ave, Corona (☏718/478-3194).

Pollos a la Brasa Mario

Chickens are dancing in the windows of family-style Colombian restaurants throughout Jackson Heights and nobody's doing a thing to stop them. The sizzling hit that's making their bodies spin, pollo a la brasa ("chicken on the live coal"), is number one with a pullet. "It's typical for Columbia," noted Mike Fandino, a manager at Pollos a la Brasa Mario. "In Bogotà, you'll see five different chicken restaurants on one block, and

$7–25

Address 81-01 Roosevelt Ave at
81st St; plus other locations
☎718/639-5555
Transportation 7 to 82nd St
Open Daily 24hr
Accepts Cash only
Reservations Not accepted

COLOMBIAN

they're all busy. Everyone has their favorite marinades." The best marinades for a dish that's popular throughout South America are rarely overpowered by individual spices or hot pepper. Though residual garlic and pronounced saltiness can be detected with every luscious bite, the remaining flavors—possibilities include rosemary, oregano, cinnamon, cumin, bay leaf, paprika, pepper, black pepper, cilantro, celery, onion, shallots, and olive oil—melt into the mushy, moist, and marvelous meat.

The chickens at Mario, the neighborhood's best pollos, dissolve into succulent perfection by spinning and rotating in chorus-line precision over lava coals for about ninety minutes. The round-the-clock rotisserie positioned beside the window holds up to sixty glistening birds on six long spits. A half-chicken is $3.50; a whole, $6.95. The quarter chicken platter with rice, chicken consommé, a boring salad, and tedious fries ($7.85) is inconsequential beside the Mario's Special ($12). It includes a quarter-chicken, a grilled skirt steak, a grilled pork loin (not the whole loin), sliced avocado, an arepa (corn cake), white beans (yes, there's pork fat in there), and rice. But take away the chicken and the only other component of real interest is the beans, which can be ordered as a side dish. All the rest is done better at Mario's sister restaurant, Cositas Ricas (see p.388).

The red and white eatery, with its laminate tables and quick service, resembles a fast-food franchise decked out to evoke a Colombian chicken ranch. The daily menu extends beyond chicken to a number of typical dishes, among them fried or sautéed red snapper, shrimp, and rice, beef tripe stew, and beans with crackling pork skin. None of these dances like the pollos.

Sripraphai

(🍴) This great and cheap Thai place constitutes the ultimate test of restaurant radar—that is, one's ability to navigate alien territory and track down the best dining options. The small, modest eatery is hidden on a nondescript block of a lackluster side street with little pedestrian traffic. No Italian sports cars are parked in front. A peek through the doorway reveals only harsh fluorescent lighting, faux marble Formica tables, and a doorway television set—hardly surefire clues of excellence in the kitchen. There aren't even the requisite travel posters and folkloric wallhangings as indicators of ethnic pride.

$8–30

Address 64-13 39th Ave, between 64th & 65th Sts
☎718/899-9599
Transportation 7 to Woodside-61st St
Open daily except Weds 11.30am–10pm
Accepts Cash only
Reservations Not accepted

The first temptation of many critics is to praise a menu such as Sripraphai's for its authenticity. Although the food may in fact be true to its origins, that isn't actually its most notable characteristic. Rather, it is the brightness and clarity of the ingredients that stand out: the fiery yet focused kick of the red and green chile peppers tossed with ground meat and basil and served over perfumed rice ($6). The sweet crunch of Thai eggplants the size of figs in the green curry with chicken and coconut milk ($6.50). The gritty egg roll skin that encrusts the jumbo shrimp ($7). The al dente stalks of the greenest imaginable Chinese broccoli set against the crispness of crackling fried pork nuggets and the silkiness of an oyster sauce ($6). If you try these specialties elsewhere after eating them here, you'll feel like you're dining while wearing sunglasses, noseplugs, and a tongue guard.

The waitresses proudly wear baseball hats emblazoned with red chile peppers. Though friendly and helpful, they tend to bring all your dishes at once. It's thus wise to order in stages if that's the way you prefer to eat. And do bring your own wine or beer, especially when choosing dishes marked with a star for "hot and spicy." The iced longan drink will also put out periodic fires while stimulating your appetite. A large assortment of Thai snacks, including some rather unexotic Rice Crispy treats, are packaged in plastic containers and displayed in the back of the restaurant.

Taqueria Coatzingo

For six hours on weekday mornings, Christmas and Cinco de Mayo included, the tubes of multicolored neon that spell TACOS in the storefront window of Taqueria Coatzingo go dark. This is no cause for panic. By 8am the neon is back on, the griddle is hot, a syrupy ballad of Alejandro Fernandez is pumping from the jukebox, the TV is showing the previous night's soccer highlights, the blender is frothing the day's first maracuya (passion fruit) milkshake, and there's at least one warm corn tortilla with your name on it. Named after a town

$7–30

Address 76-05 Roosevelt Ave, between 76th & 77th Sts
℡718/424-1977
Transportation 7 to 74th St–Broadway; F,E,R,V to Roosevelt Ave–Jackson Heights
Open Sun–Thurs 8am–2am, Fri & Sat 8am–4am
Accepts Cash only
Reservations Not accepted

MEXICAN

in Puebla, Mexico, this friendly if not English-fluent taqueria is the top sit-down eatery on Roosevelt Avenue for tacos, quesadillas, sopes (griddled corn-flour patties), enchiladas, chilaquiles (tortilla casseroles), tortas (Mexican sandwiches), and licuados de fruta (fresh tropical fruit shakes).

Among eleven taco varieties, the salty beef version is one of the most satisfying $2 bites anywhere. Its double layer of soft, warm corn tortillas stays at least two inches ajar, folded over too much steamy, shredded beef, creamy guacamole, roasted red chile sauce, and chopped cilantro for it to close any further. While the meat's saltiness hits you in the throat, the spicy chile buzzes your tongue, and the fresh lime and chopped cilantro cut through the grease. Elsewhere on the menu, quesadillas are trios of lightly crisped corn tortillas folded over cheese, chicken, and beef, topped with sour cream, and sprinkled with grated cheese ($6.95 with a decent salad). Enchiladas poblanas come five to an order ($7.95 with the same salad) with a choice of three sauces: green chile, red chile, or superbly rich mole.

Spicy chilaquiles ($7.95) consist of loosely layered tortillas, onions, hot sauce, and a choice of meats, including salty beef and broiled chicken. Surprisingly, the best chilaquile replaces meat with a fried egg, its broken yolk spilling into the tortillas. For sheer bulk go for the chicken milanese torta ($4.50), which, with its pounded breaded chicken thighs, beans, avocado, and jalapenos, is one solid sandwich. All that's required to make a meal of it are two hands and one mora (tropical blackberry) milkshake.

The Bronx

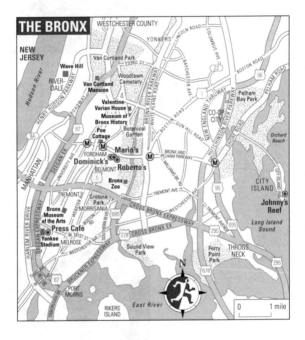

THE BRONX

WESTCHESTER COUNTY

NEW JERSEY

YONKERS

RIVERDALE

Wave Hill

Van Cortlandt Park
233RD ST.

Woodlawn Cemetery

Van Cortland Mansion

Valentine-Varian House

Museum of Bronx History

Poe Cottage

Botanical Garden

Mario's

FORDHAM

Dominick's

BELMONT

Roberto's

Bronx Zoo

TREMONT AVE.

Crotona Park

MORRISANIA

Bronx Museum of the Arts

Press Café

Yankee Stadium

MELROSE

WESTCHESTER AVE.

PORT MORRIS

RIKERS ISLAND

East River

Sound View Park

CROSS BRONX EXPRESSWAY

CROSS BRONX EX.

Ferry Point Park

THROGS NECK

PELHAM BAY PARK

CO-OP CITY

Orchard Beach

CITY ISLAND

Johnny's Reef

Long Island Sound

N

0   1 mile

Dominick's

🍴 The Bronx's Belmont neighborhood is widely known by the name of its main drag, Arthur Avenue. And dining in the Bronx's Little Italy is often associated with the name of its most famous restaurant, Dominick's. The exalted reputation of this golden oldie from the doo-wop days is surely not justified by the quality of its food. On good days, the red-sauce cooking is no better than third-best in the neighborhood. Still, were you to suggest the possibility of a Bronx without Dominick's and its tacky wood paneling and suspended acoustic ceiling, the tears of even its arch competitors and loudest detractors would be among those shed over the Naugahyde tablecloths.

$25–45

Address 2335 Arthur Ave, between East 186th St & Convent Ave
☎718/733-2807
Transportation B,D to Fordham Rd, then Bx 12 bus to Arthur Ave
Open Mon, Wed & Thurs noon–10pm, Fri & Sat noon–11pm, Sun noon–9pm
Accepts Cash only
Reservations Not accepted

Though long adored by Bronxites, Yankees fans and players, and "tourists" from the other boroughs, Dominick's most devoted followers are suburban New Yorkers. For them, the joyful dinners are wistful, "coming home" reminders of what was lost when they, their parents, or grandparents moved away from this or any of the city's old ethnic enclaves to the 'burbs. Packed around communal tables with close friends and new acquaintances, they order the way they'd like to think their ancestors did. No menus, wine lists, prices, or desserts. Just a rushed recitation of "suggestions" from the waiter and then the essential question: red or white. The storied storefront is rendered on the label of the house red, an utterly drinkable Italian merlot.

Most start with the cold antipasto, a pedestrian salad with roasted peppers, olives, thinly sliced salami, and provolone. Next up is a monstrous artichoke so overstuffed and so juicy that it collapses into its bread-crumbed spillage. To accompany good pastas like cavatelli and the stuffed shells, the chunky, peppery tomato sauce is far superior to the watery broccoli rabe. Top entrees include chicken scarpariello and the house steak (consume either and you'll be sweating garlic for a week) and the standout veal parmigiana, with its thick, tender cutlets. There is little relation between how much you eat and how much you're charged, which will be from $25 to $35 per adult.

The Bronx

Johnny's Reef

What distinguishes City Island from any quaint, charming, run-of-the-mill New England fishing village is its Bronx accent. Boroughbreds don't go to City Island; they go to (say it in a millisecond) Ciddy-I-lin. And because the many moderate-to-expensive fish houses along City Island Avenue are generally disappointing, informed daytrippers distinguish themselves by bypassing them all for the tip-of-the-island pandemonium of this 55-year-old fried-fish cafeteria. Johnny's is clearly at the southern end of the island in location, price, and atmosphere. On weekends, the interior is as noisy, chaotic, and no-frills as a school cafeteria. In good weather, it's far nicer to sit at one of the blue picnic tables on the outdoor patio, beneath fishing lines suspended overhead in horizontal rows to ward off the seagulls. Nibble on some mushy corn on the cob, squint your eyes, and you can just about make out the edges of the Gatsby mansion F. Scott Fitzgerald imagined directly across Long Island Sound.

Generously portioned fried-fish platters (mostly $7–14) come with Idaho fries and a cup of coleslaw. The (usually fresh but sometimes frozen) fish is first dunked in an egg-and-butter batter, coated with cracker meal, and then deep-fried to order. The good-sized, firm, snappy shrimp used to be the best catch, but recent examples have lacked flavor. (This is true, sadly, not only at Johnny's but all over town.) Scallops, however, are moist and sweet, clams are plentiful, and for a good, strong-flavored fish you can't go wrong with the porgy.

The best time of year to visit Johnny's is also the busiest: June and July, peak softshell crab season. The fried crabs here are amazing, with a solid coating that keeps the meat crisp, sweet, and juicy. Careful, though, not to squirt crab juice in a companion's eye. An order of three small crabs is just $10. For dessert, the soft-serve ice cream is just fine, but the thick shakes made with it are too gloppy.

$8–30

Address 2 City Island Ave, near Belden St

☏718/885-2090

Transportation 6 to Pelham Bay Park, then Bx 29 bus to the last stop

Open Sun–Thurs 11am–11pm, Fri & Sat 11am–2am

Accepts Cash only

Reservations Not accepted

Mario's

(icon) One of the frustrations of dining at Mario's, a family-run fixture in the Bronx's Belmont section, is that insiders seated in the kitschy dining room are always eating something enticing that doesn't appear on the menu of mostly Neapolitan standards. The Migliuccis themselves can be spotted at the owners' table, heartily devouring something or other—maybe a garlicky mound of shimmering broccoli rabe tossed with chopped Italian sausage ($14.50)—that has not been listed on the menu since the restaurant opened in 1919. When the warmhearted Joseph Migliucci was

**Lunch $20–65
Dinner $30–65**

Address 2342 Arthur Ave, between 184th & 186th St
☎718/584-1188
Transportation B,D to Fordham Rd, then Bx 12 bus to Arthur Ave
Open Sun & Tues–Thurs noon–10pm, Fri & Sat noon–11pm
Accepts All major credit cards
Reservations Not accepted

ITALIAN

asked why this was so, he simply chuckled and shrugged before noting that the broccoli rabe was even better with white beans and escarole. That dish too is unadvertised. Likewise, when a scene for a Sopranos episode was filmed at Mario's, Tony was served exclusively undocumented dishes, notably penne rustica ($14.95), with sausage, pancetta, butter, olive oil, and shallots; chicken royale ($17.95), with boneless breast propped over broccoli rabe and topped with prosciutto and melted mozzarella, and veal sorrentino ($17.95), layered with mozzarella, eggplant, and prosciutto.

This willingness to stray from the menu has a plus side. If you don't see something you want, osso buco ($18.50), say, or red snapper livornese ($22), Joseph will gladly prepare it for you, providing he has the necessary ingredients. And if it's lunchtime and he lacks a key ingredient, he'll send someone out to get it. Being that this is Arthur Avenue, outstanding resources for meats, fish, cheeses, breads, pastries, and all manner of imported Italian provisions are mere seconds away.

Be sure to fit the truly amazing, thin-crusted pizza into your plans. Many regulars order a large pie (from $12.50) as an hors d'oeuvre served even before the mixed cold antipasti, stuffed artichokes, clams oreganata, and octopus salad. Their anxiety is understandable. It's hard to relax, much less settle into a Mario's meal, until you've cut into a pie. You could even regard pizza as a cheese course to be enjoyed before the fresh-filled cannoli or homemade tiramisu.

The Bronx

Press Café

(🍴) It would take the longest moon shot in Yankee Stadium history to soar over the ballpark's upper deck, cross the elevated subway tracks, smash the plate-glass window of Press Café, and land in your bruschetta topped with mixed mushrooms, onions, garlic, and white anchovies. The improbability of said interruption was nearly matched in Februrary 2002 by the landing right here, a good 500ft east of Gate 6 on a residential side street in a notoriously unsafe Bronx neighborhood, of a quaint, Roman-style paninoteca. Scott Azeltine, formerly a manager at Lupa (see p.92),

$10–35

Address 114 East 157th St, between Rover & Gerard Aves
☎718/401-0545
Transportation 4,B,D to 161st St-Yankee Stadium
Open Mon–Wed 11am–5pm, Thurs & Fri 11am–11pm, Sat 5pm–midnight; also before and after Yankee home games
Accepts Cash only
Reservations Not accepted

was lured by the low rent and the proximity to both the stadium and the Bronx County courthouses. Press Café's seven copper-plate tables are occupied during weekday lunches by judges, lawyers, jurors, and felons, too. The last prefer to sit with their backs against the wall or, more precisely, the brown-painted banquettes.

Using provisions from top food purveyors in Belmont, the Bronx's Little Italy, Azeltine assembles an estimable assortment of bruschette (toasted bread slices with toppings; $3–4) and crunchy, salty panini ($6–7) distinguished by the thin-crusted ciabatta from Madonia Brothers Bakery and the salt he sprinkles on it before that choice bread hits the sandwich press. Strips of the same ciabatta even appear as croûtons in a fabulous classic Caesar tossed with vinegar-cured white anchovies (one of four salads; $5–8).

The ceci bruschetta with chickpeas, rosemary, garlic, olives, and grated grana cheese could induce a hungry judge to call an early recess. For post-acquittal or post-victory yearnings, go for the paninis: garlicky salciccia, thickly packed with fennel sausage, broccoli rabe, mozzarella, and ricotta, or the bresaola, which puts the squeeze on dried cured beef, arugula, Parmesan, and truffle oil. Sure solace in the wake of heartbreaking defeats comes from the four-cheese panino with fontina, gorgonzola, Parmesan, and Mozzarella spilling irresistibly from all sides and the dessert panino with a melted Nutella filling and, sitting on top, a ball of vanilla ice cream.

Roberto's

ITALIAN

🍴 When one of Roberto's dispas-
sionate waiters comes by to divvy
up a pasta—say the magnificently simple
farfalle with cauliflower, breadcrumbs,
garlic, and oil—the first diner served does
not wait until his companions get theirs
before digging in. When someone wisely
orders the broiled and grilled (but never
dried-out) rabbit scented with rosemary
and sided with spinach and roast potatoes (about $21), chef-owner Roberto
Paciullo himself might stop by the table
to ask if the recipient will be attacking the

$30–65

Address 632 East 186th St at
Belmont Ave
☎718/733-9503
Transportation B,D to Fordham Rd,
then Bx 12 bus to Arthur Ave
Open Tues–Fri noon– 2.30pm &
5–11pm, Sat 5–11pm, Sun 4–10pm
Accepts MasterCard & Visa
Reservations For large groups

meat with his knife or his hands. Just two responses will put a smile on
his face: "My hands," or "What's a knife?"

Despite recent renovations and the evocative photos of Paciullo's
native Salerno hung on the walls, Roberto's is clearly not for genteel
diners who care much about decor, service, presentation, etiquette, and
desserts. (Habitués are actually relieved that Paciullo neglects desserts, as
a sweetening of his tooth would only lengthen the wait for a table.) Pro-
tocol requires mostly that you follow his whims, choosing from the
specials board or, better yet, asking him what you want to eat. At this
writing the appetizers you'll be "wanting" are grilled octopus ($12) and
smoked mozzarella melted over grilled spinach, roasted peppers, and
black olives ($12).

The most fascinating development in the chef's thinking is his insis-
tence on small pasta shapes. He uses short-cut twists called strozzapretti
("strangled priest") with monkfish, shrimp, clams, and chicken and suggests that the dish be consumed with a spoon. His objection to long
pasta and the fork is that fork-twirling leaves behind most of the juice
and much of the flavor. And this loss would be considerable, as his
incomparable pastas ($14–16) are steamed over the grill with the likes
of cherry tomatoes and porcinis in a traditional method known as al car-
toccio—"in the bag" (in this instance a pouch of aluminum foil). The
objective, to trap the juice and flavor, is beautifully achieved. The one
time you might defy the chef would be if he were to advise you against
the veal affumicato ("smoked") layered with prosciutto, oozy smoked
mozzarella, and sherry wine sauce.

Staten Island

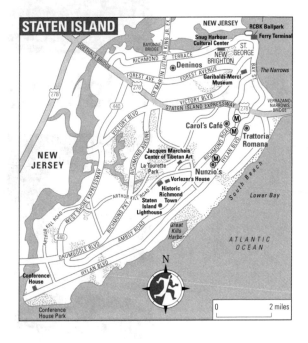

Carol's Café

Before naming any establishment after the chef, a restaurateur must consider the consequences should that chef ultimately walk out. A help-wanted ad listing the given name of Jean-Michel as a required qualification would draw a limited number of candidates. Luckily, although there are many Carols in New York, some of whom no doubt cook, there is little danger of that happening at Carol's Café. The enterprise is entirely unthinkable without sole proprietor Carol Frazzetti, an accomplished chef, cooking instructor, and Staten Island treasure who establishes a bond with her diners through the might of her personality as much as her food.

$45–90

Address 1571 Richmond Rd at Seaview Ave
☎718/979-5600
Transportation Staten Island Railway to Dongan Hills
Open Wed–Thurs 5–10pm, Fri 5–11pm, Sat 5pm–midnight
Accepts All major credit cards

Her civic pride is apparent the second you step into the historic space. The brick walls, wood floor, and ornate tin ceiling all date back to the gaslight-era depicted in old sepia photographs of Staten Island. And though there is nothing quaint about the dinner prices, which are ferociously expensive for so informal an outer-borough restaurant, there is an almost dated charm in coming across what used to be called a "Continental" menu delineated only by the passions of its author. For starters, you eat what Carol loves: crisp and golden crabcakes with a tangy sherry mayo ($12.95), say, or steamed mussels in a lyrical, spiced-to-order white wine broth ($19.90 for two). Maple-roasted bacon rolls stuffed with chicken livers ($8.95) are a favorite.

Entrees vary wildly and wonderfully, from penne with shrimp, chopped broccoli rabe, roasted garlic cloves, and good extra virgin olive oil ($22.95) through herb-roasted whole sea bass submerged under breadcrumbs ($24.95) to a foie gras-intensified wild mushroom beef Wellington ($39.95) as large and seldom seen as a man's derby. The owner's baking prowess is further evident in her reproductions from memory of cakes from Ebinger's, a dearly missed chain of New York bakeries. Your sweet tooth will be better spoiled, however, by such exclusives as an angel food cake ($7.50) so airy it nearly lifts off the table and a devilishly good peanut butter soufflé ($28 for two). The latter's mix of extravagance and whimsy is unmistakably Carol's.

Deninos

Opened by John and Mary Denino in 1937, the nondescript, red-brick tavern that is Deninos wasn't a pizza landmark then and it certainly doesn't look like one now, outside or in. The late Carlo Denino introduced pizza after he took over the family business from his parents in 1951 and slowly turned it into a Port Richmond institution. Well-concealed behind the bar and pool table up front is a utilitarian dining room where crispy-crust lovers leer at the kitchen door, waiting for the entrance of another classic pizza as rolled out by veteran baker John Comoletti.

$10–30

Address 524 Port Richmond Ave at Hooker Place

☎718/442-9401

Transportation 48 or 59 bus to Port Richmond Ave

Open Sun–Thurs 11.30am–11pm, Fri & Sat 11.30am–midnight

Accepts Cash only

Reservations Not accepted

When displaced Staten Islanders bemoan the hardships of a life away from their home borough, a large pizza ($9.20 and up) such as this invariably tops their list of laments. The crust slid out of the gas-heated brick oven is thin yet substantial, crisp yet not burned, flat yet slightly bubbly, firm yet not cardboard-like. This exceptional pizza platform lets Comoletti pile on the extra-fresh, first-rate toppings without fear of the pie turning soggy. While purists ordinarily prefer the oregano-dusted tomato and mozzarella standard, two less conventional pies also merit notice. The white pizza, with onion, garlic, and mozzarella, is spare and blissful, while the MOR (meatballs-onions-ricotta) pie is a wacky delight. A mammoth meatball the size of a softball is crumbled atop a pizza crust equipped to handle its weight. You should order that meatball on a hero sandwich if only to bear witness to its enormity. The only other food item you need to know about is the fried calamari ($6.75), a sensationally messy, crumb-and-scrap-filled pile of flour-dredged rings.

Carlo Denino never served desserts and his children Carla, Michael, and Michael (long story) have no intention of doing differently. Across the street is Ralph's (501 Port Richmond Ave), a drive-in Italian ice stand opened by Ralph Silvestro in 1949 and run today by his grandsons. The true-flavored sweetness and smooth consistency of Ralph's homemade ices represent the perfect, post-pizza treat, and are a close second on that list of homesick Staten Islanders' laments.

Nunzio's

(🍴) Bob Whiteaker had some explaining to do. It was spring 2002 and the heir to the Nunzio's pizza throne was proceeding to tear down and rebuild the little pink stucco home of New York's best pizza-by-the-slice without having the blueprints approved by his customers. As the head of a family business bought by his grandfather a year after its 1958 move from Staten Island's South Beach to Grant City, Whiteaker was certainly acting within his legal rights. But what of the public trust? What about the tens of thou-

$5–20

Address 2155 Hylan Blvd at Midland Ave
☎718/667-9647
Transportation Staten Island Railway to Grand City
Open Sun–Thurs 11am–10pm, Fri & Sat 11am–11pm
Accepts Cash only
Reservations Not accepted

sands of borough residents born after World War II who could barely fathom a world without Nunzio's? All he had to answer their concerns was a sign posted outside the construction site: "Nothing's Changing."

Were people overreacting? Sure. Did everyone know what Whiteaker meant by "nothing's changing?" Of course. But the landmark specifications of Nunzio's golden triangle needed—and need—to be protected at all costs. That means a big yes to imported Italian tomatoes, whole-milk mozzarella, and grated Pecorino Romano cheese, and a loud no to oregano and canned, pre-seasoned tomato sauces that would hide the pure flavor of the elemental Nunzio's pizza (from $1.60 per slice; from $11 for an eight-slice pie). Camouflage on these pies is left to optional toppings like sausage, peppers, onions, eggplant, mushrooms, and anchovies.

The slice's superiority cannot be explained by ingredients alone. Baking is a craft. A select number of competitors use comparable recipes, but the results fall short. Some even have coal- or wood-burning brick ovens, whose intense heat imparts a smoky flavor to the crust. The gas heat Nunzio's employs lacks that advantage. One largely overlooked factor is the way the mozzarella is handled. Instead of shredding or slicing, Nunzio's cuts its cheese into cubes that melt more slowly as the pizza bakes. The thin base still comes out crisp and lightly browned, but the mozzarella maintains its pristine whiteness. The only change of note since Nunzio's March 2003 reopening is in the building's stucco exterior, which has gone from pink to beige. That *whoosh* you hear is a collective exhale from pizza lovers all over Staten Island.

Trattoria Romana

To gain access to Anthony LeBianco and Vittorio Asoli's enormous homemade pastas, wood-oven-baked pizzas, and wood-roasted meats and fish you must allow yourself to become more intimately acquainted with the people sitting at the next table than you ever intended. Moreover, the crush felt by your knees, elbows, and eardrums marks only the beginning of the discomforts that nevertheless do not empty a single one of this trattoria's 120 sought-after seats. Your eyes may bear the strain of searching the fine print of a menu listing hundreds of tantalizing options though sometimes not, most disturbingly, the very dish you're looking for.

Lunch $15–40
Dinner $25–65

Address 1476 Hylan Blvd at Benton Ave
☎718/980-3113
Transportation Staten Island
Railway to Old Town
Open Mon–Thurs noon–10.30pm,
Fri & Sat noon–11pm, Sun 1–9pm
Accepts All major credit cards
Reservations For large groups

Repeat diners rarely bother sifting through the menu-listed appetizers and comparing them to unpublished alternatives they may have spied or heard spoken of, especially after they've been waiting on line for a half-hour, or two, or three. They instead gobble down the delectable fried polenta cubes, which are served gratis and—ouch!—steaming hot, move on to the Sicilian-style, egg-brushed stuffed artichoke (seasonal price $6.50–8.50), and then share a 12-inch pizza. These are not the hometown pizza triangles Staten Islanders fold in two and eat on the run, but rather extremely thin, rigid pies that generally require a knife and a fork. The format suits both the standard Margherita ($6) and the standout boscaiola ("woodman's style") topped with sautéed broccoli rabe (yes, it's garlicky) and crumbled Italian sausage ($10.95).

That same broccoli rabe and sausage topping is periodically fitted into ravioli ($21). If it's a special during your visit, get it. Another pasta to look out for is pappardelle, which melts first into sautéed shiitakes, garlic, white wine, and olive oil, and then into your mouth ($12.95). Any meat or fish that's roasted or grilled in the wood oven is going to be good. The grilled rack of lamb ($24) would be delicious even without the Dijon mustard and oregano. Whole roasted striped bass ($24.95) is deboned tableside. Desserts include cannoli and a tiramisu that's neither too creamy nor cakey. But some diners would happily settle for some more of those polenta cubes.

index

index of restaurants by cuisine

index of restaurants by name

A–Z note:
The Red Cat appears under R not T, La Paella under P, Il Buco under B, and Los Dos Molinos under D. But Cafe Luxembourg is a C, Bar Tabac is a B, and Les Halles an L. Well, you have to have rules.

11 Madison Park see Eleven Madison Park

71 Clinton Fresh Food   111

71 Clinton St, near Rivington St
Lower East Side
☎212/614-6960
New American

92   245

45 East 92nd St at Madison Ave
Upper East Side
☎212/828-5300
American

A   265

947 Columbus Ave, between 106th and 107th Sts
Upper West Side
T212/531-1643
French/Caribbean

À Table   323

178 Lafayette Ave at Adelphi St
Fort Greene & Clinton Hill
☎718/935-9121
French

Agnandi   359

19-06 Ditmars Blvd at 19th St
Astoria & Long Island City
☎718/545-4554
Greek

aKa Café   112

49 Clinton St, between Rivington & Stanton Sts
Lower East Side
☎212/979-6096
American

Aki on West 4th   151

181 West 4th St at Jones St
West Village
☎212/989-5440
Japanese

Al Di La   329

248 5th Ave at Carroll St
Park Slope
☎718/783-4565
Italian

Amarin Cafe   347

617 Manhattan Ave, between Driggs & Nassau Aves
Williamsburg & Greenpoint
☎718/349-2788
Thai

Amy Ruth's   239

113 West 116th St, between Lenox & 7th Aves
Harlem
☎212/280-8779
Southern

Angelica Kitchen   27

300 East 12th St, between 1st & 2nd Aves
East Village
☎212/228-2909
Vegetarian

Angelo & Maxie's   59

233 Park Ave South at 19th St
Flatiron District, Gramercy Park & Union Square
☎212/220-9200
Steakhouse

L'Annan   60

393 3rd Ave at 28th St
Flatiron District, Gramercy Park & Union Square

INDEX OF RESTAURANTS BY NAME

American

Grimaldi's   **293**

19 Old Fulton St, between
Front & Water Sts
Brooklyn Heights, Dumbo
& Downtown Brooklyn
☏718/858-4300
Pizza

Guastavino's   **253**

409 East 59th St,
between York & 1st Aves
Upper East Side
☏212/980-2455
American

**Hampton
Chutney Co.**   **127**

68 Prince St, between
Crosby & Lafayette Sts
SoHo
☏212/226-9996
Indian

Hangawi   **231**

12 East 32nd St, between
Madison & 5th Aves
Murray Hill & Kips Bay
☏212/213-0077
Korean/Vegetarian

Harmony Palace   **17**

98 Mott St, between
Canal & Hester Sts
Chinatown
☏212/226-6603
Chinese

The Harrison   **136**

355 Greenwich St at
Harrison St
TriBeCa
☏212/274-9310
New American

Hasaki   **39**

210 East 9th St, between
2nd & 3rd Aves
East Village
☏212/473-3327
Japanese

Havana Central   **73**

22 East 17th St, between
Union Square & 6th Ave
Flatiron District, Gramercy
Park & Union Square
☏212/414-4999
Cuban

Haveli   **40**

100 2nd Ave, between
5th & 6th Sts
East Village
☏212/982-0533
Indian

Heartbeat   **188**

149 East 49th St,
between Lexington & 3rd
Aves
Midtown East
☏212/407-2900
New American

Hell's Kitchen   **211**

679 9th Ave, between
46th & 47th Sts
Midtown West
☏212/977-1588
Mexican

Home   **157**

20 Cornelia St, between
West 4th & Bleecker Sts
West Village
☏212/243-9579
American

L'Impero   **189**

45 Tudor City Place,
between 42nd & 43rd Sts
Midtown East
☏212/599-5045
Italian

Indochine   **90**

430 Lafayette St,
between 4th St & Astor
Place
Greenwich Village & NoHo
☏212/505-5111
Vietnamese

'ino   **158**

21 Bedford St, between
Downing St & 6th Ave
West Village
☏212/989-5769
Italian

Inside   **159**

9 Jones St, between West

Flushing
☎718/762-6277
Chinese

Miracle Grill **163**

415 Bleecker St, between
Bank & West 11th Sts
West Village
☎212/924-1900
Southwestern

**Miss Mamie's
Spoonbread Two** **274**

366 West 110th St at
Columbus Ave
Upper West Side
☎212/865-6744
Southern

**Mr. Broadway Kosher
Deli** **181**

1372 Broadway at 38th St
Garment District & Little
Korea
☎212/921-2152
Jewish Deli/Middle
Eastern/Kosher

Molyvos **216**

871 7th Ave, between
55th & 56th Sts
Midtown West
☎212/582-7500
Greek

Mombar **364**

25-22 Steinway St,
between 25th Ave &
Astoria Blvd

Astoria & Long Island City
☎718/726-2356
Egyptian

Moustache **164**

90 Bedford St, between
Grove & Barrow Sts
West Village
☎212/229-2220
Middle Eastern

Nam **137**

110 Reade St, between
West Broadway & Church
St
TriBeCa
☎212/267-1777
Vietnamese

Naples 45 **192**

200 Park Ave South at
45th St
Midtown East
☎212/972-7001
Italian/Pizza

Nathan's Famous **316**

1310 Surf Ave at Stillwell
Ave
Coney Island, Brighton
Beach, Sheepshead Bay &
Homecrest
☎718/946-2202
American

New Green Bo **20**

66 Bayard St, between
Mott & Elizabeth Sts
Chinatown

☎212/625-2359
Chinese

Noodle Pudding **295**

38 Henry St, between
Cranberry & Middagh Sts
Brooklyn Heights, Dumbo
& Downtown Brooklyn
☎718/625-3737
Italian

Nunzio's **407**

2155 Hylan Blvd at
Midland Ave
Staten Island
☎718/667-9647
Pizza

Nyonya **104**

194 Grand St, between
Mott & Mulberry Sts
Little Italy & Nolita
☎212/334-3669
Malaysian

Ocean Grill **275**

384 Columbus Ave,
between 78th & 79th Sts
Upper West Side
☎212/579-2300
Seafood

Ocean Palace **342**

5421 8th Ave, between
54th & 55th Sts
Sunset Park
☎718/871-8080
Chinese